Syncretism p40, 67

ED; Ault, 1981, 409+

French school Morocco.

rice 47

National Integration
in Indonesia

National Integration in Indonesia
PATTERNS AND POLICIES

Christine Drake

University of Hawaii Press
Honolulu

94 93 92 91 90 89   5 4 3 2 1

Library of Congress Cataloging-in-Publication Data

Drake, Christine, 1943–
  National integration in Indonesia : patterns and policies /
Christine Drake.
    p.   cm.
  Bibliography: p.
  Includes index.
  ISBN 0–8248–1229–8
  1.   Indonesia—Politics and government—1966–   2.   Indonesia—
Economic policy.   3.   National state.   I.   Title.
DS644.4.D73   1989
959.8'03—dc19   88–39517
                                                                              CIP

⊗™   *The paper used in this publication meets the minimum require-*
ments of American National Standard for Information Sciences—Per-
manence of Paper for Printed Library Materials
                                                            ANSI Z39.48–1984

Contents

Figures

Tables

Preface

ONE of the most important problems confronting developing countries is how to promote national integration—how to bind together the various regions and diverse peoples of a country into a well-functioning and interdependent whole. Cohesive forces are essential not only to ensure the continued existence of the nation-state as one political entity and give political stability, but also to enable economic development to take place. For without some measure of integration, both human and material resources that are needed to raise living standards must be diverted instead toward coping with the centrifugal forces of regional disaffection or rebellion.

National integration is particularly important in Indonesia because of its great size and the enormous diversity of its peoples. Indonesia stretches almost 5,000 kilometers from west to east and consists of about 6,000 inhabited islands. Its population of over 175 million (the fifth largest in the world) is very unevenly distributed, with almost two-thirds of the people living on the less than 7 percent of the land area that makes up the island of Java. In addition, the levels of economic development and participation in the life of the nation vary considerably in the different regions.

This study analyzes the four basic dimensions of national integration in Indonesia, the historical, sociocultural, interaction (transportation and communications), and economic, as they manifest themselves in the country's twenty-seven provinces. Each dimension incorporates a large variety of specific characteristics, the most important of which are analyzed separately in terms of their value in promoting the integration of the provinces into the nation-state. The spatial patterns of the various characteristics in each dimension are then examined through statistical analysis and the extent to which these reinforce one another is considered. This part of the study is based on the 1980 census and other recent materials that provide data at the provincial level. Finally, government policies that relate to national integration are examined and evaluated and the problems that continue to confront the country as it attempts to increase both national cohesion and economic development are discussed.

This book was inspired by my undergraduate work at Oxford and graduate work at Rutgers, and by the opportunity to spend five years in the early 1970s living and working in the "peripheral" Indonesian province of North Sulawesi. During those five years I traveled in almost half of Indonesia's provinces and experienced first hand many of the challenges facing the nation-state. The contrast between Java and the Outer Islands was very striking in terms of infrastructure, accessibility, and the availability of commodities. Yet the plight of ordinary peasants everywhere seemed remarkably similar as they struggled to survive, to provide for their families, and to improve their standard of living. A return visit in 1985 revealed the considerable progress that had been made in many aspects of development and national integration, thanks to the increased oil revenues generated during the 1973–1983 petroleum decade. However, life for the ordinary Indonesian remains hard: the currency has been devalued several times, and wages for most workers remain below $1 per day. Resistance to integration, though muted, continues in Irian Jaya and East Timor. But overall, the country has made remarkable strides in attaining greater cohesion and is probably more fully integrated now than at any time in its history. Significant improvements have been made in all the major dimensions of integration. These are discussed in detail in the book.

The spatial patterns of the characteristics of each dimension of national integration, calculated on a per-capita or per-unit-area basis for each province, are illustrated in a number of maps. On each map the provinces have been divided into five categories by ranking their data on the characteristic under consideration and using the natural breaks in the data to delineate the categories. Technically, Jakarta, Aceh, and Yogyakarta are not provinces, although they are considered as such in this book. Jakarta is officially known as Daerah Khusus Istimewa (D.K.I. Jakarta: the Very Special Region of Jakarta), and Aceh and Yogyakarta are Daerah Istimewa (D.I. Aceh and D.I. Yogyakarta: Special Regions of Aceh and Yogyakarta). However, for convenience these special designations have been omitted in the text and tables.

Places are described using their official names at the period of history being discussed. The island known in Dutch colonial times as Celebes is referred to in the post-independence period by its authentic and official name, Sulawesi. The term Borneo is used to refer to the whole island, with the Indonesian part being referred to by its older, now official name, Kalimantan. The part of western New Guinea that is an official province of the Republic of Indonesia, known in the past as West Irian or Irian Barat, had its name changed officially in 1972 to Irian Jaya. The Spice Islands are known both by their Indonesian name, Maluku, and by their English equivalent, the Moluccas. Finally, the islands commonly known in English as the Lesser Sunda Islands are referred to by their Indonesian name, Nusatenggara. The names of provinces have been capitalized, for example West Java and North Sumatra, to distinguish them from the geographical areas of western Java and northern Sumatra, which are not coterminous.

For the sake of consistency, all Indonesian terms (including place names) are written in their modern forms, with spelling changed to correspond to the new spelling *(ejaan baru)* announced by President Suharto in 1972. Thus:

dj becomes j (as in Djakarta, now officially Jakarta);

 j becomes y (*wajang* is now officially *wayang*);

tj becomes c (*Pantja Sila* is now officially *Panca Sila,* with the c pronounced as in the English ch);

 c becomes k (Macassar is now officially Makassar);

sj becomes sy (*Sjariat* is now officially *Syariat,* with the sy pronounced as in the English sh).

Similarly, the old Dutch spelling, oe, as in Soekarno, was changed officially in 1947 to the modern form, u (pronounced oo), as in Sukarno (although traditional spelling is still widely used in proper names).

Acknowledgments

I am profoundly grateful to all who have aided in this study. Those who have contributed to the thoughts and ideas in this book include Arthur Getis, John E. Brush, Salah El Shakhs, Shanti Tangri, Karl J. Pelzer, Benedict R. Anderson, Hildred Geertz, Julian Wolpert, Robert G. Gilpin, Michael R. Greenberg, Guido G. Weigend, A. Peter Vayda, Briavel Holcomb, J. Kenneth Mitchell, Bonham C. Richardson, Josef Silverstein, Phyllis M. Frakt, Ernest L. Fogg, Ron Foresta, George W. Carey, and Charles Ogrosky. My deep appreciation is due especially to those in Indonesia, including the following who have shared with me their understanding and perspectives: Willi Toisuta, Nico Kana, John Ihalau, Sutarno, Arief Budiman, John Titaley, John Lengkong, Lieke Palenewen, Jantje and Bea Pandeirot, Bert Supit, William and Patmah Langi, and Boetje Pitna. Many others through valuable conversations have also given me a far fuller insight than they can realize into their national heritage and ideals. Gratitude is due also to several of the Indonesian government departments whose publications and correspondence have furnished much of the basic statistical material. Among the libraries I have used, three have been particularly valuable: I wish to thank the professional staff at Cornell University Library, the Library of Congress, and the Hughes Library at Old Dominion University. Inevitably, because of my extensive research and reading I may have seen and perhaps cited information whose source I no longer remember. I express appreciation to those who may have been quoted inadvertently without acknowledgment and hope that their forgiveness will be generous.

I am grateful to the College of Arts and Letters at Old Dominion University for research leave that enabled me to return to Indonesia to complete my research in the spring of 1985, and for two research grants that helped to defray some of the costs of producing the manuscript.

Thanks are also extended to Susan Cooke Hoebeke who executed the maps; to Norris Stowe and Garland White for help with the statistical analysis; to Van Buggs, Cathy Neprud, and Emily Pickering for their help with the typing of the manuscript; and to the two anonymous readers who made many helpful comments and suggestions.

Finally, my deepest thanks go to my husband, Frank, for his constant and invaluable support, ideas, involvement, and editing skills in the preparation of this book. Both his help and the forbearance and love of our children, David and Jenny, contributed so much. Of course, I remain responsible for any inaccuracies, mistakes, and errors, of which I hope there are few.

National Integration
in Indonesia

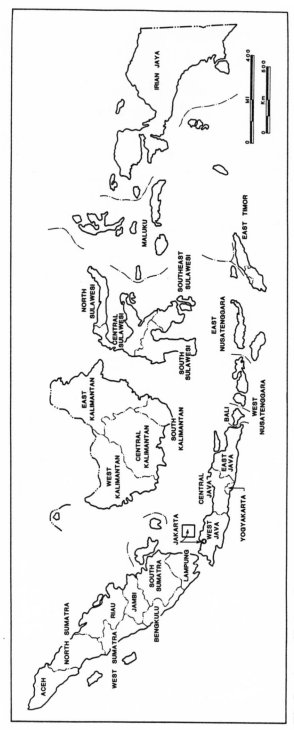

The Provinces of Indonesia

1

Introduction

WHAT is it that holds a nation-state together? Why do some countries suffer from internal conflicts that lead to regional rebellions, civil war, or even the permanent breakup of the state? Conversely, why do other countries remain united, able to contain and benefit from diversity, with strong integrative links? What are the critical elements that bind the disparate parts of a country together and nurture a common sense of unity?[1]

As with so many issues, it is easier to ask questions than to supply answers. Yet an analysis of states that have split up, such as Pakistan, the British West Indies, the Federation of Rhodesia and Nyasaland, and French West and Equatorial Africa, and an examination of countries that have undergone civil war, such as Nigeria, Chad, Lebanon, and the Republic of the Sudan, suggest that certain elements are crucial to maintaining the unity of a nation-state. Essential elements exist in the historical and political, sociocultural, interaction (transportation and communications), and economic dimensions, all of which will be explored in detail in this book.

Almost all countries are deeply concerned about national integration —the need to bind together the various regions and diverse peoples of a country into a functioning and interdependent whole. But integration is especially important in the Third World, where national boundaries were superimposed by the colonial powers without considering the wishes of the inhabitants, and where there has been insufficient time and opportunity for countries to break down the geographical and cultural barriers dividing different ethnic groups within the country. The problems are especially great in large developing countries, where greater diversity and greater distances accentuate the problem of achieving national unity. Such is the situation in Indonesia, a physically fragmented country extending more than 5,000 kilometers from west to east and containing extraordinary geographical and cultural diversity.

Cohesive forces are vital both to ensure the continued existence of the nation-state as one political entity and give political stability, and to enable economic development to take place. For without some measure of integration, both human and material resources that are needed to raise living standards must be diverted instead toward coping with the centrifugal forces of regional disaffection or rebellion. The success of a country's economic development also depends to a considerable extent on the strength of its integrative, cohesive bonds, so that the almost inevitably uneven spatial impact of development does not unduly exacerbate regional differences and tensions and lead to disintegration. An understanding of the spatial patterns of national integration is therefore essential in economic development planning.

National integration is a multidimensional, complex, and dynamic concept, involving a great variety of interlocking elements that operate separately to some extent but yet are also interacting, cumulative, and generally mutually reinforcing. Indeed, integration is a holistic concept in which the totality of the separate aspects is greater than the sum of the different parts.

National integration incorporates a number of different dimensions. Four stand out as particularly important. First, common, integrative, historical experiences obviously act as a cohesive force. These range from shared suffering to common achievements and include a great variety of historical and political experiences, both major and minor, that have become part of the common heritage of a country.

Second, shared sociocultural attributes can help give a nation-state its identity, distinguish it from surrounding states, and enable its citizens to feel a sense of unity. Shared characteristics that enhance a feeling of nationhood include a common language, common cultural features associated with religious practice as well as other cultural elements, and opportunities to belong to nationwide organizations and share in common nationwide activities.

Third, interaction among the diverse peoples within a nation-state promotes integration, especially among those who share various sociocultural attributes. Thus, all kinds of movement and communication among provinces are important, including land, sea, and air transportation links, radio, television, and telephone communications, migration, and trade.

Fourth, regional economic interdependence and some measure of regional balance in economic development are fundamental to national integration. A perception that standards of living are improving and that there is some measure of equity in the location of new industrial growth and development schemes may be of more importance to national integration than economic growth per se. Indeed, geographically unbalanced economic development, by which one area of the country or one group of people is seen to benefit disproportionately, can be decisively disintegrative.

National integration depends upon a fundamental balance among these four major historical-political, sociocultural, interaction, and economic components—a dynamic equilibrium. If one component is neglected or becomes out of balance, disintegrative forces may emerge that can threaten a state's stability or even its continued existence.

National integration is also highly complex. Part of the complexity arises from the way that the factors of integration operate at different levels; indeed, increased integration at one level may result in less cohesion at another. For example, an integrated network of extended family members with the typically deep kinship ties, expectations, and obligations found in Far Eastern cultures contrasts with hostility among major powerful families. Similarly, rural life may be integrative at the local level, with mutual help groups functioning to strengthen bonds among neighbors; but these groupings may at the same time accentuate the fact that certain people are excluded. Rural areas may seem less integrated into the whole than urban areas, especially when contact among rural communities is minimal; yet where people are brought into closer proximity and greater contact with one another in urban surroundings, disintegrative factors such as ethnic and social differences may be accentuated. Heightened ethnic awareness frequently occurs as different ethnic groups live close together in urban areas,[2] while contrasts between rich and poor, also brought into sharp relief in an urban context, can easily trigger dissatisfaction, another disintegrative force. The political implications of this dissatisfaction help to explain the greater attention characteristically given in development plans to urban centers. A disproportionate amount of investment designed to relieve disruptive, disintegrative political pressures, especially in the capital cities of developing countries, however, serves to attract greater migration and, through the process of cumulative causation, to increase the degree of primacy and the vulnerability of the city and its government to political pressure. In addition, the gap between city and countryside is also widened. One of the concerns, therefore, of developing countries is to increase the degree of integration between city and countryside, between regional capitals and their hinterlands, and to improve the integrative function of a network of urban places. Economic development is strongly related to the degree of integration at this level.[3]

Other sociocultural elements can be integrative at one level but disintegrative at another. For example, Hinduism acts as a cohesive force among the Balinese but distinguishes them clearly from most other Indonesians, who are Muslim. Another complication is that "paradoxically aspects of integration and disintegration can both occur at the same time, and may even be causally related."[4] The situation of the Chinese in Indonesia illustrates this point well. Their trading network and close cultural ties throughout the Indonesian archipelago make them an integrative force in one respect. But their conspicuous cultural differences and economic wealth and power distinguish them from the rest of Indonesian society. Yet even this disintegrative element has an ironic integrative twist, for, by being obviously different, they become a common target for the hostility, resentment, and frustration of other Indonesian citizens—thus binding these non-Chinese Indonesians more closely together than they would otherwise be.

Similarly, other seemingly integrative forces may have paradoxical effects. For example, increased commonality in one sociocultural element, such as the ability to speak a common language, may throw into relief other differences such as religion, way of life, or social status. Even such key commonalities as religion, language, and culture may vary in importance in different national contexts. Thus, linguistic differences create a barrier to national unity in Belgium but not in Switzerland, in India but not in Tanzania. Religious differences cause few tensions in the United States, but are a potent disintegrative force in Northern Ireland and Lebanon. Furthermore, sociocultural features may not necessarily be critical in and of themselves, but may assume disproportionate importance when they reinforce other differences such as the actual or perceived distribution of power or economic disparities.

Any analysis of national integration, therefore, must be attempted with extreme care. In any given situation, individual cohesive characteristics have to be considered separately in terms of their importance, their integrative roles, and their interaction with other elements.

Integration is also a dynamic concept. The subdivisions of a national entity may change in their level of integration into the national whole over time. Once integrated does not mean always integrated, as the Scottish and Welsh nationalist movements within the United Kingdom have clearly demonstrated. The degree of integration reflects clearly the political leadership and its priorities. For example, the special treatment afforded by the Dutch to the Indonesian regency *(kabupaten)* of Minahasa in North Sulawesi was not continued by the Javanese-dominated regime after independence; this led to anti-Javanese revolts there. Concern for national integration has resulted politically in suppression and increased domination by the central government and, under Sukarno, in the use of contrived external enemies to stimulate nationalistic emotions and deflect attention from internal regional tensions. The costs, however, of these policies have been considerable, in terms both of lost opportunities for economic development and of the actual costs in people and materiel. Integration needs careful nurturing to ensure that constructive, centripetal, integrative forces consistently prevail over destructive, centrifugal, divisive ones.

Yet does integration mean the extension of control by the central government into all regions and levels of society, the "increasing dominance of the core over the periphery in a spatial system," as Friedmann has expressed it?[5] Or is it shared power, fair representation, and participation by people from every part of the country in every aspect of the national life and government?

Certainly at the structural level in Indonesia, the central government has control over the entire area of the state through the channels and hierarchies of a unified framework. There are five levels of government, which extend to every tiny island, paralleled by a five-tier military command structure. Structurally, the central government has control over the political life and the educational, health, communications, and other facilities. Functionally, however, integration depends on more than just control by the central government and vertical response to it. It involves the mutual interdependence of regions and regional participation in national affairs. This distinction is comparable to the difference between national integration and nationalism. Nationalism is concerned with evoking patriotic, nationalistic emotions, feelings that are important in overcoming local regionalisms and particularisms, and emphasizes vertical links to the center. National integration, by contrast, is a much broader and more inclusive concept, concerned with lateral as well as vertical linkages. It focuses on the functioning interaction and mutual interdependence of the diverse parts of the state, ties that continue largely independently of the strength of nationalistic emotion. Obviously this is a much stronger type of relationship than the one nationalism creates on its own. It is interesting to note that the collapse of the West Indies Federation has been attributed precisely to the lack of these lateral linkages among the islands.[6]

Many studies on national integration in the past have dealt with the topic sectorally, from the perspective of the political scientist, sociologist, anthropologist, or economist.[7] In this book, the focus is upon the spatial aspects of national integration. This includes an evaluation of historical experiences: the extent to which these have been integrative and shared by all parts of the country, an analysis of the spatial distribution of sociocultural commonalities and the degree to which these are interdigitated or concentrated in particular regions, a consideration of the degree to which interaction takes place among the diverse areas and peoples of the state, and a study of the extent to which all parts of the country share in economic growth and development. These different dimensions of integration are then synthesized in an analysis of common spatial patterns of national integration.

Obviously the level of national integration does not determine the political stability of a country. Yet it does have a profound effect upon the way a country withstands the political stresses and strains imposed upon it from both outside and inside the country. It comprises the stage upon which the political actors play out their roles. As Deutsch has put it:

> A basic survey of geographical patterns, settlement, transport, areas of different language dialects, cultures, etc., would not give us an answer about the future success or failure of political unity. The final decision would come from the realm of politics—a leader, a movement, or a political party—but the surveys would help us to start out with a more detailed and realistic picture of the very uneven world in which politics must function.[8]

National integration is a matter of particular concern in Indonesia because of the great diversity of both its geographical environments and its peoples. Indonesia consists of over 13,000 islands (about 6,000 of which are inhabited) with a 1988 population of over 175 million, the fifth largest in the world, which incorporates enormous ethnic and cultural diversity. In addition, people range in their levels of development and sophistication from the Stone Age inhabitants in the inland mountainous areas of Irian Jaya to the most modern and cosmopolitan urban dwellers of the major cities.

One of the most significant geographical facts about Indonesia is its uneven population distribution. As can be seen from both Figure 1.1 and Table 1.1, the contrast is between Java and Madura, where in 1980 over 91 million people, or almost two-thirds of the Indonesian population, lived on less than 7 percent of the land area, and where average population densities in 1980 were 690 persons per square kilometer (with neighboring Bali having a slightly lower but also relatively high population density of 444 persons per square kilometer); and the Outer Islands, where average population density nowhere exceeded 139 persons per square kilometer. By way of striking example, in 1980 the entire population of Kalimantan (6.7 million) was only slightly larger than that of the capital city of Jakarta (6.5 million).

This demographic contrast underlies many of the problems and tensions of the Indonesian nation-state. It has also given rise to the general acceptance of a core-periphery model that considers Java and Bali as a congested nuclear core and the Outer Islands as an underdeveloped, sparsely populated periphery. Although this core-Outer Islands dichot-

Figure 1.1. Population density in Indonesia, 1980. Based on data from the 1980 population census in Biro Pusat Statistik, *Statistik Indonesia 1983, Buku Saku,* Table II.1.3.

Table 1.1. Area, population, population density, and percentage urban by province, 1980

Province	Area in km²	Percentage of land area	Population in 1000s	Percentage of population	Density per km²	Percentage urban
1. Aceh	55,392	2.9	2,611	1.8	47	8.9
2. North Sumatra	70,787	3.7	8,361	5.7	118	25.5
3. West Sumatra	49,778	2.6	3,407	2.3	68	12.7
4. Riau	94,562	4.9	2,169	1.5	23	27.2
5. Jambi	44,924	2.3	1,446	1.0	32	12.7
6. South Sumatra	103,688	5.4	4,630	3.1	45	27.4
7. Bengkulu	21,168	1.1	768	0.5	36	9.4
8. Lampung	33,307	1.7	4,625	3.1	139	12.5
Sumatra	473,606	24.7	28,016	19.0	59	19.6
9. Jakarta	590	0.03	6,503	4.4	11,023	93.7
10. West Java	46,300	2.4	27,454	18.6	593	21.0
11. Central Java	34,206	1.8	25,373	17.2	742	18.8
12. Yogyakarta	3,169	0.2	2,750	1.9	868	22.1
13. East Java	47,922	2.5	29,189	19.8	609	19.6
Java	132,187	6.9	91,270	61.9	690	25.1
14. Bali	5,561	0.3	2,470	1.7	444	14.7
15. West Nusatenggara	20,177	1.1	2,725	1.9	135	14.1
16. East Nusatenggara	47,876	2.5	2,737	1.9	57	7.5
17. East Timor	14,874	0.8	555	0.4	37	n.a.
Nusatenggara	88,488	4.6	8,487	5.8	96	12.0

18. West Kalimantan	146,760	7.7	2,486	1.7	17	16.8
19. Central Kalimantan	152,600	8.0	954	0.7	6	10.3
20. South Kalimantan	37,660	2.0	2,065	1.4	55	21.4
21. East Kalimantan	202,440	10.6	1,218	0.8	6	40.0
Kalimantan	539,460	28.1	6,723	4.6	12	21.5
22. North Sulawesi	19,023	1.0	2,115	1.4	111	16.8
23. Central Sulawesi	69,726	3.6	1,290	0.9	18	9.0
24. South Sulawesi	72,781	3.8	6,062	4.1	83	18.1
25. Southeast Sulawesi	27,686	1.4	942	0.6	34	9.4
Sulawesi	189,216	9.9	10,410	7.1	55	15.9
26. Maluku	74,505	3.9	1,411	1.0	19	10.9
27. Irian Jaya	421,981	22.0	1,174	0.8	3	21.4
Maluku & Irian Jaya	496,486	25.9	2,585	1.8	5	15.5
Indonesia	1,919,443	100.0	147,490	100.0	77	22.4

n.a.: not available

omy may appear simplistic in a country with the size and diversity of Indonesia, it is well established in the literature.[9]

The physical features of the Indonesian archipelago have had a strong impact upon the population distribution and the levels of development within the country. There is a clear distinction between the larger islands of Sumatra, Borneo, Java, and New Guinea, which rest at least in part on two fairly extensive continental shelves (the Sunda and Sahul shelves) and have extensive coastal lowlands fringing shallow seas; and the islands to the east of Bali and Borneo and west of New Guinea, which rise abruptly from great ocean depths and have virtually no coastal plain at all (see Figure 1.2).[10] The great coral reefs off the west coast of Sumatra and especially along the edge of the Sunda shelf in the Makassar Straits and Flores Sea have played an important part in deflecting shipping routes wherever possible to the generally coral-free sea covering the Sunda shelf between Sumatra, the Malay Peninsula, Java, and Borneo. In the eastern part of the archipelago, coral reefs and frequently swift ocean currents combine to make navigation more hazardous.

This geological background has had many effects on the geographical environment of the archipelago. It is responsible for the accessibility of much of the land area and has enabled the sea to become a common link among coastal dwellers who depend upon it for their source of livelihood, both for food and for commerce. It has led to the development of vast swamps along the edges of the islands on the continental shelf, particularly in eastern Sumatra, western and southern Borneo, and southwestern New Guinea. It has affected the topography and the types of soil found in the different islands and consequently their different potential for agriculture. And it has determined the location of mineral resources found beneath the soil: petroleum and natural gas, coal, tin, nickel, copper, and other ores.

These physical differences underlie the uneven development of the islands. Java compares favorably with many of the other islands in the archipelago in a number of ways. Its relatively central location within Indonesia, its smaller size and elongated shape, and its general freedom from coastal swamps afford greater access than that which exists in Sumatra (with its precipitous western highlands and eastern swamplands and silted rivers), Kalimantan (with its fairly short coastline, poor drainage, and lack of natural harbors), Sulawesi (with its fractured and fragmented mountainous interior), and Irian Jaya (with its rugged terrain in the north, swampland in the south, and location away from the main trading routes).

Java is endowed with many volcanoes, which are more active and provide more chemically basic ejecta than those in most other parts of

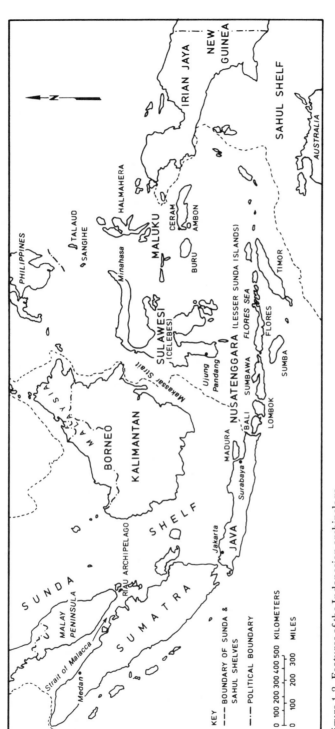

Figure 1.2. Features of the Indonesian archipelago.

the archipelago (particularly in Sumatra where the volcanoes are less active and produce more acidic ash and lava). The absence of volcanoes in other parts of the island chain means that soils have developed from very different parent rocks, which are often deficient in plant nutrients. The volcanic ejecta in Java generally produce more fertile soils that are renewed at a rate faster than the leaching process.[11] Similarly, the enormous amount of sediment carried by Indonesia's rivers provides valuable plant nutrients in the case of Java, since much of it is derived from the volcanic interior. Java's relief provides another advantage in that its scattered volcanic peaks are separated by gently sloping, interconnected valleys that facilitate terracing and the efficient use and reuse of nutrient-laden water.

Climatically, there is considerable variation in both the amount and the seasonality of the rainfall, and the ubiquitously hot sea-level temperatures (Indonesia is bisected by the equator) are modified by altitude and aspect. Although many localized dry seasons occur as a result of the topography in relation to the direction of the prevailing monsoon winds, the major climatic contrast is between much of the archipelago, which experiences constant, year-round rainfall, and the southeastern area, which experiences a marked dry season that increases in duration with proximity to the Australian continent and the influence of its high-pressure system in the months of April to September. This leads to more open deciduous forest and even to savanna vegetation in the eastern part of Nusatenggara and to reduced leaching, but increased variability in the rainfall results also in wind erosion and difficult periods of drought that affect the double- or triple-cropping potential of the land for agriculture. Java occupies an intermediate position between the continually wet lands of Sumatra and Kalimantan and the marked seasonal droughts that characterize Nusatenggara.[12]

It is, thus, easy to see that Java possesses a unique combination of favorable climate, soils, drainage, and accessibility, which underlies and helps to explain Java's greater potential for development and the decision of the Dutch colonial power to focus its attention on that island.

Physical factors contribute also to the two very different agricultural systems that are found in Indonesia: the swidden (shifting) cultivation system, which involves the use of unirrigated fields *(ladang)* and is typical of the Outer Islands; and the intensive wet-rice cultivation system *(sawah),* found predominantly in Java (and Madura and Bali).

Physical diversity in Indonesia is matched by cultural and economic variety. Scattered among the islands of Indonesia are numerous tribal and ethnic groups that vary on almost every possible index. In kinship systems, some are patrilineal (such as the Balinese), some matrilineal (such as the Minangkabau), and others bilateral (such as the Acehnese).

In location and economic activity, some inhabit isolated villages in remote, mountainous interiors where they practice shifting cultivation or rely primarily on hunting and food gathering; others live along the coasts and depend mainly on fishing; many are wet-rice farmers located in broad river valleys and extensive lowland areas; millions more are city dwellers. Some (particularly in Java and Bali but also in pockets of the Outer Islands such as parts of Minahasa and the area around Ujung Pandang in Sulawesi) live at extremely high population densities while others inhabit vast jungle areas at very low densities. Some societies have had a long history of communication and contact with the outside world; others are just now being settled in villages and brought into contact with people from other parts of Indonesia. Although 22 percent of Indonesia's population was classified as urban in 1980, there are considerable differences in the degree of sophistication of both the urban and rural masses. The people vary, too, in their religious adherence, both in terms of the religion they follow (nearly all of the world's major religions are represented, including Islam, Christianity, Hinduism, Buddhism, and Confucianism) and in terms of the degree of their commitment and the purity of their faith. Each ethnic group has its own language or dialect, customs, and culture; each varies in its degree of involvement and participation in national events.

Gross correlations have been observed between sociocultural patterns and ecological-economic divisions, and broad complexes of peoples have been distinguished. Hildred Geertz has recognized three major groups:[13] the coastal Malays, identified by their Islamic, maritime lifestyle and culture, which is more egalitarian and individualistic; the great variety of the interior tribespeople who are mainly swidden cultivators, often animistic, and relatively isolated; and the Hinduized (and now largely Islamic) wet-rice cultivators found primarily in Java and Bali, with their distinct, very highly developed, and symbolically elaborate artistic culture and hierarchical, stratified societies. However, there is no simple correlation between religion and ecology, for wet-rice agriculture is practiced by Christian, Hindu, and Muslim societies, although animistic traits are generally more pronounced among swidden groups.

There are many peoples in Indonesia, however, such as the Bataks, Ambonese, Minahasans, and Chinese, who do not fit into any one of the three main classificatory groups of Geertz, but rather combine characteristics of each. Herein lies one of the strengths of pluralistic Indonesia, as compared with Malaysia, the Sudan, or Canada, for in these latter, more dichotomized societies, differences in one sociocultural element are reinforced by contrasts in other elements and thus are more divisive. In Indonesia, cultural and social variations are interdigitated and form complex crisscross patterns, so that no one large group is totally divided from others by *all* features.[14] A basic awareness and acceptance of others' differences is evident in the common maxim, *lain desa, lain adat* (different villages have different customary rules); or, more expressively, *lain padang, lain belalang; lain lubuk, lain ikannya* (different fields have different locusts; other pools have other fish).[15] This tolerance is part of Indonesia's strength and durability.

In the face of this enormous diversity within Indonesia, building national integration is of tremendous importance. What is it that holds the country together? What bonds of integration have emerged as a result of common historical experiences? What patterns of integration exist among the sociocultural, interaction, and economic components of integration? What synthesis is it possible to obtain on the overall strength of integration and in its spatial patterns in the nation-state of Indonesia? And finally, what has the government response been to these uneven patterns of internal cohesion; how have Indonesia's independent governments attempted to promote national integration?

The purpose of this book is to provide tentative answers to these questions. Most of the data and information used in this study comes from the 1980 census and other materials available in the early 1980s. The areal unit chosen for study is the province, of which there are presently twenty-seven in Indonesia (including the special districts of Aceh, Jakarta, and Yogyakarta). The province is a logical unit for comparison for several reasons. It is the most likely unit to be able to secede and become an independent unit, because of its size. A typical Indonesian province is as large as any of a number of smaller African states that exist on their own and larger than many independent island states. On a practical level, the province has been selected as the unit for consideration because most statistical data are available only at this (or at the national) level. Unfortunately, intraprovincial differences, though known to be important, are masked when data are summarized for a whole province. Provinces vary considerably in size both in area (ranging from 590 square kilometers for Jakarta to 422,000 square kilometers for Irian Jaya) and in population (from 555,000 in East Timor and 768,000 in Bengkulu in southern Sumatra to 29,189,000 in East Java). Thus, all data in the quantitative section have been standardized to either a per-unit-area or a per-capita basis and are given in the appendixes. This study (as most geographical studies) is inevitably scale specific: the use of the province as the unit of area has a major effect upon the results of the analysis.

Warnings are also in order about the availability and quality of the data. As with most developing countries, data are not always complete or consistent, and in places their accuracy is questionable. In the past, interregional data have not always been highly valued, especially when containing politically volatile information; the government in the 1950s implicitly recognized the inflammatoriness of interregional economic data when it closed a leading newspaper for printing information on the differences among the provinces in terms of export earnings and government expenditures.[16] However, a lot of data is available on Indonesia thanks to the Biro Pusat Statistik (the Central Bureau of Statistics, whose publications include the comparatively detailed 1980 population census) and the work of economists both within Indonesia and at the Australian National University.

2

The Uneven Effect of Historical and Political Experiences

NATIONAL integration involves the way people in different areas of a country and of different ethnic, sociocultural, and economic backgrounds feel themselves to be united and function as one nation. One important component in promoting this sense of unity and national identity is that of common historical and political experiences. For it is in this historical heritage that the roots of culture and national social structures are found. In addition, feelings of oneness, of shared glory and ignominy, triumph and suffering, achievements and struggles, all help to deepen national awareness and national pride, which are basic to building national integration.

Historical experiences can be evaluated in two principal ways: first, an analysis of the extent to which particular historical events have been integrative; and second, a consideration of how much the different regions of the country have participated in those national events that have both shaped the geographical configuration of the present state and created an awareness of national identity. This chapter evaluates the integrative effect and the spatial impact of significant historical and political events on the nation-state of Indonesia.

Indonesia's history can be divided into four major time periods, each of which has had its own distinctive effect in forming the modern state and giving it its unique national character: the ancient empires, the experience of growing Western influence and colonial control, the Japanese occupation and subsequent struggle for independence, and the period of independence.

The Ancient Empires

In prehistory and very early historical times, there was nothing to distinguish those islands later to become the state of Indonesia from the

16

surrounding areas of the present-day countries of Malaysia, the Philippines, and Papua New Guinea (see Figure 2.1). Certainly the racial mix and early settlement patterns were similar to those of the Malay Peninsula. The first migration into the archipelago, probably 1.5 to 2 million years ago,[1] consisted of Australoid peoples, possibly represented today by Negritoes such as the Arafura in parts of the Lesser Sunda and Moluccan islands.[2] Later came the great waves of immigrants from southern China, including the basically Caucasoid Proto-Malays, who brought their Neolithic culture to the islands of Borneo and Sumatra and later to Java and Sulawesi. They dispossessed earlier immigrant groups, absorbing them or forcing them into marginal habitats.[3] Their stock is best represented today by the various Batak and Dyak ethnic groups of interior Sumatra and Borneo. Further to the southeast, in the Moluccas and Lesser Sundas, the Proto-Malays (and their descendants) were modified by Papuans and Melanesians who were already entrenched there; but in New Guinea the Proto-Malays were unable to penetrate beyond the coast because of the hostility of tribal warriors.

The Deutero-Malays, who were more Mongoloid in feature, brought their Bronze Age civilization particularly to the coastal districts of the large western islands, displacing those who had settled there previously. Their coastal settlements eventually became the nuclei of trading kingdoms, while the interior settlements of the Proto-Malays became centers of agriculture.[4] Ethnic groups typifying the Deutero-Malays include the Javanese (in East and Central Java), Sundanese (in West Java), Minangkabau (in West Sumatra), and Balinese.

Although a similar pattern prevailed on many islands, especially in the Greater Sundas—of later arrivals of more sophisticated peoples settling on the coast, absorbing previous groups or forcing them inland to displace still earlier people into the mountainous interiors—this pattern was not unique to Indonesia. It was as true for the non-Indonesian areas of the Malay Peninsula and northern Borneo as it was for the Indonesian islands. Indeed, there is more affinity between the inhabitants of the western islands of Indonesia and those of the Malay Peninsula than there is between the peoples of the western and eastern islands within the Indonesian archipelago. When, for example, the Portuguese finally captured the Malayan emporium of Malacca in 1511, the key entrepôt at that time of Indonesian trade, they found that the dominant political element in that great Islamic city was Javanese, its army largely Javanese, and most of its shipbuilders and other craftsmen Javanese, together with a major component of its extensive merchant class,[5] all this outside the area later to become Indonesia. By contrast, the easternmost islands of Indonesia and especially Irian Jaya, though involved in trade, were much less affected by the Javanese until well into the twentieth century.[6]

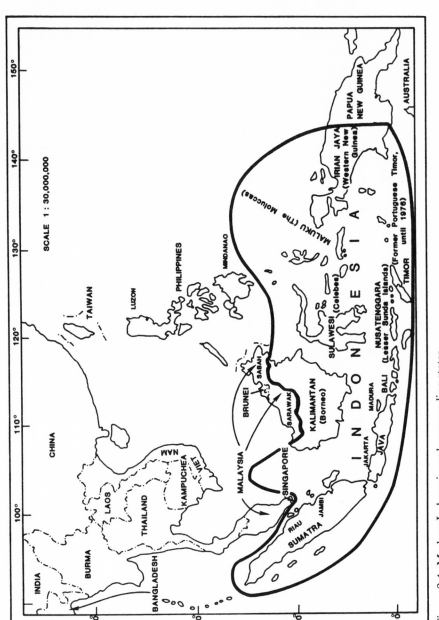

Figure 2.1. Modern Indonesia and surrounding states.

Some historians have traced Indonesia's beginnings to empires and kingdoms dating back to the pre-Christian era, including the Dong-Son period, and to the growing Indian influences felt in Dvipantara and its several rival states of Yavadripa, Jaya, Malayu, and Taruma.[7] Most Indonesian historians, however, emphasize the somewhat later kingdoms of Sri Vijaya and Majapahit as far more significant in the country's communal past. This Indian-influenced period of Indonesia's history is often idealized as a sort of Golden Age. Indeed, it has been suggested that, having won independence from the Dutch, Indonesia probably would have called itself by some old Indian or Hindu-Javanese name such as Dvipantara or Nusantara if these designations had originally been of sufficient geographical scope.[8] But these early second- to fifth-century principalities seem to have had only local extent and influence. Much of Indonesia's early history is still shrouded in obscurity.[9]

It remains to be shown to what extent historical myth and historical reality correspond. However, even a minimal correspondence would not invalidate the sense of corporate history and national identity so strongly expounded by Sukarno in his efforts to strengthen the concept of Indonesian unity:

> The national state is only Indonesia in its entirety, which existed in the time of Shrivijaya and Majapahit, and which now too we must set up together.[10]

The kingdoms of Sri Vijaya and Majapahit were only two of the many kingdoms and petty states that arose, expanded, and declined during the millennium before Western influence began to penetrate the area. They epitomize, however, the two major types of state that came into existence—the sea-based empires dependent upon control of trade and shipping, of which Sri Vijaya, based on its monopolistic control of the important Malacca Straits, is the prime example; and the inland, agricultural, and especially *sawah* (wet-rice)-based kingdoms such as Mataram and Majapahit. Sri Vijaya and other maritime principalities, which were dependent upon international trade routes, were cosmopolitan in character and had a high degree of social equality and tolerance. By contrast, the Hindu-Javanese inland kingdoms were complex, hierarchical structures, aristocratic and military in character and buttressed by magico-religious powers.[11]

Careful historical analysis suggests that the thalassocratic state of Sri Vijaya, from its center near present-day Palembang in Sumatra (and secondary node of Kedah on the Malay Peninsula), included only limited parts of western Indonesia and incorporated much of the Malay Peninsula (see Figure 2.2),[12] with possible colonies in the southern Phil-

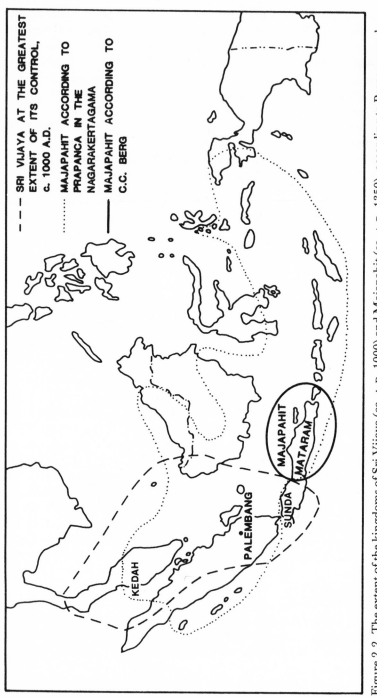

Figure 2.2. The extent of the kingdoms of Sri Vijaya (ca. A.D. 1000) and Majapahit (ca. A.D. 1350), according to Prapanca and C. C. Berg. Based on maps by Paul Wheatley, *The Golden Khersonese*, p. 299; and Jon M. Reinhardt, *Foreign Policy and National Integration*, p. 17 (used with permission).

ippines as well.[13] But its commercial links with the Spice Islands (Maluku) and other parts of the archipelago lend some credence to its claim of drawing the far-flung islands into one economic unit. Sri Vijaya's power lay in its ability, from the fifth century on, to control the Malacca Straits and enforce customs duties and port dues from ships using the prevailing monsoonal winds in their voyages from Arabia, Persia, India, and Ceylon to the Spice Islands and China.[14] Through levying tolls and providing outlets for their products, the Sri Vijayan empire transformed what would otherwise have remained small, subsistence villages into "glittering jewels strung along the thin gold thread of international trade."[15] The centrifugal forces of isolation and desired autonomy of the vassal states threatened constantly to cause the breakup of this loosely linked coastal empire. But these were counterbalanced with varying degrees of success by the wealth and prestige of the Sri Vijayan ruler, whose authority was also derived in part from generally accepted Buddhist sanctions.

Trade and the trade routes undoubtedly drew the people of the region together and helped to determine the course of their development and their exposure to foreign culture, techniques, skills, and ways of life.[16]

The kingdom of Sri Vijaya fluctuated in its fortunes from its inception sometime in the fifth century until its decline during the twelfth. Toward the end of the eighth century, the Sailandra dynasty united this Sumatran empire with Mataram, one of the earliest land-based kingdoms in Java. It was during this period that the great Mahayana Buddhist temple of Borobudur was built, in whose glory and magnificence all Indonesians are encouraged to take pride. After the Sailandra empire split into two components in the late ninth century, the Javanese kingdom returned to Brahmanistic Shiva worship and built the Prambanan temple complex, while in Sumatra the Sri Vijayan empire grew to new heights, especially in the early eleventh century through its monopoly of the growing spice trade. By the time Marco Polo visited the area in 1292, however, the once-powerful kingdom of Sri Vijaya had disintegrated into eight Sumatran kingdoms, each with its crowned king, and the center of power had moved north from Palembang to Malayu (near present-day Jambi). It seems that technological improvements in shipbuilding and navigation, fluctuations in trade, and international politics all contributed to undermining the strategic locational advantage of Sri Vijaya as an entrepôt. Because it had no agricultural base or other industries, a decline in its trading preeminence led almost inevitably to the empire's demise.

Yet the commercial empires based on the Straits of Malacca, though leaving little in the way of material remains, contributed more to present-day Indonesia than mere historic memories. Malay was used as the lingua franca of trade among the principal ports of the Sri Vijayan empire. It was this lingua franca that was later adopted as the national language of Indonesia, itself recognized as one of the strongest unifying forces in the archipelago (although not unique to it).

The other type of kingdom was the land-oriented, agrarian-based variety, found primarily in Java. The first of these, eighth-century Mataram in central Java, coexisted with Sri Vijaya and for many Javanese has more historical and inspirational significance than the latter.[17] Indeed, Legge argues that even during Sri Vijaya's period of preeminence the political center of gravity in Indonesia was really to be found for the most part on the island of Java, where

> a series of major kingdoms, at first in Central Java and then in the eastern part of the island, marked the growth of a sophisticated material culture and of a political strength which, after fluctuations and divisions, reached its apex with the rise of the kingdom of Majapahit in the thirteenth century.[18]

The early kingdom of Mataram (to be distinguished from the later kingdom of Mataram of the seventeenth century) shifted its center from central to eastern Java in the mid-ninth century and gradually expanded its agricultural base by becoming involved in maritime trade. It also promoted a resurgence of indigenous elements in art, literature, and politics. Later it was superseded by several other kingdoms, including Janggala, Kediri, and Singhasari. After Sri Vijaya's decline, Java gained a predominant position in the archipelago that has not since been eclipsed. Though its kingdoms have been rivaled at various times, most notably by the Islamic commercial empire of Malacca in the fifteenth century, the island has remained the center of political influence and the balancer of fluctuating rivalries in the area.[19]

However, the most extensive kingdom that Sukarno claimed as the foundation of present-day independent Indonesia is Majapahit. This consisted at first of a number of individual entities held together through a variety of coercive and manipulative techniques on the part of early Majapahit rulers.[20] But later it established itself not only as a coordinated, agriculturally based land power but also as a commercial empire. It attained its zenith in the fourteenth century, under the premiership of Gajah Mada, that architect of pan-Indonesia policies who is memorialized as the great unifier of Indonesia in its first university, established at the *kraton* (palace) in Yogyakarta. Almost inevitably there is controversy over the actual extent of this powerful and impressive kingdom. The Javanese court poet, Prapanca, in his long, narrative poem composed in 1365, *Nagarakertagama*, inserted a list of vassal states of Majapahit (see Figure 2.2). It included nearly all the coastal districts of Indonesia, western, eastern, and northern Sumatra, Brunei and parts of southern and western Kalimantan, Bali, the Sundas, parts of Sulawesi and Maluku,[21] and eventually the kingdom of Sunda in western Java,[22] as well as the fifteen dependencies of Majapahit in Pahang, the name by which the whole of the southern half of the Malay Peninsula was known. Several historians have argued that at the height of its power Majapahit's territory was at least coextensive with that of the modern Republic of Indonesia and included parts of present-day Malaysia as well. But many Indonesian as well as other intellectuals consider these claims vastly exaggerated. Indeed, according to Wheatley, the Dutch scholar C. C. Berg considers the impressive catalogue of Majapahit's conquests as reflecting nothing more than the geographic knowledge available in Prapanca's time.[23] The state of Majapahit at its maximum extent, he believes, comprised little more than eastern Java, Madura, and Bali (see Figure 2.2). It seems more probable, though, that there may have been a loose, temporary linkage between Java and many of the small coastal states mentioned earlier. Certainly the unknown author of the early Javanese chronicle *Pararaton (Book of Kings)* portrayed Kertanagara (king of Singhasari) and Gajah Mada (chief administrator of Majapahit at its zenith) as leaders who had endeavored to suppress the evil forces of division and to strengthen the mystic forces of unity.[24]

In any case, whatever the historic truth, the myths have been enormously important, for the kingdoms of Sri Vijaya and Majapahit have been a powerful source of inspiration and national pride for a great number of Indonesians. They thus function as an integrating force. A belief in the inherent unity of the nation, interrupted by periods of chaos and then restored again to unity, provided a tradition by which Sukarno could claim to be following in the footsteps of Airlangga (the tenth-century restorer of unity), Ken Angrok (the Just Prince of the twelfth century who founded the dynasty of Singhasari),[25] Hayam Wuruk (the king of Majapahit in the fourteenth century), and Gajah Mada (Hayam Wuruk's prime minister from 1331 to 1364, who was hailed as the last man until Sukarno to unite "Indonesia" under a single ruler).[26] Certainly Gajah Mada's unified administration and codified laws and customs lasted until the nineteenth century in essentially the same form as they had during his premiership in the fourteenth.

It was in the days of Majapahit that Indonesian sculpture, architecture, religion, and philosophy departed most markedly from the Indian prototypes from which they had developed and assumed distinctive characteristics of their own. It is little wonder, therefore, that modern

Indonesians regard Majapahit as a national and historical symbol, pointing in the direction of Indonesian unification.[27]

Thus, looking back over the history of the ancient empires, one may argue that the perception and interpretation of history may indeed be as important as the historical truth, as least for the purpose of integrating the nation. The idea that Indonesia, with approximately its present boundaries, existed and functioned as one entity at various times in the past is a powerful concept for a young country, especially one seeking to unite its very different peoples into one nation and establish its unique identity and place in the world. Equally important are the communal pride engendered in acknowledging this glorious inheritance, and the feeling of shared greatness.

Certainly some of this pride is justifiable. Indisputably, ancient empires did arise and cast their influence over many of the islands of present-day Indonesia; and the impressive heritage of Borobudur, Prambanan, and the many other temples, statues, and monuments that testify to the artistic heights reached by these Indianized kingdoms is a legitimate source of national self-esteem.

Yet, from a more objective viewpoint, it is highly questionable whether these kingdoms did in any sense *integrate* their disparate parts. Rather, they imposed a vassal or subordinate status on the many parts of their empires, a status bitterly disputed and fought over at different times. The Sundanese of western Java, for example, still retain historical memories of the ruthlessness of Gajah Mada. And it may well be that the splendor of Majapahit, appealed to by nationalist leaders as a source of inspiration and unity for *all* Indonesians, has actually deepened the divisions between the Javanese inheritors of these treasures and the "inheritors-by-extension" from the other islands. Certainly the feelings of superiority that the Javanese display toward the Outer Islanders do not help the cause of integration.[28] As Bujung Saleh, one of Indonesia's own critics, expressed it:

> The illusionary greatness of Majapahit cannot form a strong bond of unity for all our people at this time. On the contrary, it even harms national unity, for people from other regions will feel that the greatness of their own regional history is being denigrated.[29]

Finally, although the myth that the present territory of Indonesia was defined by the independent ancient empires of the past (particularly Majapahit) is immensely appealing, the cold reality is that it was the Dutch colonialists who gave Indonesia the shape it has today, with the one exception of former Portuguese (East) Timor, which was annexed in May 1976 to become Indonesia's twenty-seventh province.

The Experience of Growing Western Influence and Control

The effect of European traders and colonialists, first the Portuguese, then the Dutch (with a brief British interregnum from 1811 to 1816), was ambivalent. On the one hand, the domination of the whole area by one European power gave the area a unity not experienced before. The islands were linked more systematically in terms of administration, law, and communications into at least a nominal functional entity. Dutch colonial rule also provided exposure to Western European culture, education, values, and ways of economic development. Common colonial control in turn provided a focus for the nationalist independence movement in the twentieth century, a cause that temporarily superseded deep feelings of diversity and division. Dutch hegemony provided the rationale for adopting the boundaries of the Netherlands East Indies as the limits of the new independent Republic, and the Dutch administrative system, based upon the existing autochthonous regions of different ethnic groups within the archipelago, was taken over and substantially kept intact by the new Indonesian government at independence.

On the other hand, however, Dutch control was uneven. Not only did the Dutch preserve existing differences among the already diverse peoples and kingdoms in the archipelago, but by their unequal treatment of different areas and ethnic groups they exacerbated old rivalries and created new, deeper cleavages. They focused most of their attention on Java and later on certain select areas of Sumatra, Kalimantan, North Sulawesi, and the southern Moluccas, while ignoring vast areas of the Outer Islands. They not only treated different Indonesian ethnic groups differently, but they also encouraged and made use of the entrepreneurial skills of the Chinese immigrants and their descendants as middlemen. They even set up separate judicial systems for Europeans, Chinese, and "natives," thus legally preserving the differences among the different ethnic groups rather than helping them to be assimilated into one social fabric. In addition they increased the disparity between rich and poor in both rural and urban areas.

Thus, while at the macro level the European influence can be construed as generally integrative, at the micro level its effect was often divisive.

Dutch intentions in the first hundred years of their influence in the archipelago, as with the Portuguese before them, were to gain a monopoly of trade rather than to carve out an empire.[30] Only slowly did the Dutch East India Company (*Vereenigde Oost-Indische Compagnie,* formed in 1602) gain control of the sea lanes and then turn to protect them by becoming more involved in the internal affairs of the islands. At first, the Dutch concluded alliances with several independent kingdoms and sultanates in the archipelago, including Ambon, Bali, and Ternate, and contended with hostility from others, such as Madura and Aceh. Later, they began to intervene in internal disputes, manipulating them to their own advantage, exacting adherence to Dutch trading monopolies, and collecting tribute and later "forced deliveries and consignments" as the price of Dutch help and protection. The *Compagnie* thus gradually changed from being a purely trading enterprise to being the ruler of a territorial empire. By the mid-seventeenth century, the Dutch were firmly established in western Indonesia (at Batavia, Banten, and Gresik in Java), on the Malay Peninsula (at Malacca, Patani, and Johore), and in eastern Indonesia (at Banda and Ternate). The local empire of Mataram on Java gradually extended its control over the eastern part of that island and Madura and as far as Banjarmasin in Kalimantan. But although the historians of the period who wrote *Babad Tanah Djawi* and other histories saw Mataram as the legitimate successor to all preceding states and in particular to Majapahit, in reality its territorial extent was very limited, and it too fell to the Dutch as a result of internal disagreements.[31]

Only very slowly were the islands of the future Indonesia established as part of the Dutch colonial territory, partly through battles won against other European nations—at sea, through intrigue, or through diplomatic channels back in Europe. The Portuguese, once their naval power declined, were gradually confined to eastern Timor (in the 1680s), although their influence lingered far longer in places such as Flores, Ambon, and western Timor. The Spanish were limited to the Philippines and the Sulu archipelago (in 1663), and the British eventually to the Malay Peninsula and the northern part of Borneo. The British, however, controlled an outpost in Bengkulen for 150 years after they were driven from the western Javanese kingdom of Bantam in 1689, before they exchanged it for previously Dutch-controlled Malacca in the Malay Peninsula (in 1824);[32] and they continued to guarantee the independence of the kingdom of Aceh until 1871.

The last half of the seventeenth century saw the loss of independence and the disintegration of all the remaining major Indonesian states—Ternate, Makassar, and Bantam, as well as Mataram—both in the face of superior Dutch naval power and in the transition of the role of the *Compagnie* from a purely mercantile organization to a budding colonial power. But the imposed internal peace did little to unify or integrate the separate kingdoms; they remained mutually hostile, linked only in their shared resentment of the common vassal status they held under the Dutch, as demonstrated by their constant uprisings and struggles to regain their independence. It has been claimed that the Dutch deliberately preserved the differences among the different areas under their control in pursuit of their policy of "divide and rule."[33]

By the mid-eighteenth century, three distinct areas of Western influence could be distinguished as a result of uneven treatment by the Dutch.

In parts of eastern Indonesia Dutch influence was intensive and oppressive. By regulating and destroying the means of production and prosperity of the islanders (by cutting down unauthorized clove and nutmeg trees to maintain high prices in Europe, and by improving their monopoly on trade), the Dutch succeeded not only in breaking the power of the previously proud and independent kingdoms of the Moluccas (such as Ternate and Tidore), but also in decimating their populations and reducing the survivors to bondage and poverty.[34] In other parts of eastern Indonesia, Dutch influence ranged from nonexistent (such as in western New Guinea and many of the Lesser Sunda islands) to warmly welcomed (in northern Celebes) to bitterly resented (in southwestern Celebes around the Dutch-destroyed town of Makassar).

In much of western Indonesia (Sumatra and Kalimantan), Western influence hardly penetrated at all beyond a few strategic fortress settlements along the coast (and Padang in West Sumatra) until the development of plantations and mines and the extension of Dutch authority to more parts of Sumatra during the mid- to late nineteenth and early twentieth centuries.[35] Sumatra (and particularly Aceh) was more affected than Kalimantan by Dutch monopolistic trading policies, yet these were less stringently enforced than in the Moluccas, partly because of the presence of the British in Bengkulen and the proximity of the Asian continent (which made unauthorized trading more difficult to control), and partly because the source of peppers and other trading commodities produced in western Indonesia was not so restricted geographically. Kalimantan was culturally and economically less developed than Sumatra. There, with the exceptions of the sultanates of Banjarmasin and Sambas, the few Dutch settlements established earlier were abandoned by the end of the eighteenth century because trade was not sufficiently valuable to justify the expense of manning and defending such settlements.[36] Also, the Dutch could not compete with the highly successful Chinese traders already entrenched there. Thus, in many of the Outer Islands petty states, principalities, chieftainships, and tribal societies flourished undisturbed by the *Compagnie*.[37]

It was in Java, however, that the influence of Western domination was the greatest. The Dutch set up their headquarters in Jakarta (which they renamed Batavia) in 1619 and soon eclipsed the power of the western Javanese sultanate of Bantam. They gradually extended their control over the island, despite three wars of independence (1705–1755), as the last and greatest of the Javanese states, Mataram, succumbed to Dutch pressure. They increasingly penetrated the traditional way of life of the inhabitants and encouraged Chinese immigration and entrepreneurship, and the development of a plural, nonintegrated society in which the Dutch were on the top, the Chinese in the middle, and the indigenous Javanese at the bottom.[38] The massacre of thousands of Chinese by Javanese in 1740, along with later legal restrictions, testifies to the nonassimilation of the Chinese into Indonesian society.[39]

In their fear of the potentially unifying force of Islam, the Dutch colonial government (which replaced the Dutch East India Company at the end of the eighteenth century when the latter went bankrupt and had its assets and liabilities taken over by the Dutch government) consistently supported the *adat* rulers (those who administered traditional, customary law) against the Islamic leaders.[40] They also played off rival kingdoms against one another. They systematically reduced the power and influence of the Javanese rulers and aristocracy until, by the end of the Java War (1825–1830), they had reduced virtually all of the principalities to the status of puppet domains in the Dutch East Indian Empire.[41] Dutch emphasis on Java, first with the contingents and forced delivery system, and later through the *Cultuurstelsel* (Cultivation System, introduced in 1830),[42] led to enormous differences between Java and the other islands, especially in economic development, because only a tiny proportion of the large land area of the Outer Islands was under effective Dutch control during the period of the Cultivation System in Java. Much of the Dutch effort outside Java was limited to punitive expeditions against piracy. Only later with the great economic expansion between 1870 and 1930 was there a change in the Dutch focus on Java and in the character and emphasis of Dutch trade and interest in Indonesia. As the more traditional exports of coffee, sugar, and tobacco (grown in Java), and spices (mace, cloves, and nutmeg from the eastern islands) gave way in importance to the more industrial products of rubber, oil, and tin (primarily in Sumatra), copra (in Celebes and the Moluccas), and coal (in eastern and southeastern Kalimantan), attention shifted to the establishment of firmer administrative control in the Outer Islands.[43] Plantations, concentrated primarily in Java and northern Sumatra, were developed as corporate enterprises to produce industrial rather than garden products.[44] Although Dutch influence was motivated primarily by economic considerations and hence did not work to achieve the integration of peoples in the Indonesian islands, some recent observers nevertheless consider that the Netherlands' expansion from Java to the Outer Islands represented, in fact, the creation of modern Indonesia: this allowed the imposition of an effective unity, greater political and administrative control, the laying of the foundations of a modern economy, and the radical alteration of traditional social patterns.[45]

Yet despite the growing incorporation of the Outer Islands into Indonesia, contrasts between Java and the Outer Islands, as well as among the Outer Islands themselves, continued to grow. Direct rule in Java contrasted with a greater degree of indirect rule in the Outer Islands.[46] Contrasts between Java and the Outer Islands widened in terms of population size, growth, and density as health and sanitation measures were introduced into Java. Disparities increased also in the development of infrastructure, as communications and transportation networks were developed in Java to a much greater extent.

Thus the imprint of the Dutch was uneven both historically in terms of the length of colonial administration and politically in the impact colonialism made in the different parts of the archipelago. Some areas experienced 350 years of Dutch influence or control, while for others it was a matter of only a few decades (see Figure 2.3). Indeed, it was not until 1901 that the Dutch finally crushed the last independent state, Aceh (although sporadic outbreaks of rebellion continued until 1908). Only after the turn of the present century, then, was Dutch rule effectively extended over all the islands of the Dutch East Indies.

When the Europeans defined the territory and delimited the boundaries of the Dutch East Indies colony, they took little or no notice of ethnic loyalties or historical relationships. As with colonies in Africa and other parts of Asia, decisions were made largely in Europe. The Johore-Riau empire was dismembered and the Riau-Lingga archipelago cut off from the Malay Peninsula. The Minangkabau on the peninsula came under British control, while those in western Sumatra became part of the Dutch East Indies.[47] The Bugis (from southern Celebes) were expelled from their eighteenth-century position of dominance in Kedah on the Malay Peninsula.[48] It took decades for agreement to be reached on the precise boundaries delimiting the colonial spheres of influence. Only in 1905 did Dutch negotiations with the Germans and the British determine the frontiers in the island of New Guinea. It was not until 1907 that the British finally withdrew from Sumatra and 1915 that the British and Dutch finally agreed in detail on the present Malaysian-Indonesian border in Borneo. It is ironic that the Netherlands East Indies took on almost the exact shape of the future Republic of Indonesia precisely when the first stirrings of nationalism began to be felt at the beginning of the twentieth century. As Grant put it:

> It is as if the invader, having laboriously established the outline of his territorial possessions in the East Indies, provided the people for the first time with a definite area by which to assert their rights to national independence.[49]

Not that the struggle for independence was new. The history of the 350 years of Dutch influence and control in the archipelago is filled with

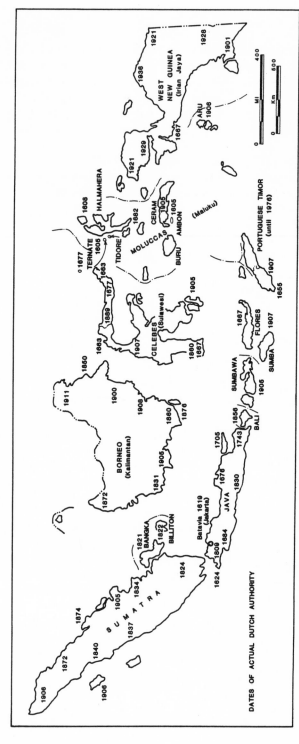

Figure 2.3. The expansion of Dutch authority in the former Dutch East Indies. Based on a map from Soedjatmoko et al., *An Introduction to Indonesian Historiography*, p. 358 (reprinted from Royal Dutch Geographical Society, *Atlas van Tropisch Nederland*) (used with permission).

revolts and insurrections against them, as individual kingdoms and sultanates fought to maintain or reestablish their independence and integrity.[50] These revolts, however, were largely isolated and uncoordinated; the unity claimed by later Indonesian historians in this "common resistance to the Dutch," at least at this stage, was experienced more in retrospect than consciously at the time. It was not until the twentieth century that these rebellions took on more than a local flavor, and Indonesians began to develop national awareness and a feeling of national unity. As the Dutch persisted in their efforts to weld Indonesia into one centrally governed administrative unit, and as the traditional authorities declined in public estimation, a new elite came into prominence—a small group of educated, upper-class Indonesians, who became aware more of the basic similarities among their countrymen than of the differences dividing them; and more aware also of their common colonial experiences and hope for a shared independent future.

These feelings of unity were encouraged by several factors: one was the worldwide rise of nationalism and national consciousness in the early twentieth century, which became increasingly apparent in other Asian countries; a second was the exposure elite Indonesians had to ideas and information about other countries through meeting people of different origins in the *hajj* (the pilgrimage to Mecca);[51] a third was the growing appreciation among Indonesians of similarities underlying regional differences, as contrasts with the intensified self-conciousness of both Dutch and Chinese became increasingly apparent;[52] and a fourth was increased education, encouraged by the Ethical Policy of the Dutch beginning in 1901. This last factor led to a recognition of Indonesia's own historic glories, a familiarity with the Netherlands' struggle against Spain (whose victory and independence the Indonesians ironically were made to celebrate), an awareness of the common suffering and oppression experienced by Indonesians at Dutch and Chinese hands, and increased consciousness of the discrimination facing Indonesians socially and in the job market. They became increasingly aware, too, of the disruption of village social patterns and the undermining of many of the village's customary certainties, caused by the new economic developments and increased penetration of Indonesian society by the government.[53] In addition, the limited number of schools, all on Java for higher education, brought together in a creative atmosphere students (and potential leaders) from different islands, who there became detached to a large extent from the framework of their own tradition and adopted a new urban culture where individual ethnic loyalties were less important.[54] Their association also fostered discussion of revolutionary ideas about a future independent Indonesia.

The Ethical Policy was a recognition that the Netherlands, having

profited for 300 years by exploiting Indonesia, should now do something in return.[55] Thus, a welfare-type program was introduced, theoretically aimed at economic, social, and political progress, including
agriculture, irrigation, public works, village sanitation, personal hy-
giene, and a very limited education for the indigenous people. However, because there were very few jobs for educated Indonesians except
in the civil service, and because the Dutch did not want to create an
intellectual proletariat to agitate for further reforms, the numbers educated were very few.[56] Exploration and surveying were intensified, rail-
ways and roads built, and interisland shipping expanded. But by its
very acknowledgment that a colony should be governed for the sake of
its inhabitants, the Ethical Policy opened the door to the inevitable, logical corollary of the principle of self-government.

The early twentieth century, therefore, witnessed the flowering of
many nationalist organizations with more than just local appeal: some
were cultural organizations, some mass movements, and others expressions of political nationalism. All served to increase national consciousness. *Budi Utomo* (Glorious Endeavor Society) was founded in 1908 with
the dual aspiration of helping the common Javanese people and creating
a movement to embrace the whole archipelago.[57] Its goals were cultural
and thus appealed to the educated rather than to the mass of society.[58]
The *Muhammadiyah,* founded in Yogyakarta in 1912 and supported both
by Javanese and by Muslims in Sumatra, became the largest and most
strongly organized movement in colonial Indonesia from the 1920s on.
Modernist in inspiration, it was devoted primarily to teaching and
social work. It too spread throughout Java and many of the Outer
Islands.

Indonesian student organizations were also active in the nationalist
movement. Soon after the foundation of *Budi Utomo,* Indonesian students in the Netherlands formed the *Indische Vereeniging* (the Indies Association), which took increasing interest in politics. In 1918 it espoused
Indonesian nationalism openly and called for full parliamentary government in the archipelago. Indonesian students in the Netherlands
later founded the *Indonesische Vereeniging* (the Indonesian Association),
which in 1925 adopted the Indonesian form of its title, *Perhimpunan Indonesia.* In 1924 this organization began publishing a militant journal entitled *Indonesia Merdeka (Independent Indonesia),* which not only justified the
name Indonesia for the Netherlands East Indies but also gave it political
content. The members of *Perhimpunan Indonesia,* drawn from all parts of
the archipelago, argued for the unity of the emerging political parties
and the formation of a single front to attract mass support on a national
basis and thus extract concessions from the colonial government.[59]
National youth congresses, held in 1926 and 1928, proclaimed Indone-

sia to be "one nation, one language, one motherland" (*"satu bangsa, satu bahasa, satu tanah air"*). They adopted a national anthem, renamed the lingua franca (hitherto called Malay) Indonesian and proclaimed it to be *the* national language, and chose the red and white colors of the Majapahit kingdom as the colors of the national flag. The motto, *Bhinneka Tunggal Ika,* was taken from *Sutasoma,* a Javanese poem also of the Majapahit period; the national emblem chosen, the Garuda, was the legendary mount of the Hindu god Vishnu and had also been used as a symbol of Majapahit.[60] They also adopted the original name of Jakarta for Batavia.

The growth of mass movements in the period of 1911–1927 was linked also to two growing world ideologies, pan-Islam and international communism. *Sarekat Islam* (the Islamic Union) was founded in 1911 by the new, Western-educated, nationalist elite, who were able for a brief period to establish enough contact with the peasantry in Java to create the first and only peasant-based nationalist organization during the entire period of colonial rule.[61] It had tremendous appeal among the masses and was greatly affected by the increasing numbers of *haji*. It reflected the growing resentment toward the Dutch colonialists and disillusionment with employment opportunities in the government civil service. This movement grew so fast, enrolling the support of more than two million members not only in Java but also in Sumatra, Kalimantan, Bali, and Celebes, that the Dutch became thoroughly alarmed and began severely to restrict contact between the Indonesian nationalist leaders and the peasantry. The government severed the ties between the central and local branches of *Sarekat Islam,* recognizing the branches but refusing to recognize the organization's central headquarters.[62] Indeed, repression by the colonial authorities so limited the political activities of the nationalist leaders that never again during the period of Netherlands rule were they able to develop the contacts with the peasantry that had been basic to the burgeoning of *Sarekat Islam.*[63]

However, it was the Indo-European party, many of whose members were Eurasians living in the large cities of Java, that developed the earliest yearnings for independence. And it is interesting to note that just as the concept of independence was first encouraged by a Eurasian, Douwes Dekker, communism was brought to Indonesia by a Dutchman, Sneevliet. From its introduction in 1914 until the Communist party's ill-conceived revolt in 1926, Marxism attracted those increasingly aware of the contrast in living standards between Javanese and foreigners, especially in the growing urban areas. But from 1920, when the *Perserikatan Komunis Indonesia* (the Indonesian Communist Union) broke off from *Sarekat Islam* and used the term "Indonesia" in its name, it emphasized awareness of national identity as one of its main planks.

Perhaps one of the most significant political institutions of the early twentieth century in the Indonesian islands was the *Volksraad,* established in 1918 as an advisory body to the governor-general.[64] Its importance lay not so much in its power, which was strictly limited, but in its existence as the colony's first popular representative organization, a symbol of national unity, and a forum for Indonesian opinion. Although the system of indirect elections to the *Volksraad* resulted in the return of lower government officials rather than the emerging political leaders of the Indonesian community, it did provide an opportunity for people from different parts of the country to work together and to give expression to their common grievances and aspirations. It thus provided some valuable political experience for a small number of Indonesians, even though the mainstream of nationalist feeling and nationalist organization passed it by.[65]

Gradually throughout the 1920s the term "Indonesia" became filled with content and extended its appeal to more and more of the inhabitants of the archipelago. Secular nationalist groups arose following the disintegration of the mass movements. The most important of these was the party founded by Sukarno in 1927—the *Perserikatan Nasional Indonesia* (the Indonesian National Union)—which became the *Partai Nasional Indonesia (PNI)* in 1928. This had as its ultimate objective an independent Indonesia and was a name and symbol that "served to transform 'Indonesia' from a concept of a few intellectuals into a living idea shared by a whole people."[66] The *PNI* grew rapidly in size and took the initiative in attempting to draw other nationalist societies into one organization. However, the resulting loose federation of parties (the *PPPKI, Permufakatan Perhimpunan Politiek Kebangsaan Indonesia*—Union of Indonesian Political Organizations) lacked real coherence and lost momentum, particularly after the banning of the *PNI* and the arrest of Sukarno in 1929.[67] Indeed, as Legge suggests, the history of organized nationalism in Indonesia was a record of a multiplicity of societies, able to enter loose alliances from time to time, but more frequently drawing apart from each other, splitting, and regrouping.[68] Division and rivalry characterized much of Indonesian nationalism, partly because of the character of Dutch rule and the nature of the Netherlands' attitude to the nationalist movement. The Indies Government alternated between tolerance and repression, becoming increasingly repressive as nationalist criticism became more radical, yet never trying to crush the nationalist movement totally. But the indecisiveness and inconsistency of government action in turn seems to have reduced the need for a tightly knit, focused nationalist organization, instead permitting, and possibly even encouraging, a variety of organizations to compete with one another.[69] Part of the disunity and rivalry can be attributed also to the elitist character of the nationalist leadership and the gap between the leaders and their mass following.

By 1930, however, the "day of Indonesia" had dawned. Indonesian party, youth, and women's congresses were held. Most associations founded after that included the almost magic word Indonesia in their titles.

The 1930s were also a period of growing confrontation between the Dutch colonialists and Indonesian nationalists. The Dutch, who were affected by the stock market crash and the worldwide depression, felt the need to extract ever more wealth from the colonies and therefore sought to suppress vigorously all the nationalist aspirations of the Indonesians (which many in the Netherlands erroneously regarded as limited to a handful of revolutionaries). As Dutch attitudes hardened and a police state was imposed, the nationalist movement once again fragmented, as Indonesian leaders disagreed among themselves about the means they should follow to attain their common goal of independence. Some advocated working within the system, pushing for self-government through an enlarged *Volksraad;* some wanted the gradual mobilization of the people; some the training of self-reliant, well-informed leaders; and some more direct confrontation. Many of the leaders, including Sukarno, Hatta, and Sjahrir, were jailed or exiled.

It was not until 1939 that the different Indonesian political associations formed a new union to improve the coordination of their activities. The *Gabungan Politik Indonesia* (*Gapi,* the Union of Indonesian Political Associations) had representatives from ninety different regional and nationalist organizations, including even such traditionally pro-Dutch organizations as the Ambon and Minahasa leagues and the Indonesian Catholic Party. *Gapi* launched an intensive campaign for an Indonesian parliament and national self-government, and officially adopted the Indonesian language, flag, and anthem. In an attempt to diffuse these demands, the Dutch instead encouraged the establishment of provincial councils, convinced that if a responsible system of government were created in the provinces, aspirations for centralized self-government could be channeled off.[70] The rift between Indonesian nationalists and the colonial government widened further.

Thus, by the beginning of the Second World War in Europe and the subsequent Japanese occupation of Indonesia, genuine nationalist consciousness had spread across much of the archipelago. Nationalist sentiment was much stronger in Java than in the Outer Islands, but members of many different Outer Island groups, especially those living in Java, participated actively in the various nationalist activities and through their ties with their areas of origin expanded nationalist sentiment there too. However, internal dissensions and ideological disputes among nationalist, Muslim, and socialist currents of opinion, along with a lack of mass support, weakened the nationalist movement as a whole. It has been estimated that of a total population in 1940 of about sixty million, the number of politically organized Indonesians totaled only about 80,700, while only around 200,000 (less than 0.5 percent) were politically or socially conscious.[71] Yet despite these small numbers, Indonesian nationalist aspirations were remarkably strong.

The Japanese Occupation and its Aftermath

The Japanese occupation (1942–1945) had a predominantly divisive effect on Indonesia, although there were certain counteracting unifying elements. The Japanese brutally subjugated the Indonesian people, disrupted trade and communications among them through strict censorship and attempts to make each regency self-sufficient, and encouraged division among the national leaders. The actions of the Japanese evoked an allied blockade that further isolated the different parts of the archipelago. From being welcomed enthusiastically as liberators from hated colonial rule on their arrival in 1942, the Japanese took barely four weeks to alienate almost the entire population. Instead of liberating and "restoring the independence of Asian peoples," as their propaganda claimed, they were more repressive than the Dutch had been even at the height of their anti-nationalist campaign. All nationalist movements were suppressed, political assemblies and demonstrations forbidden, display of the Indonesian flag prohibited, and any discussion, speculation, or propaganda regarding the political organization or administration of the country outlawed.[72] Punishment was ruthless. Further aspects of Japanese rule that particularly offended the Indonesians included the degrading punishment of flogging; Japanese emperor worship, which obliged the population to perform the ceremonial bow (saikerei) in the direction of the imperial palace in Tokyo (which deeply upset Muslims, whose prayerful bow was toward Mecca in the opposite direction); and the shaving of students' heads.[73]

But both in the intensity of their actions and in the duration of their presence, the Japanese occupation was uneven. As with the Dutch before them, the Japanese focused their attention on Java (and particularly on Jakarta), exploiting both its raw materials and labor resources. In their administrative organization of the country, the Japanese divided Indonesia into three separate commands, with little interaction among them: Java and Madura were under the Sixteenth Army based in Jakarta; Sumatra was administered from Singapore by the Twenty-fifth Army; and eastern Indonesia was controlled by the Navy, whose second fleet was headquartered in Makassar (southern Celebes).[74] The entrenched rivalry between the Japanese army and navy was also transferred to Indonesia. The army was more brutal and ruthless in its methods than the navy, although it gave considerable latitude for the Indonesian nationalist movement to develop (allowing, for example, the long-exiled nationalist leaders substantial freedom of movement and contact with the Indonesian masses). The navy, though less brutal, followed a severely repressive policy, discouraging any kind of indigenous political organization.[75] The divisiveness of the Japanese impact thus reinforced differences between the western and eastern parts of the country. In terms of the length of Japanese influence, although most of the country experienced a full three and one-half years of occupation, some of the eastern islands were liberated and reoccupied by allied forces more than a year before the rest of the country.

Yet the Japanese occupation was not without its unifying elements. The brutal treatment inflicted by the Japanese provoked deep and bitter opposition and caused common suffering that afterwards at least was recognized as a shared experience. Almost all parts of the country had their economies and ways of life disrupted, although not everywhere to the same extent. A shortage of labor, caused by conscription, resulted in neglect of estate production and irrigation works and a consequent decrease in food production; hardship and suffering thereby increased.

On the more positive side, the efficient Japanese administrative and communications networks reached down to almost every village and increased contact among the ordinary people. The Japanese organized neighborhood associations *(tonari gumi)*, the concept of which still survives today in the *rukun tetangga*.[76] Similarly, the Japanese ordered the Indonesians to establish *kumiai* in every *tonari gumi* and village, a form of cooperative society imposed from above that survived in modified form in the *koperasi* (cooperatives) of the later Guided Democracy period. In some ways Japanese policy also consolidated nationalist feeling by creating an all-embracing Muslim organization, the *Masjumi (Majelis Sjuro Muslimin Indonesia)*, comprising the *Muhammadiyah, Nahdatul Ulama,* and other groups. This was intended to provide more effective control of Muslim feeling, but in practical terms it laid the foundation for united Muslim political activity, which was to carry over into the early years of independence.[77] The Japanese propaganda system was used in disguise by the nationalists to raise villagers' political consciousness. In addition, although requiring all Indonesians to learn the Japanese language (and prohibiting the use of Dutch), the Japanese were forced in the interim to rely on the national language, *bahasa Indonesia,* to disseminate their propaganda: by so doing they unwittingly promoted and spread knowledge of Indonesian.

Further, expediency obliged the Japanese to push through a virtual social revolution as they mobilized the population and pressed everyone into their service—Muslim leaders, nationalists, princely families, and common people—without regard for their local particularisms or traditional social barriers.[78] They promoted Indonesians to many of the administrative and technical positions previously held by the Dutch. This increased opportunities for upward socioeconomic mobility among the nationalist elite, Muslim leaders, and even the old nobility and undermined the stability of society (as well as one of the most important sources of support for the Dutch regime). Old values were questioned and former social relationships were inverted and destroyed; the Japanese lost no opportunity to humiliate the former colonial masters in the eyes of the Indonesians. This inspired a new and powerful sense of self-reliance and authority among Indonesians, who found themselves both capable and competent to perform duties previously regarded as beyond their ability by the Dutch.[79] It also developed a determination among them to preserve what had already been gained.

The Japanese also set up, in 1943, what the Dutch had always resisted, an auxiliary, volunteer army, *Sukarela Pembela Tanah Air (Peta)*, which was composed mainly of members of Muslim organizations. This numbered some 120,000 men by 1945. It was this Japanese-trained but Indonesian-officered military that was to provide the principal military force behind the revolution, both in its early stages, when ironically it turned on the Japanese forces and fought them, and later, when it fought the British and subsequently Dutch forces. In addition, the Japanese gave very limited military training (but no arms) and the function of security guards to a considerable number of village and urban youth; when the *Peta* later expanded its ranks as a revolutionary army, it was able to draw on this source.[80]

On the Indonesian side, although opposition to the Japanese occupation intensified, there was no unanimity on how to respond. Some nationalist leaders, like Sukarno and Hatta, ostensibly collaborated with the Japanese while surreptitiously using the opportunities afforded them to rally support for nationalist ideas. Other leaders, like Sjahrir, organized underground resistance. Even the organizations established by the Japanese divided Indonesian opinion. At first many nationalist leaders thought they could achieve their goals by working through Japanese-approved institutions, such as the commission to study Indonesian customary law *(adat)*, the *Empat Serangkai* (literally Four-leaved Clover, referring to the four Indonesian leaders: Sukarno, Hatta, Mansur, and Ki Hadjar Dewantoro), the *Pusat Tenaga Rakyat* (Center of People's Power, *Putera*), and the *Tjuo Sangi-In* (Central Advisory Committee).

Unlike the *Volksraad* (People's Council), where the majority had never actively supported the nationalists' goal of independence, the *Tjuo Sangi-In* consisted exclusively, apart from the ubiquitous Japanese observers, of deputies who were of one mind in desiring independence.[81] But the perceived cooperation of nationalist leaders with the hated Japanese was itself divisive, as most of the Muslim groups and many regional leaders regarded them as traitors and accomplices in increasing the suffering of the Indonesian people.

The Japanese attitude toward the nationalist leaders was not consistent. Having tried at first to mobilize the population for the war effort without the help of acknowledged Indonesian leaders, the Japanese soon realized that the only way to get their economic program carried out was by using established leaders. They thus incorporated nationalist leaders in the *Putera,* which had a central bureau in Jakarta (the Japanese had adopted the native name for Batavia since the end of 1942) and branches in most provinces, and in the *Tjuo Sangi-In,* set up in Jakarta in 1943 with similar bodies *(sangi-kai)* in the provinces. Later, the Japanese replaced the *Putera* with the *Jawa Hokokai* (Javanese People's Loyalty Movement) to mobilize and control better the *priyayi* (gentry), particularly the lesser *priyayi* or, as they were now more often called, the *pamong praja* (administrative corps).[82] The Indonesian nationalists, although retaining key positions in the new movement, were incensed by the creation of *Jawa Hokokai,* partly because it deprived them of the organizational independence they had enjoyed in the time of the *Putera,* partly because this Japanese-titled organization reflected only too clearly the occupiers' policy of Nipponization, and partly because they were sandwiched between the military and the *priyayi,* neither of whom were interested in encouraging ideas of independence among the masses.[83]

Furthermore, the Japanese were not consistent in their attitude toward independence for Indonesia. At first they held out the possibility of independence (1942), but quickly changed this to membership in a Greater East Asian Co-Prosperity Sphere (March 1943), then incorporation into the Japanese empire (May 1943), followed by permission to "cooperate in government" (June 1943), and finally, after growing Nipponization, a deceptive promise of independence (September 1944). Yet despite the disappointment and frustration of gradual annexation and Nipponization, and despite the denial of future independence, nationalist sentiment grew and the nationalist leaders, particularly in Java, never lost their fervor nor stopped putting pressure on the occupation regime for self-government and independence. As Hatta put it in 1943:

It was perhaps necessary for strategic reasons to divide Indonesia into separate areas of military administration, but Indonesians will not give up the
desire and determination they have shown over the past forty years to unite
these territories into one glorious nation.[84]

Thus, tremendous changes took place during the brief three and one-
half years of Japanese occupation, out of all proportion to the pace of
developments earlier in the century. Not only was political consciousness raised on a wide scale, but also, especially toward the end of the
occupation, plans were made and organizations created to prepare for
forthcoming independence.

Although the first nationalist organizations under the Japanese were
limited to the Java-Madura command only, they were not restricted to
those living only on Java. There were many active nationalist leaders
from different ethnic groups throughout the archipelago. Although
nationalism was strongest in Java and most of the organized movements and resistance to the Japanese took place there, nationalism had
developed a pan-Indonesian appeal. There were frequent rebellions
against Japanese rule in the Outer Islands that were often hard to suppress. Although people from Java predominated in the councils and
organizations that pressed for a share in government, the Outer Islands
had similar advisory committees and provincial municipal councils,
beginning in 1944. Sumatra, for example, had a single council set up in
March 1945 at Bukit Tinggi consisting of Acehnese and representatives
of western, eastern, and southern Sumatra.[85]

It was not until May 1945, however, that a nationwide committee
was established to deal with the problems of independence (and not
until August that Indonesian nationalists from the navy-administered
areas were permitted to come to Java to consult with Javanese and
Sumatran leaders).[86] This was the *Badan Penyelidikan Kemerdekaan Indonesia* (the *BPKI*, the Committee for the Investigation of Independence for
Indonesia), which consisted of sixty-three nominated members from all
classes of the population and all shades of opinion in the nationalist
movement, and included Outer Islanders living in Java. Nationalists,
federalists, unitarians—all had different ideas about the size, shape,
partitioning, and administering of the new country-to-be.[87] It was at the
first session of the *BPKI* that Sukarno proposed the *Panca Sila* (Five
Principles of State) as the basic ideology of the future state: belief in one
God, nationalism, humanitarianism, social justice, and popular sovereignty. It is probable that this national philosophy, with its fusion of
ideologies in keeping with the ancient Javanese tradition of syncretism,
met with acceptance only because of the strength of outside pressures—

the approaching end of the Japanese occupation and the possibility of independence. It papered over deeply rooted differences rather than resolving them.

The *BPKI* adopted a republican form of government and drafted a constitution based in theory on the Indonesian democratic principles of consultation *(musyawarah)*, consensus *(mufakat)*, and cooperation *(gotong royong)*. Sovereignty was to reside in the *Majelis Rakyat Indonesia* (the Indonesian People's Congress), which was to consist of the *Dewan Perwakilan Rakyat (DPR,* a parliament chosen by direct vote) together with additional deputies who were to represent provinces and groups in proportion to their population and size. The Congress was to elect a president and vice-president by simple majority for a five-year term and a *Dewan Pertimbangan Agung* (Advisory Council of State). Ironically, however, the whole constitution reflected more the authoritarian principles of Dutch and Japanese rule that had been so violently criticized than the more flexible consultation and consensus processes regarded as more "Indonesian."[88]

Considerable disagreement arose over the precise shape of the future independent state. Hatta wanted to limit Indonesia to the former Dutch East Indies but without New Guinea, though possibly including Malaya. Yamin, supported by Sukarno, demanded the whole of New Guinea, Portuguese Timor, the British possessions in Borneo, and Malaya as far as the frontier with Thailand. A third group, consisting mostly of former civil servants, wanted the territory of the Dutch East Indies precisely as it stood. Interestingly, in the voting Yamin's Greater Indonesia won an overwhelming majority,[89] illustrating again how unsolidified the concept of Indonesia still was in 1945. It was not until later that year, when the Indonesian Independence Preparatory Committee was constituted, with eight of its twenty representatives coming from the Outer Islands,[90] that the decision was made to confine the new independent country to the territory of the former Dutch East Indies. Independence was declared on August 17, 1945, and took only hours to be relayed throughout the archipelago and abroad.

In Jakarta, the *Komite Nasional Indonesia Pusat (KNIP,* the Central Indonesian National Committee) was set up, with 135 members chosen by Sukarno and Hatta to represent the chief ethnic, religious, social, and economic groups in Indonesia;[91] while in the eight provinces established by the Preparatory Committee (West, Central, and East Java; Sumatra; Kalimantan; Sulawesi; Maluku; and the Lesser Sunda Islands) arrangements were made for local national committees. A governor was appointed for each province by Sukarno; the *KNIP* appointed a delegate to assist each governor. Thus in the six weeks between the

Japanese surrender and the Allied arrival, the Indonesians had established a fledgling republican government with its own civil service and with extensive militant support among the Indonesian people. The Indonesian flag was flown, the black cap or *peci* (originally a Muslim symbol but extended by Sukarno to have national significance) was worn, and *Radio Republik Indonesia* went on the air. The nationalists, led by the *Peta* (Indonesian army) and students, first struggled for control of Japanese weapons and for key cities in both Java and Sumatra and then wrestled with the British occupational forces. Only after this did they begin their major conflict, with the returning Dutch, who were unable to comprehend either the extent or depth of nationalist feeling that had so intensified in their brief four-year absence.

The next four years of struggle against the Dutch, from 1945 to 1949, were a time of growing solidarity and psychological unity for many Indonesians in their demand for a united and fully independent Indonesia. Differences of opinion inevitably arose that temporarily distracted the people and created divisive tensions, such as that between the youth and the older leaders both inside and outside the army, and by the communists (who attempted to lead a revolt against Sukarno and Hatta in Madiun in 1948), but the momentum of the nationalist movement and resistance both to the Dutch "Pacification Exercises" and to the imprisonment of Indonesian leaders strengthened national resistance and provided a strong integrative force.

Yet, as with nationalist consciousness, revolutionary fervor was by no means uniformly felt throughout the country. Support for the newly independent Republic centered in central and eastern Java, Jakarta, and parts of Sumatra. By contrast, there was no strong or active Indonesian nationalist organization in eastern Indonesia, where the Japanese had not permitted Indonesian nationalists to organize or to form militias.[92] Much of this area was occupied up to a year before the Japanese surrender by the Allied forces (Australian) and was returned easily to Dutch civil administration after the war. Most of Java and Sumatra, by contrast, remained part of the revolutionary Republic. The Ambonese continued to support the Dutch and even fought against their fellow countrymen's revolutionary struggle for independence. Inevitably by so doing, they aroused bitter resentment. Indeed, so strong was their anti-Republic sentiment that after the Round Table Conference in 1949, southern Maluku withstood considerable pressure to merge with the Republic of Indonesia in a unitary state as the other "federal states" did. It preferred instead to transfer its leaders (and 40,000 of its population who were mainly former members of the Dutch colonial army [*KNIL*] and their families, and former officials in the Dutch administration) to the Netherlands and form a government-in-exile there, waiting for the opportunity to reestablish an independent entity in those islands. (The 1975 incidents of the ambushed train and the attack on the Indonesian embassy in the Netherlands, and the 1977 school takeover and train hijacking illustrate the survival of this hope a generation later.)

Anti-Republic sentiment was also expressed by the Darul Islam movement focused in West Java, Aceh, and later in South Sulawesi and Kalimantan. This aimed at establishing an Islamic state in Indonesia and as such opposed both the Republic and Dutch domination. It supported its claim with guerrilla warfare, which lasted from 1950 to 1962.

Part of the Dutch strategy to regain control of the archipelago was to accentuate differences among Indonesians in different parts of the country. They attempted to isolate the self-proclaimed Republic from other areas of Indonesia in the hope of creating a federal order wherein pro-Republican elements would be outnumbered by Dutch-controlled component states.[93] The other part of Dutch strategy was to destroy the Republic by military means. They abrogated a number of agreements (including the Linggadjati and Renville Agreements) made with the Republic over the 1946–1949 period and ultimately forced on the revolutionary Republic's leaders a federal state in which fifteen of the sixteen member states were of Dutch creation.[94] Each of these was far smaller in size and significance than the Republic, which by 1949 comprised approximately half of Java and three-quarters of Sumatra (and a population of more than thirty-one million).

Among Indonesia's leaders there remained wide differences of opinion as to the future form and orientation of the country. Pro-Dutch, pro-Islamic state, and pro-*Panca Sila* (revolutionary Republic) nationalist sentiments existed in different parts of the archipelago. The experiences of the isolation of different areas under the Japanese and the four years of revolution against the Dutch during which the separate regions acted as highly autonomous units further hindered the growth of unity. However, counterbalancing these centrifugal forces were the psychological unity created by the goal of a united and fully independent Indonesia, an increasing sense of national identity, the consciousness of a common political purpose, and the commitment to a common revolutionary struggle against the Dutch. Yet in these strong centripetal forces and psychological bonds of unity lay the seeds of weakness. For once independence had been fully attained, the powerful negative dynamic of opposition to colonial rule was no longer applicable, and Indonesian nationalism lost much of its strength as a force for national cohesion. In the absence of strong outside pressures, ethnic and regional differences that had been submerged to some extent in the common struggle for independence soon reappeared to challenge the concept of national unity. Indeed, it has been claimed that the very success of the Indonesian revolution against the Dutch not only strengthened national political consciousness, but above all awakened regional pride based on ancient ethnic particularisms.[95]

Also, belief that independence would be a panacea for all difficulties, economic, social, and political, turned quickly to disillusionment as expectations for a better life remained largely unfulfilled (and the standard of living in Java continued to decline). In addition, appreciation of the centripetal power created by opposition to a common enemy contributed to the adoption of adventuristic policies in the new Republic, such as the continued cries to perpetuate the revolution ("against the enemies of imperialism, capitalism, liberalism, and individualism"[96]), the growing confrontation with the Dutch over the status of West Irian, and the *Konfrontasi* with Malaysia of the early and mid-1960s.[97]

The Period of Independence

The period of independence has been marked by deep divisions, regional rebellions, and even a short period of civil war (in 1958), but also by growing integration and the centralization of power. The country has survived as one political entity, unlike many other areas of the world that had also been united and kept together forcibly by colonial rule but that broke up after independence, such as the British West Indies, French West and Equatorial Africa, the Federation of Rhodesia and Nyasaland, and even the former unitary state of Pakistan. Part of the reason for Indonesia's survival has been its shared history along with certain common cultural underpinnings. Part has to do with the growing power and widening control of the military. Part, too, has been strong leadership, including the charismatic type of leadership exercised by Sukarno, and his political skill in keeping the country one[98] and in balancing the various forces of the nationalists, religious leaders, communists, and military. One way he preserved national unity was by changing the political system from the original federal to a unitary type of state in 1950, and from experimentation with parliamentary democracy in 1950–1957 to Guided Democracy (or martial law) in 1957–1965. However, the price for such unity under Sukarno was extremely high, because his concern for solidarity and national unity largely ignored both legitimate regional concerns and the basic economic foundations upon which all states depend. As economic decline, inflation, and falling standards of living intensified, tensions increased that ultimately helped to precipitate Sukarno's downfall, the murder of hundreds of thousands of Javanese and Balinese in the aftermath of the abortive coup of 1965, and the imposition of military rule under the presidency of General Suharto.

The change from a weak federal system to the stronger, more centralized unitary state in 1950 was one deliberate step toward consolidating
the fragile unity of the Republic. Sukarno's emphasis on keeping up the
revolutionary spirit and momentum, on infusing the diverse peoples
throughout the archipelago with a common national symbolism, on
reinterpreting history to foster national pride, and on obtaining worldwide recognition contributed to national integration in one respect.
Indonesia hosted the Asian Games and the celebrated Bandung Conference of Third World leaders in 1955. Sukarno successfully repudiated
the debt imposed on Indonesia as the price of independence by the
Netherlands in 1949. He nationalized Dutch economic interests and
repatriated many Dutch and Chinese, and he succeeded in attaining the
transfer of West Irian to Indonesian control. He inspired and
demanded loyalty and nurtured a sense of national unity.

But these achievements, though integrative in their intent and in
many of their aspects, were not without both disintegrative elements
and serious costs. With the removal of the powerful unifying struggle
for independence, regionalisms reemerged and threatened at times to
dismember the state. Indeed, Indonesia experienced twenty-one regional rebellions and revolts within its first twenty years of independence—ample evidence of the lack of integration within the country.[99]
Sukarno's emphasis on perpetuating the revolution through "symbol-
wielding" conflicted with the goals of the "administrators" or liberals,
based more in the Outer Islands, who sought to promote integration
through rationalized economic development and efficiency.[100] Important divisions arose also between rival ideologies; among and within
political parties, the military establishment, and government leaders;
and perhaps most important of all, between Java and the Outer Islands,
which itself is a key constituent of these other divisions.

The first national elections, in 1955, though designed to encourage
participation in a national event and though shared in by the population
throughout the country, were also a source of division. This was partly
because of the two years of intensive and often bitter campaigns, accompanied by the growth of corruption; partly because the election campaign clarified and emphasized the divisions existing in society and
forced a choice upon the people; and partly because of the frustration
that ensued when the prosperity and progress the elections had prom-
ised did not materialize. The central issue of the campaign itself was
deeply divisive: whether the state should continue to be based on the
Panca Sila or become a state based on Islam. The voting pattern demonstrated both the strength and nature of regional divisions and the depth
of divisions among the different groups in society, particularly among
the nationalist, socialist, and religious elements.[101] The Nationalists
(PNI), the Communists *(PKI)*, and the Muslim Scholars' Association

(*Nahdatul Ulama,* representing the more traditional Muslims) were all heavily supported in densely populated Java, but gleaned few votes in the Outer Islands. By contrast, the *Masjumi* (the reformist Islamic party) emerged as by far the largest party of the Outer Islands.[102]

Even the Asian Games and the Bandung Conference provoked division, in that these took place on Java and accentuated the Java-Outer Islands dichotomy that had been growing over the years.

This basic division between Java and the Outer Islands has been traced back to the old rivalries existing in the times of the ancient empires, between the sea-based, trade-oriented, Outer Island-centered empire of Sri Vijaya, and the land-based, agricultural, Java-centered Majapahit. But other historians see its roots as much older, going back to differences between the *ladang* (swidden) cultivation typical of the Outer Islands, and the *sawah* (wet rice) culture of Java, which dates back to Neolithic times. *Sawah* cultivation implies a rigid ecological technique: communal control over land, water supply, and cultivation systems is reflected in the highly formalized and hierarchical pattern of the intervillage social relations of Javanese rural society. Communal solidarity, a sensitivity to *adat* (customary law), and suffusion with a magico-religious cosmology that stresses harmony, continuity, order, and the unity of the land, people, and food cultivated, are all features of this life orientation.[103] Different strands of opinion represented by the *priyayi* (aristocracy) of the *kraton* (palace) and the *abangan* (traditional Muslims) of the village are thus held together in a harmonious, communal whole by the common ceremonies, superstitions, and mutual cooperation of traditional Javanese culture. Javanese society has also a highly absorptive character. Out of this ethos came the *Panca Sila.*

By contrast, the *ladang* system of shifting cultivation, which is much more common in the Outer Islands, has encouraged egalitarian social structures and a more individualistic, entrepreneurial spirit. The purer Muslim tradition found in many parts of the Outer Islands had little in common with the syncretic Javanese current of thought. It opposed the all-embracing *Panca Sila* philosophy with its lack of distinction between secular and sacred, and opposed colonialism through a crusading zeal against the infidel. Within this Muslim tradition were the modernists (who were prepared to combine modern technological and scientific ways with a distinctively Muslim outlook on life), the orthodox (who were able more easily to accommodate to the conservative, older generations, particularly in the rural areas), and the militants (who advocated the establishment of an Islamic state and were willing to back up this desire with force).

Whatever its origin, the Java-Outer Islands dichotomy was a division to which the Dutch added a further dimension by focusing their attention on Java. Java benefited from certain aspects of Western tradition such as health measures, sanitation, education, enforced peace between rival groups, more scientific methods of agriculture, better transportation and communications networks, and so on; but it also suffered the problems of greater exploitation and foreign control. The Outer Islands, by contrast, retained more independence in their traditional ways of life, trading patterns, and indigenous retail and distributive operations. They were able to respond positively to new economic opportunities, including the cultivation of export crops and improved trading opportunities, and developed increased political consciousness and regional and ethnic pride.[104]

As a result of this differential treatment by the colonial power, Java's population grew explosively, from 18 million people in 1875 to 35 million in 1920, and 49 million in 1940. (Explosive population growth continued after independence, with population increasing to 63 million in 1961, 76 million in 1971, 91 million in 1980, and an estimated 106 million in 1988.)[105] This growth in population on Java altered the established economic pattern of Javanese domination of the export economy. Whereas Java had been a rice-producing and rice-exporting area, producing 82 percent of Indonesia's total exports as late as 1892, Java's increase in population soon outstripped rice production, with the result that Java became a net rice-importing area. By 1955 Java contributed only 12 percent of Indonesia's exports.[106] Because 88 percent of Indonesia's foreign exchange earnings thus originated in the Outer Islands (71 percent from Sumatra alone), it is easy to understand the growing resentment aroused especially in the productive areas of the Outer Islands against the perceived parasitism of Java, when over 80 percent of Indonesia's foreign earnings was being spent on goods and services for the population in Java.[107] In addition, the regions outside Java became intensely dissatisfied with the government's failure to encourage their economic development or even to provide sufficient administrative and fiscal decentralization to allow them to undertake this themselves.[108]

Economic disparity and Javacentric economic policies, therefore, were one source of friction between Java and the Outer Islands. Others were fear of Javanese imperialism and domination of politics and culture, resentment of "Javanese arrogance and feudal class-consciousness,"[109] growing discontent with the centralized administrative control exercised from Jakarta, inadequate communications within and among the Outer Islands and between them and Java (heightened after the take-over of Dutch concerns in 1957 as the West Irian campaign backfired and the Dutch withdrew their interisland shipping fleet), and the almost inevitable inefficiency of a newly created bureaucracy. The coalition of divergent interests symbolized by the Javanese syncretic, symbol-wielding, politically oriented President Sukarno and the Sumatran, economics-minded administrator, Vice-President Mohammed Hatta, came under more and more strain, until it culminated in Hatta's resignation in December 1956 and the unilateral imposition of Guided Democracy by Sukarno the following year.

These sources of dissatisfaction, together with fear of the growing influence of communism, contributed to the *PRRI-Permesta* rebellion of 1958–1961, the most serious threat to the territorial integrity of Indonesia since independence. This centered in West Sumatra and North Sulawesi and dramatically highlighted the intensity of regional feelings.[110] Yet the lack of widely expected support from other regions and the overwhelming defeat of the rebellion demonstrated the strength of Indonesian cohesion. As a result of the rebellion, the centralized government's control over the provinces was tightened and the government became increasingly authoritarian. From speeches extolling national unity, Sukarno turned to demanding that all Indonesians give their loyalty exclusively to his government. He insisted that their devotion to national goals set by him should supersede whatever personal commitments they might have to local, ethnic, or religious communities, to professional standards, and even to humanitarian values.[111]

Sukarno relied increasingly on political and symbolic means of attaining national unity: he tried to inspire nationalistic feelings through the use of oratory and appeals to patriotism, slogans, and ceremony. The Political Manifesto of 1959 *(Manipol USDEK)* was rich in symbolism, from the mystical number of five (as in *Panca Sila*) to the major ideas themselves in the acronym *USDEK:* the 1945 constitution *(Undang-undang dasar 1945)*, Indonesian socialism *(Sosialisme Indonesia)*, Guided Democracy *(Demokrasi terpimpin)*, Guided Economy *(Ekonomi terpimpin)*, and Indonesian identity *(Kepribadian Indonesia)*. *Nasakom*, the title of the national front formed in 1961, deriving from the initial syllables of the words for nationalism *(nasionalisme)*, religion *(agama)*, and communism *(komunisme)*, was another example of Sukarno's love of acronyms and synthesizing symbolism.[112] Sukarno's oratory was superb, and through this, his consistent concern with national unity and solidarity, and his warmth and patriotism he won tremendous respect and affection from a vast number of Indonesian citizens.[113]

Guided Democracy (1957–1965), however, was accompanied by continued insensitivity to regional needs, bureaucratic inefficiencies, and deteriorating economic conditions. Even the Eight-Year National Plan, put forward in 1960, was significant more for its symbolism (it had seventeen parts, eight chapters, and 1,945 paragraphs, commemorating the declaration of independence on 17 August 1945) and wishful thinking than for its realistic approach to development.[114] Sukarno spent much of the country's resources on huge, unproductive national monuments and extravagant world tours, while inflation soared and tension increased among the major political groupings—the nationalists, Muslims, communists, and the army. Tensions finally erupted in the pro-communist abortive coup of September 30, 1965 (*Gestapu: Gerakan September Tigapuluh,* the September 30 Movement). The ensuing blood-bath, in which hundreds of thousands of communist supporters were massacred and innumerable personal scores settled, revealed the depth and bitterness of the hostilities that had built up over the years, particularly during the "imposed consensus" of the Guided Democracy period.[115] Bloodletting was greatest in syncretic Muslim Java, but was by no means confined there: Hindu Bali also witnessed extensive killings, as did North Sumatra, although far fewer deaths occurred in the Outer Islands.

The New Order *(Orde Baru),* ushered in by Sukarno's successor, General Suharto, has rejected the Sukarno model of attaining national unity and integration by symbol-wielding and revolution in favor of consistent emphasis on political stability, order, and economic development, even at the price of the limitation of democracy and the imposition of military rule (albeit with civilian technocrats incorporated into the government). Indeed, the army has presented itself as a truly national force identified with the interests of the community as a whole and therefore most fitted to rule.[116] At a seminar in 1965, the army produced the doctrine of the *Dwi Fungsi* (Dual Function) of the armed forces, justifying their dual role as both a military force and a social-political force (covering the "ideological, political, social, economic, cultural, and religious fields"). Since then the army has justified its continued domination of the state on the grounds that civilians still need the strong leadership that only the army can provide.[117] Since 1965 the army has expanded its role in politics and administration; many military leaders hold positions as governors, ambassadors, secretaries-general of government departments, and managing directors of state firms at both the national and regional levels.[118]

Indeed, the military has been increasing its political role in the country ever since 1945, when the youths who took up arms were motivated less by the desire for a military career than by patriotism and support for the Republic proclaimed by Indonesia's nationalist leaders.[119] After independence was attained, the army continued its political involvement, at first in an essentially guardian role, but later as a full participant in the affairs of state. The weak hierarchical structure and sharp rivalries among groups of officers curbed the army's effectiveness as a political force in its early days. But gradually army leaders were able to

take advantage of the various national crises (generated in part by politically oriented dissident groups within the army) and the weaknesses of
successive political systems to take wider powers. After the introduction
of martial law in 1957, the armed forces, and particularly the army,
became deeply involved in politics, civil administration, and economic
management, and thus became a key part of the government coalition
under Guided Democracy.[120] The army gained in strength and unity
also as a result of its role in putting down the rebellions of 1958–1961.

After 1957 (the imposition of Guided Democracy), and particularly
after 1965 (the abortive communist coup and the beginning of the military government under President Suharto), the army rapidly expanded
its role in the economy, as well as its political power. This took place at
two levels. First, the military sought to supplement the limited funds
they were allocated by the government by establishing various enterprises and controlling certain elements of the economy such as the state
oil corporation *(Pertamina)*, the national food trading agency, and the
general trading corporation.[121] Similar arrangements were made also in
the Outer Islands, where military officers became involved in a wide
range of business activities. By obtaining funds and foreign exchange
directly from *Pertamina* and other enterprises controlled by the military,
the army sought to free itself from domestic criticism, bureaucratic controls, and foreign pressure by creating the impression that military
expenditure was less than it really was. Indeed, by the mid-1970s, at
least half the army's operating funds derived from extragovernment
sources.[122]

Second, army officers developed their own private economic interests, establishing business partnerships with Chinese and foreign businessmen, and arranging contracts, credits, and licenses for colleagues,
friends, or relations, or in exchange for commissions. Indeed, Crouch
has suggested that many officers felt much more at home dealing with
Chinese and foreign businessmen than commanding troops in the
field.[123] The military thus acquired a stake in the regime and in defending the existing social order.

The military was also very concerned after 1965 not just to consolidate its own power but to provide the political stability necessary for
economic development to flourish. Specifically, the military leaders
incorporated civilian technocrats into the government, hoping that they
would create a favorable economic climate for Western and Japanese
investment capital and so provide lucrative economic opportunities for
the military-dominated elite.[124] The rapid expansion of the economy
through the influx of foreign aid and private capital not only enabled
the army to raise funds for its own operations and provided officers with
material satisfaction from their own private activities, but also, by pro-

viding greater revenues, enabled the government to raise salaries substantially for civil servants throughout the country, thus helping to create a broader civilian base of support for the regime.

The role of the military has had both positive and negative effects in
terms of the overall integration of the nation-state. On the positive side,
the New Order military government with its civilian technocrats has
established a large measure of political stability and continuity, which in
turn has restored investment confidence and led to real progress in economic development. Loans from the World Bank and loans and aid
from the countries in the Inter-Governmental Group on Indonesia
(IGGI), as well as investment by private investors, have all contributed
to the country's economic growth. The post-1965 period has been
characterized by the rehabilitation of the much-neglected transportation
system and great achievements in the development of new microwave
and satellite communications systems, the end of the chronic inflation of
the mid-1960s, improvement in production levels, a spectacular increase in export earnings, and a succession of four five-year economic
development plans. There has been a slow but appreciable increase in
the general standard of living for many people.

Yet not all the effects of the New Order or even of the improved economic situation have been integrative, either economically or politically. Economically, the emphasis on efficiency in development has
resulted in greater and increasingly apparent inequalities between the
military and civilians, between urban and rural areas, between land-
owners and local government officials on the one hand and the mass of
peasantry on the other, and between Java (where most development
monies have been invested) and the Outer Islands, inequalities that
have provoked widespread resentment against the government. The
army's conception of economic development has been primarily oriented toward the interests of the elite and white-collar middle class, and
toward the modern sector of the economy, at the expense of indigenous
entrepreneurs and the national good. Indeed, Crouch claims that the
entire system is designed primarily to serve the interests of the military
elite and the civilian bureaucratic and business groups closely linked
with it.[125] Only in the last two five-year development plans, *Repelita III*
(1979–1984) and *Repelita IV* (1984–1989), has the emphasis shifted to
the goals of greater equality in development and the more even distribution of the fruits of development—and there are questions as to how far
these goals are being implemented.

Politically, despite the elaborate facade of democratic elections in
1971, 1977, 1982, and 1987, the military retains control of the country.
Political parties have been forcibly amalgamated and streamlined, and
support has been coerced for the government-sponsored party, *Golkar*

(*Golongan Karya,* Union of Functional Groups). Many of the political
channels previously available as outlets for criticism and as safety valves
for feelings of resentment against the regime are now severely limited;
unacceptable political opposition is suppressed. The press is more
strictly controlled and muzzled and student criticism more muted than
before. Until late 1977, when thousands were released, more political
prisoners were in custody than at any time in the past. In contrast to
Sukarno's mobilization of the peasant population for various patriotic
causes, the New Order has encouraged political passivity. Fear of arrest
and of the powerful secret police (*Kopkamtib,* the Operational Command
for the Restoration of Security and Order, established in 1965), as well
as of the army-controlled State Intelligence Coordinating Body (*Bakin,*
founded in 1967), has further discouraged political activity. It remains
to be seen whether such lack of meaningful political participation can be
extended indefinitely, especially in the face of blatant corruption and
mismanagement.

Greater streamlining of the bureaucracy and stronger control in government, although leading perhaps to greater national coordination,
have resulted also in increased Javanese control over Indonesian life.[126]
This can be seen in the growing proportion of Javanese in the government (especially in the cabinet) and in the military leadership. This preponderance of Javanese officers occurred originally because most of the
fighting during the revolution took place in Java. But it became even
more pronounced when many non-Javanese lost their positions because
of their involvement in the 1958 rebellion. Because of Indonesia's
uneven population distribution, it is to be expected that the Javanese
should make up between 60 and 65 percent of the national leadership in
proportion to their numerical strength. But this proportionate representation is not easily reconciled with the need to grant representation on
the basis of territorial extent or ethnic balance. And in any case
Javanese domination of government offices and army leadership exceeds their proportional makeup of the population of Indonesia and has
increased significantly since 1956.[127] By the 1960s about 70 percent of
army officers were Javanese. In addition, the carefully worked-out balance in the highest leadership positions, by which the president
(Sukarno) was a Javanese and the vice-president (Hatta) a Sumatran, a
representative of the Outer Islands, was upset for more than twenty
years after Hatta's resignation in 1956; the position of vice-president
was first abolished and then, after the position was restored in 1965,
filled by Hamengko Buwono IX, the Sultan of Yogyakarta, a Javanese,
until Adam Malik, a Sumatran, was elected in 1978. From 1983 to
1988, however, the vice-president was from West Java, retired General
Umar Wirahadikusumah. In 1988, another Javanese, Soedharmono,

was elected vice-president. Javanese domination of the military and government has changed somewhat since the mid-1970s as the 1945 (mainly Javanese) generation has begun to reach retirement. They are being replaced by the so-called Magelang generation (trained at the Indonesian Armed Forces Academy [*Akabri*] in Magelang), which includes officers from all parts of Indonesia. This group includes a greater proportion of officers dedicated to greater regularization and re-form.[128]

The growing centralization of authority within the military has been another cause for concern. After the *PRRI-Permesta* rebellion, which ended in 1961, the central army leadership improved its position vis-à-vis the Outer Islands. It garrisoned the Outer Islands with forces from Java (thus in effect establishing a military occupation of the Outer Islands by Java's "central government" forces in the name of national unity); it reduced the authority of the regional military commanders; and it created a para-commando regiment under direct central control.[129] Since the 1965 abortive coup power has been so much further centralized and concentrated among the Javanese that some Outer Islanders claim that they have exchanged Dutch colonialism for Javanese colonialism and "colonelism."[130] In addition, Suharto has also consolidated authority within the armed forces themselves. Up until 1965 Sukarno had manipulated interservice rivalries and undermined the cohesion of the armed forces, expecting the air force, navy, and police to balance the power of the army.[131] After 1965 Suharto reduced the power of the other three branches and ended open factionalism within the army through the transfer of commanders. He also halted interservice rivalry with a reorganization and integration of the armed forces under a single command.

Finally, the army's integrative political power has been exercised partly through its "territorial" organization. Alongside its fighting units the army developed a network of territorial units concerned with internal security and generally watching over civilian activities. Thus, the army sought to integrate itself with the people through its territorial units, which more or less paralleled the civilian administration at every level. Martial law had been administered through these territorial units between 1957 and 1963; later in the 1960s, after emergency regulations were abolished, local commanders continued to carry out internal security functions as agents of *Kopkamtib*. Through this territorial organization and the power of the armed forces, the Indonesian government has had at least a fair level of effective control over the whole of its national territory, unlike several of its Southeast Asian neighbors. It can, perhaps, be argued that without military force it is entirely possible that the fragile state of Indonesia would have fractured.

However, this raises the question of the extent to which Indonesia's unity is coerced or free and genuine, and whether a measure of coerced unity is really the same thing as integration. Undoubtedly there is considerable pressure from the central government to maintain Indonesia's territorial integrity and achieve political stability through both coercion and the distribution of patronage. But in addition, a variety of government policies throughout Indonesia's period of independence has consistently sought to promote national integration within the country (although the methods of reaching this goal have changed over time).

In this brief survey of Indonesia's recent history, a major underlying theme has been the tension between Java and the Outer Islands as it has affected the political, sociocultural, economic, and military spheres of the national life. Even potentially integrative events and structures have been undermined by this division. Yet the dichotomy between Java and the Outer Islands is not the only source of division within the country. As might be expected in a nation as large and diverse as Indonesia, the situation is much more complex. This complexity, which strongly modifies any rigid distinction between Java and the Outer Islands, is more integrative than the situation existing, for example, within neighboring Malaysia, where historical developments have reinforced more clear-cut, ethnically based divisions. Within Java there are deeply felt divisions among the Sundanese of western Java, the Madurese, and the ethnic Javanese of central and eastern Java, in cultural as well as political orientation. In the Outer Islands there is considerably more diversity, not only among *sukubangsa* (major tribal groups) such as the Batak and Minangkabau or Ambonese and Dyak, but also among *suku* (sub-tribal groups) such as the Karo, Toba, and Mandailing Batak. The Acehnese are well known for their hostility to any outside control, be it Dutch or Indonesian. And resentment has been felt historically by the peoples of South Sulawesi against the Minahasans (of North Sulawesi) as well as against the Javanese. These examples highlight one of the key problems of Indonesian unity: in many areas, ethnic loyalty still rivals national loyalty in importance.

At the same time, certain areas outside Java have participated disproportionately in the national life of the country, both in terms of their areal involvement in the various integrative experiences of Indonesia's history and also in the number of leaders originating from them. Three or four ethnic groups stand out for their more entrepreneurial and dynamic roles in national affairs—the Batak and Minangkabau in Sumatra and the Minahasans and (to a lesser extent) the Ambonese in eastern Indonesia. These have provided national leaders far out of proportion to their numbers, and the trading network created by the Bugis and Makassarese (and, of course, the Chinese) has likewise been disproportionately influential.

Within ethnic groups there have been divisions between religious and traditional *(adat)* leaders. Furthermore, there have frequently been broader differences between coastal and interior dwellers within a single island than among coastal peoples in different islands separated by hundreds of miles. Thus, an affinity created by a similar life style (such as dependence on the sea for fishing and for communications) and by a network of trading connections has often enabled the sea to be an integrative rather than a divisive force.

The history of Indonesia, therefore, consists of a mosaic of experiences, both integrative and divisive, which have been shared to greatly varying extents by different parts of the Indonesian archipelago. Although it can be argued that many of the experiences have been uneven and even ambiguous in their effect, the cumulative impact of the past has been generally integrative. The shared history of the ancient empires and kingdoms, Dutch colonialism, the Japanese occupation, the struggle for independence, and over four decades of functioning as an independent nation-state, together with the country's ancient roots, both mythical and historical, and its existence as one political entity with basically the same political boundaries for almost four centuries, have served to provide an important common heritage for the vast majority of Indonesia's inhabitants. Most people consider themselves to be Indonesians and have a genuine sense of national pride and identity.

However, two provinces have not shared to anything like the same extent in most of the historical experiences discussed thus far: Irian Jaya, because of its geographical location at the eastern extremity of the country, its different ethnic and cultural composition, its relative neglect by the Dutch, and its somewhat later full incorporation into the nation-state of Indonesia; and East Timor, which was a Portuguese colony until 1976, when it was annexed by the Indonesians. They therefore merit separate consideration.

The Exceptional Provinces: Irian Jaya and East Timor

The problems posed by Irian Jaya and its continued incorporation into Indonesia remain considerable. The indigenous Irianese are ethnically and culturally quite different from the other peoples of Indonesia, yet their history has been bound up, albeit loosely, with that country for over 300 years and perhaps much longer. Indonesian nationalists claim that Irian Jaya was part of the great thirteenth- and fourteenth-century kingdom of Majapahit. The recorded history of Irian Jaya dates back to 1660, when Tidore, which had nominal jurisdiction over the area, became a dependency of the Dutch East India Company. This nominal rule of Tidore over Irian Jaya formed the basis of the Netherlands East Indies' boundary agreement with Great Britain in 1885 and with Germany in 1910. But an effective Dutch presence in Irian Jaya did not begin until 1898, and even then, apart from being used for camps for exiled Indonesian nationalists, Irian Jaya was basically neglected. Not until after the Second World War, in an attempt to ward off claims by Indonesian leaders that Irian Jaya was inherently a part of their newly proclaimed independent country, did the Dutch establish for the first time a permanent administration for the territory. When the Dutch finally conceded independence to Indonesia in 1949, therefore, Irian Jaya was not included.[132]

This policy led to an intensified confrontation between Indonesia and the Netherlands, which was not settled until 1962 when Irian Jaya was transferred to United Nations auspices. In 1969 an "Act of Free Choice" was conducted in which representatives of the Irianese voted in a referendum on whether they wanted to remain with Indonesia or become a separate, autonomous state. However, since this referendum was taken under Indonesian supervision and control, with few safeguards to ensure that the Irianese would be given a fair opportunity to exercise their choice, charges of Indonesian rigging of this "Act of Free Choice" abound. Irianese nationalists, determined to fight for an independent Irian Jaya, formed in 1963 the *Organisasi Papua Merdeka* (the *OPM* or Free Papua Movement). During the early 1970s sporadic armed clashes occurred throughout Irian Jaya between the Indonesian authorities and West Papuan freedom fighters. These escalated into more significant local uprisings in 1977 and 1978, coinciding with the national elections and associated with Melanesian resistance to pressures to vote for the ruling *Golkar* party. They drew renewed attention to the demand for Irianese separatism, and Indonesia's handling of the situation elicited widespread sympathy for the Irianese, especially among Irian Jaya's Melanesian neighbors.[133]

The *OPM* continues to operate, partly from outside the country, with political and propaganda activities organized from bases in the Netherlands, Senegal, and Papua New Guinea, and partly as a guerrilla force throughout Irian Jaya and particularly in the region near the Papua New Guinea-Irian Jaya border. Although the leaders claim to have 35,000 freedom fighters, most reliable sources accept an estimate of 400–600 guerrillas with an extensive network of supporters.[134] Despite numerous attempts to eradicate them, the *OPM* continues to grow stronger, claiming wider international recognition. Its strategy includes threatening vital oil, gas, and mineral facilities in Irian Jaya, causing a diversion of scarce resources to maintain security. The *OPM's* resistance to the Indonesian government is based on several grievances: forced territorial incorporation into Indonesia, cultural imperialism, loss of identity, alienation of land, and political repression.

Indeed, there appears to be considerable evidence to support Irianese claims that Irian Jaya's wealth of natural resources—petroleum, natural gas, hard minerals (especially copper), and timber—is being exploited by U.S., Japanese, and South African firms for the benefit primarily of the Indonesian central government in Jakarta, the military establishment, foreign investors, and local (often non-Irianese) officials. Few if any benefits accrue to the Irianese people; to the contrary, such investments have frequently caused havoc in the lives of the Irianese by uprooting them and undermining their way of life.

Nevertheless, the Indonesian government is determined to consolidate Indonesian control over Irian Jaya and integrate the area into the national whole, and not just for economic reasons. There are symbolic and security reasons as well. For if Irian Jaya were allowed to secede, a chain reaction of other dissatisfied regionally based minorities could follow.

Consequently, the Indonesian government has taken a number of steps to ensure the continued integration of the province. It has moved, or encouraged to move, thousands of non-Irianese from Java, Maluku, and Sulawesi to resettlement sites in Irian Jaya. By the early 1980s, over 250,000 non-Irianese had been added to Irian Jaya's 750,000 indigenous people. The newcomers dominate the urban areas, and increasingly the economic activities of the province. The transmigration (resettlement) plan for 1984–1989 anticipated the movement of a further one million people to Irian Jaya, thus threatening to reduce the Irianese to a minority in their own province (although that goal has not been reached). As critics have complained, the transmigration policy goes "in tandem with a systematic policy of Indonesianization (and even Javanization) and Islamization of Irian Jaya," the inevitable loss of indigenous land, and political repression that is part of the cost of "pacifying" the province.[135]

Other steps taken by the Indonesian government to integrate the province include efforts to assimilate the local populace by bringing Irianese at the local level into the provincial administration, the police, and the armed forces. A massive educational program has been designed to "induct the Irianese into the cultural mainstream."[136] This includes increasing their knowledge of the Indonesian language and providing opportunities for tertiary study and training in Java and

overseas. The Trans-Irian Jaya Highway is being built along the length
of the border with Papua New Guinea in an attempt to cut off the *OPM*
from its support source in Papua New Guinea. It remains to be seen
how successful these measures will be.

The situation in East Timor poses less of a threat than does that in
Irian Jaya to the continued integrity of Indonesia, despite its very different colonial history, partly because of its location and the much
greater inherent poverty of the province. But the damage done in the
past decade has been proportionately greater.

Despite centuries of historical contacts, both trading and political,
between the great Hindu empires and succeeding Muslim kingdoms in
Java on the one hand and the eastern part of Timor on the other, the
Indonesians made no attempt to incorporate East Timor into the country until 1975. Indeed, few Indonesian nationalists ever viewed East
Timor as part of Indonesia. But in 1975, uncertainty about the nature
of Portugal's revolution and its consequences for its small Portuguese
colony in Southeast Asia, and fear that a nominally independent East
Timor could lead to a leftist (possibly Chinese-dominated) subversive
government as well as possibly serve as a model for other minor but
smoldering secessionist movements in eastern Indonesia led the Indonesian government to annex the territory.[137]

Indonesia's invasion of East Timor in December 1975 was followed
by an "Act of Free Choice," arranged by an Indonesian government
that ignored the fact that more than two-thirds of the population of the
territory was behind rebel *(Fretilin)* lines.[138] The ensuing massacres,
atrocities, and looting, and the resulting misery, suffering, and humilia-
tion of the Timorese, as well as the famine and resulting starvation and
outbreaks of disease, combined to reduce East Timor's population from
an estimated 688,770 in 1974 to 329,270 in 1979, according to Roman
Catholic Church officials.[139] Even if the 1980 official census figures of
550,000 are accepted as accurate and not inflated, this still represents a
decline of over 130,000 from the population size on the eve of Indonesia's invasion. With population growing normally at about 2 percent
per year, however, the population should have been around 750,000 in
1980. When finally in 1979 aid workers from the International Red
Cross and Catholic Relief Services were allowed into East Timor, they
were shocked at the extent and depth of the human misery: between
one-tenth and one-third of the population had perished and over
300,000 were in the resettlement camps, debilitated, demoralized, and
deeply alienated.[140]

Despite ten years of repression and deplorable conditions, some 800–
1,000 *Fretilin* guerrillas are still active in East Timor, against whom the

Indonesian government has reportedly sent some twenty army battalions with around 15,000 men (despite the claim of General Benny Murdani, commander of Indonesia's armed forces, that only fourteen battalions with about 7,000 men were confronting 500–700 guerrillas).[141]

The Indonesian government claims that much has been done to integrate the province into the nation-state of Indonesia and to raise the standard of living of the people. Journalists have reported improvements in the living conditions of many, with better housing and water supplies and plans for a government sugar plantation and sugar mill.[142] However, persistent reports continue of ongoing dissatisfaction with the resettlement camps, which are termed no better than internment camps. This is because they are located so far from the inhabitants' fields, they greatly restrict people's freedom of movement, and they demand an unacceptable change in lifestyle from that of the traditional hamlets. Moreover, most of the worthwhile enterprises of East Timor have been taken over by army officers, and the economy has been generally mismanaged.[143]

The greatest challenge now for the Indonesian government is to win the hearts of the deeply alienated population and to replace unwilling submission to Indonesia's rule with nationalism and Indonesian patriotism.

Integration is a dynamic concept, one that has to be constantly nurtured and its component dimensions kept in balance. The history of many countries demonstrates that changing realities can raise dangerous tensions among regions, even in well-integrated nation-states. Even more in Indonesia, a diverse and widely dispersed archipelagic state, there is no room for complacency in the ongoing struggle to strengthen national integration.

3

The Sociocultural Dimension

JUST as integration depends upon shared historical experiences and participation in one national political system, so also it depends upon the degree to which people within that political entity share certain sociocultural characteristics and feel themselves to be one nation. It is important, therefore, both to examine the integrative nature of the dominant sociocultural features of the population and to analyze the extent to which these characteristics are shared by peoples in each province of the nation-state of Indonesia. Important shared characteristics include use of a common language, adherence to a common religion (or at least to shared cultural features that have a religious basis), and participation in a "national culture" in the sense of shared national values, customs, organizations, and institutions that transcend local and ethnic boundaries, extend nationwide, and promote national consciousness and interregional contact. A shared culture also includes exposure to common radio and television shows and nationally produced movies, and access to other nationwide services and amenities such as health care and nationally organized education.

The tremendous diversity of Indonesia's population has already been discussed. Yet underlying this mosaic of differences in Indonesian society are certain unifying features. From an anthropological perspective, these common characteristics include aspects of food, dress, sports, and attitudes toward pets, disease, and sexual roles.[1] To these can be added common attitudes toward time, the elderly, and the family, an almost ubiquitous belief in spirits, a general acceptance of authority, and an appreciation of the value of symbols.

Promoting national integration, a consistent goal of all nationalists and independent Indonesian governments, has meant trying to increase

60

and strengthen these and other shared national characteristics, to make Indonesia's motto (*Bhinneka Tunggal Ika,* Unity in Diversity) a reality. The aim has been to redirect local primordial bonds and ethnic and regional loyalties toward the larger nation-state, toward national consciousness, loyalty, and interests; and to encourage participation in a nationwide culture and way of life. Data for this chapter are tabulated in Appendix 1.

Language

A common national language has long been recognized as one of the strongest integrating forces within a nation. Its use is obvious in permitting interregional communication and the growth of mutual understanding and a common identity. Language is also a major vehicle for culture.

Yet although Indonesian is spoken by many, especially in the coastal areas of most of the islands of the archipelago, it is the second or third language for the vast majority. Most Indonesians speak one of the more than 250 mutually incomprehensible languages belonging to the Malayo-Polynesian language family. Also represented are Papuan tongues in Nusatenggara, Melanesian speech in parts of Irian Jaya, and a distinctive northern Halmaheran language group in northern Maluku.[2]

However, as a result of a history of extensive commercial ties among many of the islands in Indonesia as well as with the Malay Peninsula and northern Borneo, a common trade language developed, *bahasa Melayu pasar* (market Malay), incorporating Sanskrit, Hindi, Arabic, and a wide range of words of other origins. It was this language that was used widely in Sri Vijayan days and was the vehicle not only for trade but also for the spread of Islam, which was brought by Indian merchants in the fourteenth century. In 1928 the Second National Youth Congress adopted Malay as the country's one national language and renamed it Indonesian. This and other events, like the launching of a literary magazine, the *Pujangga Baru,* in 1932 and the first Indonesian Language Congress, *Kongres Bahasa Indonesia,* in Surakarta in 1938, all increased acceptance of the national language and had far-reaching effects on the growth of unity in the country, for they symbolized the growing nationalist movement and helped to stimulate a new national consciousness.[3]

The choice of Indonesian as the national language was of fundamental importance for several other reasons. Not only was it spoken over a much wider area than any other language, but its adoption avoided the overtones of domination by the major ethnic group, the Javanese, in a united republic. Indonesia, by using this politically neutral language, was thus able to avoid the internal conflict over language experienced by such countries as India, Burma, and Belgium. Further advantages of Indonesian over Javanese lie in its simplicity and egalitarian character. The Indonesian language has high status in modern Indonesian society partly because of the prestige and great authority of the elite groups who used it increasingly both among themselves in place of Dutch and in their capacities as administrators, functionaries, and so on.[4]

At the time of its official adoption as the national language of Indonesia in 1928, *bahasa Indonesia* was the mother tongue of only about six million of the estimated sixty million Indonesians, those living primarily in eastern Sumatra. By contrast, at that time there were well over twenty million people in Indonesia who spoke Javanese as their mother tongue. Even today only 11.9 percent of the population reportedly use Indonesian as their first language.[5]

Use of Indonesian has been and still is being actively promoted, partly by a permanent language commission (functioning as part of the Linguistic and Cultural Institute of the Faculty of Literature and Philosophy at the University of Indonesia) that continues to develop the language, decide on new terms, and establish modern scientific and technical vocabularies; and partly by the expanding communications links throughout the archipelago that have served to extend knowledge of Indonesian. Indonesian is currently used in all government departments, on all official occasions, in education, and for all nationwide communications. The number of people speaking Indonesian has been increasing rapidly: in 1971, according to the census, only 40.5 percent of the population spoke Indonesian,[6] but by 1980 this figure had reached 60.8 percent[7] (although these figures, as all census data, should be handled cautiously). However, Anwar claimed that much earlier a far higher percentage, a "very great majority," knew the language and that practically everyone had some knowledge of it.[8]

The proportion of people speaking the national language in each province varies widely (from 33 percent in East Timor to almost 100 percent in Jakarta), as Figure 3.1 illustrates.[9] Whether Indonesian is used as a lingua franca depends on two major factors: first upon whether there is a sizable number of homogeneous people in a limited area who have a strong culture and their own language, and second upon the degree of contact among different peoples where Indonesian might function as a common tongue.

The first factor clearly helps to explain the situation in Java and Bali, areas with their own distinct cultural heritage and rich, well-defined literary languages. Less use of Indonesian here is to be expected, espe-

Figure 3.1. Percentage of the population able to speak the national language, Indonesian, 1980. Calculated from data in Tables 8.3 in the twenty-seven volumes of the 1980 population census, Biro Pusat Statistik, *Sensus Penduduk 1980*, Series S.

cially when local government officials, for example in Java, are all Javanese (or in western Java, Sundanese) and where the majority of the population is agricultural.

The second factor helps to account for the below-average knowledge of Indonesian in provinces with more isolated and highly rural populations, such as West and East Nusatenggara and, despite its somewhat more urban character, South Sulawesi as well. It also explains the above-average use of Indonesian in more urbanized provinces (especially Jakarta and East Kalimantan); provinces where trading was historically of primary importance (as in eastern Sumatra); and areas favored by the Dutch, with sizable Christian populations and better educational facilities (such as Maluku and North and Central Sulawesi).

Yet in terms of language used in the home, Indonesian is only the third most widely used language in the country; far more people speak Javanese as their first language (40.5 percent of the total Indonesian population), while Sundanese is the first language of 15.1 percent (also more than Indonesian's 11.9 percent).[10] The percentage speaking Indonesian at home varies enormously among the provinces, from 1.1 percent in Central Java (and percentages of 3.0 or less in Yogyakarta, East Java, West Sumatra, and West Nusatenggara) to 91.6 percent in Jakarta (a very dubious figure, given the great ethnic diversity of the capital city and the large numbers of new in-migrants from Java especially; however, even if a much smaller proportion of Jakarta's population does speak Indonesian at home, the range is still considerable). Other provinces with relatively high usage of Indonesian at home include Maluku (49.2 percent), Irian Jaya (31.1 percent), North Sumatra (30.2 percent), and East Kalimantan and North Sulawesi (each with 27.5 percent) (see Figure 3.2).

In theory, regional languages are accepted and, according to the constitution, supported. They are used as the medium of instruction in the first two or three years of primary school and in broadcasts from many government radio stations, especially when they are directed toward the population living in the rural areas. However, for good political reasons, and for fear that the resurgence of regional language loyalty might lead to political regionalism, the government has done little to encourage the development of regional languages.[11] Instead, the Indonesian government vigorously promotes the Indonesian national language as a means of strengthening national integration and of uniting the diverse ethnic and cultural groups in the country, as a symbol of national dignity and national identity, and as the medium of communication among the provinces.[12] Use of Indonesian is thus seen as a critical integrating force.

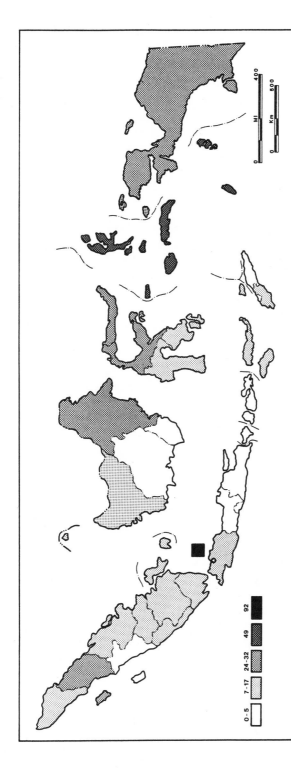

Figure 3.2. Percentage of the population speaking Indonesian at home, 1980. Calculated from data in Table 14.3 in Biro Pusat Statistik, *Sensus Penduduk 1980*, Series S, no. 2.

Religion

Shared commitment to a common religion has also long been recognized as a strong centripetal force, especially in nations of great ethnic and cultural diversity. At times, nationalism has functioned almost as a religion in colonial territories insomuch as the desire for independence and a free nation-state has become the focus of devotion and loyalty for the population. But once independence is achieved and the emotive force of nationalism spent, the role of religion proper frequently assumes greater significance as a unifying force.

The strength of religion as an integrative bond has been demonstrated in many countries, including Thailand, Ireland, and such countries in the Middle East and North Africa as Oman, the United Arab Emirates, Algeria, and Tunisia. But within Indonesia its role is more ambiguous. As to be expected in a nation as large and diverse as Indonesia, no single religion claims the loyalties of the entire population; indeed nearly all the world's major religions are represented here. And even within the religion acknowledged by the great majority (88.2 percent were classified as Muslim in 1980) there are deep differences in belief and practice.

Islam had already reached Indonesia before any Europeans arrived, but it spread more rapidly after the arrival of the Portuguese. Their capture of Malacca in 1511 caused the diffusion of Muslim traders from that major trading center, and trading rivalries further stimulated Islam's expansion. For as the Portuguese sought to concentrate all trade on Malacca, Muslim traders set up rival trading areas, first in Aceh (1515–1641), then in Banten (1526–1687) and Makassar in southern Celebes (1540–1667), and later in Banjarmasin in Kalimantan (from 1667 onwards).[13] As the Portuguese, and later the Dutch, moved further east, attempting to consolidate their strongholds along the trade routes and to monopolize the spice trade, so did Islam, which became a rallying point for those who opposed the intruders. As local Indonesian kingdoms confronted competition from European traders, their rulers called on Indian and Arab help with their trading; in exchange, they opened their principalities to Islam. By the end of the fifteenth century more than twenty Muslim kingdoms existed, scattered over Java, Sumatra, Madura, Kalimantan, Celebes, the Moluccas, the Philippines, and the Malay Peninsula.[14]

The Dutch were well aware of the potentially unifying threat of Islam. In every regional dispute they allied themselves with the *adat* leaders or traditional chiefs of a kingdom against the religious leaders of Islam (who used religion as a symbol of opposition to the Dutch, as, for example, in the Paderi War of West Sumatra, 1821–1837, the Java War of 1825–1830, and the Aceh War of 1873–1903).

Islam was important in the development of the nationalist movement. The first organization to extend its appeal outside Java was based
on adherence to Islam: the *Sarekat Islam* (the Islamic Union), founded in
1911. This Union had considerable success in binding together the disparate population of the Indies through the solidarity feelings of those
who identified themselves as Muslims. Indeed, Islam was an integrative, emotive force among many of the economic and political protago-
nists of nationalism. It is still a powerful integrating force, at least at the
macro level and particularly in provinces having an overwhelming
Muslim majority (see Figure 3.3).

However, at the micro level there are wide divergences within Islam.
The major difference is between the coastal Muslims with their characteristically purer, simpler faith and the interior Muslims, particularly in
Java, who practice a traditionalist syncretic faith, an Islam mixed with
beliefs carried over from a past of animism and ancestor worship or
Hindu beliefs, an Islam suffused with magico-religious elements. In
Java this dichotomy is expressed in the contrast between the *santri,* those
who hold the purer, more orthodox beliefs and adhere to the strict Muslim laws, and the *abangan,* who are more affected by their strong pre-
Islamic heritage and their ancestral traditions.[15]

Yet this syncretism forms a bond among peoples with different religions in the country, for the superstitions and beliefs carried over from
an animistic or Hinduistic past, including belief in the spirits of the
ancestors, the efficacy of cursing, and the power of the *dukun* (traditional
shaman), have penetrated Christianity, Buddhism, and Confucianism,
as well as Islam. Indeed, it can be argued that it is these cultural features of religious practice that are far more important as integrating elements than religious dogma, which is frequently divisive. More than 17
million non-Muslims live in Indonesia: Christians, Hindus, Buddhists,
and Confucianists. Confucianists and Buddhists in the past have been
scattered throughout the archipelago primarily among the Chinese, but
adherents of the other religions tend to be concentrated in particular
areas: Hindus in Bali, Catholics in East Timor and East Nusatenggara
(especially Flores) and to some extent in West Kalimantan, and Protestants in parts of North Sulawesi, North Sumatra, and Maluku (see Figure 3.4).

Relationships among the adherents of the different religions vary
greatly. In certain areas there is genuine tolerance; in others, especially
where the Muslim community feels itself threatened (for example, by
the growing numbers of Christians or by the economic power of Buddhists), tolerance is replaced by bitter hostility, which breaks out from
time to time in the burning of churches and even occasional killings. Yet
far more blood has been spilt among the different strands of Islam: in
the aftermath of the abortive 1965 coup it was largely *santri* against

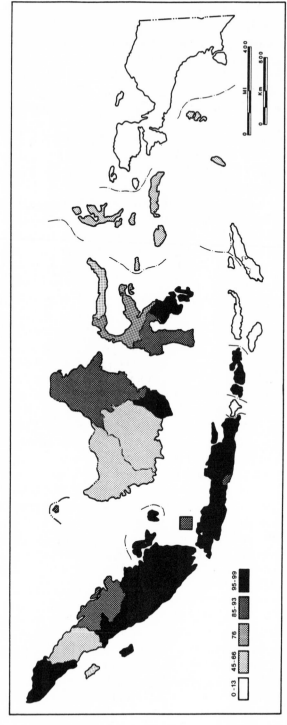

Figure 3.3. Percentage of the population classified as Muslim, 1980. Calculated from data in Table IV.4.1 in Biro Pusat Statistik, *Statistik Indonesia 1982.*

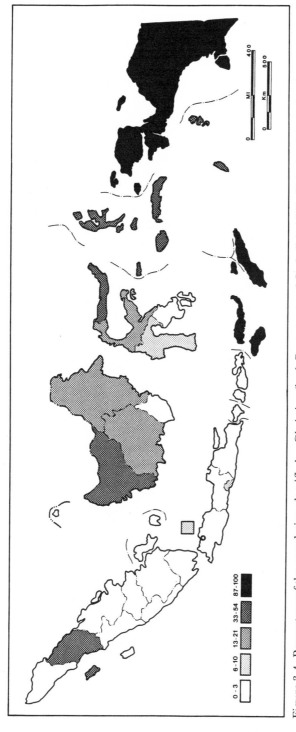

Figure 3.4. Percentage of the population classified as Christian (both Protestant and Catholic), 1980. Calculated from data in Table IV.4.1 in Biro Pusat Statistik, *Statistik Indonesia 1982.*

abangan. It is also interesting to notice in recent years a growing official emphasis not just on a passive *toleransi* (tolerance) toward adherents of the different religions, but upon the more positive *kerukunan* (social harmony).[16]

Lack of adherence to Islam, though a source of tension at one level, is not necessarily disintegrative at the national level. For Christians have shown a disproportionately large degree of leadership in the nationalist movement as well as in the economic development of the country, especially in the navy, in business, and in interisland shipping. On the other hand, Buddhism and Confucianism among the Chinese in the past have served to reinforce their cultural isolation, although this is now breaking down as many Chinese have converted to Christianity and Islam. Nowhere is this more apparent than in West Kalimantan, where the 1971 census recorded almost 40 percent of its population as Buddhist, Confucianist, or other; in 1980 these groups made up less than 3 percent of the total (and the percentage of Muslims rose from 43 to 62 percent, while the percentage of Christians increased from 18 to 35 percent).[17]

Despite its large majority of Muslims, Indonesia remains a state based on the *Panca Sila,* the first principle of which affirms the belief in one Supreme Being. Indeed five religions are officially recognized in the country: Islam, Protestantism, Catholicism, Hinduism, and Buddhism. Yet one of the major political struggles is between those who want to make Indonesia into an Islamic state and those who want to keep it tolerant of all belief in God. Obviously in a country with the religious diversity of Indonesia, a *Panca Sila* state would be, at least theoretically, far more integrative and inclusive than an Islamic state, which would discriminate in a more divisive way against all non-Muslims.

Notwithstanding the differences between the orthodox and the traditionalists, between those in favor of an Islamic state and those in favor of a *Panca Sila* state, Islam as the predominant religion still has a significant integrative role, partly through the *hajj,* which brings Muslims together from all over the archipelago in an awareness of their common nationality and religion, and partly through an increasing identification with and pride in being Muslim in the post-1973 OPEC era. This recent intensification of Islam has been characterized by a great increase in attendance at the rapidly growing number of mosques, in the popularity of the morning lecture on Islam on the radio, in the number of readers of Islamic journals and books, in the widespread occurrence of religious instruction activities, and in the higher percentage of people who pay their *zakat* (religious tax).[18]

However, the integrative role of Islam is modified by important spatial differences in the distribution of Muslims throughout the country. Adherence to Islam ranges from less than 1 percent in East Timor and

5.2 percent in Bali to 98.5 percent in Jambi and Bengkulu. In twelve of
Indonesia's twenty-seven provinces Muslims make up over 96 percent
of the population. Only in five is the proportion under 50 percent: Bali,
where 93 percent of the population is Hindu; and East Timor, East
Nusatenggara, Irian Jaya, and North Sulawesi, where 99, 91, 88, and
54 percent, respectively, are Christian. Maluku, West Kalimantan, and
North Sumatra also have sizable Christian populations. Overall, Christians (Protestants outnumber Catholics approximately two to one)
make up 8.8 percent of the population, Hindus 2.1 percent, and Buddhists just under 1 percent.

Religion, therefore, is a complex sociocultural feature with both integrative and disintegrative characteristics. But it is a very important
issue because of the strong emotional responses it evokes. It is probably
one of the least predictable elements of sociocultural integration because
of the wide diversity of intensity and tolerance among its greatly varying adherents.

Education and Literacy

Participation in a national culture and the sharing of national customs
and values are obviously important components of national integration.
One way of encouraging such participation is through education and literacy programs. In contrast to the colonial days, when the Dutch educated very few Indonesians, the Indonesian government from the very
beginning has placed major emphasis on education at all levels. A
national educational system was introduced in 1945 and has been used
to strengthen national integration and unity as well as to aid national
development. Common curricula and textbooks have served as vehicles
for expanding national consciousness, promoting the Indonesian language, and encouraging national pride.

Education is therefore an important integrative force, particularly at
the elementary level, when children are at their most impressionable
age. Children in grades one through six nationwide learn national slogans and national history; sing national songs; learn about national
heroes, values, and principles of state; and take part in national events
and celebrations. By learning to read and write, they open themselves
to national literature, newspapers, and magazines, all of which are
potentially integrative forces.

Yet the proportion of the population completing primary school
remains small. In 1980 only 43.4 percent of the population ten years of
age and over had completed elementary school, although far more had
at one time been enrolled and subsequently dropped out; yet this repre-

sents a great improvement over the 1971 figure of 26.3 percent. This 17-percent increase reflects the government's commitment to expanding and improving education.

In an effort to increase the educational opportunities available in the provinces, the government has invested major resources in education, increasing the number of primary schools by 65 percent between 1970 and 1980, junior high schools by 62 percent, and senior high schools by 53 percent. Indeed the percentage of seven to twelve year olds in school was reported to have risen since the 1978–1979 school year from 79.1 percent to 97.2 percent by 1983–1984 (involving a jump from 22.4 million to 28.9 million students).[19]

Because of the clearly integrative role education plays in Indonesia, however, it is important to note the very uneven pattern revealed by the educational data. The proportion of the population ten years of age and over who had completed the six years of primary education in 1980 ranged from 30.8 percent in West Kalimantan to 65.9 percent in Jakarta (see Figure 3.5). Outside Jakarta, Yogyakarta stands out as a cultural and educational center (with its 57.4 percent primary school completion rate). The provinces that have had a high level of Christian missionary activity over several generations (North and Central Sulawesi and Maluku) still reflect that heritage in the proportions of the population who have completed secondary school. At the elementary educational level, however, other provinces, such as East Kalimantan, North Sumatra, Irian Jaya, Aceh, and Bali have now joined the more Christian provinces in their educational achievement levels. At the other extreme are the provinces of West Kalimantan, Lampung, Bengkulu, Jambi, Central Java, and South Kalimantan.

Similarly, school participation rates of seven to twelve year olds have risen dramatically between 1971 and 1980, particularly in West and Central Java (by 26.8 and 27.2 percentage points), Riau (by 27.1 percentage points), Bali (by 27.8 percentage points), and West Nusatenggara (by 30.2 percentage points). One result of this is that the provinces are indeed much more similar in their educational levels in 1980 than they were in 1971 (in 1980 the spread was 24.5 percentage points from 66.9 percent in Irian Jaya and West Kalimantan to 91.6 and 91.4 percent in Yogyakarta and Jakarta respectively, compared with a range in 1971 of 35.6 percentage points, from 42.3 percent in West Nusatenggara to 78.0 percent in North Sulawesi) (see Figure 3.6). Impressive gains have also been made in the older age groups, and the differences among the provinces have narrowed. It is interesting to note, too, the closing gap between education of males and females. Overall, 28.2 percent of males were attending school in 1980 compared with 23.8 percent of females, but there are striking differences at the different age levels.

Figure 3.5. Percentage of the population ten years of age and over who have completed primary school, 1980. Calculated from data in Tables 6.9 in the twenty-seven volumes of Biro Pusat Statistik, *Sensus Penduduk 1980*, Series S.

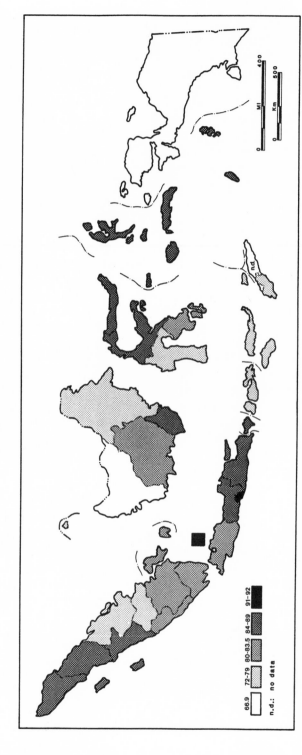

Figure 3.6. Percentage of seven to twelve year olds in primary school, 1980. Based on data in Biro Pusat Statistik, *Sensus Penduduk 1980*, Series S, no. 2.

Among five to eight year olds a higher percentage of girls than boys attend school, but the reverse is true for nine year olds upward, with the gap increasing (a 1.5-percent gap at age ten, a 10-percent gap at age fourteen, and a 14-percent gap at ages seventeen and eighteen).[20] Urban-rural differentials in primary education participation are high.

Literacy rates are a further index of integration, because they measure the ability of the population of a province to participate in national events as these are expressed in writing. A literate population is exposed in a far fuller way than a nonliterate one to the potentially integrating forces of books, newspapers, magazines, and government communications. Indeed, in a country with strict censorship laws, literacy may be regarded as particularly integrative, because only government-approved materials reach the citizens. Any critical comments in the world press relating to Indonesia (as well as unseemly materials and anything written in Chinese characters) are regularly censored from overseas-produced newspapers and magazines, and internally produced written materials are also subject to censorship, especially newspaper articles regarded as inflammatory or critical. On several occasions newspaper and magazine offices have been shut down and editors jailed for injudiciously publishing unacceptable materials.

Literacy rates have increased impressively since independence, from an estimated 10 percent literate in 1941[21] to 61 percent in 1971 and 71 percent in 1980 (see Figure 3.7).[22] As expected, literacy rates vary considerably, from 21 percent in East Timor and 52 percent in Irian Jaya to 91 percent in North Sulawesi. At the extremes, literacy rates reflect educational achievement: two of the provinces with the lowest educational standards also have among the lowest literacy rates, West Nusatenggara (55 percent) and West Kalimantan (58 percent), but the correlation is not always strong. Adult literacy programs may help to explain this anomaly. The highest literacy rates occur in the urban metropolis of Jakarta (88 percent) and in other provinces historically favored in education, notably North Sulawesi, North, West, and South Sumatra, Central Sulawesi, and Maluku, all of which have literacy rates of over 80 percent.

National Symbolism

Indonesian culture is rich in symbolism, and national symbolism has been used as a powerful tool to promote national unity.[23] Symbols have an important integrative role, especially in a nation as riven with internal contrasts as Indonesia, for they serve as a focus and expression of national as opposed to parochial feelings. Symbolism played an espe-

Figure 3.7. Percentage of the population ten years of age and over who are classified as literate, 1980. Based on data in Table 18.3 in Biro Pusat Statistik, *Sensus Penduduk 1980*, Series S, no. 2.

cially important role in the early days of the nationalist movement and in the Sukarno era. Sukarno, the great unifier and solidarity maker, took every conceivable opportunity to instill national pride through the intensive use of symbols. His government engaged in a tremendous amount of symbolic activity—gestures, ceremonies, rituals, propaganda, monuments, prestigious projects, slogans, movements, and demonstrations. Yet the integrative effect of all this activity has been disputed. Certainly it encouraged national pride, provided a sort of national anchor during times of disruptive social change, and helped to legitimize Sukarno's government. But the frenetic crescendo of symbolic activity that reached a pitch of almost hysterical intensity in the early 1960s corresponds closely to the growing economic decline and disintegration of that period. Excessive use of symbols lowered administrative and economic efficiency, not only in the amount of time and money spent on ceremonies and symbolism, but also in creating an atmosphere unfavorable to the solving of practical problems by rational means.[24]

Although used in excess by Sukarno, symbolism still has an important role in binding the disparate parts of the country together. Particularly meaningful symbols now in the post-Sukarno era, as before, are the *Panca Sila,* the national emblem and motto, the use of acronyms and names of Indonesian heroes nationwide, and the emphasis on common Indonesian values.

The *Panca Sila* (Five Principles) remains the basic philosophy of state. It was designed to appeal to Indonesians of all persuasions and ideologies. The very number five is of symbolic importance (because of the five senses, the five obligations of Islam, the five heroes in the Hindu epic Mahabharata, and so on). The symbols representing the five principles are embodied in the coat of arms on the *garuda* (a mythical bird related to the eagle and the phoenix), which is the national emblem of Indonesia. The five principles are as follows: belief in one Supreme Being, symbolized by the star in the center of the coat of arms; nationalism, symbolized by the revered banyan tree; internationalism or humanitarianism, emphasizing the broad common basis of human values of all men and women, symbolized by a golden chain with alternate square and round links; social justice, symbolized by a spray of cotton and a stalk of rice, representing the basic necessities of life; and popular sovereignty or democracy, symbolized by the head of the *banteng* or wild buffalo, an animal patient and hard to rouse, yet when roused, prepared to fight to the death to protect his herd.[25] As a national symbol, the *garuda* is portrayed as having seventeen wing feathers, eight tail feathers, and forty-five neck feathers, symbolizing the date of the proclamation of independence, August 17, 1945 (see Figure 3.8). In the

Figure 3.8. Indonesia's national symbol: the *garuda*.

claws of the golden *garuda* is a scroll inscribed with Indonesia's motto, *Bhinneka Tunggal Ika*, a Sanskrit phrase meaning "Unity in Diversity" or "they are many; they are one."

The *Panca Sila* has become of increasing importance in recent years partly as a means of legitimizing Indonesia's secular and military government, and partly to counteract and undercut other ideologies, particularly Islam. As a unifying national philosophy, it is taught in schools throughout the nation and, along with a picture of the president, is enframed and hung in every government-related office from the highest administrative levels down to the level of the village leader and school head. In addition, courses on the *Panca Sila* are obligatory for all civil servants.

Another unifying, if superficial, force has been the use throughout the nation of the names of Indonesian national heroes for mountains, rivers, airports, city streets, and so on. Thus, national personalities are commemorated and made familiar to the local inhabitants, reinforcing national awareness and prompting interest in the historical background of Indonesia. Use of acronyms is popular and often infused with symbolism. *Repelita*, the acronym for Indonesia's Five-Year Development Plans *(Rencana Pembangunan Lima Tahun)*, for example, incorporates the acronym *pelita*, which means a light or lamp, itself of significance in the process of development. Indeed, Indonesians have created enough acronyms to fill a two-volume dictionary.

Finally, certain cultural norms characteristic of most Indonesians have been glorified and appealed to in the name of national unity. Some of these common values include the idea of community interdependence and reciprocal obligation *(gotong royong);* the "Indonesian way" of reaching decisions through *musyawarah* (consultation) and *mufakat* (consensus); and the emphasis placed upon harmony and unity, control of the emotions, status, order, conformity to group norms and expectations, and the importance of face-saving devices.[26] Unfortunately, no data exist on the spatial distribution and varying intensity of the use of symbols throughout the archipelago.

The Legal System

Since Dutch colonial days Indonesia has been linked in one national legal system, although the influence of that system did not penetrate deeply into local Indonesian society. Before the Dutch, many different legal orders existed independently within a wide variety of social and political systems. Social cohesion depended not on written law but upon kinship or aristocratic status concepts in which authority was ascriptive, suffused with family and religious significance, and highly localized.[27] Yet *adat,* though varying from society to society, had certain common elements: the preponderance of communal over individual interests, the close relationship between people and the soil, a pervasive magical and religious pattern of thought, and a strongly family-oriented atmosphere in which every effort was made to resolve disputes through reconciliation and mutual consideration.[28] In addition to customary law, orthodox Muslims followed Islamic law, especially in Java and Sumatra, where religious courts functioned.

The Dutch established nationwide patterns of social and legal transactions, but created a plural legal system in which each major social group had its own law, which was applied differentially by three distinct judicial hierarchies: the European, the Islamic (family courts), and the Indonesian (based on *adat,* which varied from area to area).

Since independence the legal system has been unified, modified, and centralized. A *hukum nasional* (national law) and a national judicial system have been established, where local institutions and traditional courts have been replaced with *pengadilan negeri* (district courts). Religious courts, based on Islamic law *(syariat)* work side by side with the district courts; they deal primarily with marital and inheritance cases, but their decisions must be approved by the corresponding district courts.[29] However, controversial efforts have been made to unify matrimonial law and to subordinate *adat* to nationally oriented legal concepts and policy directives. But the traditional practice of village-level arbitration, mediated by the village headman, still prevails in most cases.

Thus, *adat,* sometimes modified by Islamic influences, continues to govern the everyday life of villagers and remains to a large extent the basis for maintaining harmony and stability at the village level.[30]

Almost inevitably these efforts to unify Indonesian law have had somewhat contradictory effects, with tension arising between the momentum of local participation in national integration on the one hand and claims that the imposition of a national legal system is nothing more than a cloak for the expansion of the Javanese system on the other. At one level, the national organization of the judiciary, public prosecution, the police, and the administrative civil service *(pamong praja)* provides a force for integration and national unity; but at another the local lower courts are more oriented toward the needs of their local clienteles than to the national perspective of the Supreme Court judges in Jakarta.

The law is still a weak institution and thus its integrative role remains muted; other ways and values are available for settling disputes and ordering society besides the formal legal channels. However, the growth and increasing influence of national law is strongly linked both to the growth of modernization, with its need for greater legal uniformity in such matters as property rights and inheritance, and to the growth of a national orientation in the country's social structure and economic behavior.

The Spread of National Organizations

One measure of sociocultural integration is the degree to which people in the various provinces participate in common, nationwide activities and organizations. National (as opposed to regional) organizations usually provide means of contact for leaders from different areas through national meetings, training sessions, and so on. They also provide for their members an integrative sense of belonging to a group that shares certain goals or values with a nationwide community. Two organizations that have more than a local or specialized appeal, and extend nationwide, are cooperatives and scouting (see Figures 3.9 and 3.10). However, there seems to be no easy explanation for the very different patterns of participation in these activities in 1980 compared with the patterns in 1971, when these nationwide organizations tended to have greater participation from people in the provinces in and near Java than in the remote or less-developed provinces. In 1971, for example, 80 percent of all cooperative members were found in Java, whereas in 1980 the figure was 68 percent, far closer to Java's 62 percent share of Indonesia's population. Membership in a social organization, as measured

Figure 3.9. Number of members of agricultural cooperatives per 100 population (average of 1979 and 1980 figures). Calculated from data in Table VIII.3.2 in Biro Pusat Statistik, *Statistik Indonesia 1983, Buku Saku.*

1.3-2.2 2.4-3.1 3.6-5.0 5.5-7.7 9.9

PER 100 POPULATION

n.d.: no data

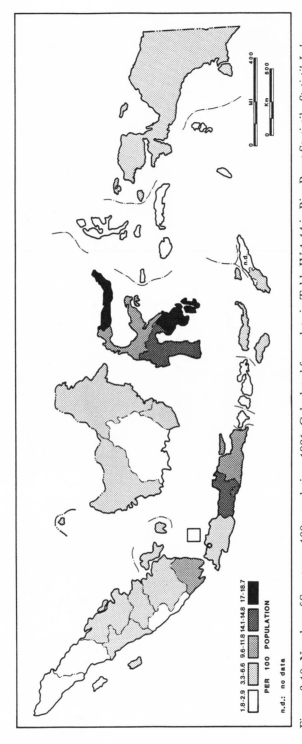

Figure 3.10. Number of Scouts per 100 population, 1981. Calculated from data in Table IV.1.14 in Biro Pusat Statistik, *Statistik Indonesia 1983*.

1.8-2.9 3.3-6.6 9.6-11.8 14.1-14.8 17-18.7

PER 100 POPULATION

n.d.: no data

by a survey in 1981, likewise shows no clear pattern (see Figure 3.11). Not only are there no clear spatial patterns of participation, but also neither membership in scouting nor membership in any social organization has a significant correlation with any other variable, sociocultural, interaction, or economic (of the more than eighty examined). The only significant correlation between membership in any national organization and any other sociocultural feature is the negative relationship between membership in a cooperative and the percentage of Asians in the population.

The Chinese

The presence of any culturally distinct and economically powerful ethnic group needs to be considered in a study of national integration: in Indonesia the Chinese form that minority. In certain respects they constitute an integrative force because they provide a common target for the hostility and frustration of Indonesians from all over the archipelago and at times serve a scapegoat function. In addition, their ethnic solidarity and commercial ties throughout the country have created a nationwide network of business and trade connections.[31] But their interregional links are not restricted to Indonesia's boundaries; they extend also to Singapore, Malaysia, Hong Kong, the Philippines, Taiwan, and the People's Republic of China. They have thus been seen to pose a threat to the national security as well as to the integration of the nation.

Yet the Chinese community itself is by no means homogeneous. It is composed of many diverse subgroups that differ from one another by reason of the length of time they have resided in Indonesia; the different ethnic groups in China from which they have come; and the differences in their occupations, political outlook, and degree of loyalty to mainland China.[32]

Chinese have immigrated to Indonesia from the seventh century onward. The vast majority of early arrivals were single men who usually married local Indonesian women and were assimilated into the local culture. It was only in the late nineteenth and early twentieth centuries that substantial immigration of both Chinese men and women took place in response to the demand for manpower in the sugarcane industry of Java and the gold mines of West Kalimantan.[33] Assimilation into the local community slowed down, and separate communities developed. The Chinese gradually took over the tax-collecting function of the colonial government and increasingly monopolized trade. Dutch colonial policies deliberately kept the Chinese separate, especially in Java, by creating a plural society with themselves at the top, the Chinese in

Figure 3.11. Percentage belonging to a social organization in the three months preceding a survey, 1981. Based on data in Table III.1.9 in Biro Pusat Statistik, *Statistik Indonesia 1983, Buku Saku.*

the middle, and the indigenous inhabitants on the bottom.[34] Upward mobility for the Chinese, therefore, meant movement away from the indigenous Javanese society toward the European elite. The Chinese thus formed a middle class predominantly of business entrepreneurs. The Dutch, seeking partly to protect the indigenous population, but also for administrative, economic, and political reasons, restricted the Chinese both in their movement (limiting their contact with interior communities) and in their place of residence (to urban centers), prohibited the alienation of land by all non-Indonesians, and legally reinforced a pluralistic society.

Since independence the Chinese have been subjected to considerable harassment both in their economic activities and in their personal lives. For example, Chinese communal associations have been severely curtailed, Chinese-language schools outlawed, and import of Chinese-language video cassettes prohibited. There is also continual criticism of the so-called Ali Baba partnership of *cukong* (Chinese businessmen) in league with politically powerful Indonesians, whereby Chinese businessmen use indigenous Indonesian businesses as a front to circumvent official government policy that gives preference to indigenous entrepreneurs.[35]

A broad distinction can be made between those Chinese born in Indonesia (the *peranakan*) and those who have migrated to Indonesia in this generation (the *totok*). Many of the *peranakan,* who make up about 70 percent of the total Chinese population of approximately three and a half million in Indonesia, are much more willing to assimilate than the Indonesian society is ready to receive them. Many have adopted Indonesian names and Indonesian cultural habits, although they are still discriminated against in a society that is very conscious of Chinese identity, whether *peranakan* or *totok.* For example, in 1979 the State Prosecutor's Office conducted a nationwide registration of everyone of Chinese descent, an action that was particularly offensive to the *peranakan* who hold Indonesian citizenship.[36]

The *totok,* by contrast, form typically insular, culturally distinct communities, held together by a powerfully integrated kinship system and separate cultural traditions.[37] However, since 1980 there has been pressure on these alien Chinese to become Indonesian citizens. In 1984 the commander of the armed forces called on his fellow countrymen to stop using what he called the divisive terms *pribumi* (indigenous Indonesians) and *non-pribumi* (referring primarily to the Chinese, naturalized or otherwise). The government subsequently has resorted to the more neutral expression *orang Indonesia asli* (native Indonesian), which purportedly includes Chinese who have already assimilated.[38]

The distinction between *peranakan* and *totok* in the past probably corresponded approximately to that between those Chinese who adopted Indonesian citizenship and those who have retained Chinese citizenship. It is interesting to notice that in both the 1971 and 1980 censuses no questions were asked about ethnic origin (a reflection of the sensitive and potentially inflammatory nature of such questions). Thus, in 1971 the presence of approximately 2,500,000 (mainly *peranakan*) Chinese was not noted; data on language, literacy, and even religion similarly fail to reveal their existence. By contrast, the presence of the approximately one million Chinese citizens was extremely accurately defined: even at the subdistrict *(kecamatan)* level citizenship along with age and sex is known. This provides an indication of how sensitive an issue citizenship is in a country concerned about national integration and security. *Statistik Indonesia 1982* gives data about the number of foreigners by province and continent of origin without specifically mentioning the Chinese population, but it is known that 95 percent of all foreigners in Indonesia are Asians and the vast majority of these are in fact Chinese.[39]

Although not revealed by the census, the spatial distribution of *peranakan* and *totok* has been quite different.[40] In Java, Madura, and Kalimantan most adult Chinese were born in Indonesia, with only about 30 percent born elsewhere. In Sumatra and other areas the *totok* are in the majority (80 percent of Chinese over thirty years of age in Sumatra were born outside the country).

In terms of citizenship, by 1981 no province had less than 97 percent of its population Indonesian citizens, and in eighteen of the twenty-five provinces for which data are available (excluding Bengkulu and Southeast Sulawesi), the figure is over 99 percent. On a per-capita basis, Chinese citizens are concentrated in West Kalimantan, Jakarta, South Sumatra, East Kalimantan, and Riau (see Figure 3.12).

In the past, the Chinese, therefore, have formed a generally nonassimilated and thus disintegrative force in Indonesian society, with their cultural differences, their connections to mainland China, their economic power, and their network of business contacts that extends beyond the boundaries of Indonesia; but serious attempts are being made to assimilate this ethnically and culturally distinct minority.

Access to Amenities

Access to amenities provides another measure of sociocultural integration, since many of these are organized on a national basis in Indonesia and extend nationwide. In the entertainment industry there is a national film distribution network, and although the provision of cine-

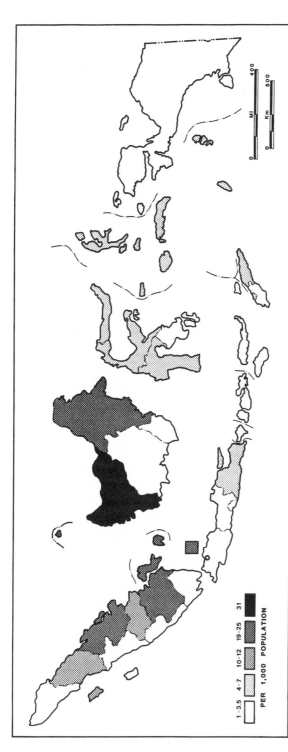

Figure 3.12. Number of foreigners claiming Asian citizenship per 1,000 population, 1981. Calculated from data in Table III.1.11 in Biro Pusat Statistik, *Statistik Indonesia 1982.*

mas also reflects comparative economic affluence and the existence of adequate electricity, the number of viewers of Indonesian-made movies (which make up approximately one-third of all movies viewed in the country)[41] is an index at least to some extent of general exposure to a "national culture." The number of people who attended at least one Indonesian-made movie in 1981 ranged from 10.0 per 100 population in East Nusatenggara to 157.1 in East Kalimantan.[42] The viewing of Indonesian-made movies is disproportionately high in Jakarta, but the rest of Java ranks surprisingly low in light of the fact that most Indonesian movies are filmed there. However, this may be a reflection of Java's own rich culture, where the *wayang kulit* (shadow puppet play) is a more popular, traditional, and less expensive form of entertainment. In addition to Java and East Nusatenggara, low attendance at Indonesian-made movies is recorded for West Nusatenggara, Lampung, Bali, and Southeast Sulawesi. Riau in Sumatra and all the provinces of Kalimantan stand out for their consistently above-average rate of viewing Indonesian-made movies (see Figure 3.13).

Exposure to nationally controlled radio programs is another index of national integration. All radio transmitters, nongovernment as well as government-owned, are required by law to broadcast certain *Radio Republik Indonesia* programs and thus, at least theoretically, have an integrating role. In developing countries broadcast media are widely expected to make a positive contribution to national integration, as well as to socioeconomic modernization and cultural creativity.[43] Radios are relatively inexpensive and require no skills (such as education or literacy) of their audience.

The percentage of households owning a radio in 1980 ranged from 13.9 percent in East Nusatenggara to 66.0 percent in Jakarta, with an average of 40.7 percent (see Figure 3.14). As might be expected, in general the pattern reflects relative wealth and urbanization. However, perhaps more indicative of exposure to radio programming are the results of a survey undertaken in 1981 to ascertain the percentage of the population ten years of age and over engaging in various social and cultural activities. This shows that 75.2 percent of Indonesians had listened to the radio at least once during the preceding week. By province, the figures ranged from 37.5 percent in East Nusatenggara and 46.1 percent in Maluku to 87.4 percent in Yogyakarta and 86.3 percent in West Java (see Figure 3.15). But one has to question the validity of the results of this survey, partly because there is a fairly low correlation between radio ownership and those listening to the radio, and partly because some of the figures seem unrealistic. For example, in Irian Jaya only 17.7 percent of households owned a radio, but an amazing (and unlikely) 70.8 percent of the population ten years of age and older said

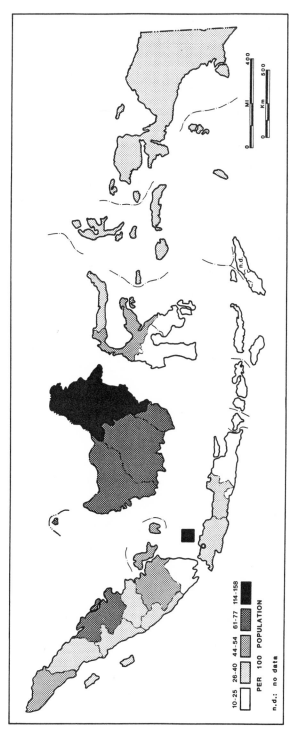

Figure 3.13. Number of people watching an Indonesian-made movie per 100 population, 1981. Calculated from data in Table 4 in Biro Pusat Statistik, *Statistik Bioskop Indonesia 1981 dan 1982.*

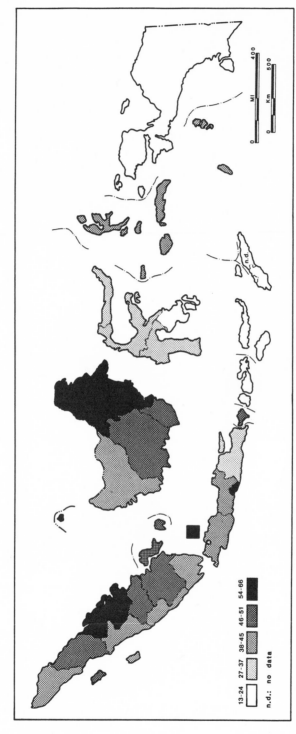

Figure 3.14. Percentage of households owning a radio, 1980. Based on data in Table 66.3 in Biro Pusat Statistik, *Sensus Penduduk 1980, Series S*, no. 2.

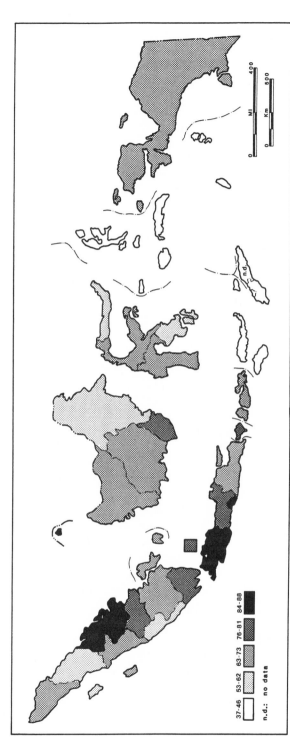

Figure 3.15. Percentage of the population ten years of age and over who listened to the radio in the week preceding a survey, 1981. Based on data in Table III.1.9 in Biro Pusat Statistik, *Statistik Indonesia 1983, Buku Saku.*

they had listened to the radio in the preceding week (a difference of 53.1 percentage points). Other comparatively high contrasts occurred in West Nusatenggara (a 45.6 percentage point difference), West Java (44.4 percentage points), Central Sulawesi (44.3), Central Java (41.3), and South Sulawesi (40.7). At the other extreme are East Kalimantan, where although 54.3 percent of households owned radios, only 60 percent tuned in the previous week, Maluku (with 38.1 and 46.1 percent, respectively), and Jakarta (with 66.0 and 76.3 percent, respectively). The data on radio ownership are thus considered to be a more accurate indicator overall of exposure to radio programs.

In contrast to radio listenership, a far smaller proportion of the population both owns and watches television. For Indonesia as a whole only 9.8 percent of households own a television set, although television service is now available throughout the archipelago. Ownership of a television set again reflects wealth and urbanization, and accounts for the range of television ownership from lows of 1.7 percent of households in East Nusatenggara and 2.7 percent in West Nusatenggara to highs of 45.5 percent in Jakarta (a dubiously high figure) and 23.0 percent in East Kalimantan (see Figure 3.16). Approximately 50.3 percent of the population sample surveyed in 1981 claimed to have watched television during the preceding week, a figure that incorporated a range from 14.3 percent in East Nusatenggara and 21.0 percent in Maluku to 87.5 percent in Jakarta and 66.1 percent in South Kalimantan. Again the correlation is not very close, as illustrated by the situation in Irian Jaya where only 3.2 percent of households owned a television set but where 63.8 percent of the population ten years old and over claimed that they had watched television sometime during the previous week (a very unlikely figure, and the same percentage as Riau with its comparatively high 17.2 percent rate of television ownership). By contrast, two provinces with approximately the same percentage of television ownership, 7.5 percent in Central Kalimantan and 7.7 percent in Maluku, had very different proportions of their provincial populations watching television: 51 percent in the case of Central Kalimantan but only 21 percent in the case of Maluku (see Figure 3.17).[44]

Newspapers and magazines play a far less important role in national integration. Only 4.6 percent of Indonesia's population regularly takes a newspaper, and only 18 percent on average had read a newspaper or magazine in the previous week, according to the 1981 survey, a figure that ranged from 8.6 percent in West Nusatenggara to 48.9 percent in Jakarta.[45]

Access to health care is another reflection of nationwide organization, for medical personnel are civil servants and are thereby integrated into a national network. Indeed, doctors and dentists are assigned by the

Figure 3.16. Percentage of households owning a television set, 1980. Based on data in Table 66.3 in Biro Pusat Statistik, *Sensus Penduduk 1980*, Series S, no. 2.

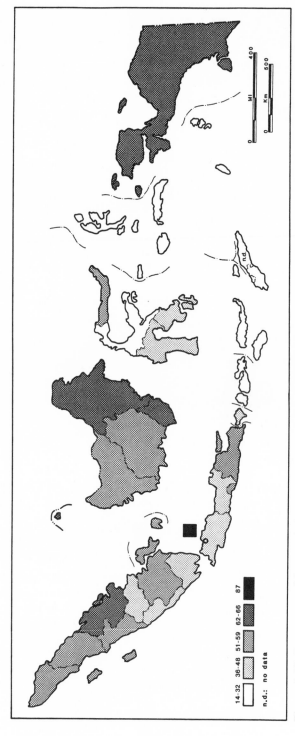

Figure 3.17. Percentage of the population ten years of age and over who watched television in the week preceding a survey, 1981. Based on data in Table III.1.9 in Biro Pusat Statistik, *Statistik Indonesia 1983, Buku Saku.*

government to their initial job for two years (in rural and more needy areas). On a per-capita basis, however, most doctors and dentists are found in the urbanized provinces of Jakarta, East Kalimantan, and Yogyakarta, and in the Protestant provinces of North Sulawesi and North Sumatra. Similarly, the provinces with the best provision of hospital beds are those with either large Christian populations (with the exceptions of East Nusatenggara and East Timor) or relatively high urbanization (see Figure 3.18). The least-served provinces are West Nusatenggara, Bengkulu, Lampung, and Jambi. Although Java's population in general is no better supplied with health facilities than that of many other provinces on a per-capita basis, from a spatial perspective a far larger proportion of Java's inhabitants is within a reasonable distance of health facilities than is the case in the Outer Islands because of Java's much higher population density. This difference is accentuated by the superior transportation system in Java, which also provides greater physical access to health care.

As with education, the government has invested major resources in improving health care throughout the country. Evidence for this can be seen in the great increase in the number of public health-care centers and mother and baby clinics, in the emphasis on family planning, and in the increasing access to piped drinking water and proper sanitation. The results can be seen in the 25 percent decline in the infant mortality rate during the 1970s and the increase in life expectancy. However, health-care facilities remain very inadequate, as the 1980 figures of seven hospital beds per 10,000 population and 31,000 persons per health center indicate.[46]

Urbanization

The level of urbanization existing in each province is relevant to the theme of sociocultural integration because urban populations participate in an urban culture that transcends provincial (and even national) boundaries. Opportunities for cross-cultural and cross-ethnic contacts exist in an urban environment in a way not found in more rural surroundings. There is also greater exposure to national symbols, values, and mores in an urban milieu than in more isolated rural environments. The correlation with knowledge of the Indonesian language has already been noted.

However, growth in the rate of urbanization does not necessarily mean increased integration. First, urbanization is known to correlate with economic development, which may or may not be integrative.[47] In other words, increasing urbanization may reflect an increase in a

Figure 3.18. Number of hospital beds (government and private) per 10,000 population, 1980. Calculated from Table IV.2.1 in Biro Pusat Statistik, *Statistik Indonesia 1982.*

dualistic economy rather than in an integrated one. Second, urbanization unaccompanied by other integrative forces may be separatist in character, because an urban environment may provide an opportunity for greater contact among people with similar needs and goals, which may be regionalist rather than nationalist in orientation. Third, urbanization per se is an inaccurate index of integration, unless employment opportunities are commensurate with urban growth. Unemployment, as well as an unbalanced employment structure with an inflated tertiary sector, is unstable and thus potentially disintegrative in character.

Thus, the role of urbanization in national integration is not all positive: increased physical proximity may accentuate social distance and provoke hostility and resentment, especially when economic or political differences coincide with ethnic or other cultural differences. Questions also arise as to the extent to which each urban node is enclave in nature and how much of an integrative role each exerts upon its hinterland and in the urban network. Only when balanced with positive, nationwide economic development and reinforced by other integrative features is increasing urbanization a positive force.

In 1980, 22.4 percent of Indonesia's population was considered to be urban.[48] The level of urbanization of each province ranged from 93.7 percent for Jakarta and 39.9 percent in East Kalimantan to a low of 7.5 percent in East Nusatenggara (see Table 3.1 and Figure 3.19). Java, with 25.1 percent of its population classified as urban, is the most urbanized island in Indonesia, followed by Kalimantan and Sumatra. This represents a dramatic change from the situation in 1971, when Kalimantan was comparatively more urbanized than Java, and reflects both the changes in the definition of urban in the 1971–1980 intercensal period and the strong growth of Java's cities over the past decade. Only four of the Outer Island provinces were more urbanized than Java in 1980, compared with eight in 1971.

The proportion of the population living in urban areas has been increasing steadily, from 14.8 percent in 1961 to 17.3 percent in 1971 to 22.4 percent in 1980.[49] However, cities have been growing at very different rates.[50] In general, the cities that have experienced the greatest growth (Jakarta, Surabaya, Tanjung Karang, Jambi, Samarinda, and Balikpapan) have been the "metropoles,"[51] those cities that are more cosmopolitan and nation-oriented than the "provincial" cities, which are more oriented to serving the provinces in which they are located, such as Yogyakarta, Cirebon, Kediri, Pematang Siantar, and Surakarta. Between 1971 and 1980, the fastest growing cities were Ambon, Padang, Medan, Balikpapan, and Samarinda, all cities in the Outer Islands (see Table 3.2 and Figure 3.20).

One integrative aspect of urbanization in Indonesia is its hierarchy of

Table 3.1. Percentage urban by province, 1961, 1971, and 1980

Province	1961	1971	1980
1. Aceh	7.7	8.4	8.9
2. North Sumatra	16.9	17.1	25.5
3. West Sumatra	14.1	17.2	12.7
4. Riau	9.7	13.3	27.2
5. Jambi	21.6	29.1	12.7
6. South Sumatra	⎫	37.0	27.4
7. Bengkulu	⎬ 18.6	11.7	9.4
8. Lampung	⎭	9.8	12.5
Sumatra		17.8	19.6
9. Jakarta	87.2	100.0	93.7
10. West Java	11.9	12.4	21.0
11. Central Java	10.2	10.7	18.8
12. Yogyakarta	16.4	16.3	22.1
13. East Java	12.8	14.5	19.6
Java		18.0	25.1
14. Bali	8.8	9.8	14.7
15. West Nusatenggara	5.6	8.1	14.1
16. East Nusatenggara	5.4	5.6	7.5
17. East Timor	n.a.	n.a.	n.a.
Nusatenggara			12.0
18. West Kalimantan	13.2	11.0	16.8
19. Central Kalimantan	14.1	12.4	10.3
20. South Kalimantan	22.7	26.7	21.4
21. East Kalimantan	32.8	39.2	40.0
Kalimantan		21.8	21.5
22. North Sulawesi	⎫ 14.9	19.5	16.8
23. Central Sulawesi	⎭	5.7	9.0
24. South Sulawesi	⎫ 15.9	18.2	18.1
25. Southeast Sulawesi	⎭	6.3	9.4
Sulawesi		16.4	15.9
26. Maluku	20.7	13.3	10.9
27. Irian Jaya	n.a.	16.3	21.4
Maluku & Irian Jaya		9.4	15.5
Indonesia	14.8	17.3	22.4

n.a.: not available

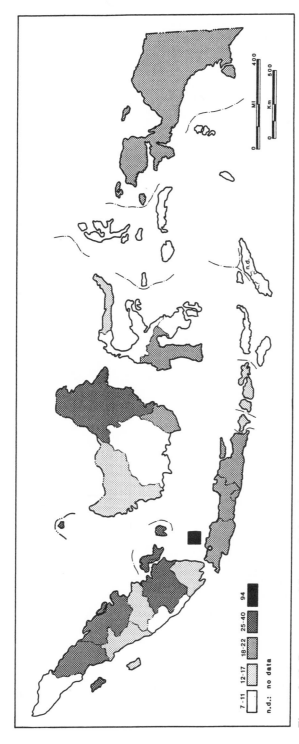

Figure 3.19. Percentage of the population classified as urban, 1980. Calculated from data in Tables 1 in the twenty-seven volumes of Biro Pusat Statistik, *Sensus Penduduk 1980*, Series S.

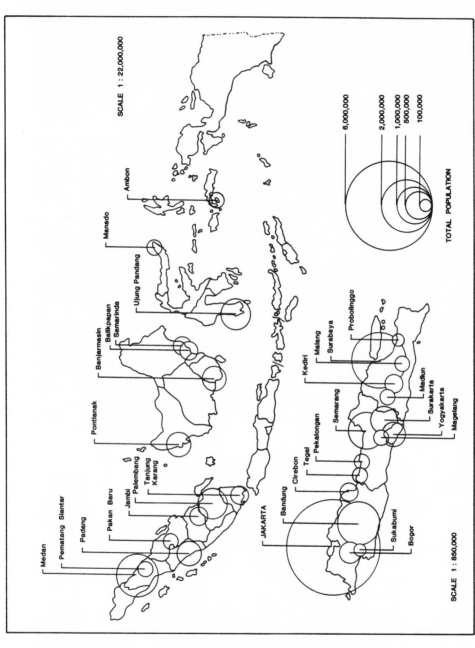

Figure 3.20. Location and population size of Indonesia's thirty largest cities, 1980. Based on a map by Sukanto Reksohadiprodjo in *Prisma* 6 (1984), p. 16 (used with permission); and data in Biro Pusat Statistik, *Sensus Penduduk*

SCALE 1 : 22,000,000

6,000,000
2,000,000
1,000,000
500,000
100,000

TOTAL POPULATION

SCALE 1 : 850,000

Medan
Pematang Siantar
Padang
Pakan Baru
Jambi
Palembang
Tanjung Karang
Pontianak
Banjarmasin
Balikpapan
Samarinda
Ujung Pandang
Manado
Ambon
JAKARTA
Bandung
Cirebon
Tegal
Pekalongan
Semarang
Kediri
Malang
Surabaya
Probolinggo
Madiun
Surakarta
Yogyakarta
Magelang
Sukabumi
Bogor

Table 3.2. Size and growth rate of Indonesia's thirty largest cities, 1971–1980

City	Size (1980)	Rank in 1971	Size (1971)	Growth rate (1971–1980)
Jakarta	6,503,449	1	4,579,303	3.9
Surabaya	2,027,913	2	1,556,255	2.9
Bandung	1,462,637	3	1,200,380	2.2
Medan	1,378,955	5	635,562	8.5
Semarang	1,026,671	4	646,590	5.2
Palembang	787,187	6	582,961	3.4
Ujung Pandang	709,038	7	434,766	5.5
Malang	511,780	8	422,428	2.1
Padang	480,922	14	196,339	10.3
Surakarta	469,888	9	414,285	1.4
Yogyakarta	398,727	10	314,629	1.7
Banjarmasin	381,286	11	281,673	3.4
Pontianak	304,778	12	217,555	3.8
Tanjung Karang	284,275	13	198,986	4.0
Balikpapan	280,675	22	137,340	8.2
Samarinda	264,718	21	137,782	7.4
Bogor	247,409	15	195,873	2.6
Jambi	230,373	19	158,559	4.2
Cirebon	223,776	17	178,529	2.5
Kediri	221,830	16	178,865	2.4
Manado	217,159	18	170,181	2.7
Ambon	208,893	31	79,636	11.6
Pakan Baru	186,262	20	145,030	2.8
Madiun	150,562	23	136,147	1.1
Pematang Siantar	150,376	24	129,232	1.7
Pekalongan	132,558	25	111,201	1.9
Tegal	131,728	27	105,752	2.4
Magelang	123,484	26	110,308	1.2
Sukabumi	109,994	28	96,242	1.5
Probolinggo	100,296	30	82,008	2.2

Source: Biro Pusat Statistik

urban places. Unlike many developing countries, and especially those in Southeast Asia that have a primate city dominating the entire nation (such as Bangkok in Thailand, Rangoon in Burma, and Manila in the Philippines), Indonesia has an extensive network of towns and cities of different sizes distributed throughout the country, thanks partly to the Dutch administrative system, partly to the growth of small transport nodes, and partly to the development of trade and small industrial centers. Such an urban network encourages integration by permitting the filtering down of national values, ideas, and concepts, and can also be used to distribute the process and effects of development and promote widespread integrated development.[52] However, Jakarta's primacy ratio has been steadily increasing, from 1.20 in 1961 to 1.34 in 1971 to 1.44 in 1980.[53] This reflects centralizing trends in government and in the direction of economic growth. The attraction of Jakarta is such that it is drawing many of the best-educated people of the other provinces in a classic "brain-drain" situation, depleting the outlying areas of the ingenuity and creativity they need for development. In the decade of the 1970s over half a million Outer Islanders migrated to Jakarta. Although this may leave the outlying regions more malleable and docile, it does not encourage strong regional participation in development or a dynamic form of integration.

The government, through its various Five-Year Development Plans (beginning in the second), has aimed at rectifying the problem of Jakarta's increasing growth and overwhelming dominance (it grew from 2,907,000 in 1961 to 4,576,000 in 1971 to 6,503,449 in 1980) by the assignment of major growth-pole functions to three of the largest urban centers—Medan, Surabaya, and Ujung Pandang. Seven other cities in addition to these three have been selected as centers for regional development, and seventeen others throughout the country have been designated as minor growth centers. Thus, there is a deliberate realization of the integrative role of an urban network and an attempt to use urbanization to promote national integration.

Many important sociocultural features, therefore, have helped to integrate the distinct and diverse peoples of Indonesia. Perhaps most important are the use of the common national language; participation in the national culture through common educational experiences; exposure to common literature and news magazines, radio and television programs, and Indonesian-made movies; the impact of powerful national symbolism; involvement in national sociocultural and economic organizations; and increasing participation in a common urban culture and environment.

4

The Interaction Dimension

INTERACTION among the many diverse peoples within a nation-state is part of the very essence of national integration, for isolation and interaction are antithetical by definition. Interaction includes all forms of transportation and communications that bring peoples from different geographical areas of the country into contact with one another. The focus in this chapter is upon interprovincial interaction, both structural linkages and functional flows (of peoples, goods, messages, and information). Because interaction data on functional integration are limited, estimates of the degree of integration of the various provinces have to be based largely upon structural information and reached from an analysis of the various transportation and communications networks within each province.

Inevitably, analysis of data at the provincial level conceals huge intraprovincial contrasts. In reality, the term transport accessibility refers only to those areas within about nine miles of major transportation nodes (such as seaports and cities) or arteries (such as navigable rivers, railroads, and major paved roads).[1] Wide contrasts therefore exist between the few areas of continuous accessibility (such as broad river valleys) and the comparatively dense transportation networks around provincial capitals on the one hand, and the vast areas of limited or extremely difficult accessibility on the other. These contrasts are particularly marked in the Outer Islands, whereas Java has a much greater density of transportation and communications networks.

Present networks are the result of long historical development, whereby areas of greatest accessibility (broad river valleys and areas of protected, indented coastlines) became indigenous core areas. The transportation accessibility of these early core areas was reinforced by the colonial establishment first of trading posts and later of administrative networks. Transportation infrastructure remains largely that inherited from the colonial period, which was geared more to the extraction of estate agricultural products and mineral wealth for the colonial homeland than to the needs of Indonesia as a nation. Short road or rail links from the estates or mines to the nearest port, together with some interisland shipping for domestic trade and administrative purposes, sufficed. An estimated 90 percent of Indonesia's land area was ignored by the Dutch.

Thus, independent Indonesia inherited an inadequate and uneven infrastructure, one that served only about 10 percent of the national territory and concentrated overwhelmingly upon Java and a few other port hinterlands, mainly in Sumatra. Even what infrastructure there was deteriorated badly during the Second World War and the subsequent struggle for independence. In the 1950s and early 1960s, problems such as regional revolts, the lack of finance and skilled manpower, and the government's tendency to give priority to directly productive investment projects as well as to noneconomic ventures contributed further to the neglect of basic infrastructure. Aside from a few limited projects, no major effort to rehabilitate and expand the economic infrastructure was made until the beginning of the New Order under Suharto in 1967.

Several difficulties arise in trying to analyze the integration of provinces into the nation-state on the basis of their structural linkages. Structural networks do not distinguish between inter- and intraprovincial communications. In addition, the provinces vary considerably in their orientation to land and sea forms of transport. Within Java most transportation takes place by land (by rail and road), whereas in Maluku the multi-island composition of the province dictates sea transportation as the predominant mode. In parts of Kalimantan river transportation is vital. Within and between many of the Outer Island provinces, sea and air links provide the only means of physical interaction, whereas in Sumatra all modes of transportation exist, although with differing combinations of usage in each province.

Transportation

Lack of detailed data on passenger flows between provinces necessitates the use of surrogates. An examination of the rail network and the numbers of passengers carried in each province gives some indication of population mobility, itself a prerequisite to population interaction. Similarly, analysis of road networks and numbers of vehicles in each province provides a general picture of comparative mobility (as well as of the level of economic development). Examination of shipping and shipping routes gives some indication of the degree of interprovincial movement, and consideration of airline traffic gives a measure of the connections among major cities. Data given, as elsewhere in the book, should be handled cautiously. It is necessary to focus on the overall picture and trends rather than assuming that the reported figures are precise. Data for this chapter are tabulated in Appendix 2.

The railroad system in Indonesia is limited to Java and Madura, and to three unconnected areas of Sumatra: Aceh and North Sumatra, West Sumatra, and southern Sumatra (see Figure 4.1). Thus, only in Java and to a limited extent in northern and southern Sumatra do railroad connections play any part in interprovincial transportation. In Sumatra the railroads were built to connect agricultural estates or tin and coal mines with ports on the coast, with the exception of that in Aceh, which was constructed originally to enable Dutch military operations to put down the Acehnese revolt in the late nineteenth century.

Most of the railroad track (71 percent) is in Java. The total length of track has decreased from over 7,360 kilometers in 1939 to about 6,700 kilometers in 1982 (4,700 kilometers on Java and Madura and 2,000 kilometers on Sumatra).[2] Passenger traffic declined during the 1961 to 1977 period, with the number of passengers falling from 144 million during 1961 to only twenty-three million in 1977, despite an increase in population of over thirty million during that time period. This was partly a response to improved road conditions and an increase in bus and truck transportation, and partly a result of the inadequate mainte-nance and renewal of railroad lines, bridges, and equipment. But since 1977 the number of passengers has increased consistently, to forty-four million by 1982.[3] The short length of the average journey in 1982 (139 kilometers for passengers in Java, 141 kilometers in North Sumatra, 260 kilometers in South Sumatra, and thirty-four kilometers in West Sumatra) suggests that most travel is intraprovincial rather than interprovincial. This factor, together with the limited areas served by the railroads, indicates that railroads have a comparatively small inte-grative role on a nationwide scale in Indonesia, with the limited excep-tion of Java. However, much interaction takes place on the trains, because people tend to converse freely with strangers and share ideas, perceptions, and news.

In an analysis of road transportation as a measure of integration, two factors need to be considered. First, the archipelagic character of Indo-nesia dictates that sea (and, to a lesser extent, air) and not road links will be more crucial among the hundreds of small islands and in the provinces consisting mostly of smaller islands. Second, the difficult ter-rain, dense vegetation, and low level of development of much of the larger islands of Kalimantan, Sulawesi, and Irian Jaya necessitate con-siderable use of small sailing craft along the coast or river systems for interprovincial passenger and freight movement.

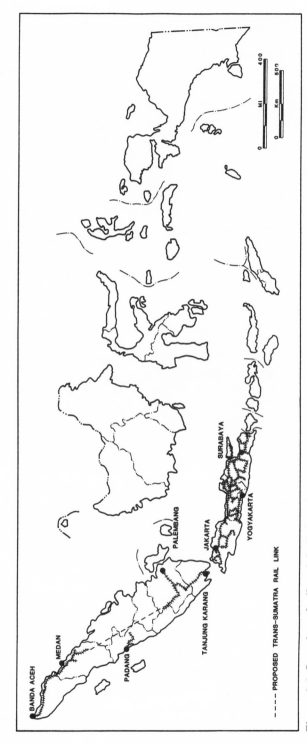

Figure 4.1. Location of railroads in Indonesia, 1980.

However, between provinces in Java, increasingly in Sumatra, and in limited areas of other provinces in the Outer Islands, road transportation is predominant. The road network is much denser in Java, and the quality of the paved roads there is much superior to that found in most of the Outer Islands. Indeed, Java, with only 6.9 percent of the total land area of Indonesia, has 27 percent of all the roads in the country and 48 percent of its paved highways.[4] In terms of total road density (in kilometers of all types of roads per 1,000 square kilometers) Java has an average of 347 compared to an average in the Outer Islands of sixty-eight (and a range from eight in Irian Jaya to 266 in North Sulawesi). Sulawesi and Sumatra have higher road densities than Kalimantan, Maluku, and Irian Jaya (see Figure 4.2).

The contrast between Java and the Outer Islands in road density is far greater when only paved roads are considered. Java has a far denser network of paved roads (249 kilometers per 1,000 square kilometers compared to thirty-six in Sulawesi, forty-one in Sumatra, and six in Kalimantan) and has a far higher percentage of its roads paved (72 percent compared to 37 percent in Sumatra, 24 percent in Kalimantan, and 23 percent in Sulawesi). There is a distinct decrease in the density of paved roads with increasing distance eastward from Java (with East Nusatenggara having 23.8 kilometers of paved roads per 1,000 square kilometers, Maluku 9.1, and Irian Jaya 1.5), although Central and East Kalimantan also rank among the lowest, with 2.0 and 3.4, respectively. Contrasts between provinces within the major islands are also enormous (see Figure 4.3).

Within the past ten years a comprehensive program of road improvement has been undertaken: a network of 18,000 kilometers of high-priority road links throughout the archipelago.[5] Indeed, some of the results can already be seen in the significant increase in total road length, from 95,463 kilometers in 1972 to 168,028 kilometers in 1982, and in the more than doubling of paved roads from 25,068 kilometers in 1972 to 69,209 kilometers in 1982 (a change from 26 percent paved in 1972 to 41 percent paved in 1982).[6]

Vehicle density has likewise increased enormously over the past decade and, as expected, ranges widely among the provinces, in relation both to the length of roads and to the size of provincial populations. In terms of the number of vehicles per kilometer of road, the Javanese provinces stand out as by far the best served (see Figure 4.4), with an average of more than three times as many as any other island group and more than seven times as many as Nusatenggara, Maluku, and Irian Jaya. Apart from all the Javanese provinces, only North Sumatra exceeds the national average of 32 vehicles per kilometer of road.

Perhaps a more meaningful measure of vehicle density is the number

Figure 4.2. Length of roads of all types and conditions in kilometers per 1,000 square kilometers, 1982. Calculated from data in Table VII.1.3 in Biro Pusat Statistik, *Statistik Indonesia 1983, Buku Saku.*

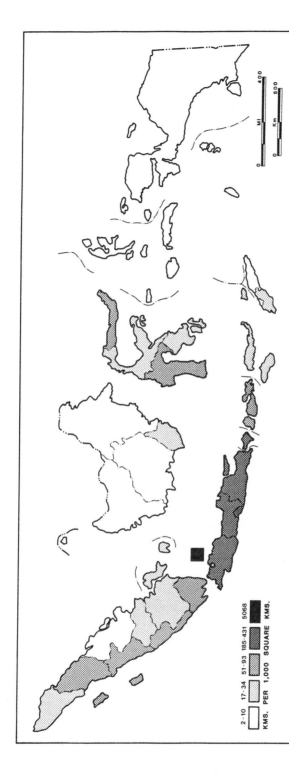

Figure 4.3. Length of paved roads in kilometers per 1,000 square kilometers, 1982. Calculated from data in Table VII.1.3 in Biro Pusat Statistik, *Statistik Indonesia 1983, Buku Saku.*

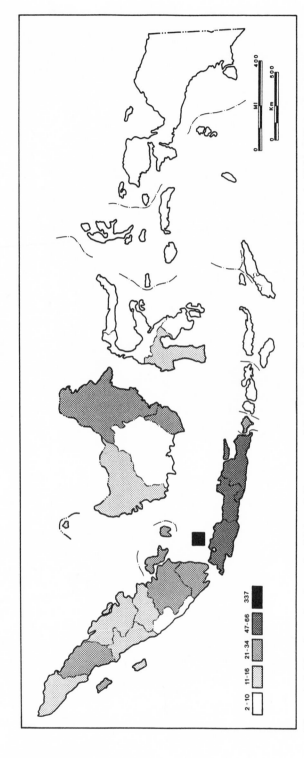

Figure 4.4. Number of registered vehicles of all types per kilometer of road, 1982. Calculated from data in Table VII.2.3 in Biro Pusat Statistik, *Statistik Indonesia 1983, Buku Saku.*

2 - 10
11 - 16
21 - 34
47 - 66
337

of registered vehicles per 1,000 population (see Figure 4.5). As might be expected, some of the more highly urbanized and developed provinces, Jakarta, East Kalimantan, Bali, and North Sumatra, have a disproportionate share of vehicles (155, sixty-eight, fifty-three, and fifty-three vehicles per 1,000 population, respectively), and East and West Nusatenggara and Maluku have the fewest (eight, thirteen, and thirteen, respectively, compared with a national average of thirty-six). Java had 65 percent of the total 5,347,716 registered vehicles in the country in 1982, a proportion fairly consistent with Java's share of the overall population (62 percent), but highly out of balance when land area is considered and when Java's rail network is taken into account. East Nusatenggara ranks lowest on both vehicular indices.

Despite the relatively small number of vehicles per 1,000 population, mobility is growing, as evidenced by the impressive increase in the number of vehicles since 1970. In that year the total number of registered vehicles was only 805,000 for a population of around 115 million (an average of one vehicle per 143 people). By 1974 this number had increased by 67 percent to 1,342,000 and by 1982 had reached an amazing 5,347,716 vehicles (for a population of around 155 million, an average of one vehicle per twenty-nine people), a 664 percent increase over the 1970 figure. The increase took place particularly in the number of motorcycles, which make up 70 percent of all the vehicles in the country, compared with 15 percent for passenger cars, 12 percent for trucks, and 3 percent for buses.[7] Once again one needs to note the considerable amount of interaction that takes place on buses and on trucks used to transport people, especially on long-distance trips.

Because of Indonesia's geographical configuration whereby 84 percent of the territory under its jurisdiction consists of sea, shipping has historically been the prime means of linking the thousands of islands and is second only to roads in importance. Interisland shipping was well organized and regular under the Dutch colonial administration, although it served only a limited number of ports. It was provided not only for economic reasons but for governmental purposes of integrating the far-flung empire, with profitable lines subsidizing other noneconomic but administratively important routes. The Dutch-owned fleet continued to serve interisland shipping needs after independence until its withdrawal in 1957; after that the situation deteriorated badly and only began to improve again at the beginning of the 1970s.

Of the five branches of the Indonesian shipping fleet, the archipelago fleet *(armada Nusantara),* the local shipping fleet *(armada lokal),* and the people's shipping fleet *(armada rakyat)* are of predominant importance in interprovincial transportation. These fleets are largely complementary, with the people's and local shipping fleets serving local harbors and

Figure 4.5. Number of registered vehicles of all types per 1,000 population, 1982. Calculated from data in Table VII.2.3 in Biro Pusat Statistik, *Statistik Indonesia 1983, Buku Saku.*

coastal villages and feeding the major ports, which are served by the interisland, archipelago fleet. Regional differences in the relative importance of the different fleets occur: people's shipping is of greater importance in eastern Indonesia, while just over half the local shipping fleet is domiciled in the west. The most important for interisland transportation is the *armada Nusantara* (interisland fleet).

The oldest, traditional form of communications among the islands was by sailing vessels *(perahu)* that made use of the seasonal monsoons in their annual voyage, sailing eastward with the westerly wind in the wet October-to-March season and westward with the northeasterly monsoon in the dry April-to-September season. By the mid 1970s, an estimated 7,500 to 10,000 of these small wooden sailing vessels, some with small auxiliary motors, served shipping needs, primarily in Sulawesi and East Java.[8] *Perahu* shipping *(armada rakyat)* accounts for approximately 10 percent of the total Indonesian interisland trade and is important for certain cargoes, particularly timber, where it has had a virtual monopoly. *Perahu* shipping has the advantage of being more flexible than other forms of transportation; the sailing vessels are virtually independent of imported materials and spare parts; they place few demands on the infrastructure of ports and dockyard services, and they are not handicapped by burdensome, bureaucratic controls. They are thus self-sufficient, labor-intensive, and, in the past especially, mostly unregulated, able to respond quickly to changes in trading needs. For these reasons, *perahu* shipping historically has been strong in periods of economic decline (such as in the late 1950s to 1960s) but has suffered increasing competition from the local shipping fleet as the economy has improved and as infrastructure and capital have been concentrated on serving the needs of the local and interisland shipping fleets.

Perahu shipping thus plays a minor though significant role in interisland trade and communications. Its importance varies considerably from area to area, partly for historical reasons and partly too because only certain routes are suitable for the *perahu* because of wind patterns. But in ports such as Banjarmasin, Semarang, and Cirebon, *perahu* shipping predominates; and in linking many of the smaller, isolated villages and harbors, *perahu* shipping has a vital role.

The *armada lokal* involves wooden- and steel-hulled motor vessels used for freight, with capacities of between 100 and 500 cubic meters, which provide feeder services to the major ports within a radius of approximately 200 miles.[9] This sector has increased its share of shipping considerably since the establishment of the New Order in 1967, and by the mid-1970s accounted for approximately 18 percent (1.9 million tons per annum) of total interisland trade. Local shipping is frequently in the hands of Chinese, who have better access to finance and cargoes, especially of consumer goods, which are so important in the outward trade from Java. Most is domiciled in Sumatra (25 percent in Riau alone), compared with only 29 percent in Java.

However, the interisland fleet of primary importance in linking all the provinces and serving the major ports for both passengers and freight is the *armada Nusantara*. Because of its recognized integrative role as well as its economic role in promoting development and regional trade, this fleet has been the main focus of attention in a nation concerned with the problems of national integration and development.

In colonial days, interisland transportation was provided by the *Koninklijke Paketvaart Maatschappij (K.P.M., the Dutch interisland shipping company)*, supplemented by the vessels of the *Kapal-Kapal Armada Pemerintah* (government fleet) to facilitate government administration and fill local transport needs. The *K.P.M.* continued to operate after independence until 1957, when it was withdrawn as a consequence of Indonesia's attempted nationalization of the fleet, which was part of its effort to wrest West Irian from the Dutch. As a result, interisland transportation declined drastically: by 1968 it was estimated that the size of the Indonesian fleet was only 30 percent of that of the *K.P.M.* fleet in 1957. By 1972, 48 percent of the interisland fleet of 389 ships was over fifteen years of age, and only 187 of the 275 ships licensed to operate on the Regular Liner Service routes were operative. Service was irregular and productivity low, with port time consuming 70–80 percent of total operating time.[10] Since 1972, however, great improvements have been made to rehabilitate seaworthy vessels; to modernize, expand, and improve the efficiency of the interisland fleet; and to improve shipyard and dock facilities. Cargo shipped by interisland shipping, for example, increased from 2.3 million tons in 1973, to 3.5 million tons in 1976, and to 4.4 million tons in 1980.

In 1980 the interisland fleet totaled 374 vessels, with a combined capacity of 379,000 deadweight tons.[11] This network was supplemented by a number of vessels designed to carry homogeneous bulk cargoes and meet overflow seasonal shipping needs. (By 1980 two-thirds of the total cargo fleet was used for the transportation of petroleum and liquified natural gas alone.) The relative importance of each province in interisland shipping can be seen in the income generated by each port, aggregated by province. The income from ports in Java (33.5 percent of the total for Indonesia) just exceeds that from Sumatra (33.3 percent), compared with Kalimantan's 21.7 percent, Sulawesi's 6.3 percent, Irian Jaya and Maluku's combined total of 4.1 percent, and Nusatenggara's 1.2 percent. However, on a provincial basis Jakarta predominates, with over 1,294 million rupiahs in income generated by its port of Tanjung Priok (17.2 percent of the total for Indonesia), followed by

East Kalimantan with 1,104 million rupiahs from its five major ports (14.6 percent), and Riau with 835 million rupiahs from its major port of Dumai (11.1 percent).[12] On a per-capita basis, however, East Kalimantan's ports generate almost twice as much as the second ranking province of Riau (1,013.5 and 538.2 rupiahs per capita, respectively), with Jakarta, Irian Jaya, and Aceh also each generating more than three times the national average of 51.1 rupiahs per capita (see Figure 4.6). Provinces with the lowest port-generated income per capita include all the Javanese provinces apart from Jakarta, as well as Bali, the two Nusatenggara provinces, and Bengkulu.

Attention has also been given to integrating especially isolated parts of Indonesia (the *daerah-daerah lemah*) by providing regular service with thirty-one special vessels (the *armada perintis* [pioneer fleet]). The motivation for this is both political and economic: to integrate and to involve those areas in mainstream Indonesian life; and to develop, by guaranteeing regular transportation, any cash crops that can be produced, as well as to raise living standards by bringing in imported goods. Areas served include the Riau archipelago, West Sumatra, West and East Nusatenggara, Sangihe and Talaud (in North Sulawesi), Maluku, and Irian Jaya. Traffic on these lines grew by over 31 percent a year between 1976 and 1980.[13]

Of the 319 registered ports, the seventeen largest (each recording an income of at least 100 million rupiahs in 1981–1982) accounted for 70 percent of the total shipping income (see Table 4.1).[14] The government has been active in rehabilitating these ports and stimulating the shipping industry through a number of regulations and construction projects. These include requiring goods purchased or sold by official agencies or enterprises to be transported on Indonesian liners and reducing berthing fees for domestic liners. In a more controversial move, the government is forcing shipowners to scrap all vessels over twenty-five years old (regardless of their seaworthiness) and sell the scrap to the state-owned Krakatau Steel (at prices well below those on the international market). Shipowners are then required to purchase standard, locally built ships from the state-owned shipbuilding company in Surabaya, which, critics claim, are being built with high-cost local materials and an inexperienced work force, thus costing far more than the preferred secondhand foreign-built vessels previously bought.[15]

Air transportation has increased enormously over the past two decades, a measure of both the increasing integration particularly of urban areas and the improving standard of living in Indonesia. Just between 1968 and 1971 the number of passengers flying on domestic flights increased from 382,000 to 993,000, an increase of 260 percent.[16] By 1974 the numbers had increased to a reported 2,229,000 passen-

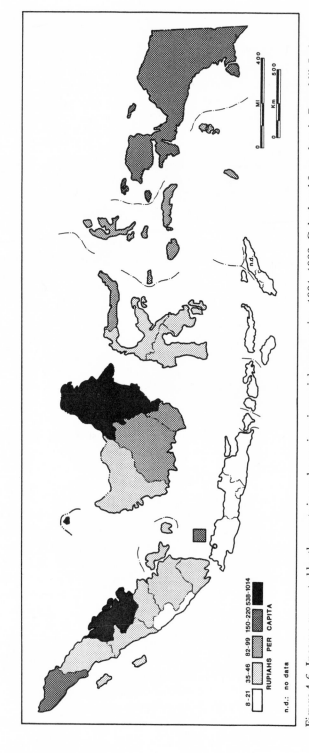

Figure 4.6. Income generated by the ports in each province in rupiahs per capita, 1981–1982. Calculated from data in Republik Indonesia, Departemen Perhubungan Laut, Direktorat Perkapalan dan Pelayaran SubDit. Kebandaran dan Awak Kapal, Seksi P.U., File No. TH 1981/82.

Table 4.1. Major ports of Indonesia ranked by income recorded, 1981–1982

Port	Rupiahs (millions)
1. Tanjung Priok (Jakarta)	1,294,006
2. Dumai (Riau)	835,426
3. Surabaya (East Java)	534,500
4. Lhokseumawe (Aceh)	339,252
5. Kuala Semboja (East Kalimantan)	286,826
6. Balikpapan (East Kalimantan)	272,765
7. Belawan (North Sumatra)	267,239
8. Bontang (East Kalimantan)	227,739
9. Palembang (South Sumatra)	181,168
10. Tanjung Santan (East Kalimantan)	161,254
11. Samarinda (East Kalimantan)	155,381
12. Manado/Bitung (North Sulawesi)	136,340
13. Banjarmasin (South Kalimantan)	133,244
14. Semarang (Central Java)	128,132
15. Sorong (Irian Jaya)	118,354
16. Ujung Pandang (South Sulawesi)	116,590
17. Cirebon (West Java)	101,784

Source: Republik Indonesia, Departemen Perhubungan Laut, Direktorat Perkapalan dan Pelayaran SubDit, Kebandaran dan Awak Kapal, Seksi P.U., *File No. TH 1981/82*

gers,[17] and by 1981 to 6,512,902, a 656 percent increase over just ten years.[18] The amount of freight carried by the airlines is still small but increased at an annual rate of 23 percent between 1969 and 1982.[19]

The number of domestic air passengers passing through the sixty-six provincial airports gives some idea of the comparative importance of air traffic relative to population size in each province and reflects economic prosperity as well as population mobility. As Figure 4.7 shows, Jakarta and East Kalimantan dominate in per-capita air travel, while provinces with the least domestic air traffic in relation to their populations are West, Central, and East Java, Aceh, Lampung, and the relatively isolated and less developed provinces of East and West Nusatenggara and Southeast Sulawesi.

Much progress has been made in increasing the number of aircraft and the number of flights on already established routes, as well as in constructing new airports and air strips, thus improving communications among previously isolated areas. Several commercial airlines serve domestic routes, and there are several special charter airlines as well. In 1983, the primary government-owned national airline, Garuda Indonesian Airways, operated seventy-seven aircraft with a combined seating capacity of 11,400, and Merpati Nusantara, incorporated into

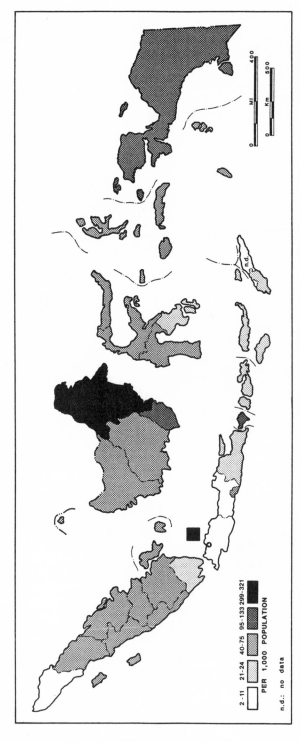

Figure 4.7. Number of air passengers recorded on domestic flights per 1,000 population, 1981. Calculated from data in Table 9 in Biro Pusat Statistik, *Statistik Angkutan Udara 1981.*

Garuda in 1978 but still run as a separate entity, operated thirty-eight aircraft.[20] Other commercial domestic airlines, such as Mandala and Bouraq, further strengthen air transportation services in the country and help to link population centers throughout the archipelago.

Communications

Mass communications are vital to integrating a nation in terms of both area and people. This has been recognized by many governments of developing countries, which have sought to improve all forms of communications. Radio and television, telephone and telegraph, mail service and the press all play a vital role in national communications. Telecommunications facilities have expanded tremendously since 1970 with the completion of the domestic satellite network consisting of two communications satellites *(Palapa)* and forty earth stations.

Of all the forms of mass-media communications considered in a 1972 sample survey of the best way to disseminate information and reach people, radio was found to be most effective (compared with the press, television, and films).[21] This is partly because of the widespread availability and relative low cost of radios and partly because a radio requires no skills of its audience. Use of traditional media (such as shadow puppet plays [*wayang*]) was also valued because of its ready acceptance by the people (in those areas such as Java where it is a traditionally accepted part of the culture).

The importance of exposure to national and nationwide radio broadcasts and television programs has already been considered under the sociocultural dimension of integration. An impressive doubling in the number of radio receivers was recorded between 1964 and 1971 (from 1.5 million to three million), and by 1980 12.3 million households reported owning a radio/cassette recorder.[22] Television accessibility throughout the country has expanded even more rapidly. By 1980, 2,940,000 households reported owning a television set, up from an estimated 10,000 in 1962. In 1973 only about 3.8 percent of the land area of Indonesia received television signals: approximately 26 percent of Java, and parts of southern Sumatra, eastern Kalimantan, and southern Sulawesi.[23] Indeed, in 1973 93 percent of all television sets were found in Java. Since then, television has become available in every province, thanks to the *Palapa* satellites. Despite the fact that television is only one-way communication, television programs are seen as a particularly effective medium for strengthening national integration and preserving and developing Indonesia's national culture, as well as for promoting rural development.[24]

Telephone communications have also been aided by the development of the satellite communications system. But even though telephone density has risen from 1.8 per 1,000 population in 1971 to 4.0 in 1981, telephone linkages remain relatively poorly developed in Indonesia. This is a reflection partly of the low level of development, but partly too it reflects the difficulties and high cost of providing telephone facilities in such a physically fragmented country. The satellite system is supplemented by microwave facilities linking Jakarta to southern Sumatra, Bali, and parts of Nusatenggara, and other high-frequency radio and high-altitude systems link the remotest islands.[25] Telephone communication is limited largely to urban areas and thus correlates closely with the proportion of the population of each province that is urban and with the level of development. As expected, telephone density is far higher in Jakarta (32.8 telephones per 1,000 population) than in any other province, with East Kalimantan a poor second at 8.5.[26] Other provinces with relatively high telephone densities are North Sumatra, Bali, and Irian Jaya, while exceptionally low per-capita telephone ownership exists in Southeast Sulawesi, East Nusatenggara, Lampung, West and Central Kalimantan, and Central Sulawesi (see Figure 4.8). As with other forms of communications, there has been a rapid expansion of telephone communications in recent years: the number of telephones has increased from 60,000 in 1968 to 263,000 in 1973 to 584,181 in 1981 and 741,322 in 1983.

Analysis of the number of minutes of telephone conversation per capita in 1980 portrays a pattern generally similar to that of telephone ownership, with Irian Jaya, East Kalimantan, Jakarta, and Bali having the highest telephone usage on a per-capita basis, and West Kalimantan, East Nusatenggara, Lampung, and Jambi the lowest (see Figure 4.9). Some interesting changes have occurred over the past decade, however, because of the development of the multichannel microwave system and the new domestic satellite communications system: whereas in 1973 Java recorded 94 percent of all telephone conversations when measured by number of minutes spoken, by 1980 that figure had fallen to 62.8 percent, approximately equal to Java's share of the total Indonesian population. The two provinces of Irian Jaya and Maluku together had far more telephone communication per capita per annum than any other group of provinces (77.1 minutes per 100 people, compared with 44.1 for Java, 43.4 for Nusatenggara [including Bali], 42.0 for Sumatra, 41.5 for Kalimantan, and 37.6 for Sulawesi).[27]

Even more than with the use of telephones, eastern Indonesia's use of telegrams for domestic communication is far higher than that of Java and Sumatra. The number of telegrams sent to domestic destinations was greatest by far in Irian Jaya and Maluku (270.6 and 231.9 per

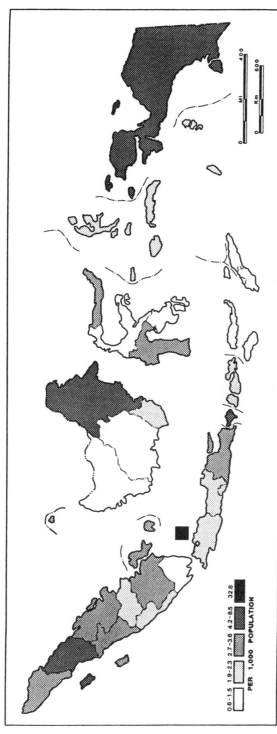

Figure 4.8. Number of telephone licenses issued per 1,000 population, 1981. Calculated from data in Table VII.5.3 in Biro Pusat Statistik, *Statistik Indonesia 1983, Buku Saku.*

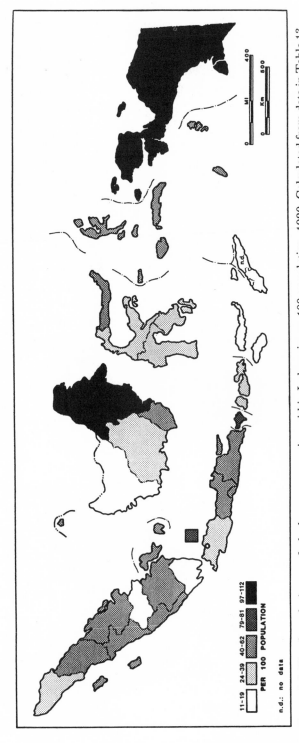

Figure 4.9. Number of minutes of telephone conversation within Indonesia per 100 population, 1980. Calculated from data in Table 13 in Biro Pusat Statistik, *Statistik Kommunikasi 1980.*

1,000 population, compared with a national average of 46.9). Other provinces with a high use of telegrams were East Kalimantan, Central and North Sulawesi, Riau, and Jakarta; those with lowest use were Lampung, North Sumatra, West, Central, and East Java, and West Kalimantan (see Figure 4.10).[28]

The provinces that stand out as having the fewest communication links with other provinces, in terms of both telephones and telegrams, on a per-capita basis, are West Kalimantan and Lampung. Telegraph communications from other isolated provinces, such as Southeast and Central Sulawesi and East Nusatenggara, are surprisingly high. For twenty-four provinces telegrams addressed to domestic destinations constituted over 95 percent of all telegrams sent. In Jakarta this figure dropped to 89 percent, a reflection of the capital's international status, and in Bali it fell to 92 percent, because of its tourism.

Interprovincial flows of mail form another index of interregional communication and thus of functional integration. However, inadequate data make detailed cross-provincial comparisons impossible.

The press, which plays such an important role in disseminating information and integrating peoples in more developed societies, has a very limited role in Indonesia. It serves a small, mainly urban clientele focused in Jakarta and a few other provincial capitals, and provides incomplete coverage of national activities. Historically, the fortunes of the press have fluctuated widely: they flowered in the mid-1950s, but underwent a spectacular decline in the period of Sukarno's Guided Democracy. After the abortive coup in 1965 the press again expanded, and in 1966 circulation rose to a peak of about two million, but then declined to under 900,000 by the end of 1967 (for a population of over 110 million).[29] It has since increased substantially. As in many developing countries, each copy of a newspaper is read by far more people than a comparable issue in a developed country.

Yet newspapers reach only a small segment of the population. On average only 18 percent of Indonesia's population ten years of age or over reported having read a newspaper or magazine in the week preceding a survey in 1981. As expected, percentages vary widely, from a high of 48.9 percent in Jakarta, and between 25 and 28 percent in North and West Sumatra, North Sulawesi, and Irian Jaya, to less than 12 percent in West and East Nusatenggara, Bengkulu, Jambi, Bali, and East Java (see Figure 4.11).[30]

Government control and interference have also varied in intensity over the years. In the late 1960s experts rated Indonesian newspapers as among the freest in Southeast Asia, but there has been considerable growth in the power and influence of the military since then and increased censorship. Several influential army-controlled dailies based

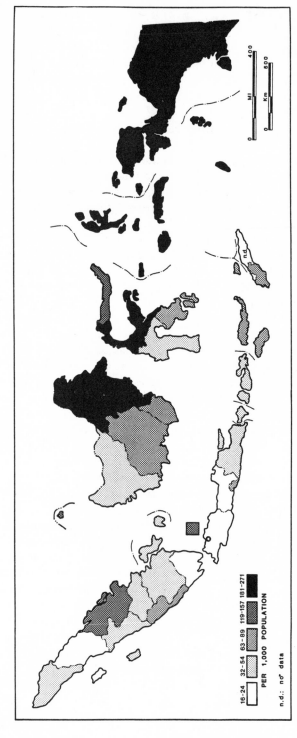

Figure 4.10. Number of telegrams sent to domestic destinations per 1,000 population, 1981. Calculated from data in Table VIII.5.5 in Biro Pusat Statistik, *Statistik Indonesia 1982.*

Figure 4.11. Percentage of the population who read a newspaper or magazine in the week preceding a survey, 1981. Based on data in Table III.1.9 in Biro Pusat Statistik, *Statistik Indonesia 1983, Buku Saku.*

in Jakarta have expanded their circulation and established affiliated
branch editions in a number of provincial towns. But some provincial
newspapers and news magazines that provide news locally have at times
been banned from being mailed to other parts of Indonesia, thereby
reducing their potential integrative effect. Press freedom was sharply
curtailed following the Jakarta riots in January 1974[31] and has fluctuated since. A fair amount of veiled criticism is currently permitted,
although there are definite limits. Indeed, a leading newspaper, *Sinar
Harapan,* was closed down in 1986 for being too outspoken. Censorship,
which theoretically may help integration by curbing inflammatory criticism, in practice may also lead to a repressive rather than an integrated
society and may restrict development.

Migration

Analysis of migration data as recorded in the 1971 and 1980 censuses
reveals much about the degree of interaction among people from the
various provinces of Indonesia, although it should be noted that the
census records only a small subset of all the population movement that
occurs within the country: that which crosses provincial borders and is
of at least six months' duration. It thus fails to take note of the considerable amount of intraprovincial movement as well as temporary migration. Other complicating factors in comparing interprovincial migration are the tremendous variation in the geographical size of the
provinces and the physical proximity of other provinces. For example,
Irian Jaya has an area of 422,000 square kilometers, whereas Jakarta
has less than 1,000 square kilometers. A person can therefore travel
only a short distance on Java by land, cross a provincial border, and be
classified as a migrant, but in Irian Jaya "migration" under this definition requires journeys of hundreds of kilometers and travel by sea or air.

   In terms of long-term interprovincial migration, the population of
Indonesia as a whole is relatively immobile. In 1980 only 7.8 percent of
the total population (11.4 million people out of 146.8 million) had
resided in a province other than that in which they were presently
located, and only 7.0 percent were living in a different province from
the one where they were born.[32] Over one-third of those who had lived
elsewhere (4.5 million or 39 percent) were residing either in Jakarta or
in Lampung in southern Sumatra, a major destination for transmigrants from Java. In general there is considerably more interprovincial
mixing in Sumatra, Kalimantan, Maluku, and Irian Jaya than there is
in Nusatenggara, Java (with the exception of Jakarta), and Sulawesi.
Very little intermixing takes place in the eight provinces where less than

5 percent of the population has ever lived in another province. This group includes both the densely populated provinces of East, Central, and West Java and Bali, and the more isolated and less developed provinces of East and West Nusatenggara and West Kalimantan, as well as South Sulawesi (see Figure 4.12).

Analysis of the generally small percentage of each province's population that has previously lived outside that province shows that in fourteen provinces over half of the immigrants came from just one or two other provinces, generally from their nearest neighbors (with the exceptions of the provinces attracting transmigrants from Java and Bali, such as North Sumatra, Jambi, South Sumatra, Bengkulu, Lampung, and West Kalimantan) (see Figure 4.13). Other provinces, however, such as East Nusatenggara and South and North Sulawesi, have immigrants from a wide diversity of other provinces, with no one province contributing more than 17 percent. In comparison with the migration data in the 1971 census, it is interesting to note that the source areas for interprovincial migrants have broadened as transportation and communications facilities have improved.

Although the percentages of people who have lived outside their present province of residence remain small, they conceal the substantial numbers involved, particularly in the case of Java. For example, although only 2.3 percent of Central Java's and 2.1 percent of East Java's population have lived previously in another province, these percentages represent 579,000 and 623,000 people respectively, significantly higher numbers than the 57,500 in-migrants in East Nusatenggara and the 69,500 in West Nusatenggara (which also constitute only 2.1 and 2.6 percent of their respective populations), or even the 150,000 in Central Kalimantan, which make up a much more significant 15.7 percent of its total population of 954,000.[33]

Three major migration flows can be identified from the 1980 census materials: first, that to Jakarta, where just over 40 percent of that special district's population formerly resided in another province. Jakarta's attractions are obvious: it is the center of government and commerce and has greater employment and education opportunities than any other province.

Over 75 percent of the in-migrants in Jakarta in 1980 had come from Java, with the highest proportions, as might be expected, from West and Central Java (33.5 and 32.3 percent, respectively) (see Table 4.2). Significant numbers had come also from North, West, and South Sumatra, West Kalimantan, and South and North Sulawesi. Indeed, Jakarta was the prime destination for migrants from North, West, and South Sumatra, West and Central Java, Yogyakarta, West Nusatenggara, and West Kalimantan. The considerable amount of interchange

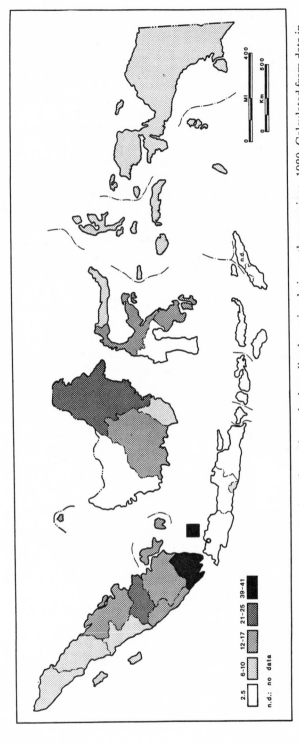

Figure 4.12. Percentage of the population in each province who have lived previously in another province, 1980. Calculated from data in Table 7.3 in Biro Pusat Statistik, *Sensus Penduduk 1980*, Series S, no. 2.

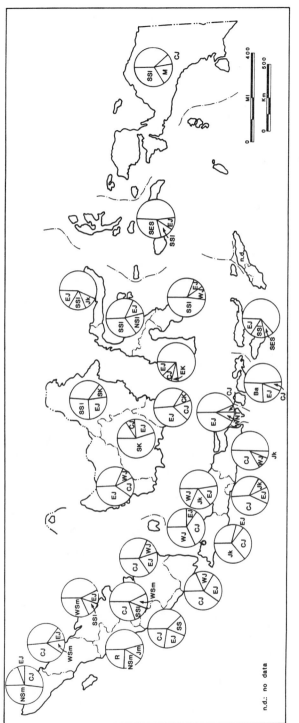

Figure 4.13. Province of last previous residence of interprovincial migrants, 1980. Calculated from data in Table 7.3 in Biro Pusat Statistik, *Sensus Penduduk 1980*, Series S, no. 2.

n.d.: no data

A Aceh	SS South Sumatra	CJ Central Java	SK South Kalimantan	SES Southeast Sulawesi
NSm North Sumatra	B Bengkulu	Yg Yogyakarta	EK East Kalimantan	Ba Bali
WSm West Sumatra	L Lampung	EJ East Java	NSI North Sulawesi	WNT West Nusatenggara
R Riau	Jk Jakarta	WK West Kalimantan	CSI Central Sulawesi	ENT East Nusatenggara
Jm Jambi	WJ West Java	CK Central Kalimantan	SSI South Sulawesi	M Maluku
				IJ Irian Jaya

Table 4.2. Migration to Jakarta

Place of previous residence of Jakarta's population in 1980	In-migrants to Jakarta	Percentage of Jakarta's in-migrant population in 1980[a]
Aceh	12,635	0.4
North Sumatra	149,513	5.8
West Sumatra	131,198	5.1
Riau	17,011	0.7
Jambi	6,576	0.2
South Sumatra	89,831	3.4
Bengkulu	3,420	0.1
Lampung	11,394	0.4
Jakarta	[3,842,898][b]	—
West Java	859,979	33.5
Central Java	828,947	32.3
Yogyakarta	62,208	2.4
East Java	211,530	8.2
Bali	7,411	0.3
West Nusatenggara	8,039	0.3
East Nusatenggara	9,009	0.4
East Timor	1,313	0.1
West Kalimantan	47,349	1.8
Central Kalimantan	2,507	0.1
South Kalimantan	12,795	0.5
East Kalimantan	6,279	0.2
North Sulawesi	27,818	1.1
Central Sulawesi	3,769	0.1
South Sulawesi	38,687	1.5
Southeast Sulawesi	2,868	0.1
Maluku	13,645	0.5
Irian Jaya	4,151	0.2

Source: Biro Pusat Statistik, *Sensus Penduduk 1980,* Series S, no. 2, Table 7.3

[a]Excluding those abroad or not stated.
[b]Residents of Jakarta who have not lived in any other province.

between Jakarta and West Java is also striking: over half the out-migrants from Jakarta live in West Java, from where a considerable number commute or engage in circular migration to Jakarta.

The second major migration flow is the movement from Java to Lampung, South and North Sumatra, and to a lesser extent Jambi and Riau, stimulated largely by the government's transmigration (resettlement) program (see Table 4.3). In Lampung 39 percent of the population had migrated from other provinces (two-thirds of them from Central and East Java), while South and North Sumatra each had over

Table 4.3. Number of government-sponsored transmigrants, 1969–1983

Province	Number of settlers
Aceh	35,516
North Sumatra	13,955
West Sumatra	29,870
Riau	114,728
Jambi	131,554
South Sumatra	358,819
Bengkulu	61,252
Lampung	140,265
West Kalimantan	66,107
Central Kalimantan	41,348
South Kalimantan	81,560
East Kalimantan	49,039
North Sulawesi	21,852
Central Sulawesi	91,599
South Sulawesi	48,426
Southeast Sulawesi	78,643
Maluku	16,678
Irian Jaya	32,927
	1,414,138[a]

Source: Republic of Indonesia, Department of Transmigration

[a]In addition to official, government-sponsored transmigrants, there are at least twice as many spontaneous transmigrants, although their destinations differ widely from those of government-sponsored transmigrants. For example, thirteen to eighteen times as many spontaneous as official transmigrants moved to Lampung and North Sumatra between 1975 and 1980. See H. W. Arndt, "Transmigration: Achievements, Problems, Prospects," p. 71. North Sumatra in 1980 recorded 617,115 people who had previously lived outside the province; in Lampung, the numbers were 1,813,900. See Biro Pusat Statistik, *Sensus Penduduk 1980,* Series S, no. 2, Table 7.3.

350,000 migrants from Java. Also increasingly affected by the government's transmigration program in the 1970s have been the provinces of South, West, and East Kalimantan, Central and Southeast Sulawesi, and, most recently, Irian Jaya. In addition to government-sponsored migration there has always been a considerably larger flow of spontaneous migration in the same direction.

The government's stated goals in its transmigration program are to provide land for the landless from Java, Bali, and Lombok (in West Nusatenggara); to improve the distribution of population; and at the same time to provide manpower for labor-scarce areas outside Java, Bali, and Lombok, so that the latter areas can develop as new centers of production. The program is also seen as a vehicle to promote "national stability and integration."[34]

However, serious questions have been raised about how *integrative* the government's transmigration program actually is. In general, the indigenous people in Sumatra, Kalimantan, and Sulawesi have not welcomed the settlement of Javanese and Balinese transmigrants among them, especially where they have threatened to become a majority in their local region. Transmigrants in Irian Jaya are strongly opposed by the local people. In a discussion of some of the sociocultural difficulties that arise in connection with transmigration, a study by the Economic and Social Commission for Asia and the Pacific noted that there was considerable resentment among poor, indigenous farmers in South Sulawesi, for example, because they were not eligible for the financial and other assistance available to transmigrants from Java and Bali.[35] Relations have been somewhat easier where there have been no conflicting land claims or where local people have benefited from employment or business opportunities opened up by transmigrant settlements. But there has been little genuine assimilation based on intermarriage, partly because of the different cultures, languages, and ways of life, but partly also because transmigrants recruited from among the poorest in Java have not usually enjoyed sufficient social standing among ethnic groups such as the Minangkabau, Bugis, or Batak.[36] In addition, there is real fear among the inhabitants of the Outer Islands of increasing Javanization.

Third, there is the movement to some of the provinces with higher gross domestic product (GDP) per capita or above-average rates of economic growth: East Kalimantan (where 25 percent of the population previously resided in another province), Jambi (21 percent), Riau (17 percent), Bengkulu (17 percent), Central Kalimantan (16 percent), and Central Sulawesi (16 percent).[37] In terms of actual numbers, North and South Sumatra had the largest flows by 1980, with over 600,000 inmigrants each. West Sumatra, Bali, East Nusatenggara, North and South Sulawesi, and South Kalimantan, as well as most of Java, registered more out-migration than in-migration in the decades preceding both 1971 and 1980.

Despite generally low interprovincial migration rates, a comparison of 1971 and 1980 census data indicates growing mobility among the population. Almost twice as many people had previously resided in another province in 1980 as in 1971 (11.4 million compared with 5.8 million). In addition, studies by Hugo, Jellinik, and others have shown a substantial upswing in all kinds of other mobility, especially commuting, seasonal migration, and circular movements, with generally shortened periodicity and longer distances involved than before.[38] Others have discussed both the great increase in commuting in connection with the improvements and expansion in transport in the 1970s, and the proclivity of certain ethnic groups (particularly the Minangkabau, West Javanese, Batak, Banjarese, Bugis, and others) to engage in circular migrations *(merantau)*.[39] In recent years the pattern of such circular migration has changed almost entirely to one of urban destinations and the taking up of occupations quite unlike those in the area of origin.[40] Such circulation between the city and the countryside not only relieves the strain on the urban infrastructure and services, but increases the dissemination of new ideas and, it can be argued, fosters understanding and integration. But, on the other hand, circulation reflects the spatial unevenness of development and helps to perpetuate the inequality between the elite among the wage-earning classes and the circulating petty producer/peasant classes.[41]

Although the low overall migration figures indicate that there is comparatively little population mixing, it is significant that most interprovincial migrants have gone to urban areas, where the potential for inter-ethnic mixing is greater than in rural areas. However, the physical presence of immigrants from another province does not, of course, necessarily mean intermingling and interaction with those born in that province. Even in urban areas, and particularly in large cities, there is a tendency for each ethnic group to live in its own *kampung* (neighborhood). In rural areas, ethnic groups frequently form separate communities having relatively little contact with other groups.

Return migration is significant for both integration and development, because migrants who return to their areas of origin generally take back with them experiences of inter-ethnic contact as well as of economic differences and innovations that can be a stimulus to local development. They are also a source of information for future migrants. The data show that the provinces where most return migrants have lived are the urban or economically developing provinces of Jakarta, Riau, Jambi, and East Kalimantan. The rates of return migration are highest in North Sulawesi, West and East Nusatenggara (although in the last two cases the actual numbers are small), and West Sumatra (with its *merantau* migration pattern revealed in its 35 percent rate of return migration).

On the basis of per-capita migration data, therefore, two provinces stand out as being particularly poorly integrated into the national whole: East and West Nusatenggara, where out-migration and in-migration together affect less than 3 percent of the provincial population. In addition, Central and East Java and Bali have relatively little in-migration. By contrast, Jakarta emerges as a melting pot for the entire nation. Although in terms of absolute numbers the majority of in-migrants have come from Java (76.4 percent of lifetime migrants), every province is a source area, with the percentages coming from other provinces ranging from 0.05 and 0.1 in the cases of East Timor and Central Kalimantan to 5.8 and 5.1 for North and West Sumatra, respectively (see Table 4.2).

Trade

Another measure of national integration is the amount of trade that takes place among the various regions within a nation. An analysis of trade data reveals those provinces that participate only minimally in the integrative trading experience, either by having very low levels of trade with other provinces in the country, or by maintaining stronger trading relationships with places outside the national boundaries than with other provinces within the country, or both.

It has been claimed that the Indonesian archipelago was probably more integrated in the seventeenth and eighteenth centuries than it was when colonial domination reoriented trade more directly to overseas markets in the nineteenth and twentieth centuries.[42] Increasingly, a separation of the different economic regions of Indonesia took place, along with a growing, dramatic split between Java and the Outer Islands in terms of production factors, income levels, and demand. This situation began to change only after 1930, in the period during and following the depression, when Java shifted from export to domestic production as a result of the slump in the sugar market and as the government began to encourage self-sufficiency in rice production, an increase in domestic manufactures, and interregional trade. Regional specialization increased and interisland trade grew. However, these trends were interrupted and reversed by the Second World War and by the Japanese occupation, which emphasized both subsistence and regional self-sufficiency and disrupted both interregional transportation and the established capital-intensive sector.

Even after independence was attained, government policy and the deep-rooted problems inherited from the past combined to reinforce economic fragmentation. A decline in prices reduced per-capita incomes and thus the market incentive for Javanese manufactured goods. Java shifted more of its resources into food production to meet the needs of its own rapidly growing population.[43] Trade tended to revert to the pattern of each island exporting and importing directly from overseas and trading within its own shores rather than with other islands, while Java used increased amounts of the revenues generated by Outer Island export earnings for its own imports of raw material and capital goods for the Javanese market.

Regional markets grew slowly. This was a function of poor agricultural growth and low per-capita incomes, together with foreign exchange policies that restricted foreign consumer imports and froze export proceeds while domestic prices rose. Interisland trade was thus subjected, at least from the viewpoint of the Outer Islands, to progressively poorer economic terms. Some local manufactures began to grow, particularly in Sumatra. But serious deterioration in transportation facilities in the late 1950s and early 1960s contributed to the further weakening of interregional trade, as did growing economic mismanagement. The distribution network remained disorganized and decentralized.

Both domestic and foreign trade have increased considerably under the new economic order in the post-1966 period. Government intervention in domestic trade has increased to "ensure the adequate supply of essential goods to Indonesian consumers, to diversify the economy in accordance with development plans, and to convert a colonial economy into a national economy."[44] This has met with mixed results: some measure of quality control of exports and the protection of certain commodities, an insistence on control of private enterprise by "Indonesian citizens," but also some inflation and speculation, and a massive, centralized bureaucracy.

In an analysis of the overall national trading pattern of Indonesia it is important to consider the disproportionate participation of the different provinces in terms of both the production of exports and the consumption of imports. The foreign trade figures for 1982 show the great importance of Sumatra, and, to a lesser extent, Kalimantan, in generating exports (primarily petroleum, liquified natural gas, and timber). Sumatra accounts for 59.1 percent of the total volume and 50.6 percent of the total value of Indonesia's exports; Kalimantan contributes 20.5 percent of the volume and 24.1 percent of the value. Java's exports, by contrast, make up only 16 percent of the total volume and 20.2 percent of the value of the whole country's exports.[45] Per-capita data on export tonnage for international and domestic destinations, presented in Figure 4.14, show a similar pattern.

Moreover, when data on cargo loaded for overseas trade are examined, Sumatra's dominant role becomes much more apparent: 80.9 percent of Indonesia's cargo by weight originates in Sumatra, primarily in

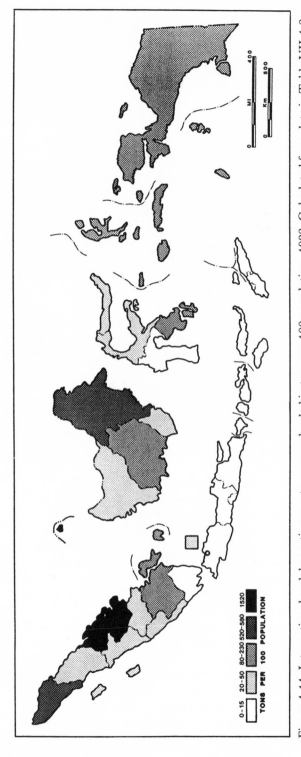

Figure 4.14. International and domestic exports: cargoes loaded in tons per 100 population, 1982. Calculated from data in Table VII.4.2 in Biro Pusat Statistik, *Statistik Indonesia 1983, Buku Saku.*

Riau (50.7 percent of all Indonesia's cargo) and Aceh (24.3 percent).[46] Java's cargoes loaded for international destinations constitute only 4.0 percent of Indonesia's total, a smaller proportion than that originating in both Kalimantan, where 7.8 percent of Indonesia's cargo destined for foreign ports is loaded, and Irian Jaya, with its 4.4 percent share.

On a per-capita basis, disparities in terms of exports are even more striking. Only seven of Indonesia's twenty-seven provinces export more than the national average of 38.9 tons per 100 population. Riau stands out with its 1,340.6 tons, Aceh is a distant second with 533.5 tons, and Irian Jaya third with 214.0 tons, all reflecting the mineral wealth of these areas. By contrast, per-capita figures of below one ton per 100 population occur in West Java, Bali, West and East Nusatenggara, and East Timor, and below five tons in Central and East Java and South and North Sulawesi (see Figure 4.15).

Imports, by contrast, flow predominantly to Java and overwhelmingly to Jakarta: 68.8 percent of imports by value enter Java, including 38.4 percent to Jakarta alone.[47] Sumatra receives 20.6 percent and Kalimantan 7.3 percent; Irian Jaya and Maluku together get 0.8 percent. These figures, however, are not greatly out of line with each island's share of the total population (Java, 62 percent; Sumatra, 19 percent; Kalimantan, 5 percent; and Irian Jaya and Maluku, less than 2 percent). On a per-capita basis, the contrasts, though wide, are not as extreme as they are for exports. Kalimantan on average receives the greatest value of imports on a per-capita basis ($182 per capita); Java's per-capita figure ($127) is only slightly higher than that of Sumatra ($124). The poor, underdeveloped islands of Nusatenggara receive least ($15), a figure that would be lower still if the relatively higher per-capita import level of Bali were not included. Jakarta's imports are more than eight times the national average on a per-capita basis ($996 compared with a national average of $114), but it is not clear from the data what proportion of imports entering Jakarta is destined for redistribution to other provinces in Java or the Outer Islands. If Jakarta's imports are averaged with West Java's, the per-capita figure falls dramatically to $227 per person, substantially lower than East Kalimantan's astounding $908 and Riau's high $387. Provinces with exceptionally low per-capita import figures are East Nusatenggara (3 cents), Bengkulu (20 cents), and West Nusatenggara and Southeast Sulawesi ($2 each) (see Figure 4.16).

In a comparison of export and import data, therefore, it is clear which islands benefit most from their incorporation into the country of Indonesia. Java obviously benefits enormously: its imports ($11,599 million or $127 per capita) far exceed its exports ($4,511 million or $49 per capita). Similar situations exist in Bali and Nusatenggara (which

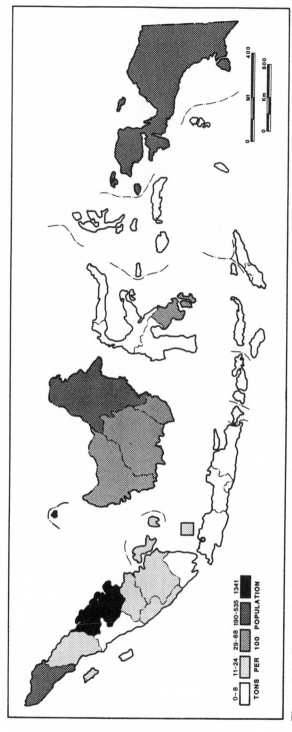

Figure 4.15. International exports: cargoes loaded in tons per 100 population, 1982. Calculated from data in Table 1 in Biro Pusat Statistik, *Statistik Bongkar Muat Barang di Pelabuhan Indonesia 1982.*

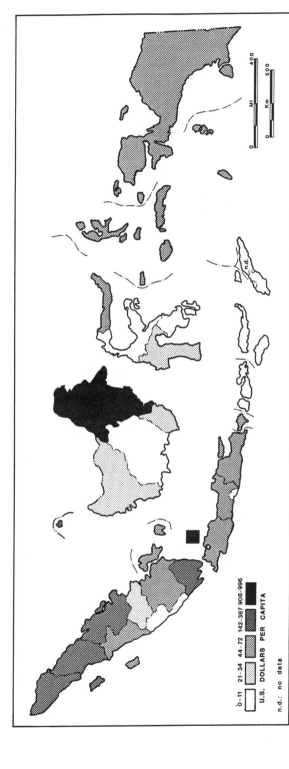

Figure 4.16. Value of imports received from international trade in U.S. dollars per capita, 1982. Calculated from data in Table 8 in Biro Pusat Statistik, *Impor Menurut Jenis Barang dan Negeri Asal,* vol. 2.

together have imports of $118 million or $15 per capita, but exports of only $22 million or $3 per capita), and, to a lesser extent, in Sulawesi (which has imports of $313 million or $30 per capita and exports of $244 million or $23 per capita). The reverse is true for Sumatra, where exports ($11,303 million or $403 per capita) exceed imports considerably ($3,474 million or $124 per capita); for Kalimantan (exports of $3,263 million or $485 per capita and imports of $1,225 million or $182 per capita); and for Maluku and Irian Jaya (exports of $868 million or $336 per capita, but imports of only $130 million or $50 per capita). One has to wonder about the integrative effect of this imbalance, particularly for Irian Jaya and Maluku, which contribute so much more to the national economy than they gain (although revenue generated by drilling or mining accrues directly to the central government and so lessens the perceived disparity between contributions to and benefits from the national economy). However, the data suggest that the situation at the beginning of the 1980s was slightly more balanced than it was in 1971. In that year 75 percent of all Indonesia's imports flowed to Java. Java had the highest value of imports on a per-capita basis of any island group, and Jakarta's imports were more than sixteen times the national average on a per-capita basis.[48] But Java obviously still consumes a disproportionate percentage of the nation's imports, both in relation to its exports and in comparison with most of the provinces in the eastern islands of Indonesia.

The export situation, though seriously unbalanced, probably does not threaten national integration as much as does the uneven import situation, because raw materials (petroleum, liquified natural gas, timber, and certain mineral and agricultural commodities) are obviously restricted in their location and exist largely as enclaval extractive industries that have little effect on the major part of the population of the provinces where they exist. The potentially explosive unbalanced import situation seems to be far more serious, as people with similar needs receive disproportionate amounts, both absolutely and in relation to what they produce for export. Differences in living standards in different parts of the archipelago are very obvious. Knowledge of where imported goods are more accessible and where higher standards of living consequently occur (in urban Java and particularly in Jakarta) contributes to the attractiveness of Jakarta and the consequent brain drain from the Outer Island provinces, as well as to some discontent in parts of the Outer Islands.

As might be expected, the contrasts among the provinces in interprovincial trade are far smaller than those in international trade, but show a similar pattern. The importance of Kalimantan and Sumatra in producing exports for domestic trade stands out both overall and on a per-capita basis (see Figure 4.17). Unfortunately, the value of exports in interprovincial trade is not available, but on the basis of tonnage per capita East Kalimantan and Riau produce far more than any of the other provinces (with 328 and 183 tons per 100 population, respectively).[49] By contrast, twelve of Indonesia's twenty-seven provinces produce less than ten tons per 100 population. As with exports for overseas, Java and the Nusatenggara provinces (Bali, West and East Nusatenggara, and East Timor) stand out for their low production of exports. However, one should note that many of Java's exports for domestic trade consist of lighter manufactured goods (as well as of cement, fertilizer, and other heavy products), whereas most of the tonnage from the high-exporting provinces consists of heavy commodities such as oil and timber.

Imports from interprovincial trade (averaged over the two-year period of 1981–1982) ranged from 14.4 tons per 100 population in Nusatenggara to 574 tons in Kalimantan, with Lampung and West Nusatenggara recording the lowest values for individual provinces (8.0 and 8.7 tons, respectively) and East Kalimantan and Riau the highest (211.9 and 123.7 tons, respectively) (see Figure 4.18). Unlike the situation with imports from overseas, on a tonnage per-capita basis in interprovincial trade, Java imports far less than all the other island groups with the exception of Nusatenggara; but it still imports more than twice as much as it exports (18.4 tons per 100 population compared with 7.8 tons), a ratio exceeded only by Nusatenggara's 14.4 and 4.3 figures.

There is more parity in interprovincial trade between exports and imports on a tonnage basis, although Kalimantan and Sumatra continue to export more than they import, unlike all the other island groups, where the reverse is true. The greatest contrasts occur in Jakarta, South Sumatra, Bengkulu, Lampung, Bali, and East Nusatenggara, which import at least three and a half times more tonnage than they export.

An examination of interprovincial trading patterns indicates limited commercial relationships and thus, one could argue, limited integration. In 1981 only Jakarta and East Java both imported and exported from every province in the country, while several (notably Aceh, West Sumatra, Jambi, Bengkulu, Lampung, Central Kalimantan, Bali, and Central Sulawesi) had significant trade (of more than 500 tons per year) with less than half of the other provinces.[50]

An interesting change from the situation in 1971 is the increased involvement in both international and interprovincial trade of Maluku, Irian Jaya, and Southeast Sulawesi. From ranking among the least integrated in this area, all three have moved much closer to the national

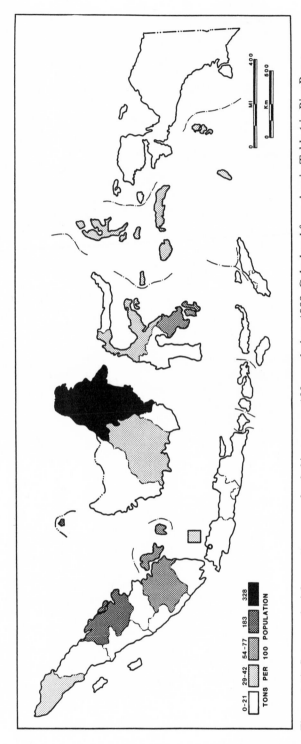

Figure 4.17. Interprovincial exports: cargoes loaded in tons per 100 population, 1982. Calculated from data in Table 1 in Biro Pusat Statistik, *Statistik Bongkar Muat Barang di Pelabuhan Indonesia 1982.*

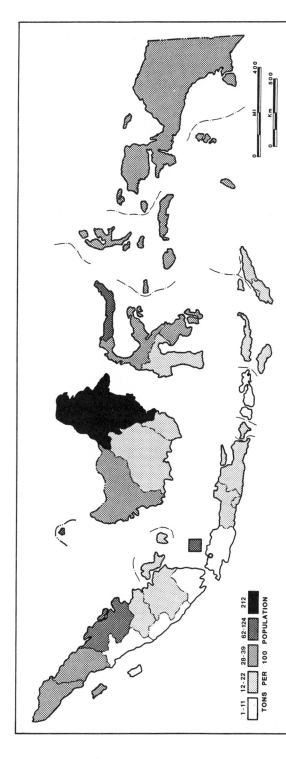

Figure 4.18. Interprovincial imports: cargoes unloaded in tons per 100 population, 1981–1982 (average). Calculated from data in Table VIII.4.3 in Biro Pusat Statistik, *Statistik Indonesia 1982* (1981 figures); and Table 1 in Biro Pusat Statistik, *Statistik Bongkar Muat Barang di Pelabuhan Indonesia 1982* (1982 figures).

1-11 12-22 28-39 62-124 212

TONS PER 100 POPULATION

averages on most trade indices and actually exceed them in terms of domestic imports and on one of the export indices (interprovincial exports for Southeast Sulawesi and Maluku, international exports for Irian Jaya). Unlike these three provinces, West and East Nusatenggara remain at or close to the bottom on all of the trade indices, demonstrating their less-developed and less-integrated status, with Central Kalimantan and Bengkulu recording particularly low figures on the import indices, which are more critical than export indices for national integration. It is encouraging to note the somewhat reduced dominance of Java in the trading statistics, with a smaller percentage of imports flowing into Java, and the fact that Sumatra and Kalimantan generally import more on a per-capita basis than Java does, a reversal of the situation in 1971.

Thus, overall Indonesia is moving toward greater integration in this interaction dimension, although the situation among the provinces remains noticeably uneven.

5

The Economic Dimension

ECONOMIC integration, both structurally and spatially, is of crucial importance to any country's national cohesion and political stability. In numerous developing countries (and in some developed ones as well) regional dissatisfaction stems from the perception of economic inequalities. This was a major underlying cause of the civil war in Sudan, and it had a definite role in the breakup of Pakistan into Pakistan and Bangladesh. Within Indonesia, too, several of the regional rebellions experienced since independence have had economic grievances at their root. Marked economic disparities are particularly disintegrative when exceptionally rich (or sometimes, poor) regions are peripherally located or economically independent of the rest of the country.

One of the major problems of economic development (whether in industry or agriculture) is that development almost inevitably exacerbates economic disparities among both regions and peoples because it takes place only in certain specific areas, rather than being spread evenly throughout an entire country. The tendency for the rich to get richer and the poor poorer is well documented in the economic development literature. But, as the Indonesian government has recognized since the early 1970s, economic growth has to be balanced with equity to attain national stability and integration.

For maximum economic integration, economic disparities among different regions ideally should be minimal, especially in such aspects as standard of living and level of development. Also, existing economic disparities should be in the process of diminishing as all areas of the country participate in and benefit from development. In addition, there should be increasing economic interdependence among the different regions of the country.

However, analysis of a large number of economic indicators available at the provincial level in Indonesia in the early 1980s reveals that, despite considerable economic development particularly since the early 1970s, Indonesia is still not very well integrated economically.

Historical Background

Some level of economic disparity within a nation-state is unavoidable because of the inevitably uneven natural resource base and because of differences in human response to varied opportunities. Thus, differences in the environment, such as in topography, climate, soil quality, and the availability of water, and also in the location and accessibility of minerals and energy sources, such as petroleum or coal, create basic inequalities in the potential for development. Similarly, many differences in the human environment—population distribution, historical development, cultural values and openness to change, varying levels of skills and entrepreneurship, and efficiency of resource use and organization—contribute to unequal rates of economic growth.

At early stages of development it is normal for differences to be exacerbated and disparities increased among the diverse regions within a state.[1] The colonial history of Indonesia well exemplifies such polarized development. The Dutch took advantage of the potential of the Javanese environment, its fertile soils, moderate climate, and accessible location, to concentrate their exploitative and developmental efforts there. A typical core-periphery situation developed between Java and the Outer Islands and lasted at least until the end of the nineteenth century. Java completely dominated the economic scene, producing most of the exports of the country and experiencing marked development of its infrastructure. By contrast, the Outer Islands, apart from some mining operations and plantations and certain privileged areas, were generally neglected and indifferently treated.

In the early twentieth century, however, an interesting inversion of this core-periphery situation began to develop. This has been attributed· partly to the world economic situation, where sugar prices dropped so dramatically. As a consequence, Indonesia shifted from dependence upon sugar as a major export crop (which had been grown almost entirely on Java) to rubber and coffee (which came from the Outer Islands, particularly Sumatra). Indeed, in the first quarter of the twentieth century Java produced three-quarters of the value of Indonesia's agricultural exports, but soon thereafter became an absorber rather than an earner of foreign exchange.[2] But this inversion resulted also from changes brought about directly by Dutch colonialism. The Dutch influence upon Java, which included development of the infrastructure and transportation and communications links, unequal urban growth, education, and health measures, led to a population increase with which productivity failed to keep pace. Thus, in spite of continued improvements in crop production in Java, standards of living have remained static or even declined during the twentieth century. In the Outer Islands, by contrast, increasing productivity outstripped population growth, and the economic dynamism and growth impetus generally associated with the core was transferred to selected areas of the Outer Islands, notably the plantation areas of North and East Sumatra, and such Dutch-favored areas as North Sulawesi and parts of Maluku (particularly Ambon).

The 1930s witnessed an increase in the economic integration of Indonesia, with a viable pattern of regional specialization and trade emerging. Java concentrated upon food (especially rice) production and domestic industrialization, providing manufactured goods for shipment to the Outer Islands in exchange for primary products produced there.[3] But this trend was abruptly halted and reversed by the Japanese occupation and the subsequent struggle for independence.

Independent Indonesia, therefore, inherited a badly damaged economy, partly because of war damage inflicted by the Japanese and the returning Dutch and partly because of Indonesia's own scorched-earth policy during its struggle for independence between 1945 and 1949. The dualistic colonial structure of export-oriented, foreign-dominated enterprises in the modern sector and peasant agriculture in the traditional sector reasserted itself in the parliamentary democracy period of 1950–1957. There was, however, a slow but steady rate of economic growth and reasonable progress in restoring an export economy, which occurred to a large extent independently of any central government action.[4] The subsequent period of Guided Economy, with its "sosialisme à la Indonesia," which followed the nationalization of all Dutch businesses in 1957–1958, was marked by aimlessness, accelerating hyper-inflation, and serious balance-of-payments deficits. These contributed to a growing gap between rich and poor, as well as to a decrease in investment and the lack of development of a firm economic base for the future.

Since independence, Indonesia's economic development has demonstrated the power of circular and cumulative causation:[5] a better-developed physical and institutional infrastructure, a ready labor force, and a large local market, as well as important political factors (of political control and local political pressures) all combined to perpetuate and accentuate the historic domination of Java over the rest of Indonesia.[6] By far the greatest share of all investment and development (except for purely exploitative mining, timber extraction, and some plantation agriculture) has been located there. Sukarno's lack of attention to the economic dimension of national integration and the imbalance he inherited in the country's economy, by which the Outer Islands generated over 80 percent of Indonesia's gross domestic product but received less than 20 percent in return, were primary causes of the regional unrest that led to a number of rebellions in the 1950s and early 1960s.

It was not until 1967, after the abortive coup and the beginning of the New Order government of Suharto with its emphasis on stability and fiscal balance, that any real attempts were made at systematic economic planning and development. But by then problems of uneven development inherited from the colonial past and the early period of independence had been exacerbated and become more entrenched. Stagnation in overall production had been matched by lack of progress in structural transformation: in other words, there had been lack of both growth and development. Surplus rural populations were not being absorbed by a growing industrial sector as in many countries; rather, they were either absorbed by the agricultural sector in a process of involution,[7] or they entered the service sector or trade. Indeed, the numbers employed in manufacturing declined absolutely in the 1931–1961 time period and declined further in the growing urban areas of Indonesia between 1961 and 1971.[8] Problems were further compounded by the great increase in population,[9] which wiped out any incremental gains in productivity that had occurred. It has been estimated that per-capita income in Java in 1969 was probably no higher in real terms than it had been thirty years previously.[10]

As a result, by the early 1970s Indonesia's economic situation was highly unbalanced, both in terms of infrastructural development, which was highly concentrated in Java, and in terms of revenue production, per-capita income, and standard of living, which were highest in certain areas of the Outer Islands, particularly in parts of Sumatra and Kalimantan.

The contrast between Java and the Outer Islands can be seen also in agriculture. Overall, only about 9 percent of Indonesia's land area is cultivated, but this figure ranges widely from region to region. Despite having less than 7 percent of the country's total land area, Java reportedly accounts for 75 percent of Indonesia's corn production, 80 percent of its cassava, 90 percent of its soybeans, 50 percent of its rice, and all of its sugar. Seventy percent of Java is cultivated year round, a figure that contrasts dramatically with the 4 to 6 percent of the total land area in the Outer Islands used for agriculture at the beginning of the 1980s. A similar contrast exists in the provision of irrigation services: over 40 percent of Java's *sawah* land is irrigated by modern facilities, whereas most of the land in the Outer Islands is in *ladang* (dry field) or swidden cultivation.[11]

Since 1967 the Indonesian economy has undergone profound change and experienced remarkable growth. This has been partly because of the New Order government's emphasis on political stability and economic development, which has promoted domestic economic growth and attracted billions of dollars of foreign investment.[12] It is also partly the result of loans (at both concessional and market rates) from international financial institutions, especially the World Bank,[13] and billions of dollars in aid and loans from the Inter-Governmental Group on Indonesia.[14]

The New Order government focused first (in its first Five-Year Development Plan, *Repelita I,* 1969–1974) upon stabilizing, rehabilitating, and developing the overall national economy, with little attention paid to regional economic differences.[15] The average annual rate of growth of the national gross domestic product (GDP) during those five years was 8.4 percent, thanks to major policy improvements (especially the control of inflation); encouragement of private and foreign investment and aid; the beginning of the rehabilitation of the economy's basic infrastructure (especially in irrigation, power, transportation, and communications); progress in the extractive industries of oil, natural gas, and timber; increased agricultural production (especially rice); and improved irrigation.[16] However, because these policies were pursued without great concern for their impact on different regions, many developments led to accentuated regional disparities.

It was only with the formulation of the second Five-Year Development Plan, *Repelita II* (1974–1979), that the balanced development of all regions became a primary objective: a most important goal for the continued political as well as economic integration of the nation.[17] In addition, *Repelita II* aimed at increasing the standard of living of the Indonesian people. Specifically, it sought to provide better food, clothing, and housing; to improve and expand infrastructure; to expand and distribute social welfare benefits equitably; and to provide greater employment opportunities. Real GDP rose at an average annual rate of 6.8 percent (4.7 percent for real per-capita GDP).[18] But neglect of balanced regional economic development in the past had led to increasing economic disparities among the regions and made the task of achieving regionally balanced development much more difficult.

The third Five-Year Development Plan, *Repelita III* (1979–1984), continued to stress regional development by placing the equitable distribution of development gains at the head of its trilogy of development goals (equity, economic growth, and national stability). In the agricultural sector it emphasized integrated rural development, and in the industrial sector it focused on the establishment of industries that create employment opportunities or that fulfill basic domestic needs.[19]

The fourth Five-Year Development Plan, *Repelita IV* (1984–1989), continues to place more emphasis on equity in the same trilogy of development goals, although it wants to ensure that all three elements are in constant harmony and mutually reinforcing.[20] Like its predecessors, its overriding goal is to "raise the standards of living, intellectual abilities, and general welfare of the people." However, plans are easier to formulate than to implement, and regional inequalities inevitably persist and in some respects seem to be widening.

In the subsequent discussion of regional inequalities, trends in regional economic disparities, and analysis of economic integration, one needs to be aware of limitations in the reliability of the statistical data. First, there is always the possibility that data have been gathered inaccurately or distorted. In addition, because the provinces vary so tremendously in size both areally and demographically, data are generally given in per-capita terms. This has the advantage of stressing the comparability of data from the vastly diverse provinces, but removes the element of size differentials from view. Finally, averaged figures for each province camouflage important intraprovincial differences, because many of the key economic activities form modern, foreign-oriented enclaves, especially in the Outer Islands, with relatively few spread or backwash effects on the provincial economies. Data for this chapter are tabulated in Appendix 3.

Regional Inequalities

The magnitude of economic disparities among regions provides some indication of the degree of economic integration of a nation-state, because in a highly integrated economy, disparities among regions are relatively small. Through the migration of the factors of production, particularly capital and labor, large differences are evened out in an integrated economic system; in a less integrated economy, substantial differences in such features as per-capita regional GDP, commodity prices, and cost of living are to be expected. Living standards, as measured by ownership of certain household items and access to electricity and to fuel other than firewood for cooking, also reveal patterns of unequal economic development. And finally, taxation data give an indication of regional differences, providing important information as to both the source of national and provincial income and the location of taxation revenue expenditures.

Perhaps the most comprehensive index of regional inequality in Indonesia is the regional gross domestic product (RGDP).[21] This ranged in 1980 from approximately 5,874 billion rupiahs (Rp) in East

Java to Rp 129 billion in Bengkulu. However, because this is partly a function of differences in the size of provincial populations, a more meaningful index is RGDP per capita. Here, too, enormous variations exist, with East Kalimantan having a per-capita income (Rp 2,846,290 per annum) more than twenty-seven times that of East Nusatenggara (Rp 104,250).[22] These figures may be misleading, however, because they include royalties generated from oil, natural gas, and other mineral production that accrue directly to the national government; and it can be argued that, as enclaval activities, they have relatively little impact on the overall welfare of the province in which they are located. But even when the petroleum and mining sectors are excluded from those five provinces where they have such a significant impact on the provincial RGDP (East Kalimantan, Riau, Irian Jaya, Aceh, and to a lesser extent South Sumatra), per-capita RGDP differences vary by a factor of eight (from Rp 846,590 in East Kalimantan to Rp 104,250 in East Nusatenggara) (see Figure 5.1). Table 5.1, which gives the relative importance of mining and agriculture in the composition of the regional gross domestic product of each province, demonstrates clearly those provinces with substantial mineral deposits (including petroleum, natural gas, and hard minerals). Riau produced more than twice as much in the value of its petroleum products in 1979 as any other province, and mining accounted for 84.4 percent of its RGDP.[23] In addition, it exports logs, plywood, other timber products, bauxite, palm oil, and rubber.

East Kalimantan also depends heavily (for 62.8 percent of its RGDP) on its petroleum and especially in recent years on its liquified natural gas (LNG) production (from the Bontang LNG plant). But in addition it has major timber resources and the largest capacity in Indonesia for producing plywood (which, together with other wood products, is Indonesia's third most valuable export, after oil and natural gas).[24] Aceh's production of liquified natural gas (from its Arun field) has risen sharply over the past fifteen years and helps to account for the high 61.1 percent of its RGDP produced by mining. Irian Jaya likewise depends for over half of its RGDP on mining (including petroleum, natural gas, copper, and gold and silver from copper concentrate).

South and North Sumatra derive a considerable amount of revenue from their mining activities, although these make up a much smaller percentage of their RGDPs. Both produce oil and natural gas, and South Sumatra has substantial coal production as well as tin (making Indonesia the second largest producer of tin in the world).[25] However, both North and South Sumatra have more developed and diversified economies, with substantial rubber and palm oil plantations, plywood production, and food, wood, chemicals, and metal-goods processing.[26]

By contrast, five provinces depended on agriculture for over 50 per-

Table 5.1. Relative importance of mining and agriculture in each province's regional gross domestic product (RGDP), 1979 (amounts given in constant 1975 market prices)

Province	Amount produced by mining in 1,000 million rupiahs[a]	Percentage of the RGDP produced by mining[b]	Amount produced by agriculture in 1,000 million rupiahs[a]	Percentage of the RGDP produced by agriculture[b]
Aceh	310.7	61.1	115.9	22.8
North Sumatra	150.9	15.0	373.3	37.0
West Sumatra	0.6	0.2	92.9	37.0
Riau				
(with petroleum)	1,409.4	84.4	61.0	3.7
(without petroleum)	14.2	6.7	61.0	28.8
Jambi	5.8	4.5	64.9	
South Sumatra				
(with petroleum)	134.0	17.7	148.0	19.5
(without petroleum)	35.0	5.8	148.0	24.6
Bengkulu	0.5	1.0	23.9	46.0
Lampung	0.5	0.2	140.9	45.0
Jakarta	—	—	26.4	1.7
West Java	218.4	9.4	704.3	30.4
Central Java	5.2	0.3	598.3	39.4
Yogyakarta	0.5	0.3	63.7	36.7
East Java	6.6	0.3	868.2	36.3
West Kalimantan	0.5	0.2	98.6	42.9
Central Kalimantan	0.4	0.3	49.7	46.6
South Kalimantan	0.6	0.3	76.9	38.0

East Kalimantan				
(with petroleum)	654.0	62.8	85.7	8.2
(without petroleum)	6.1	1.7	85.7	24.0
North Sulawesi	2.2	1.1	82.9	40.6
Central Sulawesi	0.6	0.8	43.8	53.4
South Sulawesi	3.3	0.6	254.2	50.3
Southeast Sulawesi	8.8	15.1	23.8	41.0
Bali	1.5	0.6	99.3	42.2
West Nusatenggara	3.9	3.0	68.6	52.0
East Nusatenggara	0.2	0.2	84.3	63.8
East Timor	n.a.	n.a.	n.a.	n.a.
Maluku	10.6	7.6	68.4	48.7
Irian Jaya				
(with mining)	142.4	52.9	67.8	25.2
(without mining)	0.4	0.3	67.8	53.4

n.a.: not available

[a]Biro Pusat Statistik, *Pendapatan Regional Propinsi-propinsi di Indonesia 1976–80*, Table II.A.9.
[b]Ibid., Table II.B.9.

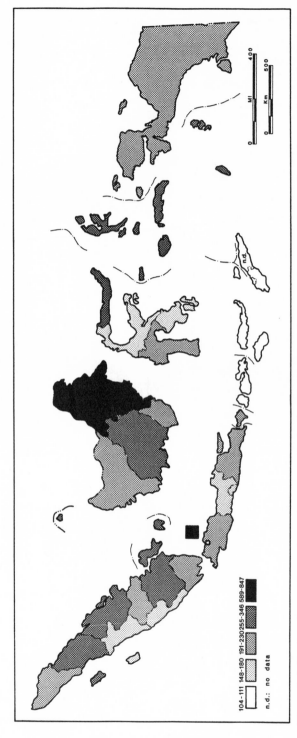

Figure 5.1. Regional gross domestic product per capita in thousands of rupiahs per capita, at current market prices, without oil, 1980. Based on data in Table X.9 in Biro Pusat Statistik, *Statistik Indonesia 1983, Buku Saku.*

cent of their RGDP in 1979, and a further eight for over 40 percent. It is significant that the provinces most highly dependent upon agriculture have the lowest per-capita RGDPs in Indonesia (for example, East and West Nusatenggara, Central Sulawesi, and Bengkulu). Also among the poorest provinces in terms of per-capita RGDP are the densely populated provinces of Central Java and Yogyakarta.

Price disparities among the provinces are inevitable because of such factors as differences in location and consequently different transportation costs, in local conditions of supply and demand, and in the concentration of private investment or government expenditure. In addition, governmental intervention through taxation or trade restrictions has affected prices in certain areas. Yet price disparities, based on the consumer price index for food, clothing, housing, and miscellaneous and general merchandise in the capital cities of each province in 1981 (the only data available), are not great. The consumer price index ranges from a low of 151.6 in Maluku to a high of 193.9 in South Sumatra (see Figure 5.2). No clear patterns emerge. Overall, prices are highest in South Sumatra and Jambi, East Java, South Kalimantan, and North Sulawesi; and are lowest in Maluku, East and West Kalimantan, Irian Jaya, Jakarta, and South Sulawesi. It appears that higher prices for some items are counterbalanced by lower prices for others.

However, when the retail price of rice in the provincial capital cities is examined, the disparities are considerably wider. The lowest prices are found in Jakarta, East Java, and Yogyakarta, prices that are over 60 percent lower than those found in Riau, East Nusatenggara, and Lampung.

Certainly, in comparison with conditions in the early 1970s, price disparities seem to have been significantly reduced. In 1972 the price index for East Kalimantan was almost double that for West Nusatenggara.[27] Then, higher prices generally corresponded to increasing distance from Java, or to the higher incomes in those provinces with oil, timber, and significant industrial activity. The higher prices in low-income provinces were of particular concern, especially when those provinces occupied geographically peripheral positions in the country, where costs could have been reduced by more direct trade with closer neighboring countries (such as North Sulawesi with the Philippines and Aceh with Malaysia). But the patterns prevailing in the early 1970s seem to have changed substantially, according to data available for the early 1980s.

Contrasts among the provinces are also exemplified in the data on the incidence of poverty and deprivation. Despite an average annual rate of economic growth of 7.3 percent during the 1970s and a decline in the incidence of poverty from a high of 57 percent in 1970, it is estimated that in 1980 approximately 39 percent of Indonesia's population (some 56,650,000 people) still lived below the poverty line (an index con-

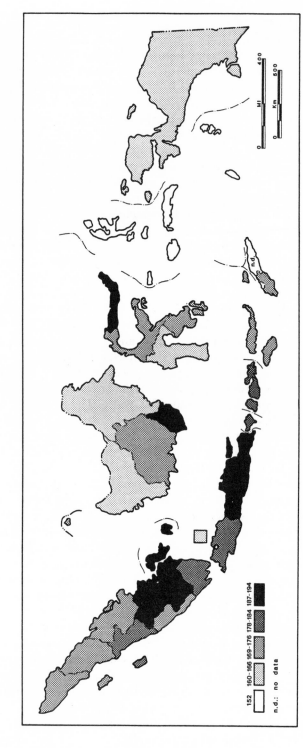

Figure 5.2. Consumer price index in the capital city of each province. Average of food, housing, clothing, miscellaneous, and general merchandise, 1981. Calculated from data in Table VIII.4.4 in Biro Pusat Statistik, *Statistik Indonesia 1983, Buku Saku.*

structed from per-capita food expenditures).[28] These proportions vary dramatically from province to province (see Figure 5.3). Irian Jaya, Jambi, and West Kalimantan record the lowest incidence of poverty (less than 10 percent of their respective populations), but three of the Javanese provinces (Central and East Java and Yogyakarta) as well as East and West Nusatenggara have over 50 percent of their populations living in poverty (with Southeast Sulawesi close at 49 percent). Compared with Java and the eastern islands (Bali, the Nusatenggaras, Maluku, and Irian Jaya), with 46.5 and 46.7 percent of their populations in poverty, Kalimantan and Sumatra appear prosperous (with low 11.5 and 20.4 percent figures), while Sulawesi matches the national average (39.3 percent).

However, an index of deprivation (defined as the proportion of people whose food needs are not satisfied) reveals a somewhat different picture: Java, despite its high level of poverty, appears as the island with the lowest incidence of deprivation (0.7 percent), compared with Kalimantan (2.6 percent), Sulawesi (3.6 percent), Sumatra (3.7 percent), and the eastern islands (with a disturbing 26.1 percent figure).[29] This low deprivation figure for Java reflects the impact of a wide series of government social welfare programs in the 1970s, which have brought at least some improvement in living standards throughout rural Java. Contrasts among individual provinces are much greater, ranging from a low of 0.3 percent in West Java (and less than 1 percent in Central and East Java, Jakarta, and North Sulawesi) to an amazing high of 44.4 percent in East Nusatenggara (and relatively high figures of 20.9 and 20.6 percent in West Nusatenggara and Bali, respectively, and 13.5 percent in Maluku) (see Figure 5.4).[30]

The very high localized incidence of both poverty and deprivation in East and West Nusatenggara, Bali, and Maluku underscores the lack of true economic integration, for this and the high costs of transport impede the flow of food (as well as of other commodities) there from food-surplus areas.[31]

Standard of living can also be measured in other ways. But differences in the size and condition of households and housing frequently reveal more about the variety of cultural customs in the country than they do about standard of living. Data on the number of rooms per household or persons per room cannot be meaningfully compared when some people live in multiple-family longhouses (such as the Dyaks in Kalimantan) and others in single-family dwellings (such as the typical Minahasan farmer in North Sulawesi). Different cultural values as well as the level of urbanization may also affect the value placed upon such conveniences as the availability of piped water, the type of toilet facility, and the mechanism for garbage disposal.

Figure 5.3. Percentage of the population living below the poverty line (an index constructed from per-capita food expenditures), 1980. Based on data in Table 5 in the World Bank report, *Indonesia: Selected Aspects of Spatial Development* (used with permission).

7-10   12-21   28-33   38-46   49-60

n.d.: no data

Figure 5.4. Percentage of the population living in deprivation (defined as those whose food needs are not met), 1980. Based on data in Table 5 in the World Bank report, *Indonesia: Selected Aspects of Spatial Development* (used with permission).

However, several indices are available that give reasonable measures of provincial differences in living standards. These include ownership of certain consumer items, the consumption of electricity, and the use of fuels other than wood or charcoal for cooking. Three measures are examined here: the percentage of households owning a sideboard; the percentage of households using electricity for lighting; and the percentage of households using kerosene, gas, or electricity for cooking. Some interesting patterns emerge.

Ownership of a sideboard may be considered indicative of a higher standard of living both because of the cost of purchasing (or making) one and because its main function is the storage of other consumer items. Overall, 46 percent of households in Indonesia reportedly own a sideboard.[32] The highest percentage is recorded, as to be expected, in the most urban province of Jakarta (69 percent), but surprisingly, South Kalimantan ranks second (67 percent), with East Kalimantan third (62 percent). Other provinces with significantly above-average figures include North Sumatra, West Java, South and North Sulawesi, and Central Kalimantan. By contrast, only 13 and 15 percent of households in Irian Jaya and East Nusatenggara are recorded as owning a sideboard, with other provinces such as West Nusatenggara and Southeast Sulawesi also having proportions of less than 30 percent (see Figure 5.5).

Economic development levels are frequently measured by consumption of electricity. It is instructive, therefore, to consider regional differences in electricity consumption. On average, only 14 percent of Indonesia's private households used electricity for lighting in 1980. As expected, there is a close correlation with urbanization, although this breaks down noticeably in the cases of Riau, Lampung, Central Java, Yogyakarta, and Irian Jaya, where consumption of electricity is far below the urban percentage of their populations (see Figure 5.6). The greatest contrast is between Jakarta, with 47.8 percent of its households recording the use of electricity for lighting, and East Nusatenggara, where only 4.3 percent of households light their homes with electricity. Yet this is a significant increase from the situation in 1971, when the range was from 23.4 percent in Jakarta to 0.4 percent in Central Sulawesi. In 1980, the more developed provinces of Jakarta, East and South Kalimantan, North and South Sumatra, Riau, Bali, and North Sulawesi stand out in having above-average use of electricity for lighting. By contrast, East and West Nusatenggara, Lampung, Central and Southeast Sulawesi, and Central Java are noticeable for their lack of development in this respect.

Another index of differences in levels of development is the type of fuel used for cooking. About 75 percent of all households use wood or

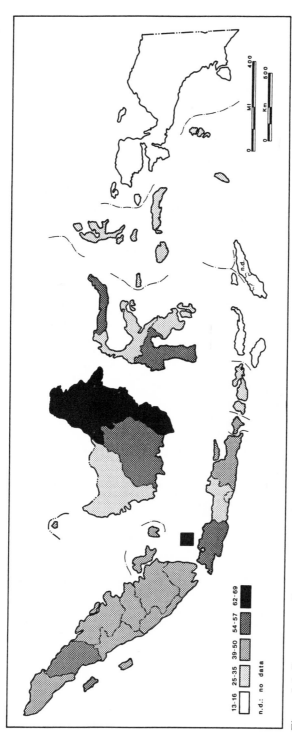

Figure 5.5. Percentage of households owning a sideboard, 1980. Based on data in Table 66.3 in Biro Pusat Statistik, *Sensus Penduduk 1980*, Series S, no. 2.

Figure 5.6. Percentage of households using electricity for lighting, 1980. Calculated from data in Table 63.3 in Biro Pusat Statistik, *Sensus Penduduk 1980*, Series S, no. 2.

charcoal, but this proportion varies considerably among the provinces. Understandably, in the urbanized province of Jakarta, wood is less available and kerosene, gas, or electricity provides the major source of fuel for a recorded 96 percent of the population. But in other parts of Java, despite the limited amount of firewood available and the increasing distances families have to go to procure it (not to mention such problems as resulting deforestation on steep slopes, soil erosion, and the choking of irrigation canals), there is a surprisingly high degree of dependence upon wood and charcoal for cooking. Less than 20 percent of the population in Central Java and Yogyakarta and less than 25 percent in East Java use kerosene, gas, or electricity. However, percentages are far lower in most of the Outer Island provinces, especially those in the less urbanized areas such as Nusatenggara, Central Kalimantan, and Central and Southeast Sulawesi (see Figure 5.7).

Information about taxation and government expenditures provides further indices of unequal regional resources and development. In 1982–1983, tax revenues made up about 27 percent of the national budget (compared with 59 percent from oil and gas production, 12 percent from foreign loans and other aid, and 2 percent from non-tax revenues); but it is from the national budget that most of the revenue used in the provinces comes. Central government funds are broken down into routine and development accounts.

Provincial governments obtain revenue for their programs from a variety of sources. Central government grants, which account for a high and rising proportion of provincial governments' income (over 70 percent), include the *Subsidi Daerah Otonomi* (the *SDO,* autonomous region subsidy) and other grants for routine expenditures, and grants for development made through the various *Inpres* programs (*Instruksi Presiden* or presidential authorization). Second, the provinces are allowed by the central government to raise revenue from royalties on such activities as gasoline sales, forestry, and mining. Third, provincial governments obtain revenue from provincial taxes, such as those on the ownership and transfer of motor vehicles and on large houses. Many other local taxes and service charges are also levied, but this income is primarily used at the *kabupaten* (district) and *kotamadya* (city district) level.

In considering spatial inequalities in the generation and expenditure of revenue, three indices are particularly pertinent. The first is the amount of per-capita tax revenue generated in the provinces.[33] This varies considerably, with East Kalimantan and Jakarta raising far more than any of the other provinces (Rp 29,800 and Rp 20,600 per capita, respectively). The other provinces in Kalimantan as well as Central Sulawesi, Irian Jaya, Aceh, and Riau all generate above-average provincial tax revenues. Almost all are mineral-rich provinces. The prov-

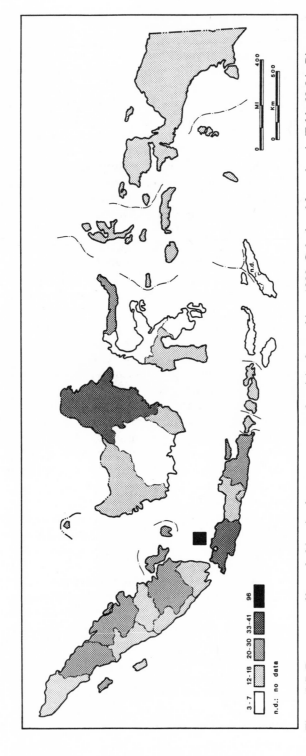

Figure 5.7. Percentage of households using kerosene, gas, or electricity for cooking, 1980. Calculated from data in Table 63.3 in Biro Pusat Statistik, *Sensus Penduduk 1980*, Series S, no. 2.

inces that raise least include both the less urbanized, less developed provinces of the Nusatenggaras, Southeast Sulawesi, and Lampung, and the poor, overpopulated provinces of East, Central, and West Java and Yogyakarta (see Figure 5.8). As to be expected, there is a strong correlation between per-capita provincially generated tax revenue and per-capita RGDP.

However, perhaps more important than local revenue generation, from the perspective of regional satisfaction and national integration, are regional government expenditures. Obviously these need to be related to some degree to provincial tax income to avert dissatisfaction in the richer, more economically advanced, and thus potentially independent provinces; but the considerable contrasts in per-capita regional expenditures, especially between Jakarta and West Java (Rp 24,100 and Rp 6,800, respectively) or between East and West Kalimantan (Rp 35,300 and Rp 12,000, respectively), can only be regarded as disintegrative, particularly as improved interprovincial communications bring more widespread awareness of such regional differences. Expenditures do not seem to be related to any minimum level of service or other gauge of equality. Indeed, central government grants that could help to even out the wide differences in the amounts generated by non-grant revenues instead tend to reinforce them. Provinces with relatively high local resources in general receive higher routine and development grants from the central government than do provinces with limited local resources. On a per-capita basis East Kalimantan and Irian Jaya spend most (Rp 35,300 and Rp 33,300, respectively), with Central Kalimantan, Jakarta, and Central Sulawesi ranking next with per-capita expenditures of over Rp 20,000. By contrast, Lampung and the three major provinces of Java have the lowest per-capita governmental expenditures (of less than Rp 7,200) (see Figure 5.9).

A third interesting indicator of spatial inequities resulting from taxation is central government support for development programs (see Figure 5.10). This has always varied considerably from province to province.[34] It seems that, once again, central government grants and transfers to the provinces in most cases compound existing inequalities. Regional grants frequently seem to favor provinces with high per-capita incomes. East and Central Kalimantan, for example, receive more than nine times as much on a per-capita basis (Rp 20,800 and Rp 16,900, respectively) as West and East Nusatenggara (Rp 1,790 and Rp 1,850, respectively), but the contrasts with the provinces in Java are greater still (East, West, and Central Java received only Rp 335, Rp 362, and Rp 386 per capita, respectively). Surprisingly, Jakarta received only a small per-capita allocation (Rp 818), although this is more than compensated for by locally generated tax revenues.

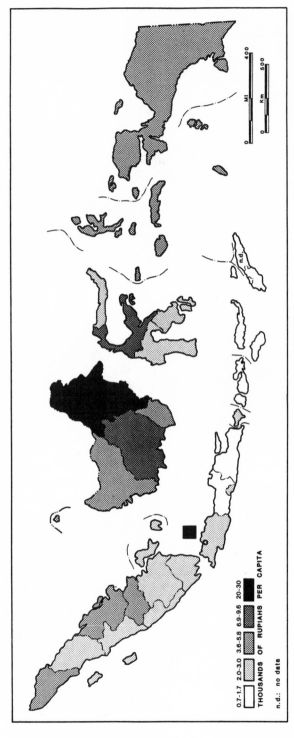

Figure 5.8. Provincial tax contributions to the central government in thousands of rupiahs per capita, 1980–1981. Calculated from data in Table 1 in Biro Pusat Statistik, *Statistik Keuangan Pemerintah Daerah, Daerah Tingkat I (Propinsi), 1975/76–1980/81.*

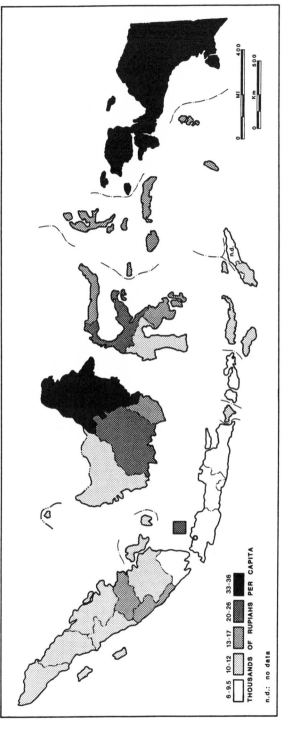

Figure 5.9. Provincial government expenditures (operating and development) in thousands of rupiahs per capita, 1980–1981. Calculated from data in Table VIII.1.5 in Biro Pusat Statistik, *Statistik Indonesia 1983, Buku Saku.*

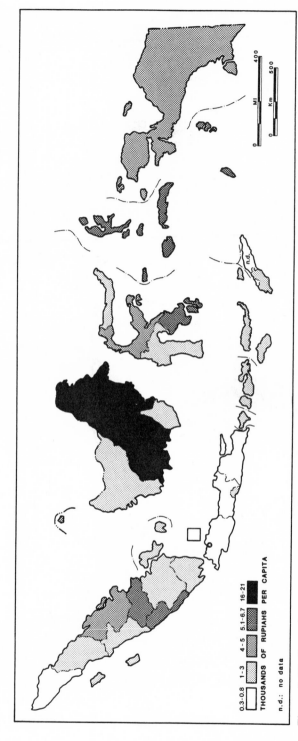

Figure 5.10. Central government support for provincial development programs in thousands of rupiahs per capita, 1980–1981. Calculated from data in Table 1 in Biro Pusat Statistik, *Statistik Keuangan Pemerintah Daerah, Daerah Tingkat I (Propinsi), 1975/76–1980/81.*

Not only did the per-capita rupiah amounts spent by the central government on development in the provinces in 1980–1981 vary enormously (from Rp 8,250 in Central Java to Rp 52,800 in East Kalimantan), but the proportions of regional expenditures provided by the central and provincial governments varied considerably as well. In West Nusatenggara and Bengkulu the provincial government contribution to development was just 1.2 percent, compared with an average of 10.4 percent, and a high of 32.2 percent in East Kalimantan. It is surprising to note the relatively low provincial government contributions of some of the richer provinces such as Riau (6.8 percent), Jambi (7.3 percent), and South Sumatra (9.2 percent). Total provincial expenditures on routine spending vary less on a per-capita basis (from Rp 7,030 in South Sumatra to the rather exceptional Rp 27,200 in Irian Jaya), but the proportion contributed by the central government varies more, from a low of 40 percent in East Kalimantan to a high of 98 percent in Irian Jaya (with an average of 80 percent). Thus, most provinces rely heavily, for 70–90 percent of their routine budgets, on central government subsidies.

Except for Jakarta and East Kalimantan, central government grants form the major source of funds for provincial expenditures. But it is interesting to notice the significant correlation between per-capita non-grant income and per-capita *Inpres* grants: the better-off provinces receive more, thus widening the gap between rich and poor.

However, it needs to be added that regional disparities might be greater still were it not for the redistributing mechanism of public finance. Most of the royalties obtained from oil and natural gas and from other minerals accrue to the central government and are derived mostly from the Outer Islands. A large proportion of this revenue is spent in Java, thus tending towards some measure of equalization of interregional income disparity at least on a per-capita basis.[35]

Trends in Regional Economic Disparities

Perhaps even more important than analysis of the static conditions of regional economic inequality is an analysis of the trends either reducing or exacerbating these differences. It has been argued that polarization is to be expected at early stages of development as limited resources are concentrated in areas of greatest potential for national economic growth.[36] Indeed, virtually all ideologies and development theories agree in predicting that in the process of a country's transition to a modern economy, the overall distribution of income will become more unequal and disparities will widen.[37] This is certainly what has happened in Indonesia, both during the colonial period and after. The evidence available suggests that income inequality and regional disparities have continued to widen, despite the regional development and social justice emphases of the last three five-year development plans.[38]

Indices that demonstrate these trends of growing regional inequality include comparative changes in regional income, different regional economic growth rates, and changes in regional allocations of new domestic and foreign investment. The growth of manufacturing industry in the country has also led to increased regional disparities.

As measured in absolute terms by per-capita RGDP, regional inequalities have increased. Whereas in 1972 the gap between the province with the lowest income (West Nusatenggara with Rp 18,000 per capita) and that with the highest (East Kalimantan with Rp 221,000) was Rp 203,000, by 1980 the income differential had increased to Rp 742,340, with average per-capita RGDP of Rp 104,250 in East Nusatenggara and Rp 846,590 in East Kalimantan, although one could argue that the relative gap had diminished.[39]

Large differences have been recorded in the annual rates of growth of the RGDP for the periods of both 1968–1972 and 1976–1980. Between 1968 and 1972 these ranged from a negative growth rate of 1.4 percent in North Sulawesi to a positive annual growth rate of 24.9 percent in East Kalimantan.[40] The 1976–1980 growth rates varied from 6.1 percent in Yogyakarta to 31.4 percent in Aceh, a spread very similar to that recorded for the years 1968–1972. In the past the richer provinces have grown faster and the poorer regions more slowly, thereby increasing disparities,[41] but the 1980 figures exhibit no significant correlation between RGDP per capita and growth rates. A spectacularly high growth rate took place only in Aceh (31.4 percent),[42] although Bengkulu also grew fast (17.2 percent) and three other provinces (North Sulawesi and Central and South Kalimantan) grew at an average annual rate of 14 percent through the 1976–1980 time period (see Figure 5.11). The growth rate in North Sulawesi is particularly significant (assuming the data are accurate) because it was the only province in the 1968–1972 period to record a negative growth rate, but both South Kalimantan and Bengkulu also experienced great improvement over their earlier sluggish 1.8 percent and 2.3 percent growth rates.

West Nusatenggara continued to experience a low average rate of economic growth. Java also, with the exception only of Jakarta, grew at below-average rates, as did Lampung and, surprisingly, Riau and Jambi (all at less than 8.6 percent). It is encouraging, though, to note the new projects funded by the United Nations Development Program and World Bank for both West and East Nusatenggara, aimed at stimulating development and alleviating poverty in these two poorest provinces of the country.[43]

Figure 5.11. Average annual percentage growth rate of regional gross domestic product at constant 1975 market prices, 1976–1980. Based on data in Table 1.6 in Biro Pusat Statistik, *Pendapatan Regional Propinsi-propinsi di Indonesia 1976–80.*

6-7.1   7.5-9.5   10-13   14-18   31

n.d.: no data

Indonesia's provinces can be divided basically into four major groups, as Table 5.2 illustrates. The first consists of those with relatively high per-capita RGDP (over Rp 210,000) and high RGDP growth rates (of 10 percent or more) in the 1976–1980 period. This group includes Jakarta and East Kalimantan, as would be expected, but also the petroleum (and natural gas) and mining provinces of Aceh, South Sumatra, and Irian Jaya. Central Kalimantan and North Sulawesi are also in this category. The second group also has high per-capita RGDP but lower rates of growth; this group includes the petroleum-producing provinces of North Sumatra, Riau, and Jambi, as well as West Kalimantan and Maluku. Third are those poorer provinces that have a per-capita RGDP of less than Rp 210,000 but relatively high growth rates of 10 percent or more; into this category fall three of the four provinces of Sulawesi and, surprisingly, East Nusatenggara, with its very low RGDP per capita but relatively high 11.7 percent growth rate. Bengkulu, Bali, and South Kalimantan are also in this category. The fourth group comprises the provinces that are both poor and slow growing: the four provinces of Java (outside of Jakarta), Lampung (which shares many of Java's characteristics), West Sumatra, and almost lowest on both indices, West Nusatenggara.

The richer provinces all have high export/RGDP ratios. It is no coincidence that Sumatra and Kalimantan, with their significant production of rubber, timber, coffee, oil, and gas and their higher dependence

Table 5.2. Per-capita regional gross domestic product (RGDP) and RGDP growth rates by province

		Per-capita RGDP, 1980 (in Rp 000), without oil	
		HIGH (over Rp 210)	LOW (under Rp 210)
RGDP growth rates 1976–1980	HIGH (over 10%)	[1] Aceh (225, 31) South Sumatra (316, 11) Jakarta (590, 10) Central Kalimantan (346, 14) East Kalimantan (847, 10) North Sulawesi (258, 14) Irian Jaya (213, 12)	[3] Bengkulu (170, 17) Bali (198, 13) East Nusatenggara (104, 12) South Kalimantan (195, 14) Central Sulawesi (174, 10) South Sulawesi (194, 10) Southeast Sulawesi (170, 10)
	LOW (under 10%)	[2] North Sumatra (299, 9) Riau (255, 7) Jambi (230, 8) West Kalimantan (214, 9) Maluku (279, 9)	[4] West Sumatra (180, 9) Lampung (191, 8) West Java (208, 9) Central Java (151, 8) Yogyakarta (148, 6) East Java (202, 8) West Nusatenggara (111, 7)

on exports, have maintained their leading position in RGDP per capita, compared with islands that have fewer resources and produce little for export on a per-capita basis, such as Java, Bali, Nusatenggara, and to a lesser extent Sulawesi. Yet the fact that most provinces depend very heavily on only one or two export commodities makes them vulnerable to price fluctuations and resulting instability.

There have been significant structural changes in the sectoral composition of the RGDP over the past decade. Every region has experienced a decline in the share of agriculture and an increase in the shares of manufacturing, construction, and commerce. But Sulawesi and the eastern islands still obtain almost half their RGDP (48.0 and 48.7 percent, respectively) from agriculture and a very small proportion from manufacturing (2.6 and 5.8 percent, respectively). They also lag far behind in commercial development. Java, by contrast, derives 16 percent of its RGDP from manufacturing and a high 30 percent from commerce. Sumatra and Kalimantan depend most on mining (22 and 27 percent, respectively). But it is interesting to note that there is no significant correlation between economic growth rates and the proportion of the population employed in agriculture, although there is a significant (though fairly low) negative correlation between per-capita RGDP and employment in agriculture.

The sector of the economy that has seen the most growth since 1966 is natural resource production. For example, petroleum and natural gas exports have multiplied almost fiftyfold in dollar terms since the mid-1960s and by over twenty times in real purchasing power. Moreover, natural resource–based commodities increased nationally from two-fifths of the total value of exports in the mid-1960s to over four-fifths in the mid-1970s. But this increased production of natural resources has been located almost entirely in the Outer Islands: petroleum and natural gas production in Sumatra, Kalimantan, and Irian Jaya; timber mainly in Kalimantan and some in Sumatra; and hard minerals in Sulawesi, Irian Jaya, and the islands off eastern Sumatra.[44] The resulting expansion of modern employment and incomes, goods, and services has led to substantially higher material standards of living for considerable numbers of Indonesians, but the expanded employment opportunities in the modern sector have not been large enough to make a major impact on the overall balance of supply and demand for labor in the traditional sector. Real wages in the traditional sector remained static during the 1970s and early 1980s (an agricultural laborer earns the equivalent of $1 per day), while traditional producers of cash crops for export received lower real incomes as a result of the resources boom. As a result there has been no overall net gain for traditional producers.[45]

Increasing disparities among provinces have occurred, partly because of differential rates of growth in sectors where there is a high degree of regional specialization. The greatest contrast is between rapidly growing Jakarta (with its concentration of industry, services, and administration) and the resource-rich provinces on the one side, and on the other the slowly growing or stagnant provinces (such as West Nusatenggara), which are dependent largely upon agriculture and have little in the way of known mineral resources, manufacturing, or other economic activities.

The regional allocation of new domestic and foreign investment has also changed. Between 1967 and 1976 it tended to confirm the pattern of unequal growth already discussed: 71 percent of all investment project approvals were concentrated in Java, with Jakarta and West Java receiving over 50 percent of all investment projects in Indonesia (excluding oil). Expressed more dramatically, more investment projects were located in Jakarta alone (32 percent) than in the entire area of Indonesia outside of Java (29 percent).[46] And if project approvals for agriculture and extractive industries (most of which are enclaval investments) are excluded, the share of investment approvals for Jakarta rises to 60 percent for foreign-financed and 35 percent for domestic projects.[47] However, the situation has changed somewhat since 1976, as the government has attempted to spread development more evenly: there has been a recent decline in the share of approvals for Java as more emphasis has been placed on increased development in the Outer Islands. Cumulative investment-project approvals for Java between 1968 and 1982 declined to 66 percent of the total for the country. During the same time period Jakarta's share of investment projects fell to 25 percent and that of the areas outside Java increased to 34 percent.[48]

On a per-capita basis Java certainly absorbed less in foreign investment capital than Maluku and Irian Jaya, Sumatra, and Kalimantan, although its domestic investment capital approximated Sumatra's amount (see Figure 5.12). With both foreign and domestic investment, Kalimantan and the Maluku and Irian Jaya provinces received above-average amounts on a per-capita basis, while Nusatenggara and Sulawesi received substantially less. As to be expected, contrasts among individual provinces are considerably larger. For foreign investment projects the per-capita figures range from highs of $323 and $234 in Aceh and Irian Jaya, respectively, to 73 cents and 98 cents, respectively, in West Nusatenggara and Yogyakarta (see Figure 5.13).[49] Contrasts are almost as great for domestic investment, with East Kalimantan receiving Rp 615 and Jakarta Rp 395 per capita in comparison with East Nusatenggara's Rp 4 and West Nusatenggara's Rp 19 per capita.[50]

Industry in Indonesia has been slow to develop. Indeed, it was not

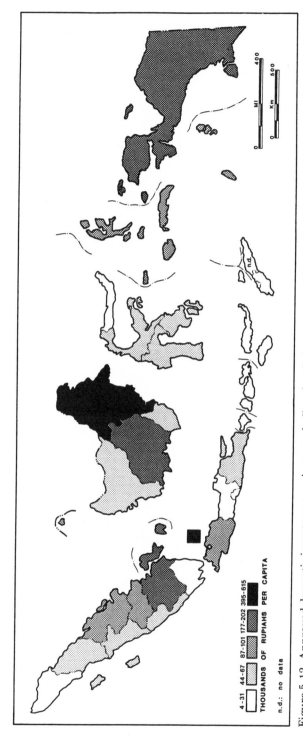

Figure 5.12. Approved domestic investment projects, excluding the oil, insurance, and banking sectors, in thousands of rupiahs per capita, 1968–1982. Calculated from data in Table IV.16b in Biro Pusat Statistik, *Indikator Ekonomi 1982.*

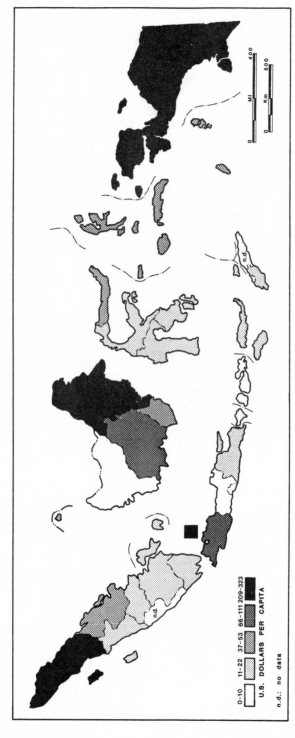

Figure 5.13. Approved foreign investment projects in U.S. dollars per capita, 1967–1982. Calculated from data in Table 16d in Biro Pusat Statistik, *Indikator Ekonomi 1982*.

until 1967 with the beginning of economic planning under the New Order that broad-based industrial growth really began. But since then, manufacturing production has increased enormously, making Indonesia the seventh largest producer of manufactured goods among developing countries (in terms of share of world manufacturing value added). Industrial growth averaged an impressive 12.3 percent annual rate during the 1970s, slowing down to 10.6 percent annually by the end of the decade as the easy stage of import substitution gradually came to an end. Growth rates have been much lower since 1981 because of the international recession and cuts in government expenditures in response to the fall in oil revenues, although the fourth Five-Year Development Plan assumes a 9.5 percent annual rate of growth in manufacturing for 1984–1989.[51] Manufacturing in 1984 grew by 24.4 percent, thanks to high growth rates in the liquified natural gas and oil refining subsectors, which grew at 53 and 30 percent, respectively. These two subsectors now account for more than half of manufacturing value added. The non-oil-and-gas component grew at only 4.7 percent.[52] Manufacturing thus has the highest planned growth rate in *Repelita IV.* It is expected to be the leading growth sector and to play a role in the creation of employment opportunities and the expansion of non-oil exports.

Indonesia has greatly diversified the structure of its manufacturing sector. Import substitution industries, including textiles, electrical, and automobile assembly, dominated early development, to be joined later by electronics, cement, tires, chemicals, paper, and aluminum. There has been major growth in iron and steel, electrical machinery, transport equipment, rubber, wood, and fabricated metal products, but much slower growth in the traditional industries related to the agricultural sector: food processing, beverages, tobacco, and textiles. A gradual shift from consumer goods has taken place in favor of intermediate and capital goods. However, it is significant that the production of consumer goods in the traditional industries is carried out mainly by private enterprises, whereas the newer, more capital-intensive industries such as cement, fertilizer, automobiles, petrochemicals, and basic metal products are primarily state-owned industrial enterprises, held either independently or in joint ventures with foreign firms.[53]

In terms of employment, in the early days cottage firms were overwhelmingly important, even though added value per worker was estimated as forty times higher in medium and large firms.[54] In the mid-1970s 3.6 million people or 7 percent of the work force were employed in manufacturing activities, with large- and medium-sized firms (defined as those employing twenty or more workers) accounting for one-fourth of these jobs. By the beginning of the fourth Five-Year Development Plan in 1984, the comparable figures were closer to five to six million or between 8 and 9 percent of the labor force. Employment in large- and medium-scale manufacturing rose by an annual average rate of only 7 percent during the 1970s, from 487,000 in 1970 to 1,067,000 in 1982.[55] Yet this increase of 0.5 million jobs during the decade corresponds to less than one-fourth of the average *annual* increase in Indonesia's labor force, and thus has failed to contribute significantly to the solution of Indonesia's employment problems. Small-scale and household or cottage industry, meanwhile, accounted for 80 percent of total manufacturing employment in 1979. Growth in manufacturing employment as a whole rose at an annual rate of only 5 percent during the 1970s. But even if an annual 10-percent increase in employment in industry could be attained, this would absorb only a small proportion of the over 2.5 million added to the work force each year.

Inevitably, spatial contrasts in industrialization are considerable, particularly those between Java and the Outer Islands. Indeed, at the beginning of the 1970s, 78 percent of all industry and 86 percent of total manufacturing employment were concentrated in Java.[56] Java has substantially more workers (relative to population size) in all three categories of firms—large and medium, small, and cottage industries—than any of the Outer Islands. The greatest contrast, however, is in the large and medium category, where in 1974–1975 Java had seventy-three manufacturing establishments per one million population, compared, for example, with only twenty-eight per million population in Kalimantan. Indeed, the Outer Island provinces had hardly any modern industry until very recently.[57] In most provinces just one or two agriculturally based industries dominated the industrial sector, such as rubber remilling and sawmilling in six of the eight provinces in Sumatra and in Kalimantan, and vegetable oil production in Sulawesi. Only Java had greater diversity, with its traditional textile and tobacco industries in the large- and medium-scale category, and bamboo and rattan weaving and coconut sugar production in the cottage industry category. However, new, diverse, large industries have expanded rapidly within the past ten years, including steel, fertilizer, cement, crumb rubber, plywood, and paper manufacture (mostly in the state-owned sector).

Industries outside Java face more difficulties both in obtaining inputs and in marketing, because of less reliable transportation services, high transportation operating costs, inadequate port facilities and other infrastructure, and other problems with inefficiency, bureaucracy, and corruption.

But the regional disparities in per-capita income that might be expected because of this spatial imbalance in industrial location, as well as by the systematic income transfers from oil and other natural resources of the Outer Islands to Java, do not materialize, because of the large numbers of the poor in overpopulated Java.

Despite the stated government goals of altering this regional concentration both by encouraging new industries to locate in rural areas and by providing incentives to invest in the Outer Islands, relatively little change in regional distribution of investment has occurred so far. Jakarta and West Java remain particularly favored provinces. The advantages of locating new factories in already-established areas (and especially in or near the capital city) are common throughout developing countries: access to senior government officials to deal with complex bureaucratic problems, availability of better transportation and communications facilities and a major port, proximity to the main financial institutions and other industries, and the personal preference of entrepreneurs for living in larger cities.

Industrial development, at least through the 1970s, has resulted in the broadening rather than the deepening of industrial structure. Industries have expanded and grown more or less independently rather than in a mutually reinforcing or integrating way. Interindustrial linkages in the past, both backward and forward, generally have not been strong.[58] However, recent development policies have focused on encouraging these linkages.

Although data are available only for interprovincial comparisons, it can be argued that intraprovincial economic disparities may be just as critical to political stability and thus to national integration. It is frequently the highly visible contrasts between rich and poor, most obviously manifest in urban areas, that provoke most tension. Evidence from household expenditure data indicates that during the 1970s inequalities increased in urban Java, especially in Jakarta.[59] There is evidence to suggest that the contrast between rich and poor has been increasing in rural areas also, as Green Revolution technology has benefited the wealthier farmers more than the poor, who cannot afford the investments or the risks involved. A study on farm size, land use, and the profitability of food crops in Indonesia in the early 1980s found that the richest households earned fourteen times as much as the poorest from the cultivation of food crops; after allowing for the transfer of rents and crop shares, they earned twenty-four times as much.[60]

In Java increasing fragmentation and decline in average farm size present major problems, as does the increase in landless households.[61] But in contrast to many other developing countries where tenant farming is more common, 75 percent of all farms are owner-operated. Changes in the structure and social organization of Javanese agriculture as it moves to greater use of high-yielding varieties of rice, however, are fundamentally labor-displacing and lead to increased social and economic disparities. A greater central government presence within the rural sector has helped to enhance the position of the more privileged classes and likewise led to a widening gap between rich and poor within the rural society. These findings are consistent with the findings of other researchers who contend that economic growth leads inevitably to a more unequal distribution of wealth among social groups, and even to a significant absolute decline in the economic and social position of the lowest income groups in developing countries.[62]

Economic Integration as Depicted by Sectoral and Regional Economic Interdependence

Economic integration depends not only upon the factors already discussed, such as approximate equality in living standards throughout the country and a trend toward reduction of regional disparities, but also on the interdependence of the various parts of the national economy, both sectorally and regionally.

Regional specialization can be an indication of both development and national integration so long as it is accompanied by interdependence among all the provinces, with each supplying the others with the specialized products of its region and obtaining from the others its many and diverse needs. For provincial self-sufficiency is, by definition, the antithesis of economic integration. In Indonesia, however, instead of mutual interdependence there has grown up an autarkic core-periphery relationship, with Java supplying the manufactured goods for much of the nation (supported by central government restrictions on the Outer Islands' ability to obtain similar economic goods more easily and inexpensively from neighboring countries) and drawing on the primary products of the Outer Island provinces. This has resulted in weak lateral links, as the earlier analysis of trade links among the provinces of Indonesia has demonstrated (see chapter 4).

Regional specialization is only integrative when it is reinforced by such integrating forces as the complementarity of regional economies and good interregional trade facilities. It threatens national economic integration when one region's specialization is not integrated into the whole through the mechanism of trade, when one province is economically independent of other parts of the country, or when it has more bilateral trade or other linkages with other nations than it does with other parts of its own national unit. Unfortunately, data are not available to compare the relative strength of extra- as opposed to intranational linkages, although it is possible that North Sumatra, for example, has stronger economic links with Singapore and Malaysia than it does with most other parts of Indonesia. The danger to national integration is obvious: such a region may consider it more economically advantageous to seek independence or to unite with its closer neighboring country than to remain within its historical national framework, particularly if that neighboring state is more economically advanced than other areas within the original nation-state.

The degree of regional specialization gives some indication of the degree of concentration of economic activity and of the degree of participation of the various provinces in the overall national economy and their stages of economic development. As already discussed, data on the location of industry and employment reveal a pattern of concentration of agriculture, mining, and extractive industry in the Outer Islands and of secondary and tertiary industry in Java. But from the perspective of employment, few economic activities are overwhelmingly concentrated. The most highly concentrated economic activities are mining and quarrying; the most widely distributed are agriculture and community service.

However, the pattern of agricultural activity varies considerably, with certain provinces relying to a much greater extent than others on agriculture. Bengkulu, West Kalimantan, East Nusatenggara, and Lampung all have over 75 percent of their provincial populations employed in agriculture (see Figure 5.14). On average throughout the country, 56 percent of the recorded employed population in 1980 was involved in agriculture, a figure that ranged from 48 percent in West Java and East Kalimantan (excluding the 1.9 percent figure in Jakarta) to 80.4 percent in Bengkulu.[63] Java had the lowest population percentages employed in agriculture, with East Kalimantan, Bali, West Nusatenggara, and North Sulawesi the only other provinces with below-average employment in agriculture. Although agriculture's share of the GDP was projected to drop (to 26.4 percent in fiscal 1988–1989), agriculture was expected to grow by 3 percent annually and to continue to be the mainstay of Indonesia's economy, employing (together with fishing and forestry) about 55 percent of the labor force.[64]

Examination of the participation of each province in the nine major labor divisions (agriculture; mining and quarrying; manufacturing; electricity, gas, and water; construction; trade; transport and communications; financing and insurance; and community services) shows the very low participation of certain provinces in everything except agriculture and extractive industries, the two economic activities most influenced by the environment. This is the situation particularly of some of the provinces in the Outer Islands, such as Bengkulu, Lampung, West and Central Kalimantan, Central and Southeast Sulawesi, East Nusatenggara, and Maluku, indicating the low level of their economic inte-

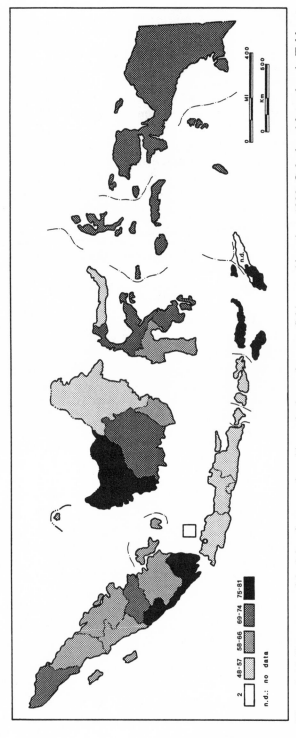

Figure 5.14. Percentage of the labor force employed in agriculture, forestry, fishing, and hunting, 1980. Calculated from data in Table 44.9 in Biro Pusat Statistik, *Sensus Penduduk 1980*, Series S, no. 2.

gration. By contrast, all the provinces of Java, together with those of South, West, and North Sumatra, Riau, Jambi, South and East Kalimantan, North and South Sulawesi, and Bali have much greater involvement in all the national economic sectors.[65]

Serious questions arise over the integration of the Indonesian economy from a structural point of view, although the situation has improved considerably in the past few years with the development of more forward and backward linkages between the agricultural and nonagricultural sectors.[66] In the past, agriculture has been undercapitalized, with government policies reflecting an urban bias in turning the terms of trade against agriculture, while the urban-based industrialization strategies have generated few linkages with the rural sector. Even now, one has to question the advisability of developing aircraft assembly and manufacturing, and the production of steel, oil tankers, patrol boats, and telecommunications equipment, which are both very costly and capital intensive, when the country badly needs more labor-absorbing industry. During the 1970s the share of manufacturing output of consumer goods, whose production techniques are generally more labor intensive and simpler, roughly halved, while that of intermediate and capital goods rose approximately threefold.[67]

Unemployment and underemployment are major problems, claiming in 1983, according to *Asian Business,* a total of seventeen million people, with the figures swelled by a further two million each year.[68] But the greatest problem, according to Arndt, is that of low productivity, for the great majority of the poor work long hours for minimal returns. Indeed, he suggests that emphasis should be placed on a productivity-oriented development strategy rather than an employment-oriented one, for modern technology is essential to attain the quality of products demanded in the export markets.[69] As he puts it, the crucial test of development performance is not employment, but the rate of growth of income and the degree of equity in its distribution.

Greater economic integration is hindered by a number of factors. One of the most influential is the high cost and difficulty of transportation within an archipelago consisting of over 6,000 inhabited islands flung over a west-east distance of over 5,000 kilometers. High port charges and high distribution costs because of underdeveloped transportation facilities linking docks with their hinterlands compound the problem. Traditionally, provincial customs duties were charged to provide vital revenue for each province, but these served also to hinder the flow of interprovincial trade and were ultimately abolished. In addition, bureaucratic red tape, corruption, and poor provincial administration and management have further limited economic integration.

Yet compared to the old Federation of the West Indies or the present

Caribbean Community, Caricom, Indonesia's prospects for greater economic integration are bright.[70] There is more regional specialization, standardization of telecommunications and transportation, and monetary integration within the Indonesian archipelago than there is among the members of Caricom, which is the most similar geographically of all other regional trading groups. Indonesia also has the advantages of strong, centralized political and administrative authority and a common national language.

The pattern that emerges in Indonesia in the early 1980s, therefore, is one of significant economic disparities among the provinces. These disparities are increasing in their magnitude, partly as a result of the normal power of circular and cumulative causation, whereby initial locational advantages especially of infrastructure are exploited first and become compounded, partly because of the growing centralization of power that has encouraged centralization of economic activity, and partly because of policies concerned with reestablishing economic stability and promoting rapid economic growth after the Sukarno era. However, there is current government commitment to spread development and its benefits more evenly throughout the country and to increase economic interdependence among the regions, although this is limited partly by the high costs of transportation and partly by numerous administrative and bureaucratic barriers.

6

Spatial Patterns

IN THE three previous chapters the various dimensions of integration have been discussed and analyzed separately. Each dimension has been shown to consist of a number of variables with varying degrees of interrelationships, as a comparison of the various maps already presented clearly demonstrates. In this chapter, these interrelationships will now be considered more rigorously, through statistical analyses, to obtain a more complete, composite picture of national integration in Indonesia. Two types of analysis have been used: correlation analysis, to consider the relationships between each pair of variables; and factor analysis, to extract the common elements from a number of variables in each dimension of integration. The relationships among the factors thus extracted are also examined. Finally, factor scores for the provinces are analyzed and the spatial patterns of overall integration delineated.

The indices selected for inclusion in the statistical analysis were the most significant and relevant ones for which complete and detailed data were available for the early 1980s. Obviously they are subject to certain limitations. They are aggregate data, a fact that masks important intraprovincial differences. They are also not completely accurate, but subject to the differential honesty and professionalism of the census takers and other data collectors, sorters, and editors, and to a certain amount of political manipulation (although in general Indonesian census data are regarded as remarkably accurate). Nor are the indices chosen always ideal; for example, data on interprovincial movements of people would have been preferable to structural indices on road networks and vehicle numbers. But, given these constraints and caveats, one can still argue that the indices selected do indeed have considerable validity, relevance, and reliability. The data point out serious disparities among the provinces: certainly the government could have suppressed or altered particularly embarrassing data to give a more rosy picture of Indonesia's conditions had it so desired.

For the purposes of this analysis, moreover, all data were standardized to accommodate the large differences in size of both area and population among the different provinces.[1] For most of the sociocultural, interaction, and economic variables, the standardization was in terms of population (percent, per 10,000, and so forth as appropriate) for each province, but for a few variables (such as road density) the standardization was in terms of unit area. Such standardization, however, necessary as it is for valid statistical comparison, also camouflages very basic differences, particularly between Java and the Outer Islands, that are strikingly obvious to the observer; for the concentration of infrastructure, the size and sophistication of urban centers, and other signs of economic development in Java are diluted when averaged over the enormous population of Java (91.3 million in 1980). Logarithmic transformation of the data was carried out on those variables that had one disproportionately high value, to avoid distortion of the mean and standard deviation for that variable and increase the chances for linear relationships between each pair of variables.[2]

The correlation matrices for each dimension (using the Pearson product-moment correlation coefficients) were scrutinized to ascertain which indices were statistically significant. Indices with correlates of over 0.95 were judged to be measuring the same factor; the correlation matrix was therefore simplified to include only one of the indices thus clustering together. At the other end of the scale, indices that showed correlations of less than 0.50 with any other variable were likewise excluded on the grounds of their confusing further analysis with unnecessary noise.

In the factor analysis, the varimax orthogonal type of rotation was selected as being most valuable in this study because by this method of rotation the best fit vectors (factors) extracted are independent of one another.

Because of the large number of variables (over eighty were considered) and the small number of provinces (twenty-five were included in the statistical analysis), it was impossible to achieve statistically valid results if the variables were all included in one factor analysis at the same time.[3] The three major dimensions of integration were therefore analyzed separately, and the common factors from each dimension were examined subsequently for their correlations. Factor scores were then examined to ascertain the spatial patterns (of the degree of integration obtaining in each province on each factor) so that the overall patterns of integration of the different provinces into the nation-state of Indonesia could be determined.

Initial analysis of the three dimensions demonstrated that the inclusion of Jakarta distorted the results. Although each province is unique in its combination of sociocultural, interaction, and economic characteristics, Jakarta's "uniqueness" is overwhelming. This can be seen in most of the maps in the earlier chapters of the book. It is typified by Jakarta's special character as an almost all-urban province in a country whose average degree of urbanization is only 22.4 percent and as the province where economic and political power is concentrated. Jakarta almost consistently exhibited disproportionate indices. This confused the analysis by unduly affecting the size of the mean and standard deviation for each variable and thus distorted the overall pattern for the other provinces. As a result, Jakarta was excluded from the statistical analysis. East Timor was also omitted, because of its recent incorporation into Indonesia and the consequent lack of comparable data.

Only a proportion of the variation within the correlation matrices is accounted for by the factors extracted. This ranges from 76.3 percent for the interaction dimension, through 79.9 percent for the economic, to 84.8 percent for the sociocultural dimension. This is to be expected, partly because not all the variables that are relevant to the question of integration are available and partly because the variables selected are also measures of forces other than integration. For each dimension several computer runs were undertaken to obtain the matrix with the most significant variables, where each variable had a communality of above 0.49 and loaded specifically on one factor. This led at times to the exclusion of certain variables theoretically considered relevant to the concept of national integration, such as the migration data.

Out of the wealth of information available in the sociocultural dimension of national integration, twelve key indices were selected for inclusion in the statistical analysis. These variables and their Pearson product-moment correlation coefficients are shown in Table 6.1. Some interesting relationships emerge. The language variable measuring the percentage of the population able to speak the Indonesian language correlates highly (0.74), as might be expected, with literacy rates, but surprisingly little with any of the education variables (0.20 with the percentage of the population ten years of age and over who have completed primary school, 0.40 with the percentage who have completed senior high school, and 0.22 with primary school participation rates). Likewise, the low correlation between literacy rates and the education variables are unexpected (0.11 with primary school completion rates, 0.42 with secondary school completion rates); only with elementary school participation rates does literacy correlate at a significant level of 0.68.[4] It was this last education variable, therefore, that was chosen for inclusion in the statistical analysis, both on the basis of its higher correlation with literacy rates and on theoretical grounds that it best measures basic educational opportunities among the provinces.[5] It is interesting to

Table 6.1. Correlation matrix of selected sociocultural variables

Variable	LANG	ISLAM	CHRSTN	EDUCNP	LITRCY	COOPMB
LANG	1.00	-0.10	0.28	0.22	0.74**	-0.40
ISLAM	-0.10	1.00	-0.79**	0.27	0.24	0.05
CHRSTN	0.28	-0.79**	1.00	-0.37	-0.14	-0.17
EDUCNP	0.22	0.27	-0.37	1.00	0.68**	0.29
LITRCY	0.74**	0.24	-0.14	0.68**	1.00	-0.19
COOPMB	-0.40	0.05	-0.17	0.29	-0.19	1.00
ASIANS	0.38	0.04	0.02	-0.37	0.07	-0.51*
INDFLM	0.38	0.16	-0.10	0.08	0.24	-0.40
RADIOW	0.28	0.35	-0.52	0.40	0.47*	-0.31
HOSPBD	0.47*	-0.39	0.48*	0.10	0.19	-0.07
TVOWNR	0.44	0.25	-0.27	0.18	0.43	-0.35
URBAN	0.19	0.13	-0.09	-0.06	0.04	-0.25

*Significance level 0.01   **Significance level 0.001

Meanings of the variables selected and their sources:

LANG (Language). Percentage of the population in 1980 able to speak the Indonesian language. *Source:* Biro Pusat Statistik (B.P.S.), *Sensus Penduduk 1980,* Series S, Tables 8.3.

ISLAM (Adherents of Islam). Percentage of the population in 1980 classified as Muslim in the 1980 census. *Source:* B.P.S., *Statistik Indonesia 1982,* Table IV.4.1.

CHRSTN (Christian). Percentage of the population in 1980 classified as Christian (both Protestants and Catholics) in the 1980 census. *Source:* B.P.S., *Statistik Indonesia 1982,* Table IV.4.1.

EDUCNP (Education participation). Percentage of seven to twelve year olds in school in 1980. *Source:* B.P.S., *Sensus Penduduk 1980,* Series S, no. 2.

LITRCY (Literacy). Percentage of the population ten years of age and over classified as literate in the 1980 census. *Source:* B.P.S., *Sensus Penduduk 1980,* Series S, no. 2, Table 18.3.

COOPMB (Cooperative membership). Number of members of agricultural cooperatives per 100 population (average of 1979 and 1980 figures). *Source:* B.P.S., *Statistik Indonesia 1983, Buku Saku,* Table VIII.3.2.

note, however, that the correlations between language and completion of primary school, and between literacy and completion of primary school, were much higher in 1971 (0.56 and 0.83, respectively) than in 1980.[6]

Of the two religion variables considered, Islam correlates significantly (in a negative direction) only with Christianity, whereas Christianity (including both Protestantism and Catholicism) correlates both with the provision of hospital beds and (negatively) with radio ownership. Among the various indices measuring participation in a cross-provincial, nationwide organization (cooperatives, scouts, and membership in a social organization in the three months before a survey was taken in 1981), only cooperative membership correlates significantly with any other variable, negatively with the presence of foreigners claiming Asian citizenship. This latter variable, the percentage of non-

ASIANS	INDFLM	RADIOW	HOSPBD	TVOWNR	URBAN
0.38	0.38	0.28	0.47*	0.44	0.19
0.04	0.16	0.35	−0.39	0.25	0.13
0.02	−0.10	−0.52*	0.48*	−0.27	−0.09
−0.37	0.08	0.40	0.10	0.18	−0.06
0.07	0.24	0.47*	0.19	0.43	0.04
−0.51*	−0.40	−0.31	−0.07	−0.35	−0.25
1.00	0.55*	0.37	0.23	0.60**	0.51*
0.55*	1.00	0.47*	0.34	0.79**	0.61**
0.37	0.47*	1.00	0.11	0.77**	0.47*
0.23	0.34	0.11	1.00	0.44	0.57**
0.60**	0.79**	0.77**	0.44	1.00	0.79*
0.51*	0.61**	0.47*	0.57*	0.79**	1.00

ASIANS (Non-Indonesian Asian citizens). Number of foreigners claiming
Asian citizenship, 1981. *Source:* B.P.S., *Statistik Indonesia 1982,* Table
III.1.11.

INDFLM (Indonesian-film watchers). Number of people watching an Indonesian-made movie in 1981 per 100 population. *Source:* B.P.S., *Statistik
Bioskop Indonesia 1981 dan 1982,* Table 4.

RADIOW (Radio ownership). Percentage of households owning a radio,
1980. *Source:* B.P.S., *Sensus Penduduk 1980,* Series S, no. 2, Table
66.3.

HOSPBD (Availability of hospital beds). Number of hospital beds per
10,000 population in 1980. *Source:* B.P.S., *Statistik Indonesia 1982,* Table
IV.2.1.

TVOWNR (Television ownership). Percentage of households owning a television set, 1980. *Source:* B.P.S., *Sensus Penduduk 1980,* Series S, no. 2, Table
66.3.

URBAN (Urban population). Percentage of the population classified as
urban in the 1980 census. *Source:* B.P.S., *Sensus Penduduk 1980,* Series S,
Tables 1.

Indonesian-citizen Asians, correlates positively with viewers of Indonesian-made movies, while both these variables correlate positively with
television ownership and the percentage urban. Both the Indonesian-
movie viewing and television ownership indices also correlate strongly,
as might be expected, with a number of other nonsociocultural indices,
particularly those measuring economic development and communications links.

These twelve variables were subjected to a principal components factor analysis with a varimax rotation, which condensed and ordered
them into four orthogonal and thus statistically independent factors.
The first factor depicts the urban- and media-related characteristics of
television ownership, the viewing of Indonesian-made movies, radio
ownership, and access to hospital facilities. The second factor depicts
religion and the associated variables of health-care facilities (as mea-

sured by the availability of hospital beds) and, to a lesser extent, radio ownership. It is interesting to note here the positive association of radio ownership with Islam in contradistinction to the association of Christianity with health care (a reflection of past Christian missionary activity). The third factor relates literacy to education and knowledge of the Indonesian language. The fourth factor combines membership in a cooperative (a positive integrating measure) with the presence of non-Indonesian Asian citizens (evaluated as a negative force). Cooperative membership is also loosely linked to elementary school participation rates (see Table 6.2). Eigenvalues and the percentage of the variance in each factor are given in Table 6.3, and communalities in Table 6.4.

The factor scores for these four factors reveal some important spatial differences among the provinces, as Table 6.5 demonstrates.

The first factor, dealing with urban- and media-related variables, highlights the exceptional province of East Kalimantan with its disproportionate scores,[7] but it also depicts clearly the more urban provinces of North and South Sumatra, Riau, South Kalimantan, and Yogyakarta, all in the western part of the country (see Figure 6.1). Their more urbanized populations, as might be expected, are more exposed to radio, television, and Indonesian-made films. The provinces with the lowest scores on this factor are among the least urban and least developed: East Nusatenggara, Central and Southeast Sulawesi, and Lampung.

The second factor illustrates the contrasts associated with religion and its related attributes (radio ownership with Islam and the provision of hospital beds with Christianity). The highly Christian-influenced provinces of Irian Jaya and East Nusatenggara stand out with their extreme scores, and fairly high scores are recorded for North Sulawesi, Maluku, and North Sumatra. In clear contrast are the highly Muslim provinces in the rest of Sumatra, all of Java, and southern Sulawesi, as well as South Kalimantan and West Nusatenggara (see Figure 6.2).

The third factor deals with the important integrative characteristics of literacy, knowledge of the Indonesian language, and education. It clearly depicts the most highly developed provinces in this aspect: North Sulawesi, Maluku, and North Sumatra (where former Christian missionary activity contributed much). However, not all predominantly Christian provinces or provinces with a notable Christian presence benefited equally, as the very high negative scores for Irian Jaya and West Kalimantan demonstrate. Similarly, the relatively high scores of Central Sulawesi and particularly West Sumatra cannot be attributed to a Christian presence (Central Sulawesi's population is only 21 percent Christian, and that of West Sumatra is just 1.6 percent Christian). Yet the difference is very striking in the two least-developed provinces of

Table 6.2. Rotated factor loadings in the sociocultural dimension

Variable	Factor 1	Factor 2	Factor 3	Factor 4
LANG	0.22	−0.31	0.76	0.40
ISLAM	0.10	0.86	0.10	−0.01
CHRSTN	−0.12	−0.95	−0.04	0.16
EDUCNP	0.03	0.27	0.75	−0.53
LITRCY	0.09	0.13	0.96	0.09
COOPMB	−0.14	0.05	−0.15	−0.86
ASIANS	0.53	0.01	−0.05	0.69
INDFLM	0.72	0.09	0.12	0.39
RADIOW	0.56	0.49	0.41	0.16
HOSPBD	0.65	−0.64	0.25	−0.15
TVOWNR	0.87	0.21	0.31	0.24
URBAN	0.93	0.01	−0.07	0.07

Note: Underlined numbers indicate the variables that have the most significant loadings on each factor; dashed lines indicate those variables contributing somewhat less.

Table 6.3. Eigenvalues and percentages of the variance in the sociocultural dimension

Factor	Eigenvalue	Percentage of the variance	Cumulative percentage
1	4.40	36.7	36.7
2	2.67	22.2	58.9
3	1.91	15.9	74.8
4	1.20	10.0	84.8

Table 6.4. Communalities in the sociocultural dimension

Variable	Communality
LANG	0.88
ISLAM	0.76
CHRSTN	0.94
EDUCNP	0.92
LITRCY	0.95
COOPMB	0.78
ASIANS	0.76
INDFLM	0.70
RADIOW	0.75
HOSPBD	0.92
TVOWNR	0.95
URBAN	0.88

Table 6.5. Factor scores of the sociocultural factors

Province	Factor 1 Urban/ Media	Factor 2 Religion	Factor 3 Literacy/ Language	Factor 4 Coop membership/ Asians
Aceh	-0.48	0.76	0.43	-0.16
North Sumatra	0.96	-0.96	1.27	-0.16
West Sumatra	-0.17	0.48	0.88	-0.77
Riau	0.92	0.81	0.13	1.54
Jambi	-0.65	0.94	0.29	1.37
South Sumatra	0.90	0.47	0.38	0.76
Bengkulu	-0.79	0.85	0.18	-0.22
Lampung	-1.14	0.74	0.45	0.79
West Java	-0.15	0.79	-0.02	-0.10
Central Java	-0.01	0.71	-0.60	-0.75
Yogyakarta	0.77	0.40	0.25	-1.82
East Java	0.14	0.68	-0.87	-1.06
Bali	0.14	-0.36	-0.63	-1.22
West Nusatenggara	-0.51	0.52	-2.18	-1.31
East Nusatenggara	-1.60	-2.06	-0.62	0.60
West Kalimantan	0.48	-0.27	-1.57	2.32
Central Kalimantan	-0.65	0.34	0.51	0.63
South Kalimantan	0.89	0.67	0.22	-0.53
East Kalimantan	3.23	-0.17	0.00	0.88
North Sulawesi	0.52	-1.74	1.80	-1.37
Central Sulawesi	-1.19	-0.14	1.08	0.34
South Sulawesi	0.13	0.87	-1.13	-0.44
Southeast Sulawesi	-1.11	0.34	-0.27	0.08
Maluku	-0.74	-1.12	1.71	0.49
Irian Jaya	0.13	-2.78	-1.68	0.11

West and East Nusatenggara, where West Nusatenggara's last place and high negative score (and 0.4 percent Christian population) contrasts with East Nusatenggara's more modest negative score (and its 91 percent Christian population) (see Figure 6.3).

The fourth factor links the integrative variable of membership in cooperatives with the disintegrative variable of the presence of non-Indonesian-citizen Asians. It shows the more integrated provinces on this characteristic, Yogyakarta, North Sulawesi, West Nusatenggara, Bali, and East Java, standing in sharp contrast to three provinces that have disproportionate numbers of non-Indonesian-citizen Asians (and low cooperative membership), West Sumatra, Riau, and Jambi (see Figure 6.4).

The sociocultural dimension thus consists of four very different strands, each with its own spatial patterns. Only East Nusatenggara has

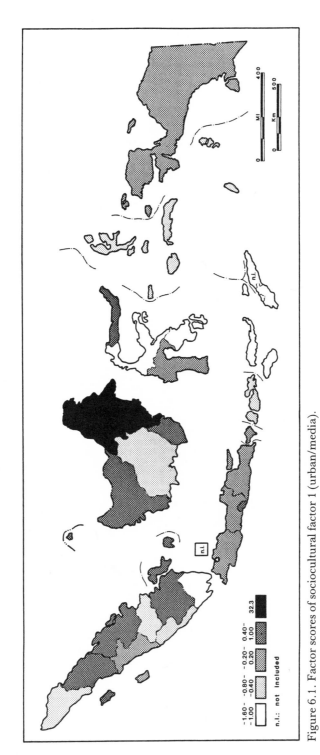

Figure 6.1. Factor scores of sociocultural factor 1 (urban/media).

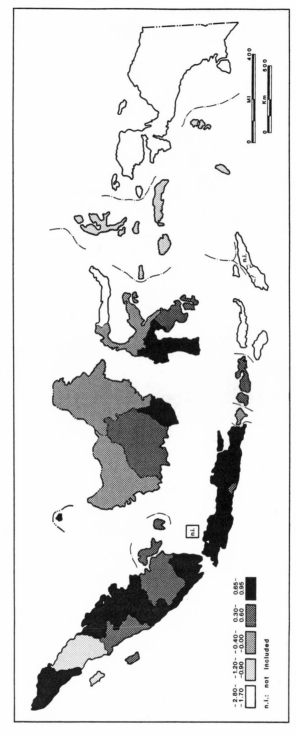

Figure 6.2. Factor scores of sociocultural factor 2 (religion).

Figure 6.3. Factor scores of sociocultural factor 3 (literacy/language).

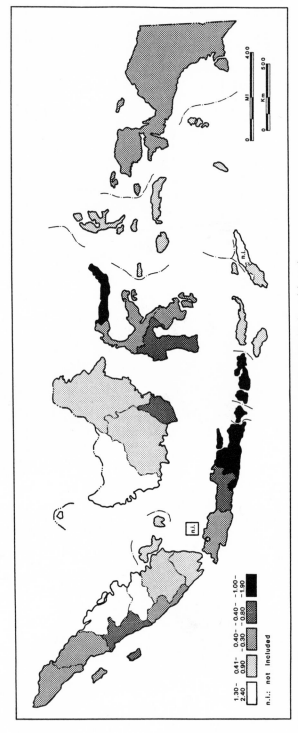

Figure 6.4. Factor scores of sociocultural factor 4 (cooperative membership/Asian citizens).

negative scores on all four factors,[8] while West Kalimantan, Central and Southeast Sulawesi, Maluku, and Irian Jaya have negative scores on three of the four factors.

Statistical analysis of the interaction dimension of national integration is particularly difficult because of the different land-sea orientation of different parts of archipelagic Indonesia. Some provinces consist predominantly of land areas on one of the major islands of Sumatra, Java, and Kalimantan, where overland or river transportation is most important; other provinces are made up of a number of smaller islands, where coastal shipping is of greater significance. A further problem is that the same index may have widely differing implications in different areas: for example, the railroad in Java links the different provinces, whereas in Sumatra the three sections of railroad are unconnected and thus serve predominantly local, not interprovincial, transportation needs. A further difficulty arises over standardizing for both the area and the population of each province.

However, out of all the variables pertaining to the interaction dimension, nine key variables (which correlated with at least one other significant variable and for which there were relatively accurate and detailed data) were selected for the statistical analysis. It is interesting to note that theoretically important indices of interaction, such as newspaper circulation and population mobility (including migration data), had to be excluded because of their lack of significant correlation with any other interaction variables. The variables selected and their Pearson product-moment correlation coefficients are shown in Table 6.6. When subjected to a factor analysis with a varimax rotation, these were condensed and ordered into a dichotomous factor structure (see Table 6.7).

Interpretation of the factors is difficult. The first factor consists of loadings from variables associated with greater urbanization and higher per-capita economic development: telephone and vehicle ownership, passengers using air transportation, and the two trade variables measuring interisland and international imports. The second factor has two poles, one relating sea transportation and telegram use, the other reflecting high road density (which is associated with high population density). These two factors account for 76.3 percent of the variation in the matrix. Eigenvalues and percentages of the variance in each factor are given in Table 6.8, and communalities in Table 6.9. Factor scores for the interaction dimension are given in Table 6.10.

Factor scores of the first factor, dealing with the urban and economic orientation of the transportation and communications network, depict the dominant position of East Kalimantan (with a factor score of 3.40). Bali, North Sumatra, and Riau are the only other provinces that have significant, relatively high scores on this factor; while at the other

Table 6.6. Correlation matrix of selected interaction variables

Variable	ROADNS	VEHCLP	LGSEAT	AIRTRF	TELPHN	TELGRM	IMPDOM	LGIMPI	LGPOPD
ROADNS	1.00	0.30	-0.58*	-0.02	0.08	-0.32	-0.23	-0.05	0.73**
VEHCLP	0.30	1.00	0.30	0.64**	0.79**	-0.02	0.49*	0.54*	0.08
LGSEAT	-0.58*	0.30	1.00	0.60**	0.53*	0.58*	0.75**	0.55*	-0.72**
AIRTRF	-0.02	0.64**	0.60**	1.00	0.83**	0.49*	0.77**	0.37	-0.44
TELPHN	0.08	0.79**	0.53*	0.83**	1.00	0.32	0.74**	0.59**	-0.18
TELGRM	-0.32	-0.02	0.58*	0.49*	0.32	1.00	0.50*	0.10	-0.63**
IMPDOM	-0.23	0.49*	0.75**	0.77**	0.74**	0.50*	1.00	0.46*	-0.40
LGIMPI	-0.05	0.54*	0.55*	0.37	0.59**	0.10	0.46*	1.00	0.01
LGPOPD	0.73**	0.08	-0.72**	-0.44	-0.18	-0.63**	-0.40	0.01	1.00

*Significance level 0.01   **Significance level 0.001   *Significance level 0.001

Meanings of the variables selected and their sources:

ROADNS (Road density). Length of roads (of all types and conditions) per 1,000 square kilometers, 1982. *Source:* Biro Pusat Statistik (B.P.S.), *Statistik Indonesia 1983, Buku Saku*, Table VII.1.3.

VEHCLP (Vehicles per 1,000 population). Number of registered vehicles of all types per 1,000 population, 1982. *Source:* B.P.S., *Statistik Indonesia 1983, Buku Saku*, Table VII.2.3.

LGSEAT (Sea-traffic-generated income, log-transformed). Income generated by sea traffic in the ports of each province in rupiahs per capita (calculated from recorded data for 285 ports, agglomerated by province), 1981–1982. *Source:* Republik Indonesia, Departemen Perhubungan Laut, Direktorat Perkapalan dan Pelayaran SubDit. Kebandaran dan Awak Kapal, Seksi P.U., *File No. TH 1981/82.*

AIRTRF (Air traffic). Number of domestic air travelers, recorded for sixty-six airports and agglomerated by province, per 1,000 population, 1981. *Source:* B.P.S., *Statistik Angkutan Udara 1981*, Table 9.

TELPHN (Telephone ownership). Number of telephone licenses issued per 1,000 population, 1981. *Source:* B.P.S., *Statistik Indonesia 1983, Buku Saku*, Table VII.5.3.

TELGRM (Telegrams). Number of telegrams sent to domestic destinations per 1,000 population, 1981. *Source:* B.P.S., *Statistik Indonesia 1982*, Table VIII.5.5.

IMPDOM (Imports from domestic sources). Number of tons of cargo unloaded in interprovincial trade per 100 population (average of 1981 and 1982 figures). *Source:* B.P.S., *Statistik Bongkar Muat Barang di Pelabuhan Indonesia 1982*, Table 1.

LGIMPI (Imports from overseas, log-transformed). Value of international imports in U.S. dollars per capita, 1982. *Source:* B.P.S., *Impor Menurut Jenis Barang dan Negeri Asal*, vol. 2, Table 8.

LGPOPD (Population density, log-transformed). Population density per square kilometer, 1980. *Source:* B.P.S., *Statistik Indonesia 1983, Buku Saku*, Table II.1.3.

Table 6.7. Rotated factor loadings in the interaction dimension

Variable	Factor 1	Factor 2
ROADNS	0.20	−0.84
VEHCLP	0.89	−0.23
LGSEAT	0.53	0.77
AIRTRF	0.82	0.34
TELPHN	0.94	0.11
TELGRM	0.24	0.72
IMPDOM	0.75	0.47
LGIMPI	0.70	0.04
LGPOPD	−0.06	−0.93

Note: Underlined numbers indicate the variables that have the most significant loadings on each factor.

Table 6.8. Eigenvalues and percentages of the variance in the interaction dimension

Factor	Eigenvalues	Percentage of the variance	Cumulative percentage
1	4.53	50.3	50.3
2	2.34	26.0	76.3

Table 6.9. Communalities in the interaction dimension

Variable	Communality
ROADNS	0.74
VEHCLP	0.84
LGSEAT	0.87
AIRTRF	0.79
TELPHN	0.90
TELGRM	0.58
IMPDOM	0.79
LGIMPI	0.49
LGPOPD	0.87

extreme, several provinces stand out for their lack of integration as measured by this factor: East Nusatenggara (especially), West Nusatenggara, Southeast Sulawesi, Central Kalimantan, and Bengkulu, all less-developed and more-isolated Outer Island provinces (see Figure 6.5).

On the second factor, however, the Javanese provinces, along with

Table 6.10. Factor scores of the interaction factors

Province	Factor 1 Urban-related	Factor 2 Sea transportation/ Road density
Aceh	0.19	0.44
North Sumatra	0.90	-0.62
West Sumatra	-0.07	-0.19
Riau	0.88	1.41
Jambi	-0.25	0.08
South Sumatra	0.38	-0.01
Bengkulu	-0.82	-0.07
Lampung	-0.64	-0.35
West Java	-0.36	-1.26
Central Java	-0.17	-1.26
Yogyakarta	0.47	-1.60
East Java	0.12	-1.01
Bali	1.63	-2.25
West Nusatenggara	-1.00	-0.42
East Nusatenggara	-1.64	-0.13
West Kalimantan	-0.64	0.49
Central Kalimantan	-0.82	1.04
South Kalimantan	0.13	0.22
East Kalimantan	3.40	1.43
North Sulawesi	0.23	0.05
Central Sulawesi	-0.63	0.76
South Sulawesi	0.05	-0.38
Southeast Sulawesi	-0.94	0.60
Maluku	-0.56	1.28
Irian Jaya	0.14	1.75

the most extreme case, Bali, cluster together at one pole, demonstrating their high population density and correlated high road density and their difference from the rest of Indonesia. At the other pole, Irian Jaya, East Kalimantan, Riau, Maluku, and Central Kalimantan illustrate the importance of sea travel and telegram communications (see Figure 6.6).

In the statistical analysis of the economic dimension, difficulties arise in trying to separate indices measuring economic integration from those illustrating economic development. Indices such as the ownership of a sideboard or consumption of electricity are measures as much of economic development as they are of participation in and integration into the national economic life. Yet it can be argued that economic development is a necessary though not sufficient condition for economic integration and that the extent to which the different provinces are involved

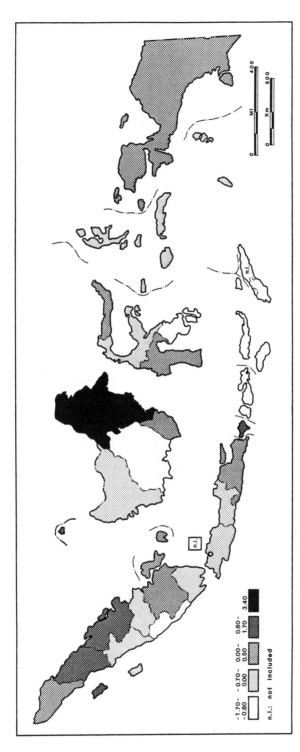

Figure 6.5. Factor scores of interaction factor 1 (urban-related)

Figure 6.6. Factor scores of interaction factor 2 (sea transportation/road density).

in economic development is an indication of their integration into the nation-state.

Of all the variables relating to the economic dimension, eleven were selected for their particular relevance, the completeness and consistency of their data, and their correlation with other variables. These variables and their Pearson product-moment correlation coefficients are shown in Table 6.11. When subjected to factor analysis with a varimax rotation, these variables were condensed and partitioned into three distinct factors (see Table 6.12). Eigenvalues and percentages of the variance in each factor are given in Table 6.13, and communalities in Table 6.14. Factor scores are shown in Table 6.15.

The first and most important factor, which accounts for 47.4 percent of the variance, summarizes those variables contributing to national development (provincial income and domestic investment levels, provincial participation in the national economy through taxation, and the amount spent upon development by both central and provincial governments). Factor scores depict a pattern of striking contrasts between several of the economically dynamic provinces in the Outer Islands, dominated overwhelmingly by East Kalimantan but also including Central Kalimantan and Irian Jaya; and the provinces of inner Indonesia, with their negative per-capita contributions to the national economy, particularly the provinces of Java but also Bali and the two Nusatenggara provinces (see Figure 6.7). These contrasts underscore the claim made earlier about the exploitation of the Outer Islands for the benefit of Java.

The second factor, by contrast, highlights the more modernizing forces of altered economic life-styles associated with changes from agricultural to other forms of employment, which involve greater personal interdependence. This factor is characterized by a relatively low percentage of the population employed in agriculture; a comparatively high use of kerosene, gas, or electricity as a fuel for cooking (in place of the traditional firewood); a relatively high use of electricity for lighting; and a high rate of ownership of one of the symbols of development, a sideboard.[9] This household-modernizing economic factor illustrates the differences between much of the eastern part of the country (the lowest factor scores recorded are for East Nusatenggara, Irian Jaya, and Southeast and Central Sulawesi) and the other parts of the country. East Kalimantan and West Java score highest on this factor, followed by South Sumatra, Riau, and North Sumatra (see Figure 6.8).

The third factor focuses on the dynamic element of economic growth as measured by the average growth rate in RGDP between 1976 and 1980 and the associated variable of approved foreign investment projects in the 1967-1982 period on a per-capita basis. Not surprisingly,

Table 6.11. Correlation matrix of selected economic variables

Variable	REGGDP	SIDEBD	FUELCM	ELECCM	REGEXP
REGGDP	1.00	0.47*	0.64**	0.75**	0.63**
SIDEBD	0.47*	1.00	0.56*	0.67**	-0.03
FUELCM	0.64**	0.56*	1.00	0.70**	0.04
ELECCM	0.75**	0.67**	0.70**	1.00	0.33
REGEXP	0.63**	-0.03	0.04	0.33	1.00
TAXGVT	0.93**	0.33	0.45	0.60**	0.74**
CGVDVT	0.79**	0.26	0.17	0.44	0.79**
GROWTH	0.03	0.10	-0.17	-0.03	0.14
AGREMP	-0.25	-0.39	-0.59**	-0.37	0.12
LGDINV	0.71**	0.42	0.50*	0.61**	0.59**
INTINV	0.48*	0.09	0.27	0.17	0.50*

*Significance level 0.01   **Significance level 0.001

Meanings of the variables selected and their sources:

REGGDP (Regional gross domestic product). RGDP in money terms (excluding oil) in thousands of rupiahs per capita, 1980. *Source:* Biro Pusat Statistik (B.P.S.), *Statistik Indonesia 1983, Buku Saku,* Table X.9.

SIDEBD (Sideboard ownership). Percentage of households owning a sideboard, 1980. *Source:* B.P.S., *Sensus Penduduk 1980,* Series S, no. 2, Table 66.3.

FUELCM (Fuel consumption). Percentage of private households using kerosene, gas, or electricity for cooking, 1980. *Source:* B.P.S., *Sensus Penduduk 1980,* Series S, no. 2, Table 63.3.

ELECCM (Electricity consumption). Percentage of private households using electricity for lighting, 1980. *Source:* B.P.S., *Sensus Penduduk 1980,* Series S, no. 2, Table 63.3.

REGEXP (Regional expenditure). Provincial government expenditures (operating and development) in thousands of rupiahs per capita, 1980–1981. *Source:* B.P.S., *Statistik Indonesia 1983, Buku Saku,* Table VIII.1.5.

TAXGVT (Provincial tax contributions to the government). Locally raised

given its first-place position on both these individual variables (see chapter 5), Aceh's factor score totally dominates the factor score structure (4.14, compared with its nearest rival, North Sumatra, with a score of 0.86). At the other extreme, Yogyakarta and West Nusatenggara record both low economic growth and little foreign investment (see Figure 6.9). However, the provinces at both extremes on this factor have changed since 1971, as a comparable study using early 1970s data demonstrates.[10] Then, East Kalimantan, Maluku, and Riau stood out along with Aceh as economically dynamic provinces, contrasting especially with North Sulawesi, which was the only province to experience a negative economic growth rate during the 1968–1972 time period on which the earlier study was based. West Kalimantan and Bengkulu also recorded fairly high negative scores at that time.

Significantly, only East Kalimantan has positive scores on all three of

TAXGVT	CGVDVT	GROWTH	AGREMP	LGDINV	INTINV
0.93**	0.79**	0.03	-0.25	0.71**	0.48*
0.33	0.26	0.10	-0.39	0.42	0.09
0.45	0.17	-0.17	-0.59**	0.50*	0.27
0.60**	0.44	-0.03	-0.37	0.61**	0.17
0.74**	0.79**	0.14	0.12	0.59**	0.50*
1.00	0.84**	0.08	-0.18	0.64**	0.46
0.84**	1.00	0.03	0.04	0.65**	0.29
0.08	0.03	1.00	0.27	-0.06	0.59**
-0.18	0.04	0.27	1.00	-0.03	0.07
0.64**	0.65**	-0.06	-0.03	1.00	0.37
0.46	0.29	0.59**	0.07	0.37	1.00

tax revenue in thousands of rupiahs per capita, 1980–1981. *Source:* B.P.S., *Statistik Keuangan Pemerintah Daerah, Daerah Tingkat I (Propinsi), 1975/76–1980/81,* Table 1.

CGVDVT (Central government support for development). National government support for development programs in thousands of rupiahs per capita, 1980–1981. *Source:* same as above (TAXGVT).

GROWTH (Growth rate of RGDP). Average annual growth rate of RGDP 1976–1980 at constant 1975 market prices. *Source:* B.P.S., *Pendapatan Regional Propinsi-propinsi di Indonesia, 1976–80,* Table 1.6.

AGREMP (Agricultural employment). Percentage of the population employed in agriculture, forestry, fishing, and hunting, 1980. *Source:* B.P.S., *Sensus Penduduk 1980,* Series S, no. 2, Table 44.9.

LGDINV (Domestic investment, log-transformed). Approved domestic investment projects excluding the oil, insurance, and banking sectors, 1968–1982 in thousands of rupiahs per capita. *Source:* B.P.S., *Indikator Ekonomi 1982,* Table IV.16b.

INTINV (International investment). Approved foreign investment projects, 1967–1982, in U.S. dollars per capita. *Source:* B.P.S., *Indikator Ekonomi 1982,* Table IV.16d.

these economic factors. Indeed, East Kalimantan is the only province even to record positive scores on the first two most significant factors, demonstrating again its predominant position as Indonesia's richest and most developed and developing province on a per-capita basis.[11]

At the other extreme, however, there are several provinces with significant negative scores on all three factors: West and East Nusatenggara and Lampung. This indicates their lack of economic development and integration into the national whole. In addition, there are several provinces that have significant negative scores on two of the factors:[12] West Sumatra, West, Central, and East Java, Yogyakarta, West Kalimantan, Central, South, and Southeast Sulawesi, and Maluku. Of this latter group, the Javanese provinces, together with West Sumatra and South Sulawesi, have positive scores on the second, modernizing factor but negative scores on both the economic development and growth-

Table 6.12. Rotated factor loadings in the economic dimension

Variable	Factor 1	Factor 2	Factor 3
REGGDP	0.82	0.50	0.14
SIDEBD	0.13	0.79	0.14
FUELCM	0.22	0.88	0.00
ELECCM	0.48	0.74	0.03
REGEXP	0.90	−0.16	0.18
TAXGVT	0.88	0.30	0.14
CGVDVT	0.93	0.04	0.02
GROWTH	−0.05	−0.10	0.94
AGREMP	0.10	−0.74	0.23
LGDINV	0.75	0.34	0.05
INTINV	0.38	0.09	0.80

Note: Underlined numbers indicate the variables that have the most significant loadings on each factor.

Table 6.13. Eigenvalues and percentages of the variance in the economic dimension

Factor	Eigenvalues	Percentage of the variance	Cumulative percentage
1	5.22	47.4	47.4
2	2.24	20.4	67.8
3	1.33	12.1	79.9

Table 6.14. Communalities in the economic dimension

Variable	Communality
REGGDP	0.93
SIDEBD	0.66
FUELCM	0.82
ELECCM	0.78
REGEXP	0.87
TAXGVT	0.88
CGVDVT	0.87
GROWTH	0.89
AGREMP	0.61
LGDINV	0.69
INTINV	0.80

Table 6.15. Factor scores of the economic factors

Province	Factor 1 Economic development	Factor 2 Modernization	Factor 3 Growth/ Investment
Aceh	-0.89	-0.17	4.14
North Sumatra	-0.38	0.91	0.86
West Sumatra	-0.38	0.18	-0.40
Riau	-0.05	0.93	-0.55
Jambi	0.39	-0.09	-0.71
South Sumatra	-0.05	1.07	-0.18
Bengkulu	0.05	-0.67	0.67
Lampung	-0.50	-0.62	-0.39
West Java	-0.83	1.60	-0.20
Central Java	-0.80	-0.01	-0.67
Yogyakarta	-0.55	0.00	-1.02
East Java	-0.75	0.66	-0.53
Bali	-0.71	0.73	-0.04
West Nusatenggara	-0.68	-0.47	-0.95
East Nusatenggara	-0.67	-1.87	-0.12
West Kalimantan	0.19	-0.55	-0.42
Central Kalimantan	1.78	-0.95	0.39
South Kalimantan	-0.34	0.75	0.42
East Kalimantan	3.58	1.93	0.18
North Sulawesi	-0.41	0.84	0.35
Central Sulawesi	0.51	-1.27	-0.48
South Sulawesi	-0.54	0.56	-0.22
Southeast Sulawesi	0.20	-1.34	-0.44
Maluku	0.56	-0.48	-0.42
Irian Jaya	1.28	-1.67	0.73

investment factors, while the others have positive scores on the first, economic development, but negative scores on the other two factors.

However, as discussed earlier, it is almost impossible to measure economic integration without also measuring economic development. Although economic integration depends upon some degree of development, economic development does not necessarily lead to greater economic integration. It is difficult, therefore, to be sure that Aceh's seemingly greater degree of economic integration as measured by the indices selected here truly reflects increased integration and not what is more likely, substantial investment and development. Similarly, it would seem that Lampung's negative scores on all three factors reflect its general poverty and lack of development as much as its lack of national integration.

The problem of promoting both economic development and eco-

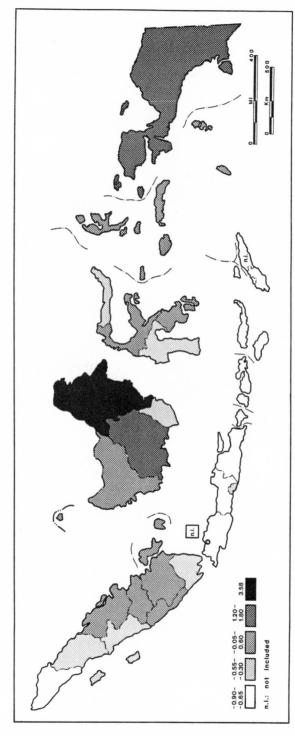

Figure 6.7. Factor scores of economic factor 1 (economic development).

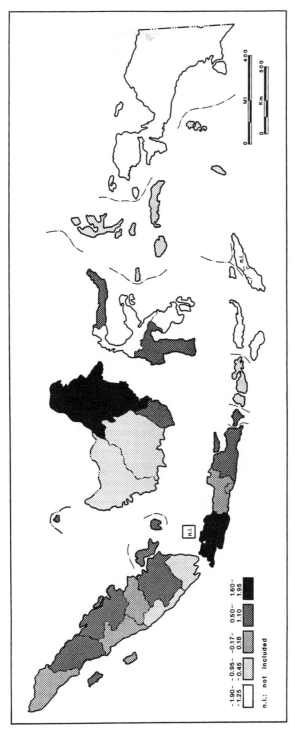

Figure 6.8. Factor scores of economic factor 2 (modernization).

Figure 6.9. Factor scores of economic factor 3 (growth/investment).

nomic integration remains a major one for the government and peoples of Indonesia. National economic growth cannot continue to be pursued at the cost of ever-widening disparities in economic well-being among the provinces. Nor, on the other hand, can uncontrolled regional development be promoted without concern for its impact on the nation as a whole. Both are prescriptions for disintegration. Only in a balance between the two, in which regional development takes place within a national framework of economic growth where other bonds of national interdependence are constantly being strengthened, can true economic development and integration take place.

Because the three dimensions of integration had to be analyzed separately to achieve statistically valid results, the interrelationships among the dimensions have thus far not been examined. However, these are shown in the correlation matrix of the nine factors extracted in the factor analyses (see Table 6.16). Two sets of significant interrelationships emerge.

The first set, with the highest correlations, consists of the urban-related factors: the first sociocultural factor (which had loadings from variables measuring television and radio ownership, exposure to Indonesian-made movies, and access to hospital beds, as well as the percentage urban), the first interaction factor (which had loadings from variables associated with greater urban and per-capita economic development, including telephone and vehicle ownership and participation in air transportation and trade), and the second economic factor (which was labeled the modernizing factor because of its more urban-related characteristics of relatively low employment percentages in agriculture, relatively high household ownership of a sideboard, and comparatively high consumption of electricity for lighting and use of fuels other than firewood for cooking).

The second set, with somewhat lower correlations among the factors and less inherent meaning, links together the fourth sociocultural factor (with its positive loadings on the presence of non-Indonesian-citizen Asians and its negative loadings on the more integrative variable of cooperative membership) with the second interaction factor (which had positive loadings from sea travel and telegrams and negative loadings from population density and road density). This second interaction factor also correlates significantly with the first economic factor, that concerned with national development (with its positive loadings from provincial income, domestic investment, provincial participation in the national economy through taxation, and the amount spent on development by both central and provincial governments).

The correlation matrix demonstrates also the very high degree of

Table 6.16. Correlation coefficients of the nine factors extracted in the analysis of the sociocultural, interaction, and economic dimensions of national integration

Factor	SocCult 1	SocCult 2	SocCult 3	SocCult 4
SocCult 1	1.00	0.00	0.00	0.00
SocCult 2	0.00	1.00	0.00	0.00
SocCult 3	0.00	0.00	1.00	0.00
SocCult 4	0.00	0.00	0.00	1.00
Intact 1	0.87**	−0.01	0.11	−0.07
Intact 2	0.08	−0.28	0.13	0.61**
Econfac 1	0.42	−0.21	0.07	0.44
Econfac 2	0.76**	0.33	0.21	−0.15
Econfac 3	0.02	−0.09	0.18	−0.01

**Significant at the 0.001 level.

independence of the remaining three factors: the second sociocultural factor (concerned primarily with religious differences in the country), the third sociocultural factor (including literacy, language, and education), and the third economic factor (dealing with economic growth and foreign investment); all of these had correlations of under 0.35 with any other factor. It thus appears that these are genuinely independent factors, measuring separate aspects of the whole concept of national integration.

The factor analysis and the ranking of the provinces on the basis of their factor scores demonstrate two distinct aspects of national integration within Indonesia.

On the one hand, factors such as the fourth sociocultural factor (cooperative membership and Asian citizens), the second interaction factor (high population and road density and low use of sea transportation and telegrams), and the second economic factor (household modernizing) highlight the dichotomy between Java (and Bali) and the Outer Islands. This is the very dichotomy that has been consistently recognized in the literature about Indonesia: the "sharp contrast between Java and Bali on the one hand and the outlying islands on the other," which has given rise to the acceptance of Java as the "core" of Indonesia and the other islands as the "periphery."[13] Thus, the far greater population density in Java and Bali, their more developed infrastructure (in terms of road density and vehicle concentration), their greater participation in certain nationally oriented organizations such as village social associations and cooperatives, and their greater exposure to modernizing influences (as indicated in their higher levels of consumption of electricity and kerosene and their lower employment levels in primary agricultural activities) contrast with conditions existing in the Outer Islands.

Intact 1	Intact 2	Econfac 1	Econfac 2	Econfac 3
0.87**	0.08	0.42	0.76**	0.02
-0.01	-0.28	-0.21	0.33	-0.09
0.11	0.13	0.07	0.21	0.18
-0.07	0.61**	0.44	-0.15	-0.01
1.00	0.00	0.42	0.72**	0.14
0.00	1.00	0.68**	-0.28	0.21
0.42	0.68**	1.00	0.00	0.00
0.72**	-0.28	0.00	1.00	0.00
0.14	0.21	0.00	0.00	1.00

Yet on the other hand, a closer examination of the factors and their spatial patterns reveals that in at least two different ways this "core-periphery dichotomy" conclusion is inadequate. First, the factors that demarcate Java as a distinct "core" are not as crucial as those factors synthesizing other features. In both the sociocultural and interaction dimensions, the major factor extracted from the factor analysis fails to distinguish Java from the Outer Islands on a per-capita basis (see Figures 6.1 and 6.5); in the economic dimension it is the second (household modernizing) factor that fails to make that distinction (see Figure 6.8). Rather, the contrast is between certain of the Outer Island provinces and other provinces also in the Outer Islands. In other words, the contrasts among the Outer Island provinces are greater and more significant than those between Java and the Outer Islands, at least on a per-capita basis.

Second, the factor analysis shows that from a per-capita perspective Java is not a true core, because in each dimension the Javanese provinces lack several of the key characteristics expected of a national core.

In the sociocultural dimension, a higher proportion of the population speaks the national language in most of the outlying areas in the Outer Islands (such as North and Central Sulawesi, Maluku, all of Sumatra, and East Kalimantan) than in Java (see Figure 6.3). Indeed, in Java less than 62 percent of the population can speak Indonesian (with the exception of Jakarta). Yet widespread knowledge of a common, nation-wide language is one of the most important integrating forces in any nation-state and consequently should characterize the core of any country. Literacy and educational levels are similarly below the national average in most of Java. In terms of access to medical facilities and other amenities on a per-capita basis, the Javanese have fewer hospital beds and mother-and-baby clinics and less exposure to Indonesian-made movies than the population in many of the Outer Island provinces (especially East Kalimantan, North Sulawesi, and the provinces of Sumatra). Indeed, the provinces of Java outside Jakarta are not even the most urbanized on a per-capita basis. North and South Sumatra, Riau, and East Kalimantan all have a higher percentage of their provincial populations classified as urban than any of the four provinces in Java included in the statistical analysis.

On the interaction level, although Java has by far the most highly developed land transportation network (road, rail, and vehicular density), the comparative underdevelopment on a per-capita basis of its sea transportation system and other non-land-based interaction indices, as demonstrated by the non-land-oriented interaction factor, is striking in this sea-oriented island nation (see Figure 6.6). Similarly in terms of population interaction and mixing, on the basis of the 1980 migration data Java emerges as a very homogeneous area: less than 4 percent of its population (outside Jakarta) has lived in another province, a characteristic hardly to be expected in a national core.

The same is true with the economic dimension. The national development economic factor distinguishes Java (along with provinces in the Outer Islands such as West and East Nusatenggara and Aceh) as an economically *under*developed area on a per-capita basis, an area lacking the dynamic characteristics normally associated with a core region (see Figure 6.7). Despite the fact that Java has received a disproportionate percentage of both domestic and foreign investment, and is the center of manufacturing industry in Indonesia, provincial income levels and provincial contributions to the national economy are lower per capita than in most of the Outer Island provinces. This inverted core-periphery situation has been discussed earlier (see chapter 5).[14] On a per-capita basis therefore, Java is a net economic drain on the national economy, not an economically dynamic, pulsating center from which spread effects extend to an underdeveloped periphery.

Thus, it is obvious that Java (outside Jakarta) and Bali do not form the economically dynamic and heterogeneous heartland, containing truly national core characteristics. Only in its political relationships, in its political domination of the periphery, can Java be considered a core. In other ways the Javanese provinces and Bali form a part of the periphery, albeit a very distinctive part.

Only Jakarta, the national capital city, stands out with true core characteristics. Only Jakarta has a highly urban character, a high economic growth rate, high income, and marked cosmopolitan features (with the greatest heterogeneity of population of any province in Indonesia). Indeed, Jakarta has been labeled "the most, even the only truly *Indonesian* city, because of its function as one of the few crucibles in which the nation's ethnic groups interact in their daily lives."[15] Jakarta alone is the center of investment; the headquarters of finance, administration, and government; and the focus of most communications and transportation links in the country.

When only Jakarta is recognized as the national core of Indonesia, the pattern of national integration appears significantly different from the dichotomous Java-Outer Islands model traditionally accepted in the literature about Indonesia. Comparison of factor scores and the rankings of the six major factors (see Table 6.17), together with other elements discussed earlier in the book, suggests a fourfold classification of the levels of integration of the provinces in Indonesia based on per-capita characteristics (see Figure 6.10).

Of the nine factors that resulted from the factor analysis of the three major dimensions of integration, six are conceptually more important than the remaining three. In the sociocultural dimension the first and third factors are most significant: the first, accounting for 37 percent of the variance, links the urban- and media-related characteristics; and the third, accounting for 16 percent of the variance, combines the important variables of literacy, education, and knowledge of the Indonesian language. The second factor, depicting religious differences, demonstrates the contrasts between the predominant religion of Islam and the minority Christianity; but, as discussed earlier, adherence to Islam cannot necessarily be construed as being more integrative, because Christians have contributed to national development and integration disproportionately to their numbers. The fourth sociocultural factor is likewise ambiguous in meaning, for it combines the integrative cooperative membership variable with the disintegrative presence of non-Indonesian-citizen Asians.

Both interaction factors are inherently valuable because they measure different, positive aspects of interaction. With the economic dimension, however, the first two factors (measuring national economic development and participation in the national economy, and household modernizing forces of changing economic life-styles) are more significant than the third. This last factor, accounting for only 12 percent of the variance, is concerned with economic growth during a rather limited time period (1976–1980) and with approved foreign investment projects from 1967 to 1982, and reflects the existence of economic wealth and potential rather than economic integration. The groupings of the provinces, therefore, are based on their factor scores on the six most important factors, two in each major dimension.

First, the five provinces of West, Central, and East Java, Yogyakarta, and Bali form a fairly distinct group with similar scores on most of the factors, although it is interesting to notice that they form a less uniform

Table 6.17. Ranks of the provinces based on the factor scores of the six most pertinent factors

Province	Sociocultural		Interaction		Economic	
	Factor 1	Factor 3	Factor 1	Factor 2	Factor 1	Factor 2
Aceh	16	8	8	9	25	15
North Sumatra	2	3	3	20	13	5
West Sumatra	15	5	13	16	13	11
Riau	3	14	4	3	10	4
Jambi	18	10	15	11	6	14
South Sumatra	4	9	6	13	10	3
Bengkulu	21	13	21	14	9	20
Lampung	23	7	19	17	16	19
West Java	14	16	16	22	24	2
Central Java	13	18	14	22	23	13
Yogyakarta	6	11	5	24	18	12
East Java	9	21	11	21	22	9
Bali	9	20	2	25	21	8
West Nusatenggara	17	25	24	19	20	16
East Nusatenggara	25	19	25	15	19	25
West Kalimantan	8	23	19	8	8	18
Central Kalimantan	18	6	21	5	2	21
South Kalimantan	5	12	10	10	12	7
East Kalimantan	1	15	1	2	1	1
North Sulawesi	7	1	7	12	15	6
Central Sulawesi	24	4	18	6	5	22
South Sulawesi	11	22	12	18	17	10
Southeast Sulawesi	22	17	23	7	7	23
Maluku	20	2	17	4	4	17
Irian Jaya	11	24	9	1	3	24

CATEGORY

| 1 | 2 | 3 | 4 |

1 Least integrated & developed
2 Java – Bali Group
3 Average
4 Most integrated & developed

n.l.: not included

Figure 6.10. Provinces grouped according to their common characteristics, 1980.

group than they did ten years ago. They rank below average on the literacy-education-language sociocultural factor, on the second interaction factor (which has high loadings on sea transportation and telegram use and negative loadings on high road and population density), and on the most important economic factor (that measuring economic development and contribution to the national economy on a per-capita basis). And they rank at or a little above average on the other three major factors. As already suggested, Java and Bali seem only partially integrated into the whole Indonesian nation-state. In some ways they constitute a nation-state of their own, with their own distinct cultures symbolized in their rich art forms and language traditions, which are not those of the nation as a whole. They are attached politically (though frequently in a colonial-type relationship) to the other parts of the Indonesian archipelago and are certainly economically dependent on them for revenue generation; yet in other ways Java and Bali seem independent, culturally aloof, and unwilling partners when it comes to regional equality.

Second, five spatially separate provinces in the Outer Islands stand out as being the most economically developed and highly integrated. These provinces, East Kalimantan, North and South Sumatra, Riau, and North Sulawesi, rank among the top seven on at least three of the major factors and have generally above-average scores on the others. They are provinces with comparatively high levels of urbanization, each with a major urban core. East Kalimantan stands out in its first position with its overwhelmingly high scores and first-place rankings on four of the six major factors (and second place on a further one). Its only relatively low ranking (fifteenth) is on the literacy-education-language sociocultural factor.

Historically these five provinces consist of two different types. The provinces of North and South Sumatra and North Sulawesi, with their nuclear centers of Medan, Palembang, and Manado, are old historic cores.[16] North Sumatra is the home of the Bataks and the locus of important late-nineteenth- and twentieth-century agricultural estates, and it has a favorable position with regard to trade with the Malay Peninsula across the Straits of Malacca. South Sumatra traces its historic roots to the Sri Vijaya empire of the seventh to the thirteenth centuries and is the focus of a network of trading routes and connections extending through much of the archipelago. North Sulawesi developed later as a core area and owes its comparatively high degree of development to its favored position under the Dutch. This is reflected in its sociocultural tradition, with its European emphases on literacy, education, Christianity, medical facilities, and so forth, and on its economic development as a center for the production of copra and certain of the spices (cloves, nutmeg, mace, cinnamon, and vanilla). Its decline from a position of preeminence among the Outer Islands has to be understood in the light of the Javanese control of the economy after independence, the *Permesta* rebellion, and the central government's restrictions on trade (with the nearby Philippines) and regional development.

The second type of province, including East Kalimantan and Riau, reflects particularly, though not exclusively, the exploitation of their economic resource base in the more recent past, especially timber, petroleum, and natural gas. North and South Sumatra are also rich in natural resources.

Third, a group of ten provinces exhibits an average or less-than-average degree of overall integration. This group can be subdivided into three categories: first, those that are somewhat more integrated and developed, that rank within the top ten provinces on at least two of the factors and include one or two other relatively high or average rankings: South Kalimantan, Aceh, and Jambi; second, those that are somewhat below average in most of their rankings: South Sulawesi and West Sumatra; and third, those with great contrasts in their rankings on the different factors: Central Sulawesi, Irian Jaya, Maluku, and West and Central Kalimantan.

Central Sulawesi, Maluku, and Central Kalimantan all rank remarkably high (within the top six provinces) on the literacy-education-language sociocultural factor, the second interaction factor (sea transportation-telegram use), and the first economic factor (economic development and participation in the national economy), but have very low rankings (within the bottom eight) on the remaining three major factors. Irian Jaya and West Kalimantan, by contrast, share very low rankings on the important literacy-education-language sociocultural factor, but rank higher on the first (urban- and media-related) sociocultural factor; they share similarly high rankings on the second interaction factor and first economic factor with the three other provinces in this subgroup. Irian Jaya stands out as having the greatest contrasts in its rankings: first and third on two (the second interaction and first economic factors), but next to last on two others (the second sociocultural and second economic factors). In other words, it is a province with considerable economic resources (particularly petroleum and copper) and has comparatively high interaction by sea and telegrams on a per-capita basis, but it shares little in the cultural heritage (as represented by the literacy-education-language factor) and in the economically modernizing forces of the country. Economic development here tends to be enclaval in nature, with greater impact on the towns and in the vicinities of resource extraction, and on its numerous in-migrants than on the indigenous inhabitants.

South Sulawesi's low level of integration as measured by the factor scores is somewhat surprising, given the role of its provincial capital, Ujung Pandang (formerly Makassar), as a thriving port and metropolis, a major center for communications, and the economic and administrative center for much of eastern Indonesia. South Sulawesi's population is more heterogeneous than most, and in addition the Bugis trading network is an important factor in integrating South Sulawesi into the rest of Indonesia;[17] yet these traits are not reflected in any of the indices. The explanation for the anomalous position of South Sulawesi may have to be sought both in its past development and in the size of its provincial population. Although historically an important center before its sacking by the Dutch in 1669, South Sulawesi developed slowly, partly because of a lack of emphasis on education and training of the local population.[18] An important rice- and copra-producing region, South Sulawesi was dominated for over 300 years by either Javanese or Minahasans (from North Sulawesi), until the 1958–1961 *Permesta* rebellion when it threw off North Sulawesi's control. The Dutch regarded South Sulawesi much as they did Aceh, as an area of perennial unrest, even after they pacified it in 1905–1910.[19] The impression of Ujung Pandang as a thriving, bustling city and the influence of the Bugis are diluted by the large size of the provincial population (6,062,000 in 1980, or over half the entire population of the island of Sulawesi).[20] The province of South Sulawesi includes some remote and isolated areas, and the contrast between the city *(kota)* and the hinterland *(hutan,* literally forest or jungle) is striking. But the designation of Ujung Pandang as a major growth center and regional capital for all of eastern Indonesia suggests that South Sulawesi will become more integrated and developed in the years ahead.

It is interesting to notice how much more developed and integrated Aceh seems now than ten years ago. In a comparable study based on early 1970s data, Aceh seemed rather poorly integrated, with low rankings and negative scores on both the interaction and economic dimensions.[21] Now, although it still has negative scores on both major economic factors, it has positive scores on both interaction factors and, in addition, totally dominates the third economic factor, with its highest per-capita economic growth rate and foreign investment rate. It appears that real progress has been made both in developing Aceh's economic resources and in integrating this province, with its peripheral position, its fanatical Muslim character, and its history of continuous rebellion against any outside power, whether Dutch or Javanese, into the national whole.

Fourth, five provinces stand out as least integrated and least economically developed, having generally low rankings on almost all the major factors and ranking among the lowest six on at least three of them. This group includes Bengkulu and Lampung in Sumatra, Southeast Sulawesi, and West and East Nusatenggara. It is the last two provinces, however, that emerge as by far the least integrated and developed in the country: they have negative scores on all six major factors; indeed, East Nusatenggara ranks last on one major factor in each dimension. The two Nusatenggara provinces have the lowest regional gross domestic product per capita in the country by far and the fewest natural resources. In addition, East Nusatenggara is the least urbanized of all the provinces (with only 7.5 percent of its population being classified as urban). Together these two provinces stand out as the most underdeveloped and most neglected of all the provinces of Indonesia.

In addition to the four groups of provinces discussed thus far are two provinces excluded from the statistical analysis: East Timor because of lack of comparable data and Jakarta because of its overwhelming primacy.

East Timor was forcibly annexed by Indonesia in 1976 and, almost inevitably, is still poorly integrated into the national whole. Problems of neglect and lack of development by the former Portuguese colonial power are being attacked by Indonesian government investment in developing the infrastructure and economic base of the province,[22] but East Timor is poor in natural resources and will continue to be a drain on the national economy. As to be expected, residents of East Timor have by far the lowest knowledge of the Indonesian language (33 percent) and the lowest literacy rate (21 percent) of any Indonesian province. East Timor therefore joins West and East Nusatenggara as the least integrated and most underdeveloped of Indonesia's provinces. In addition, continued Timorese resistance to Indonesian control and the fact that a military presence is still required to control the province indicate lack of genuine integration, despite the efforts of the Indonesian government to incorporate East Timor more fully into the country through development and firmer structural linkages.

In contrast to all the other provinces is the Special District of Jakarta (*Daerah Khusus Istimewa*). It is not technically a province, although it functions as a separate administrative unit comparable to a province. As already discussed, Jakarta stands out as unique, with its dominant core characteristics.

As might be expected, no simple spatial pattern of national integration in Indonesia emerges from the analysis. The most highly integrated and developed provinces on a per-capita basis are spatially separated both from one another, and from the national capital of Jakarta. They include provinces in the northern and western parts of the archipelago, and on three of the four larger islands, Sumatra, Kalimantan, and Sulawesi. The provinces that stand out most obviously as a distinct, more homogeneous group, those of Java and Bali, form a compact geographical bloc. The least integrated and least developed provinces of West and East Nusatenggara, Bengkulu, Lampung, and Southeast Sulawesi flank Java and Bali on the west and east. Immediate proximity to the capital city, the true core of the country, seems to have little impact on the level of integration. Provinces closest to Jakarta—Lampung, Bengkulu, and Central and South Kalimantan, as well as West and Central Java—are *not* the most integrated and highly developed. Rather, they form a broken circle of less integrated provinces separating those provinces that are most integrated and developed on a per-capita basis (North and South Sumatra, Riau, East Kalimantan, and North Sulawesi) from the national core of Jakarta. Distance from the core, however, may contribute to the feelings of remoteness and estrangement experienced in Aceh, Irian Jaya, East Nusatenggara, and East Timor.

Indonesia's pattern of integration, therefore, is uneven. It does not show the more regular decline in cohesion with increasing distance from the core that is characteristic of most developing countries. Rather, the level of integration in Indonesia declines at first with distance from the core in the provinces nearest to it, but then peaks in the more developed and prosperous provinces beyond the less integrated group, before declining again toward the remote boundaries of the country. The complexity of this pattern is not surprising, given the size and archipelagic character of Indonesia, with its geographic, demographic, and economic diversity.

This refined understanding of the spatial pattern of national integration in Indonesia has major implications for the country, both for its continued progress in integration as a nation-state and for its direction in economic development.

The weak integrative links of some of the provinces detract from the overall strength of the country and pose a potential threat to the continued unity of the nation-state. This is particularly so when such provinces have peripheral locations and/or greater economic strength than the nation as a whole. Aceh, Irian Jaya, and West Kalimantan are among those that seem most vulnerable in this respect. Similarly, provinces that are poorly developed from an economic perspective weaken the entire country's economy. West and East Nusatenggara and East Timor are obvious examples here.

For some provinces (such as Irian Jaya, East Java, and South Sulawesi) the predominant need is for stronger sociocultural bonds through increased literacy, use of the Indonesian language, and basic education. For others (including West Sumatra and Central Kalimantan) the most important need is to increase spatial linkages or interaction, not only with the capital city but with other provinces as well. Many provinces need increased economic development. Several provinces need in-creased attention in two of the three major dimensions: West Kaliman-tan, Jambi, Bengkulu, and Southeast Sulawesi in both the sociocultural and interaction areas of integration; Lampung and Central Sulawesi in both the interaction and economic spheres; and Bali in both the socio-cultural and economic dimensions. West and East Nusatenggara stand out as urgently requiring development in all three major dimensions.

Indonesia's leaders have long been aware of the challenges of the country's size, complexity, and uneven development and have sought in a variety of ways to weld the country into a more cohesive unit. The next chapter analyzes and attempts to evaluate the various policies that have been followed to meet this goal.

7

Government Response to the Need for National Integration

THE problems of Indonesia's great diversity and uneven development were recognized by Indonesia's leaders long before the country proclaimed its independence in 1945. From the earliest stirrings of nationalism in preindependence days to the present, Indonesia's leaders have sought continually to counteract the potentially divisive threat of the differences existing within the far-flung islands of the archipelago by seeking to bind together the various regions and peoples into a better-functioning and more mutually interdependent whole. Methods and emphases have changed over the years, but the goal has consistently been to promote greater national integration.

In preindependence Indonesia, it was not until the early twentieth century that Indonesians began to develop a national awareness and feeling of national unity. Although nationalism was limited at first to a small group of educated upper-class Indonesians, it gradually spread throughout much of the archipelago, helped by various nationalist organizations such as *Budi Utomo,* the *Muhammadiyah,* and *Perhimpunan Indonesia.* The role of the united youth congresses in 1926 and 1928 in propounding the concept of one people and one country and in gaining acceptance for the idea of one national language, a national flag, and a national anthem has already been discussed (see chapter 2).

Under Sukarno, during the *Orde Lama* days, government policies toward national integration varied. At first, during the revolutionary struggle against the Dutch (1945–1949), there was an emphasis on symbolism and political solutions for the problems caused by the lack of cohesion. In 1950 the political system was changed from a weak federal system to a stronger, more centralized unitary state. Then, between 1950 and 1957, during the period of parliamentary democracy, policies focused more on promoting economic stabilization, internal consolidation, and rational development. Efforts were made to preserve a balance among the different ideas of the various peoples and political parties. However, after 1957 and the imposition of the authoritarian Guided Democracy political system, the government pursued national integration particularly through emotive political and sociocultural policies. Sukarno sought to raise nationalist, patriotic emotions through perpetuating the revolution against Indonesia's perceived enemies of continued imperialism and capitalism.[1] He believed that the cause of national integration was best served by keeping up the revolutionary spirit and momentum, by infusing the whole people with a common national symbolism, by moving civil servants around within the country, by promoting "Indonesian" ways of doing things, and by developing national pride and worldwide recognition through conspicuous foreign policy moves.

But through promoting national cohesion and unity at the emotional level, and in the political and sociocultural dimensions only, Sukarno ignored the reality of people's other deeply felt needs and thus in some ways exacerbated divisions within the country. Some of the dissatisfaction found expression in the twenty-one regional revolts that Indonesia experienced during its first twenty years as an independent nation.[2] Needs not met included those of economic development, improved standards of living, increased infrastructure within, and interaction and trade among, the provinces, and the extension of social benefits to a larger proportion of the population. Valuable resources urgently needed for development were used instead on noneconomic and prestige projects, on elaborate and expensive presidential world tours, and on adventuristic foreign policy ploys, such as the *Konfrontasi* policy against Malaysia.

The New Order government of President Suharto that came to power after the abortive communist coup of 1965 thus inherited a country with a low level of national integration. Since then, national integration, national stability, and economic development have been its major goals. The government has attempted to pay close attention to all the different essential dimensions of national integration and to achieve a better balance among them. Many of the government's efforts to promote national integration have already been mentioned in the chapters dealing with the separate dimensions of integration. The purpose of this chapter is to examine these in more detail and to evaluate them.

Policies Relating to the Sociocultural Dimension

In the sociocultural dimension, the Suharto government has sought to strengthen national identity and national unity by developing a truly national and nationwide culture that both transcends and incorporates regional differences and overcomes the disintegrative threats of modernization.[3]

Major emphasis has been given to the promotion of the Indonesian language, *bahasa Indonesia*.[4] It is the sole official language of government, the medium of instruction beginning no later than the third grade, and the dominant language of radio and television. The government has also actively promoted literacy in Indonesian as a means of integrating the population.

The national education system, which was introduced in 1945, has been carefully crafted to further national cohesion. All schools use centrally produced curricula and textbooks, written in Indonesian, that intentionally promote national pride and patriotism. To foster national unity, the curriculum at all levels includes courses on the *Panca Sila*, Indonesia's basic national philosophy. Indeed, critics have charged that at times instruction on these matters tends toward indoctrination and that the whole educational pattern in fact teaches intellectual conformity, requiring mostly memorization, despite a theoretical commitment to the development of a scientific attitude, a critical ability, and a willingness to solve problems. Similarly, at the higher education level, despite official encouragement for students to engage in creative thinking and national dialogue, the government has taken a sharply repressive attitude toward politically oriented stu lent activism and has attempted to restrict student activities to scholarly societies.[5]

The governments of Indonesia have consistently sought to expand education at all levels throughout the archipelago and to reduce the regionally unequal educational opportunities inherited from Dutch colonial days (when educational facilities were highly concentrated in Java). Universal education is regarded as an end in itself as well as a means to improve living standards and the productivity of people and to unify the nation. Impressive steps have been taken to provide greater opportunities for education, particularly at the primary level, where attendance is now compulsory. Tens of thousands of new schools and classrooms have been built and hundreds of thousands of new teachers trained, with the result that the government now claims that almost every child of elementary school age is enrolled in school.[6] Although the government's estimates are almost certainly overoptimistic,[7] it is clear that both the numbers and the percentages of school-age children in elementary school have increased substantially. This is also true at the secondary level.[8] However, disparities among the regions are still considerable, with much higher proportions of primary-school graduates able to find a place at lower secondary schools in Jakarta than in the Outer Islands (and especially in West Nusatenggara). Wide variations in test scores indicate also that a higher quality of education is available in Jakarta than in eastern Indonesia (where the average test scores in 1980 were 44 percent lower on a test administered nationally to ninth graders).[9]

The geography of higher education is a simple extension of these disparities. Despite the establishment of government universities in the capital city of every province, most of the public universities and almost all private universities are in Java, and the quality of teaching is higher there too.

But recently, major efforts have been made to increase both the availability and quality of higher education. The percentage of nineteen to twenty-four year olds going on for higher education reportedly doubled between 1979–1980 and 1984–1985, from 2.5 percent to 5.1 percent.[10] In 1984 the government established an open university *(Universitas Terbuka),* with an initial enrollment of 66,000 students, in a further attempt to spread higher education into the more inaccessible parts of the archipelago, as well as to make it available to more of the over 400,000 applicants for university (of whom only 70,000 were accepted at the forty-three public universities in 1984).[11] The nationwide radio and television networks are also being used as part of this outreach.

In another attempt to bring equity of access to quality teachers to all regions of the country, especially the less-developed areas, twelve universities in the eastern part of the country have been linked to the agricultural university in Bogor via satellite in the new Indonesian Distance Education Satellite System (Indess).[12] In an earlier overhaul of the universities, policies were adopted to raise standards, improve efficiency, and standardize the subject credit system so that students could transfer credits from one institution to another.[13] The traditional system of university senates electing their own rectors and deans was replaced by direct presidential appointments. Part of the purpose behind many of these reforms has been to integrate as well as to upgrade the national education system.

Official government policy toward the religious diversity within the country has been consciously integrative. Although 88 percent of the population is at least nominally Muslim, the government has tried assiduously to be inclusive rather than exclusive in its public policies. It has done this by stressing *Panca Sila* as the state philosophy, thereby giving equal recognition to all the major religions and attempting to incorporate and unite peoples of very different persuasions and cultures under the first *sila,* which affirms belief in one Supreme Being. *Panca Sila* has been emphasized also as a way of undercutting the strength of Islamic organizations.

Since the overthrow and total discrediting of the Communist party in

1965, the greatest perceived threat to the unity of the country has been from the more fanatical Muslim groups, especially in the light of the recent resurgence of Islam in the Middle East. The government has sought, therefore, to reduce the power and influence of Muslims within the country, and to depoliticize Islam by separating the political aspect of Islam from the religious and social, discouraging the former while claiming to encourage the latter.[14] It has strenuously resisted Muslim pressure for an Islamic state. Government checks on Muslim missionary activity (*dakwah*) have been imposed in an effort to assuage feelings of anxiety among many religiously concerned Protestants, Catholics, Hindus, and Buddhists, who feel threatened by the very visible and much-felt dominance of the Islamic majority.[15] The traditional link between the long school holidays and the annual Islamic fasting month of Ramadan has been cut despite vigorous Muslim opposition. And the government (dominated as it is by Javanese Muslims who practice a syncretic, Javanese spiritualism, based on earlier Hindu-Buddhist beliefs, known as *kebatinan*) has redefined Javanese mysticism as *kepercayaan terhadap Tuhan yang Maha Esa* (belief in One Supreme Being), thus qualifying it for inclusion under the first *sila* of the *Panca Sila*. To practice *kebatinan* is thus officially to uphold the *Panca Sila*.[16] Since 1974 the government has encouraged a series of dialogues at local and national levels among leaders of all five official religions to reduce conflict among them. A Religious Consultative Body of the five official religions has been established to promote social harmony (*kerukunan*) and tolerance both within and among the different religions in this pluralistic society.

Yet the government has also made concessions to the Muslim community. It has restricted the missionary activity of other religious groups (particularly Christian) by requiring that religious propagation be directed only at persons not already professing faith in one of the five official religions. It has subsidized the building of mosques and religious schools and the establishment and operation of Muslim educational as well as social organizations.[17] It has even pursued a deliberate Islamization policy in the provinces of Irian Jaya and East Timor, where the indigenous population is overwhelmingly Christian, by constructing mosques in the centers of all-Christian villages. In response to Muslim criticism, the government has also banned all gambling as mentally and morally destructive to society and contrary to the religious tenets included in the *Panca Sila*.[18]

Politically, Islam has been on the defensive in Indonesia ever since independence. In the wording of the constitution and its preamble, Muslim pressure was rejected when the phrase "with the obligation of Muslims to practice the shariah (Islamic law)" was omitted in the Jakarta Charter. More recently, during the New Order regime, Muslims lost in their bid to revise the marriage laws to require all Muslims, including nominal ones, to be married in Islamic ceremonies. In the simplification of the political party system after the 1971 elections, the New Order government forced several Muslim political parties to merge and become the Development Unity Party *(Partai Persatuan Pembangunan, PPP)*, deliberately rejecting any reference to Islam in the *PPP*'s name.[19] In 1983 the government even went so far as to force this Muslim political party, as well as all other religious, social, and political organizations, to accept the *Panca Sila* as their sole ideological basis. This has been a particularly difficult issue for Islamic groups, whose faith enjoins them to implement their religion in their public as well as their private lives. But in compliance with government demands, Islam is now no longer openly the ideological foundation of the *PPP;* as a result, it has lost some of its attraction as a vehicle for channeling Indonesia's Muslim aspirations.[20]

This move has been seen by some as unnecessarily provocative and divisive, causing a growing cleavage between institutionalized Islam, led largely by well-to-do Muslims in the towns and countryside, and the increasing numbers of more radical Muslims, who regard the *Panca Sila* policy as blatantly anti-Islamic and the regime as fundamentally hostile to Islam. The government has also been criticized for perpetuating the status quo by stressing unity and harmony over social change and mobilization, and for concentrating too much power in the state bureaucracy, thus threatening the autonomy of social organizations and some personal freedoms.[21] Indeed, as Awanohara has expressed it:

> The great stress on *Pancasila* underlines the government's extreme concern for security and stability in a country where national unity is still fragile. However, the irony is that the *Pancasila*-as-the-single-principle policy, which is meant to consolidate national unity by eliminating all conflicts based on ideological differences, because of the way it has been so forcibly pushed, runs the risk of provoking a backlash that could threaten the very unity it has set out to achieve.[22]

Friction has also arisen over the government's banning of the *kerudung* (veil) and *jilbab* (women's headdress) in state-run schools.

Despite government pressure and determination that Islam should be developed and practiced only in the context of Indonesia's national culture (and despite the spread of Christianity in some areas, the government's encouragement of Javanese spiritualism, and the general wave of secularization accompanying economic development), Islam as a religion has been gaining strength. It has permeated the secular schools, government offices, and even the military. Nearly every major building has a prayer hall or prayer room, and mosques have sprung up every-where. At universities mosques have become centers of Islamic activity, organizing both daily prayers and social work. Over 80,000 pilgrims a year make the *hajj,* and more are paying the *zakat* tax for the benefit of the poor.[23] The Islamic revival is reportedly creating groups of religious fundamentalists and political radicals, although these are a small minority; for there has always been considerable diversity within Islam. Not only is there a difference between traditional, nominal *abangan* and devout *santri,* but there is a significant gap between fundamentalists and moderates, between those who believe it is impossible to separate reli-gion from politics or any other aspect of life, and those who support the depoliticization of Islam, believing that a pragmatic differentiation between religion and politics is necessary for Indonesia to cope with the demands of modern times.[24]

The *Panca Sila,* as the basic, integrative national philosophy, has been promoted increasingly in a variety of different government strategies and policies. The government has established an institute to interpret and teach *Panca Sila.* In 1978 it began a series of courses for all Indone-sian citizens, beginning with civil servants, known as the *P-4* courses (a contraction of the Indonesian term *Pedoman Penghayatan dan Pengamalan Panca Sila,* meaning a Guide to the Comprehension and Practice of *Panca Sila*). Under this program, approved by the People's Consultative Assembly *(MPR),* up to two million civil servants (including all below the rank of cabinet minister) have been required to attend two-week upgrading courses, organized throughout the archipelago, whose pur-pose has been solely to examine and understand *Panca Sila* within the framework of the New Order. As an official in the program expressed it, "the purpose of the program is to unite the nation behind a sound ideol-ogy that all will enthusiastically embrace."[25] The courses have since been extended to the universities and high schools, to religious leaders, and to other groups.

In the *P-4* courses, *Panca Sila* has been explained as a traditional phi-losophy of life, the articulation of the historical experience of the Indo-nesian people, and something already existing within the people rather than imposed upon them from outside (in a deliberate attempt to disso-ciate the *P-4* courses from the *indoktrinasi* that took place under Sukarno during the Guided Democracy period). It has emphasized the unity and cohesion of society rather than new directions or changes in the social order (and as such has been criticized for being an extraordinarily static ideology, long on rhetoric and sentiment but short on specific prescrip-tions).[26]

Inevitably, the costs associated with the implementation of the *P-4* courses have been considerable, both directly in providing the facilities and instructors for the large numbers required to attend and indirectly in the vast amount of time lost from carrying out regular government, teaching, or other business. Yet the fact that these costs are considered worthwhile demonstrates the seriousness with which the New Order government sees *P-4* as providing an important justification for its policies and its ongoing emphasis on national unity.[27]

Besides language, education, religion, and philosophy of state, the Indonesian government has pursued integrative policies in other sociocultural fields as well. Yet its policy toward the Chinese minority (which numbers about 3.8 million out of a total of 165 million, about 2.3 percent of Indonesia's population) has been somewhat ambiguous. On the one hand the government has brought pressure to bear on the Chinese to become Indonesian citizens, change their names, and be assimilated. It has liberalized the nationalization law and reduced the waiting time for citizenship. In 1979, to "help develop Indonesian culture and nurture unity among the people,"[28] the government banned the import, sale, and distribution of any literature printed in Chinese characters, although it has been suggested that the real goal of the decree was for all Chinese Indonesians to lose their command of the Chinese language.[29] The government has also tried to protect Chinese enterprises, businesses, and people when anti-Chinese riots have broken out, as they have periodically.

However, on the other hand, the Chinese continue to face both official and unofficial discrimination. In 1979 the ethnic Chinese were required to be registered again and later were issued identity cards marked by a special code to distinguish them from *pribumi* (indigenous Indonesians).[30] A presidential decree *(Keppres 14A/1980)* provided for preferential treatment for economically weak *pribumi* firms and local businesses in the selection of contractors for certain government projects,[31] and a number of additional stipulations were aimed at providing the "economically weak groups" with more facilities to enable them to compete with the "economically strong group" (i.e., the Chinese). Even though Suharto argued that this policy of upgrading the economically weak groups was not a form of racial discrimination but was intended to achieve "equity in distribution,"[32] it is dubious how many Chinese saw it as such. As Arndt has put it:

> The problem in Indonesia has been how to strengthen the weaker economic groups of *pribumis* vis-à-vis the Chinese with their superior business skills and resources, and how meanwhile to retain the indispensable contribution of the Chinese to the nation's commercial life while preventing communal tensions from erupting into open friction.[33]

With ambivalent government support, the Chinese continue to be hated and resented, particularly by young, under- or unemployed *pri-*

bumi. The Javanese have long held the view that the Chinese are cultur-ally and economically arrogant. Most Indonesians feel especially bitter toward the Chinese businessmen who finance and manage the business concerns of the *pribumi* government and military officials and amass unacceptably great wealth to the detriment of the ordinary citizens of the country. The close ties between the presidential family and the wealthy Chinese tycoon, Liem Sioe Liong, are deeply resented.

In other policies relating to the sociocultural dimension of integra-tion, the government has encouraged a variety of organizations and programs to spread nationwide, transcending regional and provincial boundaries. These include scouts, agricultural cooperatives, and village social associations. Major efforts have been made to expand both the availability and quality of health care by increasing immunizations, building new community health centers and subcenters, increasing the number of health professionals including both doctors and paramedics, expanding the family planning program, and so on. In the arts, the gov-ernment has encouraged local artistic expression through the establish-ment of increasing numbers of art centers and traditional arts groups and the documentation of regional intellectual and ceremonial tradi-tions. The goal has been to create a new and vibrant Indonesian cul-ture, incorporating diverse local, traditional elements while nurturing regional cultures and upholding regional traditions. Policies have also been established to guide the national culture to cope with the "influ-ence of negative foreign culture" while absorbing those positive alien values that are needed for development.[34] The government has even set up an Institute for the Advancement of National Unity *(Badan Pembina Kesatuan Bangsa).*

Thus despite the difficulties, problems, and continued shortcomings, much has been accomplished in the sociocultural dimension of national integration in welding the very diverse and geographically scattered peoples of the archipelago into one nation, and in giving them the sense of a shared historical heritage and national pride, a feeling of participa-tion in one national culture, and a common Indonesian identity.

Policies Relating to the Interaction Dimension

Great efforts have been made, particularly since 1967, to improve the transportation network and communications systems in an attempt to integrate the country more effectively. The results have been spectacu-lar. As discussed in chapter 4, independent Indonesia inherited an uneven and inadequate infrastructure from the Dutch, one geared more to the needs of a colonial regime than to those of a new nation-state.

Even the limited infrastructure that existed was badly neglected in the early years of independence, because of the Sukarno government's primary concern with symbolism and political integration rather than with economic development. It was not until 1967 that attention seriously began to be paid to the need to improve the transportation and communications systems.

In the light of this history, the New Order government has made impressive strides in improving and integrating the country's transportation system. Thousands of kilometers of Indonesia's roads have been rehabilitated and upgraded, and the road network has been substantially expanded. A number of World Bank loans and loans from the United States, Australia, and the Asian Development Bank have helped in the construction of the trans-Sumatra highway, the trans-Sulawesi highway, road projects in Kalimantan, and the beginning of a new trans-Irian highway parallel to the Irian Jaya–Papua New Guinea border. Several new toll roads have been built and major highways in Java improved and repaired. Many bridges have been replaced and there has been a steady upgrading of rural and rural-to-urban roads. City roads with heavy traffic are continually being upgraded and new bypasses constructed, and ferry crossings have been made more frequent and efficient. The intention has been to improve transportation while reducing costs and to promote economic activity, as well as to improve the integration of areas thus linked together.

Some of the success of the improved road-building program can be seen in the large increase in the number of vehicles in the country. The number of buses increased from 20,000 to 160,000 in the 1969–1983 period (an average annual growth rate of 16 percent), while passenger vehicles increased at an 11 percent average annual rate, from 212,000 to 870,000, during the same period.[35] Particularly important, too, has been the great increase in the number of minibuses, pickups, and small trucks plying short-distance local routes, integrating villages, towns, and cities. Indeed, a virtual revolution seems to have occurred, at least in Java. For whereas fifteen years ago there was still some substance in the stereotype of villagers who had never visited their neighboring town, now in many villages most people under forty have spent at least some time working in the city and have brought back with them a much more dynamic outlook to the village when they returned.[36] The psychological distance between village and city has been shortened dramatically. The improved and better-integrated transportation system (and particularly the quick, cheap, and frequent bus service between cities) has led to greater labor mobility, with the result that workers now move much more freely and spontaneously from low- to high-wage employment; so much is this true that there were signs in rural Java of an emerging labor shortage in early 1982 (despite a population of over ninety million in an area approximately the size of New York State) as villagers moved to obtain higher-paying construction and other work in cities both in Java and in the Outer Islands. And this increase in labor mobility is not restricted to Java, but is apparent throughout the entire archipelago, extending even as far as Irian Jaya.[37]

Railroad transportation also has been improved and modernized. One of the goals of the fourth Five-Year Development Plan *(Repelita IV)* is to make rail travel inexpensive, fast, and safe by improving management, rehabilitating and reconstructing railroad tracks and bridges, and adding and rehabilitating passenger coaches, freight cars, and locomotives. Plans to upgrade and extend the rail network beyond the existing 6,700 kilometers of rail track began to be carried out in 1981.[38]

Lake and river transportation has also been given attention as an integral part of the surface transport network. Attempts have been made to expand facilities and make them more efficient.

Improved transportation has also been achieved at sea. Major efforts have been made to modernize, expand, and improve the efficiency and capabilities of the interisland and local fleets, as well as to improve ferry crossings and shipyard, dock, and port facilities.[39] The capacities of both the national interisland merchant fleet and the local fleet increased by an average of 7 percent a year between 1969 and 1982, while tonnage increased by 20 percent annually on ocean vessels and 6 percent on local over the same time period.[40] Passenger traffic likewise has risen enormously. Recent government efforts have focused on increasing efficiency and productivity at the ports by reducing overregulation and corruption, by simplifying administrative procedures, by rationalizing harbor handling and anchorage fees, and by reforming the corruption-ridden customs system.[41] An *Inpres (Instruksi Presiden)* Decree of April 1985 abolished the protection previously received by domestic ocean shipping companies by opening up a large number of ports to foreign vessels.[42]

Yet despite all the attention devoted by the government to interisland shipping, its performance still falls well below that of the early 1950s, when the Dutch-owned *Koninklijke Paketvaart Maatschappij* maintained very efficiently a comprehensive network of services that was closely integrated through transshipment with the deep-sea lines.[43] Indeed, Dick argues that the improvements in interisland shipping have come about in spite of, rather than because of, government policies. He claims that it has been competition leading to better organization in the use of space and in traffic flow rather than physical upgrading that has led to improved shipping, and that government regulations have tended not to promote but to retard this process (as, for example, the compulsory scrapping of ships more than twenty-five years old and the restrictions on importing new and secondhand ships).[44] The regulatory system has tended also to discourage the more efficient firms from expanding, while helping the least efficient to stay in business. However, as Dick acknowledges, this is not entirely the fault of the government, as the Shipowners' Association has consistently lobbied for the "rights" of the weak (generally *pribumi* companies) while giving no support to the further expansion of the strong (often non-*pribumi* companies).[45]

The fourth Five-Year Development Plan proposes improvements for four gateway ports (Jakarta, Surabaya, Ujung Pandang, and Belawan) to replace transshipment via Singapore, fourteen collector ports, and twenty-five distributor ports. Port facilities are to be rehabilitated through the construction of new berths and storage facilities, the procurement of equipment for cargo handling and storage, dredging of the harbors, and dockyard rehabilitation.[46] The plan aims at increasing the total capacity of vessels in the interisland and local shipping fleets, the traditional sailing fleets, and the vessels serving remote communities and outlying islands.

The government continues to support and subsidize pioneer transport services to serve areas that are not attractive to commercial carriers. The pioneer fleet, which was designed to assist farmers on isolated islands in marketing their produce and in buying essential goods, serves about 175 small ports.[47]

There has also been an impressive expansion of air traffic, particularly over the past eighteen years. Beginning with a broken-down fleet of thirty-five aircraft in 1968, the major government airline, Garuda, has more than doubled and substantially upgraded the number and size of its aircraft,[48] and other internal airlines have expanded as well. New airports have been constructed and older airports and airstrips improved. Passenger and freight volume on domestic routes has increased at annual average rates of 20 and 23 percent, respectively, between 1969 and 1982.[49] Pioneer routes to outlying regions that offer very few passengers are subsidized by the government in the interests of national integration.

An enormous investment in the interisland communications network has been made by a government very conscious of the vital role of mass communications in integrating a nation of such great diversity and widespread geographical distribution. Perhaps most important has been the domestic satellite communications system, *Palapa*, first launched in 1976 and now in its second generation of satellites (the *Palapa B* satellites). This has revolutionized Indonesia's telex, radio, television, and facsimile- and data-transmission services. Among other advantages, the system permits direct telephone dialing to any major city in Indonesia and has made telephone communication with isolated areas possible also. A multichannel microwave system supplements the domestic satellite communications system with its forty earth stations. Long-distance domestic telephone calls increased at an annual rate of 6 percent between 1969 and 1983, while local telephone calls increased at an astonishing 33 percent annual rate.[50] During *Repelita III*, 232,000 automatic telephone lines were added to the system, and the number of telephone lines available to business and residential users is expected to double during *Repelita IV* as the state-owned telephone utility, *Perumtel*, installs some 750,000 additional lines. Modern digital switching exchanges, over 16,000 additional telex lines, and 100 small earth-satellite communication stations are also planned for the 1984–1989 five-year development period.[51] Domestic telexes increased at a 35 percent annual rate between 1969 and 1983.

It has been especially through the expansion of television, however, that the government has sought to promote national unity; an understanding and appreciation of Indonesia's diverse cultures; and pride in its national cultural, economic, and athletic achievements. It has worked to develop a truly national culture, to integrate the entire archipelago, and to inspire and encourage national development. The geographical area covered by television broadcasting more than quintupled between 1975 and 1984, reaching an estimated audience of ninety-six million people in 1984 (up from forty million in 1975).[52] In addition, the number of television sets increased from 410,000 in 1975 to 5,343,000 in 1984, while the number of transmission stations grew from twenty-three to 200 during the same time period. Thirty-eight thousand public television sets have been placed in villages in an attempt to achieve greater evenness in information distribution.[53]

Radio broadcasting by *Radio Republik Indonesia* has likewise been extended both geographically, with the increase in the number of radio transmitters, and in the number of broadcast hours per day. One recent development has been the great increase in the use of ham radios (by an estimated one million amateur radio operators). In some provinces (such as Bali), the number of transmitters is thought easily to exceed the number of telephone lines.[54] The potential of radio broadcasting for increasing national integration and its effect on the national identity could be enormous.

The value of the satellite communications system in integrating the country was demonstrated convincingly during the 1982 elections, when television coverage from all over the archipelago was able to "drive home to many Indonesians that they had just participated in a great national undertaking." It also enabled the votes to be counted more quickly than in past elections.[55]

Postal services have been expanded to cover all of Indonesia's regions, including remote villages and new transmigration settlements. Eight hundred new post offices are planned to be established during *Repelita IV,* enabling 58,028 of the country's 65,000 villages to benefit from regular postal service.

Thus, great progress has been and is being made to integrate the country in terms of improved transportation and communications systems.

Policies Relating to the Economic Dimension

It is probably in the economic field, however, that the greatest threats to national integration occur. For it is the gap between the rich and the poor, the problems of unemployment and underemployment particularly in the cities, the contrast between cities and rural areas, and the unequal standards of living and inequality of opportunity among provinces that provoke the greatest dissatisfaction and unrest. Even the ethnic problem between the Chinese and *pribumi* Indonesians is largely an economic one.

Economic disparities among the provinces exist partly because of the uneven spatial distribution of the resource base, but partly too because of very uneven treatment by the government both during the colonial era and in the early years of independence. By the beginning of the Suharto era in the late 1960s, therefore, there were already strong regional inequalities and contrasts among the provinces, as already demonstrated in the previous two chapters. Only then did attention seriously begin to be paid to national economic planning and development. Indeed, it has been one of the major premises of the Suharto government that economic development and growing prosperity promote national integration and blunt friction among the different ethnic groups within the country.[56]

Even though the Suharto government recognized these regional disparities as being important, the first Five-Year Development Plan (1969–1974) focused upon the reestablishment of political and economic stability.[57] It emphasized economic growth, rather than equality, to secure the main needs of society and to reestablish the country's economic credibility. An impressive 8.4 percent annual growth rate during *Repelita I* was indeed attained, but the Plan's stress was upon strictly sectoral planning.[58] Consequently, the greatest growth occurred in those provinces already well endowed with infrastructure or already experiencing growth. In addition, economic protection given to the modern sector, to medium- and large-scale enterprises, resulted not in

phasing out the dual structure of the economy, but instead in reinforcing the dichotomy between urban and rural labor markets. It also
created a new dualism between the formal and informal sectors, particularly in urban areas.[59] The cost of economic growth during the first
Five-Year Development Plan was, therefore, a further increase in the
economic disparities among both peoples and regions.

Part of the purpose of *Repelita II* (1974–1979),[60] therefore, was to confront the unequal rates of development between rich and poor provinces, and to "raise the living standards of the whole people."[61] This
plan sought to widen opportunities for employment and achieve a more
equitable distribution of income.[62] It emphasized regional development
and set out to achieve a balance between regional and sectoral growth
by including regional targets in the planning activities of each of the
central government's sectoral ministries. It contained goals in five basic
areas: (1) to reap the highest possible benefits from the potentials of the
different regions, both from the national development point of view and
from that of the individual region; (2) to harmonize the rate of growth
among the provinces and to improve conditions in the poorest provinces
by allocating at least a proportion of all development activity to them;
(3) to help provincial governments solve their large-scale provincial
problems; (4) to encourage regional development through the establishment of provincial planning boards *(Badan Perencanaan Pembangunan
Daerah [Bappeda])*; and (5) to integrate the Indonesian economy into one
economic unit.[63]

To achieve these goals, the country was divided into a hierarchy of
development regions, each with its prospective growth centers: four
major regional metropolises, ten regional development centers, and
eighty-eight smaller subcenters (see Figure 7.1).[64]

Theoretically, attention has been given all along to the goal of economic equity, from the earliest days of Indonesia's independence. The
fifth *sila* of the *Panca Sila* speaks of social justice for all the people of
Indonesia. It was not until the third Five-Year Development Plan
(1979–1984), however, that equity was placed first in the trilogy of
Indonesia's interrelated development goals: equity or spreading the
benefits of development *(pemerataan)*, a reasonably high economic
growth rate, and healthy and dynamic national stability.[65] Major
emphasis was placed on attaining greater equality in eight areas of
socioeconomic development: meeting basic needs; providing more
equal opportunities in obtaining education and health care; obtaining
more equal distribution of income, with special attention to the lowest
income groups; the creation of more employment opportunities with
high priority on employment-generating and labor-intensive projects;
more equality in business opportunities, especially for the economically

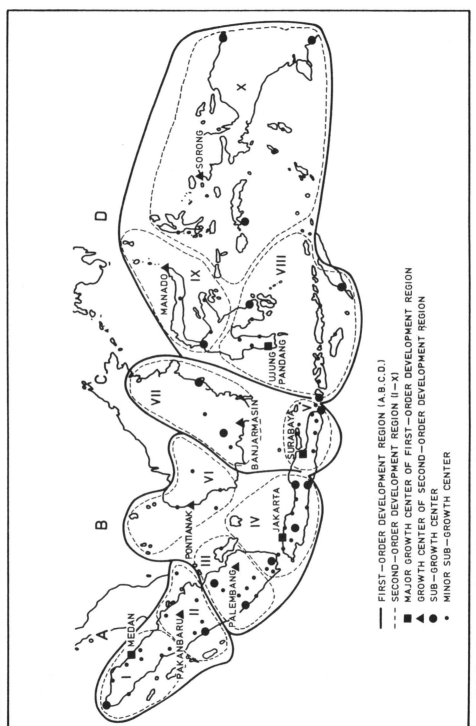

FIRST−ORDER DEVELOPMENT REGION (A.B.C.D.)
SECOND−ORDER DEVELOPMENT REGION (I−X)
■ MAJOR GROWTH CENTER OF FIRST−ORDER DEVELOPMENT REGION
▲ GROWTH CENTER OF FIRST−ORDER DEVELOPMENT REGION
● SUB−GROWTH CENTER OF SECOND−ORDER DEVELOPMENT REGION
● SUB−GROWTH CENTER
• MINOR SUB−GROWTH CENTER

Figure 7.1. Development regions and growth centers in Indonesia.

weak groups; more equal opportunities to participate in the development process, especially for youth and women; more equitable distribution of development activities throughout all the regions of Indonesia;
and more equal opportunity of obtaining justice before the law.[66]

The government's commitment to greater equity in economic development has been constantly reiterated in official pronouncements. In
his 1981 Independence Day speech, President Suharto stressed the New
Order's determination to "enhance the material and spiritual wellbeing
through efforts that give priority to the equitable distribution of development gains leading towards the creation of social justice."[67] The
Broad Outlines of State Policy *(Garis-garis Besar Haluan Negara)* adopted
by the People's Consultative Assembly *(MPR)* in 1983 directed that the
overriding goal of the fourth Five-Year Development Plan (1984–1989)
should be to raise the standards of living, intellectual abilities, and general welfare of *all* the people. They also stated that *Repelita IV* should
create an environment that provides every incentive and opportunity
for all to participate and perform fully and harmoniously in the national
development effort; that more emphasis should be given to equity in the
development trilogy, while at the same time ensuring that the three elements of equity, economic growth, and national stability are in constant
harmony and mutually reinforcing.[68] At the fortieth anniversary celebrations of Indonesia's independence in 1985, President Suharto again
confirmed his commitment to distributional equity and recommended
boosting the development of outlying regions, spreading around infrastructural development projects, and stepping up transmigration. As
one critic put it, the government's growing preoccupation with the
problem of equity stems from an awareness that staying within the limits of tolerable inequities is a condition for maintaining the momentum
of development as well as for staying in power.[69]

Various strategies have been tried to fulfill government promises of
greater equity in the fruits of development and thus help the poor
achieve some benefits from the economic growth of the country. In the
1970s huge government subsidies on food and fuel were established,
and regulations were implemented to control the prices of nine essential
commodities *(bahan pokok,* including rice, sugar, salt, kerosene, and fertilizer).

Policies have been formulated to try to synchronize the pace of development in the regions. The relatively less-developed regions have been
encouraged to achieve higher rates of growth in conformity with their
potentialities, while equity has been promoted within each region itself
by having both central and regional governments give special attention
to isolated, less fertile, and other problem areas. Efforts have been
made to develop greater transportation and communications links

between these least-developed regions and other, more prosperous areas. Increased central government grants to the regions through the *Inpres (Instruksi Presiden)* program have been used for the development of infrastructure and the provision of drinking water, health facilities, elementary schools, irrigation, credit schemes to aid rural hawkers and others in the rural population, and other social services. There has been an emphasis on job-creating public works programs and labor-intensive enterprises in both rural and urban areas. The government is committed to a further expansion in public spending, which is expected to lead to an increase in the demand for consumer goods and in spending on labor-intensive programs. This in turn should "directly improve the position of those sectors of the population whose increases in income have lagged behind the average in recent years and whose standards of living have remained very low."[70]

But there is also recognition among government policy-makers that economic equity has to be balanced with economic growth, especially in a country with a fast-growing population and in an era of rising expectations. In overall terms, Indonesia has experienced an impressive rate of growth. Between 1969 and 1980 the economy grew at an average rate of 7.4 percent. (Population grew during the same period at a rate of 2.3 percent, leaving an actual annual increase in the gross domestic product of 5.1 percent.)[71] These solid gains resulted mainly from increased OPEC oil prices and increased liquified natural gas sales, but manufacturing production also rose impressively during the 1970s, at an average rate of 12.3 percent.[72] Major efforts to boost rice production have met with enormous success: Indonesia went from being the world's largest importer of rice in 1975 to self-sufficiency by 1985.[73] New technologies in many sectors of the economy have raised productivity, as have economies of scale (realized when larger factories produce more items at a lower unit cost).[74] Electricity production increased at an average annual rate of 17 percent between 1973 and 1984 (from 2,494 million to 13,296 million kilowatt-hours).[75] However, economic growth slowed in the early 1980s to less than 5 percent per annum, thanks to the world recession, persistent high interest rates, growing worldwide protectionism, drought in the countryside, and the falling price of petroleum (which still made up about 70 percent of Indonesia's export earnings at the beginning of 1985).[76]

Manufacturing industry has been strongly encouraged by a government that wants to lessen its dependence upon oil and gas exports; indeed, government policies have met with considerable success. Manufactured goods have increased from a tiny 2 percent of all exports at the beginning of the 1970s to an impressive 17 percent in 1984.[77]

However, it has been in the more capital-intensive rather than in the labor-intensive industries that most growth has taken place, even though it is the small-scale and household or cottage industries that account for about 80 percent of the total manufacturing employment.[78] Yet it is this very duality that poses a dilemma for policy makers. Should effort and resources be directed to labor-intensive, small-scale, and cottage industries to increase employment and reduce poverty, or should they be concentrated on medium and large firms in the modern sector where labor productivity is much higher, to promote greater economic growth? Unemployment and underemployment affected approximately 26 percent of the formal labor force in 1984.[79]

Since 1969 there have been interesting changes in the government's objectives for industrial development. *Repelita I* emphasized industries ancillary to agriculture; *Repelita II* emphasized social objectives, particularly employment and the protection of *pribumi* entrepreneurs. Broad-based industrial development based on domestic oil, mineral, timber, and other natural resources, and labor-intensive manufactures for export were the focus of *Repelita III;* in the current plan, *Repelita IV,* manufacturing is to take the place of the oil sector as the main focus of growth, to provide a stronger and more diversified base for economic development. The plan aims at further expanding import substitution, increasing net foreign exchange earnings, and providing a substantial number of jobs for the estimated 9.3 million workers who are expected to enter the labor force over the next five years.[80] The goal is to promote machinery, machine-tool, and export industries, especially those that process raw materials into intermediate products with higher value added. This, it is argued, would also help to correct the regional imbalance of manufacturing industries, as most of the raw materials are found in the Outer Islands (and so far most of the manufacturing industries are in Java). Several resource-based growth centers are thus expected to emerge in the Outer Islands, based on oil and gas, wood, fertilizer, and aluminum-smelting industries in North Sumatra; oil and gas, coal, tin, forest, plantation products, petrochemicals, steel, and cement industries in South Sumatra; oil and gas, petrochemicals, and forest-based industries in East Kalimantan; and iron, nickel, paper, cement, and shipping industries in South Sulawesi.[81] *Repelita IV* also recognizes the need for better integration of small, medium, and large industries, so that development of medium and large industries will directly accelerate the development of small ones. In addition, it should assist small-scale industry in the Outer Islands to overcome problems such as low productivity, intermittent employment, inadequate financing, limited marketing, poor quality control, and other management problems.[82]

The recent rapid growth in manufactured exports illustrates the government's policy of export substitution in the plywood and crumb-rubber industries (even though the net economic benefits of this policy of regulated industrialization are small).[83] This, as expected, has decreased exports of unprocessed timber and rubber.

New technologies have flooded into many sectors of the Indonesian economy, raising productivity: Green-Revolution technology, with its emphasis on improved hybrid seeds and use of chemical fertilizers, pesticides, and irrigation, has affected rice cultivation especially. Improved transportation and communications services, the increased availability of electric power, improvements in management and the numbers of skilled people, and increased economies of scale have been other important components.[84]

But the government has not been concerned just with economic growth. Rural development has been a major objective since the beginning of the third Five-Year Development Plan. It emphasized community participation in planning and implementing rural development programs, and better village administration and coordination of development activities. An ambitious ten-year program to increase the plantation sector's level of earnings has focused on small-holder plantation development, in keeping with the government's priority of seeking a wider geographical dispersion of development and a more equitable distribution of income.[85] The government has shifted to a far greater reliance on incentives, extension, and local participation in the area of rice production than in the past.[86] Some squatter farmers and shifting cultivators have been given title to land and helped to produce export crops through the Nucleus Estate Program, begun in 1977. Cooperatives have been strongly encouraged, not only to distribute fertilizer and rice, but to deal with all basic needs, including other small-holder crops, kerosene, handicrafts, fisheries, shipping, and transport.[87] Electricity facilities have been extended to rural areas to upgrade rural business enterprises and small-scale industries, agriculture, and education.[88]

Urban development has focused on specific growth centers; small and medium-sized cities have been encouraged rather than the growth of large cities. Indeed, *Repelita IV* aims at accelerating the development of industrial growth centers and industrial zones, and at establishing centers for small industries throughout the country to facilitate the growth of small-scale manufacturing. Meanwhile a "Neighborhood Improvement Program" has been directed at improving the quality of life of lower-income groups in urban areas through the construction of low-cost housing and the provision of social services such as safe water supplies and health and educational services.[89] Investment outside Java has been particularly encouraged through a mixture of incentive and disincentive measures as another means of evening out development.

Decentralization of the development budget has been one of the government's most important tools in its new policy emphasis on equity. The *Inpres Kabupaten* scheme, inaugurated in 1970, and the provision of earmarked grants to the provinces first began this trend of channeling development expenditures through local governments rather than through central government departments. By the early 1980s there were eight *Inpres* programs in operation: grants to provinces, *kabupaten* (districts), and villages; grants for the construction of primary school buildings, for health infrastructure, particularly clinics; for road rehabilitation; and for reafforestation/regreening.[90] Grants to the provinces in 1981–1982 ranged from Rp ten billion each for provinces in Java to Rp 7.5 billion each for provinces outside Java. *Kabupaten* development grants for construction of infrastructure were based on population size; plans had to be approved first by the provincial government, then by *Bappenas* (the National Development Planning Agency). But the use of the subsidies to the villages (Rp one million per village, of which at least Rp 200,000 were designated for women's activities) had to be approved only by *kabupaten* officials and not by any higher authorities. The result has been that more projects have been accomplished more quickly, and regional government officials have gained in both experience and skill.

Inpres grant procedures thus take account both of high population densities through per-capita grants and of low density and poor infrastructure through proportionately larger increases in provincial grants to provinces outside Java.[91] Regional officials now administer ten times as much revenue as they did ten years ago. And, in an attempt to overcome the lack of technical skills at regional levels, detailed specifications, especially for buildings, have been provided by the central government.[92] Greater local participation in government contracts, in contrast to previous heavy reliance on large national contractors, has resulted from a series of regulations issued in 1979 as presidential decrees *(Keputusan Presiden* or *Keppres). Repelita IV* promises a continuation of the *Inpres* funds to be made available directly to provincial, district, and village authorities, thereby allowing these bodies to continue to exercise local judgment on development planning. It also calls for better coordination among the disparate projects in the region and among government agencies and argues for the strengthening of the regional development planning bodies *(Bappeda)*.

Other evidence of the government's commitment to *pemerataan* includes the establishment of a Directorate for Regional Development. This Directorate has undertaken programs in about half of Indonesia's provinces to reach the rural poor through credit, employment, industrial, and other activities; to develop greater capability in planning and executing programs at the provincial and *kabupaten* level; and to increase the capability of central government agencies to support the development of local government.[93] These programs concentrate on more densely populated *kecamatan* (subdistricts) and can be directed toward any of a number of projects such as production, employment, infrastructure, or welfare. Direct grants have been made to the poor, and technical assistance and training programs have been funded for provincial *kabupaten* and *kecamatan* planning units.[94]

Recent experiments to enhance equity and encourage local initiative through wide-ranging pilot projects have been undertaken through the Provincial Area Development Program (PDP). This program has focused on aiding underdeveloped districts and on assisting low-income people directly through numerous small projects rather than concentrating investments on strategic growth poles and hoping that the benefits will trickle down to the masses. The PDP is seen as an important way to increase participation in development and bottom-up planning.[95]

Government-financed credit programs have been made increasingly available for small businessmen, craftsmen, and traders through the *Bank Rakyat Indonesia,* and at the provincial level through regional development banks. At the *kecamatan* level, loans through the *Badan Kredit Kecamatan (BKK,* the subdistrict credit board) have been particularly effective in channeling assistance to poor rural households.[96]

The government's transmigration (resettlement) program has been expanded to a multi-objective program from its original purpose of moving people from overcrowded areas of Java and Bali to the Outer Islands to achieve a more even distribution of population in the country. It is also intended to provide manpower for the labor-scarce areas outside Java, Bali, and Lombok, so that they can develop as centers of growth, particularly for agricultural production. It is hoped that this will both attract the spontaneous migration of landless peoples, thus improving their living conditions,[97] and increase regional development. Transmigration is designed also to be "a vehicle to promote national stability and integration."[98] However, as discussed earlier, it is also perceived as an attempt to extend central government control over, and achieve Javanization of, parts of the Outer Islands.[99]

At least in theory, therefore, the government is committed to a trilogy of development goals that are regarded as mutually reinforcing and interdependent: equity (or the evening out of inequalities, *pemerataan*), economic growth, and national stability.[100] However, although the economic planners insist that such goals are harmonious, critics have argued that the evidence suggests otherwise. Encouraging growth through greater efficiency at Indonesia's ports, for example, has led to more streamlined operations and increased containerization; yet the

costs and fruit of this have been distributed very unevenly. One underlying cause of the riots in Tanjung Priok, Jakarta's port, in 1984 was the
poverty and increasing suffering of dock workers negatively affected by
these changes. Increased use of new hybrid, high-yielding varieties of
rice has led to the greater use of scythes in harvesting. But such harvesting needs fewer laborers (men) and thus eliminates a traditional source
of women's income (harvesting with the traditional single-bladed knife,
the *ani-ani*).[101] Meanwhile, stability has been purchased by increased
centralization of authority and repression rather than by greater participation and by seeking consensus on how to overcome the tensions
created by growth and uneven development. The greater central government presence within the rural sector has led to the decline of village
self-government and traditional patterns of reciprocity and to the
advancement of the more privileged local classes within rural society,
with their greater access to government resources and their ability to
control them. Sociopolitical stratification has undermined the goals, for
example, of agricultural cooperatives and rural banks, for these have
become dominated by local elites, who have prevented many small
farmer and lower-income households from gaining access to the various
benefits and services that these institutions were designed to provide,
such as agricultural credit, fertilizer, extension information, and marketing services. Without basic structural reform at the village level to
allow greater access to land and other productive resources, it is dubious how much real development and equity can be attained.[102]

But overall, national economic growth and relative political stability
have led to a general improvement in living standards throughout the
country. According to a July 1980 public-opinion poll conducted by the
respected Indonesian newsweekly *Tempo,* a considerable majority of the
population felt substantially better off than they did ten to fifteen years
earlier.[103] Certainly, the government assessment of the general level of
popular welfare is favorable. In his Independence Day speech in August
1985, President Suharto stressed that the "various basic necessities for
people, such as food, clothing, public housing, education, and health
facilities, are increasingly better and more evenly distributed."[104] And
improvements in transportation and communications and in the variety
and availability of goods even at the village level are striking to any
returning visitor.

Yet critics have also been quick to point out that there is a wide gap
between the impressive plans and theories of economic development
espoused by the government and the implementation of these policies;
and that although *pemerataan* is much talked about, uneven development
has continued and even been promoted by government policies, leading
to growing interregional disparities and an increasing gap between rich

and poor. Paauw claims that much of the income generated by the upsurge in export earnings from extractive products (particularly petroleum and natural gas) has been narrowly distributed within the capital-intensive sector, with a large share accruing to the government and to individuals associated with large-scale government enterprise. Employment opportunities have not kept up with the growth of the labor force, so that increasing numbers are being forced into low-income agriculture and underemployment or unemployment in the urban sector. He suggests that the distribution of income, productive assets, and wealth have thus become more unequal during the past decade of Indonesia's planned growth.[105] MacDougall charges that economic progress has failed to improve living standards among the bottom 30 percent of citizens and has not dealt with the grave problems of unemployment; underemployment in low-paying, low-productivity jobs; severe disparities of income; and corruption.[106] White found that inequality had increased significantly in his village-level studies of employment and income in some of the poorer communities of rural Java;[107] and Hughes and Islam conclude that although there has probably been an overall decline in rural inequality in Java, there has been an increase in rural inequality in the Outer Islands because of the general decline there in rural expenditure levels relative to the national level.[108] They also found that urban inequality had risen very sharply in Java and that there had been a large increase in urban-rural income disparity in Java as well.[109] In general, therefore, it appears that although the proportion of the population in poverty has dropped significantly, from 57 percent of the population in 1970 to about 40 percent in 1980, absolute numbers of poor people have remained fairly stable over the past decade.[110]

The plight of the poor thus remains very serious. A World Bank Report in 1980 noted that "a significant portion of Indonesia's population remains among the poorest in the world," and that the development process has not really had a favorable impact on the welfare of rural poverty groups.[111] In 1976 the per-capita consumption of more than fifty million Indonesians was less then $90 per annum; life expectancy at birth was a low forty-eight years, and 600,000 infants died each year below the age of one. Illiteracy rates were high, and over 100 million people had no access to safe drinking water. Nearly half the population received less than 85 percent of the recommended daily allowance of calories.[112] Since then, the rupiah has been devalued three times: in 1978 by 33 percent, in 1983 by 28 percent, and in 1986 by a further 31 percent.[113] The subsequent rise in prices has hurt particularly those at the bottom. Increased consciousness of their poverty and of the lifestyles of the wealthy has serious implications: a public-opinion poll in July 1981 showed that more than 50 percent of those questioned consid-

ered the greatest danger to national unity to be social disturbances
between rich and poor.[114] The World Bank's 1984 restricted report
states that the still very high magnitude of poverty constitutes the major
challenge the country faces.[115]

Equality is easier to legislate than to implement. For example, when
poverty in the rural areas results partly from the concentration of land
in the hands of a few individuals, when up to 50 percent of the population in some villages do not own land, and unemployment is high, it is
still much easier to discuss land reform than to bring it about.[116] Little
has been done since the 1960s; and even when attempts at land reform
have been made, these have not always been successful. Government
land-reform policies promoted rural unrest in both 1978 and 1979, and
the riot in Jenggawah in East Java apparently originated from the
unfair redistribution of land. It seems that many of the programs that
have been aimed at the poor in fact have reached only limited numbers,
and some government measures that were designed to achieve greater
equality in economic development may actually have done the opposite.
Even Suharto's strong support for increased rice production, on the
grounds that it is crucial for political stability as well as for successful
economic development, seems to have been biased in favor of urban
consumers and benefited farmers who produce surpluses rather than
helping poorer subsistence farmers.[117]

Similarly, the government subsidies on food and fuel (which amount-
ed to $2.4 billion in the 1981–1982 budget)[118] in practice benefited those
who purchased these commodities rather than those who lived at subsistence levels (and used firewood for fuel). It has been charged that the
subsidy on kerosene especially in Java, though helping to preserve the
ecological balance in an environment that is seriously threatened by the
cutting of firewood on steep slopes, encouraged overconsumption and
waste. Domestic consumption of kerosene in the late 1970s grew at 7
percent per annum, far faster than the 2.3 percent rate of population
growth, while domestic consumption of all petroleum products grew at
an annual rate of 12 percent.[119] Oil was thus diverted from export purposes (and foreign-exchange earnings), while subsidies took an increasing proportion of the budget that could otherwise have been used for
further development projects. This was finally recognized in 1983,
when subsidies were cut substantially: the food subsidy was discontin-
ued and the oil subsidy cut back, although the fertilizer subsidy was
retained.[120] The government's goal now is to have the prices of essential
commodities reflect their market value by the end of *Repelita IV* in
1989.[121]

Questions have also been raised about whether the government vil-
lage-aid programs *(Inpres)* for the construction of roads, bridges, and

schools encourage local initiative and development efforts or instead kill local creativity and bolster dependence on the government; and whether the much-sought-after "participation" in development is instead actually perceived as a burden, as orders to be carried out. In many village "self-help projects" the poor frequently become passive observers rather than active participants.[122] Even cooperatives have not worked well. They have been promoted by the government rather than growing from local community initiatives. Thus, they suffer from lack of effective control by the members themselves and consequently are not trusted.[123] Indeed, critics have asked whether the government would even accept, let alone welcome, competition from community-based initiatives.

Despite the government's oft-repeated commitment to greater equality and to raising living standards through labor-intensive projects and small and middle-sized industry, much has been spent on large, highly capital-intensive enterprises and on the import-intensive sectors of power generation, industry, and mining.[124]

Use of money on projects such as the Nurtanio aircraft plant is highly questionable. Between 1976 and 1985 over $500 million was spent on Nurtanio's development plan, and tens of millions more in state funds will be needed before the company is able to stand on its own a decade from now. Yet Suharto's prestige is intimately bound up with its success, because he unilaterally initiated the program and has steadfastly supported it in his belief that it would help Indonesia take off industrially in the mid-1990s.[125]

In response to the slump in the world economy in the early 1980s and the decline in oil prices in the mid-1980s, the government decided to continue its level of investment in most major industrial and "developmental" projects. Projects were thus kept going that created profits for the regime's leaders (and foreign backers), while the three major devaluations of the rupiah against the U.S. dollar and the reduction or abolition of subsidies on basic commodities increased the cost of living and thus disadvantaged the ordinary people. Retrenchments, cuts in wages and allowances, and shorter working weeks have all added to people's difficulties.[126]

As oil revenues decline further and as more revenues have to be generated from taxes on goods, services, and property and from taxes on international trade, lower-income people will be even more seriously affected. Their share of the tax burden will increase, because among lower-income groups the proportion of consumer expenditures used to buy the commodities most affected by excise taxes (*kretek* [clove] cigarettes, sugar, alcohol, and beverages) is quite large.

Meanwhile, the benefits from export revenues have accrued disproportionately to the small section of the urban population with better education and access to government jobs.[127] Even though Garnaut argues that the accompanying expansion of modern employment and income has resulted in significant numbers of Indonesians enjoying substantially higher material standards, the expanded employment opportunities in the modern sector have not been large enough to have a major impact on labor in the traditional sector. Real wages have not risen, while unemployment and underemployment have. And while employees in the traditional sector have gained little or nothing in higher wages, the traditional producers of cash crops for export have received lower real incomes as a result of the resources boom.[128]

Although some of the huge increases in natural-resource revenues in the past have been used for subsidies and public projects such as rural facilities and schools, the great bulk of public expenditure has been concentrated in activities that have provided few direct benefits to people in the traditional economy. Meanwhile, much work remains to be done on rural village infrastructure: roads and small bridges, irrigation canals, small dams, rural water-supply projects, warehouses, markets, and so on. Booth and McCawley conclude that although the 1970s was the best decade in Indonesia's recorded history for sustained economic growth, too many opportunities for reform were missed as development efforts remained oil-dependent, capital-intensive, and Jakarta-centered.[129]

Increases in protectionism between 1983 and 1985, seen in the growing list of goods that cannot be imported because they are produced locally, have also had mixed results, stimulating the production of domestic engineering and industrial products, but also creating inefficiencies and misallocation of investment and hindering economic growth. A good example of this two-sided effect of protectionism is the import ban on new and secondhand ships: this has protected the domestic shipbuilding industry but has significantly raised costs for transportation and thus prices for goods that are shipped. The ban is also inconsistent with the objectives of the important Presidential Instruction (*Inpres* No. 4) of April 1985, which were to reduce handling and transport costs for exports as well as to simplify the administrative procedures governing interisland and foreign trade.[130]

It has been argued that the government with its overregulation and bureaucracy seems more concerned with measurable, tangible results than with the *process* of development and changes in orientation and attitudes. Decentralization in the system of planning, implementation, and supervision is needed, so that the aspirations and potential of the community can be fully accommodated in programs developed "from below."

Hendrata has commented that a major problem thwarting development is the traditional paternalistic bureaucracy which has a much stronger orientation to above than below, an overly strict observance of procedure even if it means sacrificing efficiency; an aversion (or perhaps an inability) to act as a creative and dynamic manager taking calculated risks to achieve optimal results in line with sound business principles; an emphasis on appearing to be a "ruler" rather than a "servant" of the community; a paternalistic attitude toward the people and subordinates based on the conviction that "Father knows best"; plus a doubt as to the ability of the people to find solutions for their own problems.[131]

Meanwhile, the inequality between Java and the Outer Islands continues. Despite a theoretical commitment to the evening out of economic inequalities by encouraging economic development in the Outer Islands, most investment, both domestic and foreign, has been in Java. From 1967 through April 1984, the government licensed 787 foreign investment projects worth some U.S. $9,368 million. Of these, 560 (71.2 percent) were located in Java (with ninety-five projects worth $2,957 million in Sumatra, fifty-eight projects involving $447 million in Kalimantan, and eleven projects worth $274 million in Irian Jaya).[132] In addition, development funds from aid donors have been heavily concentrated in resource-rich or already relatively industrialized areas.[133]

Arndt argues that the regional imbalance between Java and the Outer Islands has been aggravated through the still further concentration of industry, urban development, and decision-making power in Jakarta and through the relative neglect of the least-developed regions, particularly in eastern Indonesia.[134]

Even within Java there is considerable concentration of industry. Despite the official goal of encouraging new industries in rural areas, over half of all the employees in large and medium-sized industries in the early 1970s were concentrated in just twenty of Java's eighty-two *kabupaten,* and that pattern seems to have been continued. Despite a government commitment to the growth of small and medium-sized cities, Jakarta has almost tripled its population over the past twenty-five years, from 2.97 million in 1961 to 4.58 million in 1971 to an estimated 8.16 million in 1986.[135]

Meanwhile, within the Outer Island provinces, despite a government commitment to rural and equal development, huge industrial enclaves have been created, such as the Asahan aluminum project in North Sumatra and the natural-gas-based, large-scale industrial complex around Lhokseumawe in Aceh, that have few trickle-down effects on the regional economy.

Perhaps at the root of the problem is the controversy over the underlying assumptions of Indonesia's development program. The government's position has been that a basic condition for reaching the targets of development is undisturbed national stability. This explains, at least according to some critics, why the New Order government is actually pursuing a "trickle-down" strategy of development, despite its official commitment to *pemerataan* (the equitable distribution of development efforts and their benefits); for it is committed to maintaining the social order without fundamental change.[136] Critics charge that the government has overemphasized security, the fear of regional disintegration, and the threat of communism in efforts to hold on to its own power, thus curbing freedom of thought and action, creativity, and basic human rights.[137] They maintain that the increasingly centralistic and authoritarian government has become rigid and is stifling local initiative.[138] Even the Director of the National Institute for Economic and Social Research, Education, and Information noted the existence of too much paternalistic government bureaucracy, overregulation, and excessive supervision.[139] Despite official recognition of the need to devolve authority for regional development to the provinces themselves, power instead has been increasingly centralized. Measures taken to promote economic integration have frequently backfired: in 1975, for example, provincial customs and export duties were prohibited in order to promote greater economic integration of the country and to stimulate interisland trade. But this move left the provinces with no legal source of foreign exchange and thus financially weak. As power has become more concentrated in Jakarta, a brain drain of the more able and better-trained provincial leaders to Jakarta has occurred. The effect has been, on the one hand, provocation of regional and local resentment and, on the other, the further development of dependent attitudes among provincial administrators remaining in the *daerah* (regions). These attitudes have made local officials hesitant to take development initiatives and too accustomed to central government handouts to do anything but wait for anticipated central government help and directives.

Currently, nearly 80 percent of total public expenditure in the provinces is disbursed through the national budget and controlled by ministries and agencies headquartered in Jakarta, leaving only about 20 percent of the funds to be administered by the provincial governments. Of this 20 percent, about half comes from *Inpres* funds; only half comes from locally raised taxes and levies, and these tax sources are strictly controlled by the central government. There is a strong need for more decentralization and deconcentration to allow local governments and regional branches of national bodies headquartered in Jakarta to make more decisions.[140]

The government has also been unable to deal firmly with the increasingly pervasive problem of corruption. Although periodic attempts are made to control corruption, only minor officials have been apprehended, while flagrant abuse among senior government officials goes unheeded and is carefully covered up. Yet there is an awareness that the fall of a number of Third World governments has had its roots in corruption that riddled the state; there is also a recognition that the experience and lessons of history had better not be ignored.[141] Editorials in newspapers and newsmagazines in Indonesia periodically focus on the corruption issue, recognizing the institutionalized corruption in the country and calling for enforcement of the Anti-Corruption Law. Renewed government efforts to deal with the acknowledged widespread corruption in all government departments, though, seem to have met with only limited success.

Pauker, however, argues that corruption may not be as harmful to the economic system as is generally assumed. Certainly the petty corruption that results from inadequately low salaries for civil servants delays and obstructs the economic process and is "a socially harmful form of indirect taxation." But he argues that the much bigger form of corruption that comes from the "symbiotic relationship between political power and economic entrepreneurship actually expedites economic growth." Politically influential Indonesian military men and civilians, who often lack business skills, help authentic entrepreneurs, who are often foreigners or ethnic Chinese, to implement projects that would otherwise be obstructed by the graft-seeking lower bureaucracy. They also help to obtain credits from official sources for those most capable of using the money productively.[142] As Pauker sums it up, the harm done by corruption in high places is not so much economic as sociopolitical: it erodes the authority of the ruling elites, causes distrust in government, and lowers resistance to radicalism.[143] It has been suggested that such corruption is likely to lead either to destabilizing radical political upheavals or to the increasingly harsh repression of its critics by the government, the latter of which appears to be taking place.

However, the damage done to the economy is nevertheless considerable. Import and other monopolies in such major sectors of the economy as steel, plastics, cement, insurance, and food restrict competition and thus lead to inefficiency and permit mismanagement. In addition the companies controlling these monopolies, which have links with Suharto's family and friends, provide enormous profits for their owners. It has been "conservatively estimated that the entire system of privilege generated hundreds of millions of dollars in revenue each year for the companies involved."[144] Much of this profit supports extravagant lifestyles and is invested outside the country.

Indonesia's economic policies came under heavy criticism in the early 1980s from World Bank experts in a confidential draft document entitled "Selected Issues of Industrial Development and Trade Strategy." The report charged the government with creating policies that misallocated economic resources and thus thwarted Indonesia's long-term economic and social development goals. Using the principle of comparative advantage as its underlying premise, the report advocated fewer government controls rather than better controls over economic activity.[145]

Perhaps here is one of the clearest examples of cultural misunderstanding and opposing social and political value systems. World Bank experts, with their emphasis on capitalism, growth, economic efficiency, and the free-market system, are not culturally attuned to Indonesia's priorities or fully cognizant of the importance of social and political constraints impinging on economic decision making in Indonesia. Granted, there is the generally accepted need for economic reform through reducing licensing inefficiency and unwieldy bureaucracy, and for the simplification and reduction of government regulations, but the Bank's recommendations for a shift toward a more outward-looking, export-oriented trade policy run counter, at least to some extent, to the government's officially accepted goal of *pemerataan* (equitable distribution), which at least in the past implied domestic production and import substitution rather than export-oriented manufacturing for earning foreign exchange. Similarly, the Bank's recommendation for a shift from "an administratively determined allocation system to a price-determined one" is in direct opposition to Jakarta's emphasis on encouraging *pribumi* (indigenous Indonesian) entrepreneurs through preferential treatment. The free-market World Bank theories grated also against the Indonesian government's inherent distrust of an uncontrolled private sector, and the Bank's desire to open up the Indonesian economy to attract greater Western investment ran up against the Indonesians' great sensitivity to economic domination by foreigners.[146] As one critic summed up the situation, for Jakarta's technocrats the World Bank's recommendations may have been theoretically neat, but they were politically and historically inept.[147]

But despite all the criticisms of the government's economic policies, the assessment of Awanohara, Habir, and Handley in a recent overview of Indonesia is that economic progress has been shared remarkably evenly throughout the vast Indonesian archipelago, given the urgent needs and superior political clout of the cities, the difficulties of transport and communications, the faltering bureaucracy, and the inclination of the military-dominated central government to concentrate power in Jakarta. Evidence can be seen in the consistent growth of rice output over the past fifteen years; in the construction of roads, schools, and piped water; and in other new economic activities throughout the archipelago, much of which would not have happened without these government policies.[148] Certainly, the country's agricultural sector has grown rapidly, industrial output has increased dramatically, average per-capita income has soared (from about $100 per annum in 1965 to $650 in 1985), and a substantial middle class has developed since Indonesia declared its independence in 1945; and the disparate elements of commerce, industry, and agriculture have been forged into a national economy with a considerable degree of national economic unity.[149]

Conclusion

Government policies, therefore, have been of great importance in promoting and strengthening national integration. In the sociocultural field, diverse peoples from a great variety of ethnic and cultural backgrounds have been encouraged to emphasize their common sociocultural unity and identify more closely with one another as fellow Indonesians. Knowledge and use of the national language have been strongly promoted, and, through a variety of educational, social, and cultural organizations, greater cohesion attained.

In the interaction dimension, great progress has been made in improving and expanding the transportation and communications networks, thus reducing the former isolation of many peoples and areas, especially in the Outer Islands. Mobility has increased significantly. And through the domestic satellite communications system especially, the different parts of the country have been brought into much closer and more effective communication with one another.

In the economic dimension, government policies have been important not only in encouraging and directing economic growth but also in attempting to ensure that the benefits of development are distributed more equitably than they would be in a free-market economy. Not all of the government's economic policies have been successful, however, and progress toward the goal of greater economic equity has been undermined also by corruption and bureaucratic mismanagement.

Inevitably, Indonesia still has a long way to go in creating a fully integrated nation-state, but the distance the country has come already is both impressive and encouraging.

8

Retrospect and Prospect

As the earlier chapters have illustrated, national integration is a vast, multifaceted, and enormously complicated concept. Not only does it consist of a number of major dimensions, each with a multitude of component parts, but these dimensions are integrally intertwined, each affecting and being affected by the others. Moreover, events or trends in each dimension can produce integrative results at one level and disintegrative effects at another. This book has attempted to draw together a wide variety of material from many diverse sources in a comprehensive study of the geographical aspects of national integration. It has included an examination of the major dimensions of integration, an analysis of their spatial patterns, and a consideration of the impact of government policies on the country's patterns of cohesion. This chapter includes both an overview and a discussion of some of the major problems confronting Indonesia's national integration in the late 1980s.

The concept of national integration itself is remarkably complex. Obviously, this book is not a conclusive study: more could be added to the discussion of the four major dimensions that have been considered here—historical and political, sociocultural, interaction, and economic —as they relate to national integration. And further work needs to be done in analyzing more precisely the interrelationships of their many components. Inevitably, questions also remain about the best way to quantify the dimensions once defined. The present analysis has been limited by the available data. The lack of data has both necessitated the omission of significant aspects of the concept of national integration, such as the feelings, perceptions, and attitudes of people in different parts of the country toward the nation-state, and at times forced the use of surrogates, such as road density rather than the preferred numbers of interprovincial travelers. In addition, some of the available data are of dubious validity, meaning that both they and the statistical analysis based on them have to be regarded cautiously and critically.

Another problem relates to the time element. Although integration is a dynamic concept, and the historical chapter has examined changes in the levels and processes of integration in the past, the major part of this study has been concerned with the conditions of national integration as they exist at a cross section of history, during the limited time frame of the 1970s and early 1980s.

The results of the analysis are also a reflection of the scale selected. As discussed in chapter 1, the province has been used as the unit of analysis mainly for practical reasons, as most data are available only at that level. However, the great contrasts in both area and population size among the provinces necessitated standardization of the data, leading inevitably to the introduction of certain distortions, because no index can adequately encompass both population and area differences at the same time. The use of the province as the areal unit of analysis has also camouflaged wide intraprovincial differences, which at times may be of more significance than interprovincial differences in assessing the strength of national integration. In particular, the role of the urban centers in their respective provinces may have been distorted, because their data have been averaged with those of the entire population of the province in which they are located. This seems to have affected particularly the status of South Sulawesi in the overall analysis of integration and may also have unduly accentuated Jakarta's preeminence at the expense of West Java. The patterns of national integration would be found to be much more intricate if a smaller unit of analysis, such as the *kabupaten* (district) had been used.[1] But even use of the *kabupaten* would have presented difficulties, as it too is related more to areal than to population size.[2] Indeed, no unit can be perfect in measuring differences in both population and area, especially when the geographic realities include such great contrasts in population distribution as exist in Indonesia (where Java contains 62 percent of the population of the country but has less than 7 percent of its land area).

However, despite the limitations caused by problems of expressing the concept of national integration in Indonesia in measurable terms and of obtaining relevant, accurate, and sufficiently detailed data, the study depicts a very interesting, complex pattern of integration. In place of the Java-Outer Islands core-periphery model that has been used so widely in the literature to describe Indonesia, the study demonstrates convincingly that a far more complicated pattern exists. In many ways, at least as far as per-capita characteristics are concerned, Java has been mislabeled as the core, for despite its high population density and well-developed infrastructure, it does not exhibit many of the characteristics associated with a core, especially in the sociocultural and economic dimensions of national integration. Java generates less than a

third of the country's gross national product while consuming a disproportionate share of the country's revenue; meanwhile, almost three-
quarters of Indonesia's poor live in (mainly rural) Java. In reality, only
Jakarta emerges as the national, dynamic, urban core, surrounded by a
diverse periphery, with no obvious decline in the level of integration
associated with increasing distance from that core. The contrasts among
the Outer Island provinces on a per-capita basis, particularly between
some in Sumatra and Kalimantan on the one hand and some in eastern
Indonesia on the other, are far more striking than any Java-Outer
Islands dichotomy. The poverty and underdeveloped character of West
and East Nusatenggara, even in comparison with Java, is especially
marked and contrasts sharply with conditions particularly in East Kalimantan and North and South Sumatra.

If this new interpretation of the core and periphery is accepted, it
helps our understanding of the unequal development patterns of the
past and can affect regional planning and policy decisions for the future.
As demonstrated in chapter 5, Jakarta has been the focus of a disproportionate amount of both domestic and overseas investment, largely
because of its status as the capital city and core of the country, with its
cumulative advantages of a more highly developed infrastructure, labor
pool, local market, and center of decision making. The importance for
business and industry of physical proximity to this center of economic
and political power cannot be overemphasized in a country like Indonesia where telephone communications are less dependable and less effective than in the West, and where personal contacts are so important in
cutting through the maze of bureaucracy.

Yet this excessive investment in and around Jakarta has provoked
widespread resentment. As one of Indonesia's own critics, Alisjahbana,
so expressively described it in the late 1960s, Jakarta, as the source of all
finance and decision making, has become the leech, sucking blood from
the body of the fish, growing fatter while the fish (Indonesia), losing
blood, gets thinner.[3]

Jakarta's location on Java and its domination by Javanese have had
widespread ramifications for the pattern of economic development in
Indonesia as a whole.[4] Political pressure from tens of thousands of poor
Javanese and Sundanese migrants to Jakarta (the great majority of
whom come from West Java), and from the educated unemployed in
the city, is obviously far more immediate than pleas for attention and
investment from more remote Outer Island provinces, especially the
poor ones. In addition, there is a natural tendency for Javanese leaders
to favor their own *suku* (people) before attending to others in the Outer
Islands, whose different cultures and needs are both strange to them
and not clearly understood or respected. Thus, the amount of govern-

ment revenue spent in Java, and especially in Jakarta and West Java, is out of proportion to its comparative land area and even to its relative population size.[5] Furthermore, imports flow into Java far in excess both of its exports and of imports into other parts of Indonesia.

Yet the government, aware of the need for greater spatial equality in development, has made *pemerataan* (the evening out of development) a top priority in its interrelated trilogy of development goals—spreading the benefits of development, economic growth, and national stability—and has made efforts to disperse investment and government projects to all areas of the country. But policies designed to attain a better balance in economic development among the different regions of the country run into an almost insoluble dilemma. Obviously, for the sake of regional development and spatial economic equity, it is necessary to restrict uncontrolled economic growth in Java and encourage manufacturing activities in the Outer Islands; yet efficiency and growth considerations, not to mention the severe problems of poverty, unemployment, and underemployment on Java, underscore the essential need for increased investment there.

Thus, the problems Indonesia faces in terms of both national integration and national development remain enormous. Population pressure continues to rise inexorably. The 1980 census revealed that population had grown in the previous intercensal period (1971–1980) at an annual rate of 2.34 percent, despite vigorous government support of family planning.[6] This figure translates into a population increase of twenty-eight million between 1971 and 1980 and an estimated further growth of seventeen million between 1980 and 1985.[7]

Meanwhile, population distribution has become increasingly uneven, in real even though not in percentage terms, despite government commitment to the transmigration program, which relocates landless people primarily from Java and Bali to more sparsely populated areas in the Outer Islands. Indeed, the transmigration program is able to resettle only a small proportion of the annual population *increase* of Java, and at enormous cost.[8] The disparity in population densities between Java and the Outer Islands has increased significantly over the past twenty years. From an average density in 1961 of 476 per square kilometer in Java and nineteen in the Outer Islands, average densities increased to 690 and thirty-one, respectively, by 1980.[9] Obviously, these figures camouflage the even greater contrasts existing among individual provinces (for example, between Central Java, the province with the highest population density [outside Jakarta and Yogyakarta], with 742 per square kilometer on the one hand, and the province with the lowest density, Irian Jaya, with three per square kilometer on the other). The gap between Java and the Outer Islands thus grows ever wider, at least as far as population numbers and density are concerned. And the over half a million Outer Islanders who have moved to Java over the past fifteen years have partly counteracted the government's transmigration efforts, both by adding to the numbers already in the urban areas of Java and by draining some of the most creative and dynamic talent from the Outer Islands.

The pressure on land resources in Java is immense. Of Java's estimated 100.5 million people in 1985, over thirty-five million were landless, and these numbers are increasing yearly. Another estimated forty million do not own enough land to live on, as the average size of land holdings continues to decline.[10] One unfortunate result of Green Revolution technology, which has boosted rice production and helped to make Indonesia self-sufficient in rice, has been the growing gap between rich and poor farmers. Only richer farmers can afford both the added costs of hybrid seeds, fertilizer, pesticides, and so on, and the element of risk involved. In consequence, cultivated land has become increasingly concentrated in the hands of the few. By 1980, 60–70 percent of the cultivated land in Java was owned by just 10 percent of the population,[11] and the percentage of small farmers having less than half a hectare rose from 46 to 63 percent between 1973 and 1980.[12]

Rural-to-urban migration is another major problem, because not only do the new urban migrants swell the numbers of the unemployed and underemployed, but they also put great strain on the existing social fabric as well as on already inadequate physical facilities (water supply, fuel, sanitation, housing, and so on). Although the rates of urban growth have been relatively low (Indonesia is considered only 22.4 percent urban now, compared with 17.2 percent in 1971, and the growth is due partly to a change in both the definition of urban and the location of urban boundaries), the sheer numbers of new urban dwellers are staggering: 12.3 million in less than ten years. Nowhere is the problem of rapid urbanization more clearly seen than in Jakarta, which has increased its population by over three and a half million people in just the past fifteen years.[13] Its population in 1986 totaled an estimated 8.2 million (more than the entire population of Kalimantan's four provinces) and probably is considerably higher than these official estimates, as thousands live in West Java, outside Jakarta's official boundaries, and commute to work or take up short-term residence in the city and so are not counted as permanent residents. It is estimated that more than 70 percent of Jakarta's population live below the poverty line (earning less than $22.50 per month), inhabiting slum dwellings with almost no potable water, sanitation facilities, or medical services.[14]

To avert growing dissatisfaction, particularly among the young unemployed, the government has located investment disproportionately in the cities, rather than focusing it in the rural areas in an attempt to keep people there, assure reasonably full employment, increase rural incomes, and thus reduce rural-to-urban migration. The gap between urban and rural areas has thus widened over the past twenty years. Indeed, it has been suggested that Java might do well to emulate the South Korean and Taiwanese experience of village development; in these two countries villages are both 100 percent literate and 100 percent electrified. Locating small-scale industries in the villages of South Korea and Taiwan has also ensured not only an extra source of income for farm families but virtually no rural unemployment as well. In contrast, at the beginning of the 1980s Java's 35,000 villages were only about 65 percent literate and less than 10 percent electrified. As a survey in 1979 indicated, better irrigation, better roads, more schools, more credit for small-scale industries and workshops, and more technical training were objectives Javanese villagers sought.[15] It has also been argued that although rural development is not a sufficient condition for rapid economic growth, it is a major necessary condition in the early stages of that growth.[16] The widening income gap between agricultural and nonagricultural workers also needs to be addressed.[17]

Other major economic problems remain. Despite the fact that the World Bank upgraded Indonesia's classification to that of a lower middle-income country in 1982 (with an estimated average gross national product per-capita figure of $560 in 1985),[18] over fifty-seven million people remain extremely poor.

Part of the national economic problem arises from the dependence of Indonesia upon the petroleum sector for almost 70 percent of its total budget, a reality that has left the country vulnerable to price fluctuations. Plans based upon continued projected increases in oil prices had to be scaled back when OPEC in the early 1980s reduced Indonesia's production allocation in response to falling oil prices, the world recession, and an increase in non-OPEC-produced oil. By 1986 economic problems caused by the major slump in world oil prices had begun to shake the country. These were accentuated and compounded by the reduced demand for some of Indonesia's other exports, such as tin, rubber, and palm oil; by decreased foreign investment in the country; and by growing protectionist sentiments in the West against Indonesia's increased export of manufactured goods. Further, continued spending on imports and a significant problem with capital flight have caused difficulties in the balance of payments and added to a steeply rising foreign debt burden.[19] The grave drop in government income has necessitated a cutback in government spending and a total revision of the country's development plans. The question now seems to be whether Indonesia will be able to meet the rising expectations of its population (which have been brought about to some extent by the increase in both the interaction and economic aspects of national integration) or whether people's growing discontent and frustration with economic austerity will spill over into political and social unrest. Government concern with this problem, however, began long before the 1986 crisis: as early as April 1981 commercial advertising was banned from national television, in large part because it led to rising expectations that the government could not hope to fulfill.[20] But the situation is much more critical now.

Another major economic-related problem is the growing and increasingly conspicuous gap between rich and poor, both between the rural poor and urban rich and between the urban elites and the extremely poor city dwellers. Partly because of television coverage and improved communications, ordinary Indonesians are much more aware of the wealth of multimillionaire generals, government leaders, and relatives of the president, and of the luxurious life-style of the rich and powerful in contrast to their own struggles to survive. They hear of how land formerly owned by poor transmigrants has become part of extensive, privately owned plantations; of the wealth of the Chinese and other foreign traders with high government connections; and of the increased profits of middlemen even though commodity prices do not change. They struggle with the higher prices they have to pay because of import monopolies, protectionist regulations, and government controls of the economy. They hear about the illicit fortunes amassed by the families of deposed presidents such as Duvalier in Haiti and Marcos in the Philippines and have no trouble recognizing the analogy to their own country.

In the political field the country faces similar dilemmas of trying to balance national with regional needs, and the need for political control and stability with that for political participation.

The political consensus in Indonesia has always been fragile because of the existence of ethnic, religious, cultural, and historic diversities and conflicts. Despite the considerable progress that has been made in developing a feeling of "Indonesian identity" among the widely differing peoples of the archipelago, deep-seated regionalisms and local ethnic pride continue to thwart full political as well as sociocultural integration. The political problem centers on how much to allow these regional differences to be reflected in regional autonomy and how much power to retain in the central government. The newly independent government of Sukarno quickly discarded a federal form of government for a unitary system. And despite the arguments of former Vice-President Hatta that a devolution of political, administrative, and fiscal authority would be more responsive to local needs and conditions, the New Order government of Suharto has sought to centralize power and exert ever-increasing control over the entire archipelago. This policy inevitably has met with resistance.

Serious regional discontent and unrest still fester in a few areas of the country. In Aceh (northern Sumatra) the National Liberation Front of Aceh (NLF) is still active in its struggle for independence from Indonesia (which its separatist leaders proclaimed at the end of 1976), and claims of large-scale military repression have been made.[21] Simmering discontent survives in areas of Maluku, and in many other areas there is unhappiness with the power and pervasiveness of the central government.

In East Timor there remains deep disenchantment with and resistance to Indonesia's annexation of the territory in 1976. Reports from its Jakarta-appointed provincial assembly have charged that corruption, brutality, and other abuses of power (including ignoring local customs and behaving as conquerors) by some in both the army and administration are causing growing fear and anti-government feeling as well as economic hardship there.[22] Despite Jakarta's financial assistance, it is claimed that living conditions have worsened.[23] In addition, there is considerable resistance to and resentment of the government's much vaunted goal of *asimilasi*.

Irian Jaya remains the locus of further regional dissatisfaction and periodic unrest. Although the government has gradually and effectively consolidated its control over the province, and although the *Organisasi Papua Merdeka (OPM,* Free Papua Movement) is officially banned, its followers continue to be active, especially in the eastern border area, in their secessionist attempts to wrest Irian Jaya from the Indonesian government and achieve independence. As in the other areas of unrest within the country, much of the cause of the trouble is attributable to the presence of "outsiders," predominantly Javanese, who run the affairs of the province and who, with their culturally superior attitudes and insensitivity to local customs, as well as their Islamic faith, offend the indigenous inhabitants. The transmigration of Javanese to all three areas is perceived by some not as a "civilizing mission to promote their welfare and lagging economic development," but as one of the "most blatant land robberies in history."[24]

Indeed, Javanese influence is a problem throughout the Outer Islands and is one dimension of the whole core-periphery problem, because the government is excessively controlled by Javanese. Not only has the government experienced increased Javanization, but so too has the military. For example, by 1980 all twelve territorial military commands in the Outer Islands were in the hands of officers from Java (eleven Javanese and one Sundanese [from West Java]); thus not a single Outer Islands territorial command was held by a "native son," whereas the commands in Central, West, and East Java were all held by native sons. The overwhelming power of the Javanese in the high commands can be seen also in the officer corps; 89 percent of military officers were either Javanese (80 percent) or Sundanese (9 percent).[25]

The conflict between the need for political control and political participation is also sharp. Suharto believes in strong political control partly to ensure national stability, itself a basic condition for development and integration.[26] Indeed, over the past twenty years Indonesia has enjoyed a relatively high level of political stability, unlike many developing countries. But escalating criticism has emerged, particularly in the last few years, that the Suharto government has become increasingly authoritarian and repressive as its support base has narrowed.[27] Notwithstanding Suharto's appeal to the *Panca Sila* and the 1945 Constitution, there have been serious signs of discontent among some of the country's former senior government leaders and politicians, discontent that has been firmly put down. The result is a growing isolation of the New Order's hierarchy from the people, with only a few reaping the benefits of power.[28]

Little has been done to develop the political and judicial institutions that the country so badly needs. In addition, there is serious concern that Suharto is personally adapting the New Order concepts to preserve his own executive control over the electoral process; that he has legitimized such extra-constitutional institutions as *Kopkamtib* (the Operational Command for the Restoration of Security and Order);[29] and above all that he is attempting to become the personification of the *Panca Sila* and the Constitution of 1945, so that any criticism of him is interpreted as being an attack on the basic institutions of the state. Awanohara reports a vague but widely held notion that Suharto is becoming more and more like a Javanese king and Indonesia like a traditional Javanese empire, feudalistic, stultifying, and unsuited to meeting the challenges of modern times.[30]

Discontent with poverty, social injustice, and abuses of power by the authorities in the rural areas is widespread. Perhaps at the root of the pervasive dissatisfaction is a general disillusionment about the New Order society and the government's ability to deal with the country's many ills. Two main issues stand out: the lack of real political participation despite the veneer of democratic institutions, and a misguided economic development program that has fueled corruption on a grand scale and exacerbated the gap between rich and poor.[31]

Political participation is encouraged only during the elections that take place under highly controlled conditions every five years. Elections are regarded by the Indonesian government as an important demonstration of democracy (despite the existence of a military-dominated administration), a legitimation of the regime, and an endorsement of the government's development policies. However, elections are also to impress foreign democratic governments, particularly those of the Inter-Governmental Group on Indonesia, and to ensure their continued support. However, only 39 percent of the 920 delegates to the People's Consultative Assembly *(MPR, Majelis Permusyawaratan Rakyat)* are elected by popular vote and then only after careful screening of the candidates by government security forces.[32]

Fear that the strength of the political parties would undermine the power of the Suharto regime (as well as the officially given reason that uncontrolled political parties and elections would accentuate tensions and divisions among the populace as they did in 1955 during Sukarno's time) led the New Order government to place severe constraints on the political process. Political parties have been restricted in their campaigning, and *Golkar* (Union of Functional Groups), an army-initiated and government-sponsored organization, has been actively promoted as an alternative to the traditional parties.

After the 1971 elections, when nine major political parties competed, the government sought to streamline the process and create two weak parties that could easily be controlled and manipulated.[33] It therefore forcibly consolidated the various Muslim parties into one umbrella organization, the *Partai Persatuan Pembangunan* (*PPP,* Development Unity Party), and the remaining five non-Muslim parties into the *Partai Demokrasi Indonesia* (*PDI,* Indonesian Democratic Party). These restructured parties have suffered from destructive internal factionalism, weak leadership,[34] and a series of government rules and regulations restricting political activity to the *kabupaten* (district) level and progressively decreasing the preelection campaign period (to sixty days in 1977, forty-five in 1982, and twenty-five in 1987).

Meanwhile, although the government denies that *Golkar* is a party, it functions very much like one. Yet as an official, government-sponsored institution, it has a number of advantages over the political parties: for example, it has access to government facilities in finance, transportation, and communications; it has greater freedom to campaign at all levels in Indonesian society; and it has been able to exert considerable political pressure by coopting, coercing, and manipulating local village officials.[35]

In addition, *Golkar* institutionalizes the army's role in political and civilian life. As Pye put it:

Golkar represents a remarkably effective organ for enforcing and legitimizing the domination of the military in Indonesian politics. Hostility toward army rule is directed against *Golkar,* yet since *Golkar* represents all elements in Indonesian society through its functional groups, it is hard to be hostile toward it.[36]

The armed forces in each election have become actively involved on behalf of *Golkar,* despite the fact that they are represented directly in the *Dewan Perwakilan Rakyat (DPR,* House of People's Representatives) by 100 delegates (out of a total of 460) selected by the president.

Unrest has focused both on the composition of the People's Consultative Assembly *(MPR)* and on the continuing domination of the military in the government. The Working Group of the Petition of Fifty (an opposition group of former senior ministers and political leaders) has openly questioned whether the president should continue to appoint one-third of the Assembly, claiming that this arrangement was adopted in 1967 as a temporary measure only, with the idea that subsequently the whole body would be elected.[37]

Distinctly controversial also is the continuing and increasing role of the military in government administration; for the military, who make up only 0.36 percent of the population, form a distinct ruling class, controlling all essential governmental bodies and state-owned enterprises.[38] By 1982, active or retired military men occupied half the positions in the Indonesian higher central bureaucracy; at the highest levels military penetration is nearly complete (the president and his principal immediate aides) or has increased (coordinating ministers) over the course of the New Order regime.[39] Military personnel dominate the affairs of every Cabinet department. Their involvement in almost every facet of public life is considered by the government to be part of their *dwi fungsi* (two functions): the military's role not just to protect the nation in wartime but also to help with nation building. Inevitably, however, there are those who would like to see the restoration of a fully civilian government and the return of the military to their barracks.

The role of Indonesia's economic development program in promoting national integration has also come under attack on a number of counts. The government's main expectation, that economic development would lead almost automatically to greater cohesion and political stability as more people were satisfied and had their needs met, is highly debatable; for economic development always leads to rising expectations, which are all but impossible for a government to meet. In addition, economic development, by unleashing new forces in society, almost inevitably creates as many new problems as it solves. It has been argued that economic development leads to such changes as industrialization, urbanization, and increases in literacy and mass-media exposure, which in turn expand political consciousness, multiply political demands, and broaden the desire for greater political participation on the one hand, but also tend to undermine traditional sources of political authority and traditional political institutions on the other.[40] The problem, therefore, arises of how to adjust the political system so as both to preserve political stability and to allow for greater political participation and development. Oey argues that under the New Order, political consciousness and demands for greater participation have increased tremendously; yet these have not yet been absorbed constructively by new and strong institutions.[41] The *MPR* and *DPR,* which could channel at least some of this development, lack legitimacy because of their undemocratic basis. *Golkar* also is not in a position to act as a strong institution because it is government controlled and lacks the genuine support of the masses at the grass-roots level. Oey concludes that the inevitable result will be an increase in political instability and disorder in the years ahead.[42] The recent waves of student demonstrations and bombings; the arbitrary arrest, intimidation, interrogation, beating, and imprisonment of opposition leaders and of anyone who dares to criticize the government; the mysterious killings by the death squads; and the muzzling of the national press are but some of the evidence of this increasing authoritarianism and repression.[43]

Critics of Indonesia's economic development program point also to the increasing disparities in the income and development levels in different parts of the country as demonstrated in this study, disparities that result from uneven economic growth and government policies that have frequently exacerbated rather than reduced them. In addition, they are concerned about the collusion between government and big business and about how the development program has affected corruption in the country. For the problem of corruption has grown enormously in magnitude in recent years, partly because of the increased opportunities offered by a vast bureaucracy administering a pervasive regulatory system of government controls over all aspects of economic life and partly from the plethora of money entering the country from foreign governments, companies, and international organizations, and from oil and other revenues. As discussed in chapter 7, corruption now affects almost every part of Indonesian life and society and may even have become accepted as the norm by the younger generation upon whom power will devolve. Attempts to deal with corruption appear to have been more symbolic than substantive.

Although almost all observers of the Indonesian scene agree on the major problems, they vary considerably in their evaluations and judgments about them. On the more condemnatory side are those who regard the system as so immensely corrupt and incompetent, with its embedded nepotism and its conspicuous luxury in a setting of extreme poverty, that the situation is irretrievable and almost inevitably explosive.[44] On the other hand, other Indonesia watchers, while recognizing the corruption and inefficiencies endemic in the system, conclude that the present Indonesian government has accomplished an enormous amount both in promoting economic development and in strengthening national integration.[45] Certainly there could be much more corruption. More foreign exchange earnings could be misused in extravagant modernization projects or glamorous buildings (as they were in Sukarno's day).[46] Funds currently used for development could be diverted for the acquisition of sophisticated new weaponry, as has happened in a number of other Third World countries.

These very different evaluations of Indonesia's achievements in nation building are comparable to the juxtaposition of the rather optimistic picture painted by the statistical section in the earlier part of this book and the somewhat more pessimistic conclusions reached in this present chapter. The situation presented in this chapter emphasizes the key problems facing Indonesia. These include the effects of population growth, distribution, and pressure on the country's resources; rural-urban contrasts; problems arising from Indonesia's economic overdependence on the petroleum sector; rising expectations and growing unemployment; the growing gap between rich and poor; and political problems arising primarily from Java's dominant influence, Suharto's style of government (with its lack of meaningful participation), and the role of the military in government and commerce. Unquestionably, these issues represent a formidable challenge to the New Order government in its public commitment to equity, economic growth, and national stability. They also present a threat to the country's continued integrity, probably a more serious one than that presented by the conditions measured in the statistical analysis.

The statistical analysis of national integration based on provincial per-capita characteristics, however, provides a different perspective on the overall picture of national integration. It gives an objective insight into the geographical stage on which the political, economic, and historical events take place. As discussed in chapter 1, the geographical background (the spatial patterns of various integrative forces) does not determine the future of national integration in any country. But it does demonstrate the relative vulnerability of the country as a whole, and of certain areas in particular, to disintegrative forces and events.

Many indices in the sociocultural, interaction, and economic dimensions show that integration among the provinces is growing. More people speak the national language, take part in the national educational system, receive better health care, belong to nationwide organizations that acknowledge (if forcibly) the state ideology of *Panca Sila* as their sole basis, have access to national radio and television programs, and are linked together through improved transportation and communications networks and through increased interprovincial trade than at any time in the past. Increasingly, Indonesians from all over the archipelago are being bound together into mutual webs of common interests, financial and communication linkages, and a shared sense of nationhood and national unity. Overall standards of living have risen for the majority of Indonesians (at least until recently),[47] and even the poorest areas have experienced some improvements as a result of the resources boom and economic development of the 1970s.[48] Despite its great diversity, the country has also been progressively welded into one functioning political entity.[49]

With the exceptions of the two areas most recently added to the country, Irian Jaya and East Timor, widespread regional unrest seems to be a phenomenon largely of the past.[50] The major threat to Indonesia's continued national integration comes not so much from regional as from transregional economic and political sources, particularly the conspicuous and growing gap between the rich and the poor, population pressure, the growing Javanization in government, and increasing repression in the political arena. But the statistical analysis demonstrates a growing (albeit uneven) level of integration in Indonesia.[51]

In spite of the differences in these two evaluations, however, there is no real incongruence between the picture discussed in this chapter's overview of problems confronting the country and that drawn by the statistical analysis. Each of these approaches deals with different facets of integration. Both describe aspects of the reality of Indonesia. Both the integrative and the disintegrative aspects of Indonesia's national integration are true at the same time.

This is so for two major reasons. First, the generally integrative picture drawn by the statistical section is concerned with provinces and their averaged per-capita characteristics, whereas the nonstatistical part deals more with national, intraprovincial, rural-urban, and other scales and facets of integration. Second, as discussed in the first chapter, national integration is a multifaceted, highly complex, and at times paradoxical concept, in which factors of integration operate at different levels and indeed increased integration at one level may result in decreased integration at another. To have aspects of integration moving in opposite directions at the same time is to be expected with such a complex and complicated phenomenon. Thus, the statistical sections are dealing to some extent with different aspects and levels of integration than the nonstatistical sections. From a structural point of view, Indonesia is indeed becoming more integrated as greater unity is forged among the diverse ethnic groups and greater interaction takes place among people from its different areas. However, serious issues of inadequate national integration as well as other economic, political, and social problems also remain. But it is quite probable that the country could have experienced far greater tensions and unrest had it gone through the severe problems discussed in this chapter without the growing integration portrayed in the statistical analysis, for the setting in which the problems of Indonesia are occurring is more integrated and protective of national unity than would have been the case even a decade ago.

This study has illustrated that continuing provincial disparities do exist and in some respects have been accentuated by uneven development. However, it can be argued that the current situation is considerably more stable because of the government's commitment to increasing national integration and ameliorating the greatest economic contrasts through its policy of *pemerataan,* the evening out of spatial inequalities in development.

Indonesia thus remains a diverse and fascinating country, one in which great progress has been made toward the fuller integration of its many islands and peoples, yet one where enormous problems, particularly demographic, economic, and political, remain. As the Indonesian government is aware, integration is a dynamic concept, a condition that has to be constantly nurtured, one where peoples of different social and cultural backgrounds and economic levels have to be bonded continually into a better functioning and more mutually interdependent whole. In this process much has been accomplished, but much yet remains to be done, as Indonesia pursues its goal of "Unity in Diversity."

Appendixes

APPENDIX 1.

Provincial Data for the Eighteen Major Variables in the Sociocultural Dimension

(see Figures 3.1–3.7 and 3.9–3.19 for sources)

Province	Percentage able to speak Indonesian 1980	Percentage speaking Indonesian at home 1980	Percentage Muslim 1980	Percentage Christian (Catholic and Protestant) 1980
1. Aceh	63.7	7.7	97.6	1.8
2. North Sumatra	77.7	30.2	62.3	33.6
3. West Sumatra	63.7	2.2	98.1	1.6
4. Riau	73.4	11.9	92.4	2.8
5. Jambi	68.3	12.3	98.5	1.1
6. South Sumatra	69.8	9.8	96.1	1.8
7. Bengkulu	63.2	7.9	98.5	1.1
8. Lampung	67.5	9.5	95.5	2.2
Sumatra	70.5	14.8	86.2	11.3
9. Jakarta	99.5	91.6	85.0	9.3
10. West Java	61.2	10.1	98.4	1.1
11. Central Java	51.0	1.1	96.8	2.6
12. Yogyakarta	58.9	2.0	92.7	6.8
13. East Java	50.9	2.2	97.1	2.1
Java	57.7	10.6	96.4	2.6
14. Bali	52.3	3.3	5.2	0.8
15. West Nusatenggara	46.6	3.0	96.5	0.4
16. East Nusatenggara	57.2	14.0	8.9	91.0
17. East Timor	33.3	1.2	0.8	99.1
Nusatenggara	50.8	6.4	36.6	33.8
18. West Kalimantan	63.4	9.6	62.1	35.1
19. Central Kalimantan	61.8	4.1	65.9	16.2
20. South Kalimantan	60.6	2.5	98.2	1.2
21. East Kalimantan	78.5	27.5	85.3	13.9
Kalimantan	65.0	9.7	78.8	17.2
22. North Sulawesi	82.0	27.5	45.8	53.5
23. Central Sulawesi	77.2	24.0	76.5	20.6
24. South Sulawesi	51.2	7.9	90.0	9.0
25. Southeast Sulawesi	61.4	16.3	96.3	2.4
Sulawesi	61.6	13.9	79.8	19.0
26. Maluku	88.5	49.2	55.5	44.4
27. Irian Jaya	63.7	31.1	12.1	87.8
Maluku & Irian Jaya	77.6	40.1	36.4	63.5
Indonesia	60.8	11.9	88.2	8.8

n.a.: not available

ᵉ: estimated

Percentage completing primary school 1980	Percentage of seven to twelve year olds in primary school 1980	Percentage literate 1980	Membership in cooperatives per 100 population 1979–1980 average	Number of Scouts per 100 population 1981
47.0	86.2	74.5	4.6	2.1
48.1	87.3	84.3	2.4	2.9
41.8	88.8	81.8	5.0	3.3
42.2	78.2	77.3	1.3	4.7
38.6	79.0	76.2	1.5	6.6
40.9	83.1	81.4	2.2	4.6
37.5	82.4	74.4	5.7	1.9
33.0	80.6	77.5	1.9	11.0
42.4				
65.9	91.4	88.2	2.7	2.7
43.1	82.4	74.9	3.6	4.7
38.8	85.1	66.4	4.6	14.1
57.4	91.6	69.5	6.4	14.8
42.5	84.6	63.1	6.1	9.6
43.9				
46.5	84.5	62.1	6.1	2.9
39.1	72.5	55.0	9.9	2.8
41.4	76.4	65.0	2.5	6.5
n.a.	n.a.	21.4	n.a.	n.a.
42.4				
30.8	66.9	58.2	1.6	4.3
43.3	82.6	78.9	2.1	2.5
39.2	85.2	77.5	4.4	4.0
48.4	78.9	75.9	1.3	5.0
39.1				
44.1	88.9	91.1	7.7	18.7
45.3	86.4	82.1	4.6	11.8
44.7	78.8	62.0	4.0	14.3
45.7	81.1	68.5	3.6	17.0
44.7				
48.7	85.7	82.9	3.1	1.8
47.4	66.9	51.9	2.9	6.3
48.3				
43.4		71.1	4.3	8.1

Province	Percentage belonging to a social organization 1980	Number of Asian citizens per 1,000 population 1981	Number watching an Indonesian-made movie per 100 population 1981	Percentage of households owning a radio 1980
1. Aceh	55.8	2.4	53.1	39.9
2. North Sumatra	66.4	10.3	38.6	46.7
3. West Sumatra	51.7	1.8	38.8	43.7
4. Riau	49.7	19.8	63.7	55.4
5. Jambi	56.5	11.5	34.0	50.1
6. South Sumatra	51.4	21.9	44.4	47.5
7. Bengkulu	41.4	1.6ᵉ	33.0	41.8
8. Lampung	40.9	2.3	14.8	42.8
Sumatra		9.6		
9. Jakarta	20.8	24.9	114.1	66.0
10. West Java	28.6	1.9	28.1	41.9
11. Central Java	48.8	2.1	37.3	39.6
12. Yogyakarta	57.9	1.3	18.0	56.2
13. East Java	55.1	4.4	24.2	36.7
Java		4.4		
14. Bali	70.9	3.0	19.4	46.4
15. West Nusatenggara	50.7	2.4	13.8	17.4
16. East Nusatenggara	49.0	2.9	10.0	13.9
17. East Timor	n.a.	5.8	n.a.	n.a.
Nusatenggara		3.0		
18. West Kalimantan	29.9	31.4	68.8	44.3
19. Central Kalimantan	43.5	2.0	61.9	49.0
20. South Kalimantan	70.7	3.2	77.1	47.8
21. East Kalimantan	45.0	20.1	157.1	54.3
Kalimantan		16.5		
22. North Sulawesi	74.1	6.7	37.5	36.2
23. Central Sulawesi	45.0	6.9	49.9	27.2
24. South Sulawesi	41.1	6.3	24.7	29.9
25. Southeast Sulawesi	49.0	2.7ᵉ	21.1	23.2
Sulawesi		5.9		
26. Maluku	39.2	6.7	26.8	38.1
27. Irian Jaya	50.3	1.7	30.4	17.7
Maluku & Irian Jaya		4.4		
Indonesia		6.0	37.2	40.8

n.a.: not available

ᵉ: estimated

Percentage listening to the radio 1980	Percentage of households owning a TV set 1980	Percentage watching television 1980	Number of hospital beds per 10,000 population 1980	Percentage urban 1980
65.6	10.2	52.8	4.4	8.9
60.0	13.4	57.8	13.5	25.5
66.9	8.6	53.3	8.0	12.7
84.0	17.2	63.8	4.9	27.2
78.0	9.3	45.0	3.4	12.7
68.0	13.6	54.4	8.3	27.4
61.9	7.0	36.6	3.0	9.4
77.6	5.9	45.1	3.2	12.5
			8.0	19.6
76.3	45.5	87.5	19.5	93.7
86.3	9.3	44.4	4.0	21.0
80.9	6.2	44.9	5.3	18.8
87.4	9.4	51.6	9.5	22.1
72.7	7.4	53.1	5.2	19.6
			6.0	25.1
76.0	8.2	47.2	6.7	14.7
63.0	2.9	31.7	2.7	14.1
37.5	1.7	14.3	5.4	7.5
n.a.	n.a.	n.a.	3.9	n.a.
			4.8	12.0
70.4	10.4	58.8	6.8	16.8
70.8	7.5	51.0	4.4	10.3
79.0	14.3	66.1	7.6	21.4
60.0	23.0	62.0	13.6	40.0
			7.9	21.5
57.6	11.2	56.2	14.2	16.8
71.5	3.6	28.6	4.4	9.0
70.6	7.0	39.4	8.6	18.1
53.4	3.8	40.5	5.1	9.4
			8.9	15.9
46.1	7.7	21.0	9.2	10.9
70.8	3.2	63.8	12.8	21.4
			10.9	15.5
75.2	9.8	50.3	6.7	22.4

APPENDIX 2.

Provincial Data for the Sixteen Major Variables in the Interaction Dimension

(see Figures 4.2–4.12 and 4.14–4.18 for sources)

Province	Length of all roads (kms) per 1,000 km² 1982	Length of paved roads per 1,000 km² 1982	Number of registered vehicles per km of road 1982
1. Aceh	120.0	23.5	15.4
2. North Sumatra	185.2	83.8	33.6
3. West Sumatra	150.5	66.2	14.6
4. Riau	55.6	9.6	15.0
5. Jambi	91.6	17.4	11.4
6. South Sumatra	85.7	34.2	23.6
7. Bengkulu	149.0	56.5	7.4
8. Lampung	112.1	66.7	21.2
Sumatra	110.7	40.5	20.8
9. Jakarta	5,067.8	5,067.8	337.3
10. West Java	268.0	184.6	56.9
11. Central Java	414.7	294.4	47.8
12. Yogyakarta	648.8	359.7	63.7
13. East Java	295.7	212.9	65.9
Java	346.5	249.3	75.5
14. Bali	1,017.8	431.0	23.3
15. West Nusatenggara	177.9	86.6	9.8
16. East Nusatenggara	233.5	23.8	2.0
17. East Timor	84.5	6.0	9.2
Nusatenggara	245.1	60.7	9.3
18. West Kalimantan	26.2	7.5	14.0
19. Central Kalimantan	13.4	2.0	9.2
20. South Kalimantan	98.8	23.1	21.8
21. East Kalimantan	14.9	3.4	27.3
Kalimantan	23.4	5.5	18.7
22. North Sulawesi	265.5	93.2	9.8
23. Central Sulawesi	78.2	16.6	6.5
24. South Sulawesi	218.6	51.2	13.2
25. Southeast Sulawesi	130.2	27.1	4.9
Sulawesi	158.8	36.0	10.4
26. Maluku	28.1	9.1	8.9
27. Irian Jaya	8.0	1.5	8.8
Maluku & Irian Jaya	11.0	2.7	8.9
Indonesia	87.5	36.1	31.8

n.a.: not available
*Combined

Number of registered vehicles per 1,000 population 1982	Income generated by provincial ports (Rp per capita) 1981–1982	Number of domestic air passengers per 1,000 population 1981	Number of telephone licenses issued per 1,000 population 1981	Minutes of telephone conversation per 100 population 1981
39.2	149.6	10.7	2.8	26.6
52.7	43.7	41.7	4.9	54.2
32.0	39.1	41.1	2.9	54.0
36.4	538.2	73.2	3.6	47.5
32.6	44.0	60.5	2.3	19.2
45.2	46.2	74.6	3.4	47.4
30.2	10.8	46.2	2.2	62.3
17.1	36.2	20.9	1.3	15.5
38.9	89.6	44.3	3.3	42.0
155.1	220.0	321.4	32.8	81.0
25.7	7.8	1.7	2.1	32.1
26.7	9.0*	9.0	1.9	47.1
47.6	9.0*	58.1	2.2	53.8
32.0	21.1	23.9	3.1	43.7
37.9	27.6	35.3	4.6	44.1
53.3	10.6	133.3	4.8	79.4
12.9	10.4	23.4	2.0	39.4
8.2	11.7	20.5	1.0	14.8
20.8	n.a.	n.a.	0.6	n.a.
23.7	10.9	56.6	2.4	43.4
21.7	46.3	53.4	1.5	10.7
19.6	98.9	64.5	1.5	32.2
39.3	91.7	95.3	2.3	50.1
67.9	1,013.5	299.4	8.5	96.8
35.2	242.9	112.4	3.0	41.5
23.6	82.3	64.9	3.4	52.9
27.7	36.5	50.1	1.5	37.1
34.7	35.0	67.2	2.7	34.5
18.8	45.5	21.3	1.0	23.9
30.1	45.7	60.5	2.5	37.6
13.2	92.7	54.6	2.3	48.2
25.3	151.9	118.7	4.2	112.0
18.7	119.6	83.7	3.2	77.1
36.3	51.1	44.2	4.0	43.5

Province	Telegrams sent to domestic destinations per 1,000 population 1981	Percentage reading a newspaper or magazine 1981	Percentage who have lived in another province 1980
1. Aceh	48.5	20.1	6.3
2. North Sumatra	22.4	28.7	7.4
3. West Sumatra	53.0	27.7	7.3
4. Riau	156.8	20.2	17.2
5. Jambi	42.6	11.3	21.3
6. South Sumatra	38.8	23.5	14.0
7. Bengkulu	63.0	10.1	17.0
8. Lampung	15.6	12.3	39.2
Sumatra	42.7		15.4
9. Jakarta	137.2	48.9	40.7
10. West Java	16.1	17.5	4.6
11. Central Java	24.4	13.7	2.3
12. Yogyakarta	82.1	19.3	8.3
13. East Java	33.7	11.7	2.1
Java	34.6		5.8
14. Bali	50.0	11.1	3.3
15. West Nusatenggara	47.8	8.6	2.6
16. East Nusatenggara	82.5	12.4	2.1
17. East Timor	n.a.	n.a.	n.a.
Nusatenggara	60.5		2.6
18. West Kalimantan	32.4	14.9	4.8
19. Central Kalimantan	69.5	17.0	15.7
20. South Kalimantan	83.2	23.1	7.8
21. East Kalimantan	188.4	21.0	25.0
Kalimantan	81.5		10.9
22. North Sulawesi	118.9	25.8	6.6
23. Central Sulawesi	180.5	19.0	15.6
24. South Sulawesi	53.7	16.1	2.9
25. Southeast Sulawesi	89.4	17.1	12.7
Sulawesi	85.9		6.1
26. Maluku	231.9	13.6	10.0
27. Irian Jaya	270.6	28.1	9.1
Maluku & Irian Jaya	249.5		9.6
Indonesia	46.9	18.0	7.8

n.a.: not available
*Combined

International exports (tons per 100 population) 1982	Interprovincial exports (tons per 100 population) 1982	Value of imports from overseas ($U.S. per capita) 1982	Cargoes unloaded in interprovincial trade (tons per 100 population) 1981–1982	International and domestic exports (tons per 100 population) 1982
533.5	41.8	172.5	28.9	575
22.5	12.8	142.1	32.8	35
7.6	14.3	67.6	10.3	22
1,340.6	183.4	386.5	123.7	1,524
20.4	5.4	23.5	12.3	26
12.4	76.5	62.2	17.5	89
22.3	1.7	0.2	9.8	24
5.1	1.1	160.0	8.0	6
165.7	36.8	124.0	28.4	203
11.9	28.7	996.0	104.0	41
0.3	2.1	44.4	1.8	2
2.0*	8.7*	71.2	17.7*	11*
2.0*	8.7*	11.0	17.7*	11*
3.1	8.2	70.7	15.6	11
2.5	7.8	127.1	18.4	10
0.1	5.0	45.5	21.3	5
0.0	5.7	2.0	8.7	6
0.7	2.6	0.0	13.8	3
0.4	3.1	n.a.	n.a.	3
0.3	4.3	14.9	14.4	5
34.2	9.1	21.5	28.4	43
68.1	29.6	6.3	17.2	98
29.6	20.3	28.5	19.8	50
194.2	327.9	908.4	211.9	522
66.6	73.2	182.1	57.4	140
4.3	19.8	46.2	62.3	24
7.5	40.9	6.3	29.5	49
2.1	11.3	33.9	16.8	13
53.5	54.6	2.0	38.7	108
7.9	20.6	30.1	29.6	28
59.2	34.1	49.1	35.6	93
214.0	13.5	51.9	37.7	227
129.5	24.8	50.4	36.5	154
38.9	17.3	114.3	22.9	56

APPENDIX 3.

Provincial Data for the Fourteen Major Variables in the Economic Dimension

(see figures 5.1–5.14 for sources)

Province	RGDP per capita (Rp 000) without oil 1980	Consumer price index in provincial capitals 1981	Percentage living below the poverty line 1980
1. Aceh	224.6	171.4	8.8
2. North Sumatra	298.5	175.5	20.4
3. West Sumatra	180.3	182.9	14.0
4. Riau	255.0	175.6	13.3
5. Jambi	230.1	193.5	7.9
6. South Sumatra	315.9	193.9	13.6
7. Bengkulu	169.9	169.6	21.0
8. Lampung	191.0	181.6	45.5
Sumatra			20.4
9. Jakarta	589.5	165.0	16.9
10. West Java	207.7	183.7	32.7
11. Central Java	150.5	189.3	57.9
12. Yogyakarta	148.4	187.8	59.9
13. East Java	202.2	192.3	54.9
Java			46.5
14. Bali	197.9	178.2	38.3
15. West Nusatenggara	111.0	178.8	50.0
16. East Nusatenggara	104.3	173.0	56.6
17. East Timor	n.a.	n.a.	n.a.
Nusatenggara			48.6
18. West Kalimantan	214.1	164.3	9.4
19. Central Kalimantan	345.5	169.7	12.3
20. South Kalimantan	194.5	190.7	12.5
21. East Kalimantan	846.6	160.3	13.4
Kalimantan			11.5
22. North Sulawesi	257.9	190.6	32.7
23. Central Sulawesi	173.7	173.5	28.8
24. South Sulawesi	193.6	165.8	42.3
25. Southeast Sulawesi	169.5	170.0	49.1
Sulawesi			39.3
26. Maluku	278.7	151.6	39.0
27. Irian Jaya	213.2	163.2	7.8
Maluku & Irian Jaya			34.7
Indonesia			34.3

n.a.: not available

Percentage living in deprivation 1980	Percentage owning a sideboard 1980	Percentage using electricity for lighting 1980	Percentage using kerosene, gas, or electricity for cooking 1980
1.6	39.9	9.7	16.0
2.6	56.8	17.5	26.0
3.3	46.2	12.6	17.8
6.7	49.9	17.8	29.6
2.4	44.4	19.7	17.4
3.8	48.6	26.7	26.0
8.9	49.0	12.0	14.5
5.1	43.6	6.3	11.9
3.7		15.7	21.1
0.6	69.0	47.8	95.9
0.3	56.1	13.9	33.1
0.7	33.2	8.1	16.5
3.6	32.1	11.4	17.9
0.7	45.2	12.1	23.9
0.7		13.7	28.8
20.6	48.0	18.7	17.7
20.9	25.4	7.3	12.1
44.4	15.3	4.3	3.8
n.a.	n.a.	n.a.	n.a.
28.9		9.9	11.2
5.3	33.3	16.7	16.9
insignificant	54.6	12.8	6.7
0.9	66.9	21.8	12.0
8.8	62.3	33.7	41.0
2.6		20.9	18.1
0.6	54.1	22.3	20.1
4.1	31.7	9.0	6.5
4.2	54.7	14.6	17.7
5.3	28.3	6.4	5.4
3.6		14.8	15.7
13.5	34.3	15.4	16.6
5.9	13.4	10.4	13.2
12.5		13.0	14.9
3.3	46.1	14.2	25.1

Province	Provincial tax contributions in Rp 000 per capita 1980–1981	Provincial government expenditures in Rp 000 per capita 1980–1981	Central government support for development programs (Rp 000 per capita) 1980–1981
1. Aceh	5.05	11.6	0.5
2. North Sumatra	2.87	10.5	1.2
3. West Sumatra	2.56	10.7	1.5
4. Riau	4.25	11.8	4.0
5. Jambi	3.75	13.9	6.0
6. South Sumatra	2.97	9.1	2.2
7. Bengkulu	2.74	15.1	6.7
8. Lampung	2.17	6.4	1.3
Sumatra	3.09	10.1	1.8
9. Jakarta	20.60	24.1	0.8
10. West Java	2.03	6.8	0.4
11. Central Java	1.69	7.2	0.4
12. Yogyakarta	2.22	11.8	1.6
13. East Java	1.34	6.4	0.3
Java	3.04	8.2	0.4
14. Bali	2.93	10.6	2.1
15. West Nusatenggara	1.26	8.3	1.8
16. East Nusatenggara	0.69	10.7	1.8
17. East Timor	n.a.	n.a.	n.a.
Nusatenggara	1.58	9.8	1.9
18. West Kalimantan	5.78	12.0	2.4
19. Central Kalimantan	9.63	25.9	16.8
20. South Kalimantan	4.87	13.5	2.5
21. East Kalimantan	29.77	35.3	20.8
Kalimantan	10.39	14.7	7.8
22. North Sulawesi	2.69	17.3	2.8
23. Central Sulawesi	6.92	20.5	4.5
24. South Sulawesi	2.98	10.4	1.1
25. Southeast Sulawesi	2.09	16.0	5.3
Sulawesi	3.33	13.6	2.2
26. Maluku	3.61	16.3	6.3
27. Irian Jaya	5.43	33.3	4.4
Maluku & Irian Jaya	4.43	24.0	5.5
Indonesia	3.32	9.8	1.4

n.a.: not available

Average percentage growth rate of RGDP 1976–1980	Approved domestic projects (Rp 000 per capita) 1968–1982	Approved foreign investment projects ($U.S. per capita) 1967–1982	Percentage employed in agriculture 1980
31.4	30.4	322.7	70.5
9.4	54.8	209.0	65.9
9.0	64.7	20.5	62.1
7.1	87.4	46.6	58.9
7.5	98.5	11.3	71.8
11.0	192.4	18.8	64.9
17.2	56.8	n.a.	80.4
7.9	28.7	18.9	75.6
	77.0	105.4	67.5
10.0	395.0	270.2	1.9
8.5	96.0	66.9	48.0
8.2	25.6	9.1	54.3
6.1	17.6	1.0	52.8
8.1	44.2	16.9	56.4
	78.8	47.3	50.1
12.8	22.6	9.8	51.2
7.1	19.0	0.7	54.0
11.7	4.0	12.3	76.8
n.a.	n.a.	n.a.	n.a.
	14.9	7.6	61.2
9.4	66.2	6.3	79.0
14.1	202.0	110.3	72.7
14.0	62.1	37.2	59.7
10.3	614.6	214.1	48.3
	183.5	68.2	67.7
14.1	20.0	38.7	54.7
10.0	49.5	14.3	70.4
10.0	51.9	18.7	58.9
10.4	51.2	21.1	69.0
	45.1	22.4	60.5
8.9	100.8	52.4	70.8
11.7	177.7	233.6	73.7
	135.7	134.7	72.2
	81.6	63.3	55.8

Notes

Chapter 1

1. These questions have all been asked before. Political geographers, as well as political scientists, have long been interested in the existence and functioning of the state. For example, Friedrich Ratzel recognized implicitly the need for internal national integration when he described the state as an organic being and a complex system of interacting parts (see Harm de Blij, *Systematic Political Geography,* p. 140). Richard Hartshorne, in "The Functional Approach in Political Geography," distinguished between centripetal forces working for national integration and political cohesion, and centrifugal or divisive forces pulling the state apart. Jean Gottmann focused on the major centripetal or cohesive forces in his discussion of the "spirit" and iconography of each nation ("Geography and International Relations").

2. G. William Skinner, ed., *Local, Ethnic, and National Loyalties in Village Indonesia: A Symposium.* However, Immanuel Wallerstein, ("Ethnicity and National Integration in West Africa," pp. 665–670) found that ethnic loyalties facilitate integration into urban communities.

3. Brian J. L. Berry, "Hierarchical Diffusion: The Basis of Developmental Filtering and Spread in a System of Growth Centers"; Salah El Shakhs, "Development, Primacy, and Systems of Cities."

4. Ernst B. Haas, "The Uniting of Europe and the Uniting of Latin America," p. 315.

5. John Friedmann, "A General Theory of Polarized Development," p. 94.

6. W. A. Douglas Jackson and Edward J. F. Bergman, "On the Organization of Political Space," p. 155.

7. Karl Deutsch, for example, describes integration as "the attainment, within a territory, of a 'sense of community' and of institutions and practices strong enough and widespread enough to assure, for a 'long' time, dependable expectations of 'peaceful change' among its population." Karl W. Deutsch et al., *Political Community and the North Atlantic Area,* p. 2. The Dimensionality of Nations program at Northwestern University and the Yale Political Data Program have been concerned with quantifying indices related to national integration and the political solvency of governments. In a cross-national comparison, these programs have examined the national resources, administrative capabili-

ties, and popular support for particular governments and their formal and informal commitments, but with little consideration of the spatial dimension. See Rudolph J. Rummel, "The Dimensionality of Nations Project"; and Karl W. Deutsch et al., "The Yale Political Data Program." See also Amitai Etzioni, *Political Unification: A Comparative Study of Leaders and Forces;* Philip E. Jacob and James V. Toscano (eds.), *The Integration of Political Communities;* Joseph S. Nye, "Comparative Regional Integration: Concept and Measurement"; Leon N. Lindberg, "Political Integration as a Multidimensional Phenomenon Requiring Multivariate Measurement"; Myron Weiner, "Political Integration and Political Development"; David E. Apter, *The Politics of Modernization;* Fred M. Hayward, "Continuities and Discontinuities Between Studies of National and International Integration: Some Implications for Future Research Efforts"; Karl W. Deutsch and William J. Foltz (eds.), *Nation-Building;* and Bela Balassa, *The Theory of Economic Integration.*

8. Karl W. Deutsch, *Nationalism and Social Communication,* pp. 63–64.

9. Clifford Geertz, for example, in *Agricultural Involution: The Process of Ecological Change in Indonesia,* divided Indonesia into two ecological zones: Inner Indonesia, corresponding to Java and characterized by wet-rice agriculture, fertile volcanic soil, high agricultural productivity, and high population density; and Outer Islands, centered upon swidden agriculture, alkaline soils, low agricultural productivity, and low population density. Brian J. L. Berry, Edgar C. Conkling, and D. Michael Ray, in *The Geography of Economic Systems,* pp. 400–402 and 408, contrast the inner Indonesian heartland of Java, Madura, and Bali with the Outer Islands; the high-density, inner-Indonesian core with a set of sparsely populated, agriculturally oriented hinterlands. Charles A. Fisher, in *South-East Asia: A Social, Economic and Political Geography,* pp. 377–381, writes of "Java versus the Outer Territories"; and William A. Withington, in *Southeast Asia: Realm of Contrasts,* of "Indonesia: Insular Contrasts of the Java Core with the Outer Islands."

10. Fisher, *South-East Asia,* p. 17.

11. G. J. Missen, *Viewpoint on Indonesia: A Geographical Study,* p. 23.

12. Clifford Geertz, *Agricultural Involution,* p. 39.

13. Hildred Geertz, "Indonesian Cultures and Communities," p. 30.

14. James L. Peacock, *Indonesia: An Anthropological Perspective,* p. 149.

15. Hildred Geertz, "Indonesian Cultures and Communities," p. 95.

16. Clifford Geertz, "The Integrative Revolution: Primordial Sentiments and Civil Politics in the New States," p. 212.

Chapter 2

1. A. G. Thorne, "The Longest Link: Human Evolution in Southeast Asia and the Settlement of Australia," p. 35.

2. Peter Bellwood, "Plants, Climate and People: The Early Horticultural Prehistory of Austronesia," p. 57.

3. Wilfred T. Neill, *Twentieth Century Indonesia,* p. 208.

4. Ibid., p. 210.

5. George McT. Kahin, "Indonesia," p. 474.

6. There were, however, Javanese settlements dating from at least the fifteenth century in Ternate, Hitu, and Ambon in the Moluccas. D.J.M. Tate, *The Making of Modern South-East Asia,* vol. 1, *The European Conquest,* p. 29.

7. See Bernhard H. M. Vlekke, *Nusantara: A History of Indonesia;* and Neill, *Twentieth Century Indonesia.*

8. Neill, *Twentieth Century Indonesia,* p. 225. The name Indonesia itself is a recent creation. The British ethnologist G. R. Logan, in 1850, was probably the first to call the Netherlands East Indies "the Indonesian archipelago." The term Indonesia was first used by Indonesian students in the Netherlands who formed their own *Indonesisch Verbond van Studeerenden* in 1917. Its first use in a political context was by the *Perserikatan Komunis Indonesia* (the Indonesian Communist Union) in 1920; it was then adopted by other organizations. The name gained acceptance partly through Suprapto's 1928 authorship of a national anthem for the infant nationalist movement, called "Indonesia Raya," and partly through its acceptance as the nation's name during the Japanese occupation (1942–1945). In 1945, when the Republic was proclaimed, Indonesia was its official name.

9. As is apparent in Gertrude J. Resink, *Indonesia's History Between the Myths.*

10. Bruce Grant, *Indonesia,* p. 25.

11. John D. Legge, *Indonesia,* p. 29.

12. Paul Wheatley, *The Golden Khersonese: Studies in the Historical Geography of the Malay Peninsula Before A.D. 1500,* p. 298.

13. Neill, *Twentieth Century Indonesia,* p. 244.

14. Ailsa G. Zainu'ddin, *A Short History of Indonesia,* p. 42.

15. Ibid., p. 44.

16. Tate, *The Making of Modern South-East Asia,* vol. 1, *The European Conquest,* pp. 10, 31.

17. "Dari Dieng memantjarlah untuk pertama dari Indonesia sinar kebudayaan Mataram-Kuna meliputi seluruh Nusantara. . . ." ("It was from Dieng [the location of the original kingdom of Mataram in central Java] that the rays of the ancient civilization of Mataram radiated for the first time from Indonesia, enfolding all of Nusantara. . . ."), "Bhinneka Tunggal Ika Terbabar," p. 218. The early Mataram kingdom left some of the earliest of Java's temple remains on the Dieng Plateau in central Java.

18. Legge, *Indonesia,* p. 28.

19. Jon M. Reinhardt, *Foreign Policy and National Integration: The Case of Indonesia,* p. 14.

20. Jeanne Blamey, "Ancient Indonesian Empires," p. 29.

21. Tate, *The Making of Modern South-East Asia,* vol. 1, *The European Conquest,* p. 38.

22. Formerly Pajajaran. See Vlekke, *Nusantara,* p. 70.

23. Wheatley, *The Golden Khersonese,* pp. 302–303. Wheatley refers to C. C. Berg's article, "De sadeng-oorlog en de mythe van Groot-Majapahit."

24. Vlekke, *Nusantara,* p. 84. For a further discussion of the problem of the historicity of the events of this period see Legge, *Indonesia,* pp. 20–41.

25. Legge, *Indonesia,* p. 30.

26. Grant, *Indonesia*, p. 7.

27. Neill, *Twentieth Century Indonesia*, p. 247.

28. See Resink, *Indonesia's History*, p. 21.

29. Quoted in Justus M. van der Kroef, "Indonesia: Centrifugal Economies," p. 214.

30. Legge, *Indonesia*, p. 70.

31. Vlekke, *Nusantara*, p. 148.

32. Tate, *The Making of Modern South-East Asia*, vol. 1, *The European Conquest*, p. 121.

33. Zainu'ddin, *A Short History of Indonesia*, p. 112.

34. Vlekke, *Nusantara*, pp. 159, 166, 203–204.

35. Legge, *Indonesia*, p. 73.

36. Zainu'ddin, *A Short History of Indonesia*, p. 107.

37. Tate, *The Making of Modern South-East Asia*, vol. 1, *The European Conquest*, p. 94.

38. Neill, *Twentieth Century Indonesia*, p. 286.

39. This characteristic was by no means unique to Indonesia, however; it is typical of many Southeast Asian countries.

40. This was true outside Java as well as in Java. For example, in western Sumatra the Dutch supported the *adat* (traditional) leaders in the Padri Wars. Legge, *Indonesia*, p. 77.

41. Tate, *The Making of Modern South-East Asia*, vol.1, *The European Conquest*, p. 83.

42. The Cultivation System entailed both the growing of commercial crops (such as sugar) on Javanese peasant land and the establishment of vast, state-owned plantations of coffee, indigo, tea, tobacco, cotton, pepper, kapok, and quinine, cultivated by forced labor, to ease the Dutch financial crisis in the homeland. For over a century Dutch colonial activity concentrated on Java, but spread to a few favored districts in Sumatra, particularly western Sumatra.

43. Legge, *Indonesia*, pp. 79–80.

44. Ibid., p. 82.

45. Ibid., p. 81.

46. Ibid., p. 85.

47. Tate, *The Making of Modern South-East Asia*, vol. 1, *The European Conquest*, p. 121.

48. By the British. Ibid., p. 104.

49. Grant, *Indonesia*, p. 16.

50. The Java War of 1825 and the struggle of western Sumatra against the Dutch in the 1820s and 1830s are examples of these movements of resistance.

51. Bernhard Dahm, *History of Indonesia in the Twentieth Century*, p. 41.

52. Zainu'ddin, *A Short History of Indonesia*, p. 169.

53. Legge, *Indonesia*, p. 116.

54. Ibid., p. 93.

55. Neill, *Twentieth Century Indonesia*, p. 296.

56. This is exemplified in the civil service figures for 1940, where out of 3,039 civil service positions classified as "higher rank" only 221 were held by Indonesians. See Kahin, "Indonesia," p. 491.

57. Dahm, *History of Indonesia,* p. 28.

58. Legge, *Indonesia,* p. 128.

59. Dahm, *History of Indonesia,* pp. 61–62.

60. Fisher, *South-East Asia,* p. 368.

61. Kahin, "Indonesia," p. 483.

62. Legge, *Indonesia,* pp. 129–130. *Sarekat Islam* (the Islamic Union) claimed over 360,000 members in 1916: 277,277 in Java and Madura, 5,574 in Kalimantan, 75,859 in Sumatra, 1,064 in Bali, and 599 in Celebes (Dahm, *History of Indonesia,* p. 275). It was thus the first mass political organization in the Netherlands East Indies, but floundered rather purposelessly in a welter of religious, social, and economic ideas (William J. O'Malley, "Second Thoughts on Indonesian Nationalism," p. 602).

63. Kahin, "Indonesia," p. 483.

64. After 1903 some provision was made for Indonesian participation in local government, and this experiment was extended in a more systematic fashion after 1922. Local councils were established in regencies and in municipalities, and later at the provincial level, but these had very limited powers. Legge, *Indonesia,* p. 123.

65. Legge, *Indonesia,* p. 124.

66. Dahm, *History of Indonesia,* p. 65.

67. Legge, *Indonesia,* p. 128.

68. Ibid., p. 127.

69. Ibid., p. 130.

70. Dahm, *History of Indonesia,* p. 73.

71. Ibid., p. 76.

72. A. Arthur Schiller, *The Formation of Federal Indonesia, 1945–1949,* p. 80.

73. Dahm, *History of Indonesia,* p. 83.

74. Ibid., p. 84.

75. Kahin, "Indonesia," p. 494; Neill, *Twentieth Century Indonesia,* p. 315.

76. Khaidir Anwar, *Indonesian: The Development and Use of a National Language,* p. 40.

77. Legge, *Indonesia,* p. 132.

78. Dahm, *History of Indonesia,* p. 93.

79. Kahin, "Indonesia," p. 495.

80. Ibid., p. 496.

81. Dahm, *History of Indonesia,* p. 91.

82. Ibid., p. 92.

83. Ibid., p. 93.

84. Quoted in Dahm, *History of Indonesia,* p. 89.

85. Dahm, *History of Indonesia,* p. 108.

86. Kahin, "Indonesia," p. 497.

87. Neill, *Twentieth Century Indonesia,* p. 319.

88. Dahm, *History of Indonesia,* p. 105.

89. Ibid., p. 104.

90. Three represented Sumatra (one each from Batak country in northern Sumatra, western Sumatra, and Aceh) and five eastern Indonesia (one each from northern and southern Sulawesi, Kalimantan, Bali, and Ambon).

91. Kahin, "Indonesia," p. 503.

92. Ibid., p. 498.

93. Ibid., p. 499.

94. Fisher, *South-East Asia*, p. 363.

95. Van der Kroef, "Indonesia: Centrifugal Economies," p. 212.

96. Legge, *Indonesia*, pp. 156–157.

97. Dahm, *History of Indonesia*, p. 145.

98. It can also be argued, however, that Indonesia's continued unity has been forced, and its unitary type of government superimposed upon a number of unwilling parts.

99. Berry, Conkling, and Ray, *The Geography of Economic Systems*, p. 418.

100. Herbert Feith, "Indonesia's Political Symbols and Their Wielders."

101. Zainu'ddin, *A Short History of Indonesia*, p. 253.

102. Fisher, *South-East Asia*, p. 374.

103. Van der Kroef, "Indonesia: Centrifugal Economies," p. 199.

104. Modern plantation development was started in certain areas of Sumatra and Sulawesi in the nineteenth century by the colonial government. The east coast of northern Sumatra, for example, was transformed from a swampy to a productive agricultural region through the introduction of export crops and the development of infrastructure.

105. Widjojo Nitisastro, *Population Trends in Indonesia*, pp. 5–6, 126, 174; Biro Pusat Statistik, *Statistik Indonesia: Statistical Pocketbook of Indonesia, 1970 and 1971*, p. 23; Biro Pusat Statistik, *Sensus Penduduk 1980*, Series L, no. 3.

106. Peter Lyon, *War and Peace in South-East Asia*, p. 65.

107. Charles A. Fisher, "Indonesia—A Giant Astir," p. 158.

108. Kahin, "Indonesia," p. 564.

109. Zainu'ddin, *A Short History of Indonesia*, p. 247.

110. For a more complete discussion of the reasons for the details of the *PRRI-Permesta* rebellion, see Barbara S. Harvey, *Permesta: Half a Rebellion*. *PRRI-Permesta* stands for *Pemerintah Revolusioner Republik Indonesia/Perjuangan Semesta Alam* (The Total Struggle of the Republic of Indonesia's Revolutionary Government).

111. Herbert Feith, "Indonesia," p. 240.

112. Indeed, a glossary of acronyms and abbreviations published in 1970 contained over 9,000 items. See A. Morzer Bruyns, *Glossary of Abbreviations and Acronyms Used in Indonesia*.

113. After his gradual removal from power between 1965 and 1967, Sukarno was discredited for a while but has recently been rehabilitated as a great, patriotic, nationalist leader.

114. Legge, *Indonesia*, p. 154.

115. Estimates of the total number killed varied from 78,500, suggested by a Fact-Finding Commission appointed by the president at the end of December 1965, to one million, based on an army-sponsored survey conducted by students from Bandung and Jakarta. The most commonly accepted estimate is between 250,000 and 500,000. In 1976, the head of *Kopkamtib* (the Operational Command for the Restoration of Security and Order), Admiral Sudomo, estimated that between 450,000 and 500,000 had been killed (*Tempo*, July 10,

1976). A further estimated 200,000 people were arrested (*Harian Kami,* July 27, 1967). See Harold Crouch, *The Army and Politics in Indonesia,* p. 155.

116. Crouch, *The Army and Politics in Indonesia,* p. 273.

117. Ibid., pp. 344–345. However, this was significantly different from the Middle Way, formulated by General Nasution after the introduction of Guided Democracy in 1957. This ideology permitted army officers to participate actively in the affairs of government but not to seek a dominant position. By contrast under the *Dwi Fungsi* doctrine, established in 1965, no limitations were placed on the army's political role; indeed, it justified the increasing military domination of the government by stressing that the army was concerned with all fields of social life.

118. In 1966, twelve out of the twenty-four provincial governors were army officers. By 1971, the number had increased to twenty (Crouch, *The Army and Politics in Indonesia,* p. 244). This was accompanied by a similar increase at the level of *bupati* (head of a district or *kabupaten*) and mayor, where, by 1971, two-thirds were military personnel.

119. Crouch, *The Army and Politics in Indonesia,* p. 25.

120. Ibid., p. 348.

121. Ibid., p. 277.

122. Ibid., p. 321.

123. Ibid., p. 285.

124. Ibid., p. 318.

125. Ibid., p. 302.

126. "Javanese" in this context includes all three of the major ethnic groups living in Java: the Sundanese in West Java, the Javanese in Central and East Java, and the Madurese in East Java and Madura.

127. See Akio Yasunaka, "Basic Data on Indonesian Political Leaders"; and O. G. Roeder (compiler), *Who's Who in Indonesia: Biographies of Prominent Indonesian Personalities in All Fields.* For details on the military elite see Benedict R. Anderson et al., "Data on the Current Military Elite"; Benedict R. Anderson et al., "Current Data on the Indonesian Army Elite"; Benedict R. Anderson and Susan Hatch, "Current Data on the Indonesian Military Elite" (1973); ibid., (1974).

128. Crouch, *The Army and Politics in Indonesia,* p. 306.

129. Ruth T. McVey, "The Post-Revolutionary Transformation of the Indonesian Army, Part II," p. 172.

130. See Taufik Abdullah et al., "Current Data on the Indonesian Military Elite after the Reorganization of 1969–1970."

131. Crouch, *The Army and Politics in Indonesia,* p. 237.

132. Much of this section is based on the article by Ralph R. Premdas, "The Organisasi Papua Merdeka in Irian Jaya."

133. R. J. May, "Irian Jaya: West Papuan Nationalism in 1979," p. 721.

134. Premdas, "The Organisasi Papua Merdeka," p. 1061.

135. Ibid., p. 1062.

136. Ibid., p. 1067.

137. Peter Hastings, "Timor and West Irian: The Reasons Why," pp. 715–716.

138. James Dunn, *Timor: A People Betrayed*, p. 299.

139. Ibid., p. 321.

140. Ibid., p. 329. See also U.S. House of Representatives, "Famine Relief for East Timor."

141. Harold Crouch, "No Enemy in Sight," p. 34.

142. Steven Jones, "Fight for Timor Grows Quiet but Goes On." However, journalists who are allowed to visit East Timor are strictly screened first and are limited in the areas they may visit.

143. Dunn, *Timor*, pp. 336–337.

Chapter 3

1. Peacock, *Indonesia: An Anthropological Perspective*, p. 143.

2. See William A. Foley, "History of Migrations in Indonesia as Seen by a Linguist."

3. Anwar, *Indonesian*, p. 21.

4. Ibid., p. 178.

5. Biro Pusat Statistik, *Sensus Penduduk 1980*, Series S, no. 2, Table 14.3.

6. Biro Pusat Statistik, *Sensus Penduduk 1971*, Series E, Table 13.

7. Biro Pusat Statistik, *Sensus Penduduk 1980*, Series S, no. 2, Table 16.3.

8. Anwar, *Indonesian*, p. 145.

9. Most of the maps in this and subsequent chapters are based on published census data that should be accepted as approximations and illustrative of overall patterns rather than as precise facts.

10. Biro Pusat Statistik, *Sensus Penduduk 1980*, Series S, no. 2, Table 14.3.

11. Anwar, *Indonesian*, p. 138.

12. Ibid., p. 151.

13. Zainu'ddin, *A Short History of Indonesia*, p. 61.

14. Neill, *Twentieth Century Indonesia*, p. 252.

15. See Clifford Geertz, *The Religion of Java*.

16. Taufik Abdullah, "The Sociocultural Scene in Indonesia," p. 66.

17. However, the size of the change makes these figures seem doubtful, although there is no reason to doubt the trend reflected in the figures.

18. Abdullah, "The Sociocultural Scene in Indonesia," p. 74.

19. Republik Indonesia, *Rencana Pembangunan Lima Tahun Keempat, 1984/85–1988/89*, vol. 2, pp. 518–519. These percentages again illustrate the scepticism with which the published data on Indonesia should be treated. A school participation rate of over 97 percent is most unlikely!

20. Biro Pusat Statistik, *Statistik Indonesia 1983, Buku Saku*, Table III.1.1.

21. Frank W. Speed, *Indonesia Today*, p. 55.

22. However, these figures may not be strictly comparable, because the figures in 1980 and 1971 are based on the population ten years of age and over and not on the entire population as presumably the earlier estimate was.

23. See Clifford Geertz, "Afterword: The Politics of Meaning," p. 321.

24. Feith, "Indonesia's Political Symbols," p. 86.

25. Zainu'ddin, *A Short History of Indonesia*, p. 243.

26. For more details, see Ann Ruth Willner, "The Neotraditional Accommodation to Political Independence: The Case of Indonesia."

27. See Daniel S. Lev, "Judicial Institutions and Legal Culture in Indonesia."

28. Sutan Takdir Alisjahbana, *Indonesia: Social and Cultural Revolution,* p. 71.

29. Frederica M. Bunge, ed., *Indonesia: A Country Study,* p. 186.

30. Ibid.

31. It has been estimated that the Chinese controlled about 70 percent of the monetized sector of the economy in the late 1960s. See Business International Corporation, *Doing Business in the New Indonesia,* p. 4.

32. Victor Purcell, *The Chinese in Southeast Asia,* p. 385.

33. J. S. Furnivall, *Netherlands India: A Study of Plural Economy,* p. 47.

34. G. William Skinner, "Change and Persistence in Chinese Culture Overseas: A Comparison of Thailand and Java," pp. 401–404.

35. Charles A. Coppel, "China and the Ethnic Chinese in Indonesia," pp. 731–732.

36. Ibid., p. 729.

37. Nena Vreeland et al., *Area Handbook for Indonesia,* p. 103. See also G. William Skinner, "The Chinese Minority," pp. 105–108.

38. Susumu Awanohara, "The Perennial Problem," p. 26.

39. Calculated from Table IV.1.15 in Biro Pusat Statistik, *Statistik Indonesia 1982.*

40. Purcell, *The Chinese in Southeast Asia,* p. 387.

41. Biro Pusat Statistik, *Statistik Bioskop Indonesia 1981 dan 1982,* Table 4.

42. Biro Pusat Statistik, *Statistik Indonesia 1983,* p. 142.

43. Elihu Katz and George Wedell, *Broadcasting in the Third World: Promise and Performance.*

44. See Table 66.3 in Biro Pusat Statistik, *Sensus Penduduk 1980,* Series S, no. 2; and Table III.1.9 in Biro Pusat Statistik, *Statistik Indonesia 1983, Buku Saku.*

45. See Tables III.1.8 and III.1.9 in Biro Pusat Statistik, *Statistik Indonesia 1983, Buku Saku* for details.

46. Yet this is a big improvement over the 1972 figure of 50,000 persons per health center.

47. Brian J. L. Berry, "City Size and Economic Development, Conceptual Synthesis and Policy Problems, with Special Reference to South and Southeast Asia."

48. The definition of urban includes all urban centers belonging to recognized administrative categories (*kotamadya* [municipalities] and *kota administratif* [administrative cities]) and those wards *(kelurahan)* or villages that contained population densities of 5,000 or more persons per square kilometer, had more than 25 percent of households directly dependent on individuals working outside the agricultural sector, or had eight or more of sixteen designated "urban facilities." See Jeremy Evans, "The Growth of Urban Centres in Java Since 1961," p. 54.

49. These figures are not strictly comparable because of boundary and definition changes in the intercensal periods. See Evans, "The Growth of Urban Centres."

50. Gavin Jones, "The Problem of Urbanization in Indonesia," p. 1.

51. Hildred Geertz, "Indonesian Cultures and Communities," pp. 33–41.

52. Missen, *Viewpoint on Indonesia,* p. 315.

53. Evans, "The Growth of Urban Centres," p. 56.

Chapter 4

1. William A. Withington, "The Economic Infrastructure," p. 55.

2. Stephen B. Wickman, "The Economy," p. 164.

3. Biro Pusat Statistik, *Statistik Indonesia 1983, Buku Saku,* Table VII.2.6.

4. Calculated from Table VII.1.3 in Biro Pusat Statistik, *Statistik Indonesia 1983, Buku Saku.*

5. *Asia Research Bulletin* (October 1976), p. 254.

6. Calculated from Table 2 in Biro Pusat Statistik, *Statistik Kendaraan Bermotor dan Panjang Jalan 1974;* and Table VIII.1.4 in Biro Pusat Statistik, *Statistik Indonesia 1982.*

7. Calculated from Table VII.2.3 in Biro Pusat Statistik, *Statistik Indonesia 1983, Buku Saku.*

8. H. W. Dick, "Prahu Shipping in Eastern Indonesia," July 1975; and November 1975.

9. Dick, "Prahu Shipping in Eastern Indonesia," July 1975, p. 70.

10. Nena Vreeland et al., *Area Handbook for Indonesia,* p. 368.

11. Wickman, "The Economy," p. 164.

12. Republik Indonesia, Departemen Perhubungan Laut, Direktorat Perkapalan dan Pelayaran SubDit. Kebandaran dan Awak Kapal, Seksi P.U., *File No. TH 1981/82.*

13. Wickman, "The Economy," p. 164.

14. Calculated from data in *File No. TH 1981/82,* Republik Indonesia, Departemen Perhubungan Laut, Direktorat Perkapalan dan Pelayaran SubDit. Kebandaran dan Awak Kapal, Seksi P.U.

15. Susumu Awanohara, "Overboard on Ships," p. 66.

16. Indonesia, *Prospek Perekonomian Indonesia,* p. 95.

17. Biro Pusat Statistik, *Indikator Ekonomi,* Table VII.14, "Lalu Lintas di Indonesia."

18. Biro Pusat Statistik, *Statistik Angkutan Udara 1981,* Table 9.

19. Peter McCawley, "Survey of Recent Developments" (1985), p. 30.

20. J. B. Sumarlin, *Indonesia: Economic Update 1984,* p. 96.

21. Indonesia, Departemen Penerangan, Proyek Penelitian dan Pengembangan, *Hasil-hasil Polling Pendapat Umum Pelita Tahun Ke-IV.*

22. Biro Pusat Statistik, *Sensus Penduduk 1980,* Series S, no. 2, Table 66.3.

23. *Asia Research Bulletin* (August 1974), p. 2969.

24. Republic of Indonesia, Department of Information, *Indonesia 1979: An Official Handbook,* p. 273.

25. Wickman, "The Economy," p. 166.

26. Biro Pusat Statistik, *Statistik Indonesia 1983, Buku Saku,* Table VII.5.3.

27. Biro Pusat Statistik, *Statistik Kommunikasi 1980,* Table 13.

28. Biro Pusat Statistik, *Statistik Indonesia 1982,* Table VIII.5.5.

29. Judith B. Agassi, "Mass Media in Indonesia."

30. Biro Pusat Statistik, *Statistik Indonesia 1983, Buku Saku,* Table III.1.9.

31. *Asian Recorder* (April 1975), p. 12540.

32. Biro Pusat Statistik, *Sensus Penduduk 1980,* Series S, no. 2, Tables 7.3 and 6.3.

33. Ibid., Table 7.3.

34. Republic of Indonesia, *Bappenas* (National Development Planning Agency), *Repelita IV, The Fourth Five-Year Development Plan of Indonesia, 1984/85–1988/89: A Summary,* p. 47.

35. Economic and Social Commission for Asia and the Pacific, *Migration, Urbanization and Development in Indonesia, A Comparative Study on Migration, Urbanization and Development in the ESCAP Region.* Country Reports III, p. 146.

36. H. W. Arndt, "Transmigration: Achievements, Problems, Prospects," p. 64.

37. Biro Pusat Statistik, *Sensus Penduduk 1980,* Series S, no. 2, Table 7.3.

38. Graeme J. Hugo, "Road Transport, Population Mobility and Development in Indonesia," pp. 355–356.

39. Historically, *merantau* referred to the long-standing traditional practice of the Minangkabau from West Sumatra to migrate temporarily "to another island for a relatively long period but eventually return to the origin community." Graeme J. Hugo, "Circular Migration in Indonesia," p. 64. The term has been expanded by Dean Forbes and others to include circular migration by other groups. *Merantau* has been defined by Mochtar Naim as "leaving one's cultural territory voluntarily, whether for a short or long time, with the aim of earning a living or seeking further knowledge or experience, normally with the intention of returning home." Mochtar Naim, "Voluntary Migration in Indonesia," p. 150.

40. Dean Forbes, "Mobility and Uneven Development in Indonesia: A Critique of Explanations of Migration and Circular Migration," p. 57.

41. Ibid., p. 70.

42. Missen, *Viewpoint on Indonesia,* p. 224.

43. Ibid., p. 280.

44. Vreeland et al., *Area Handbook for Indonesia,* p. 381.

45. Biro Pusat Statistik, *Statistik Indonesia 1983, Buku Saku,* Tables VI.2.1 and VI.2.2.

46. Biro Pusat Statistik, *Statistik Indonesia 1982,* Table VIII.4.3.

47. Biro Pusat Statistik, *Impor Menurut Jenis Barang dan Negeri Asal,* vol. 2, Table 8.

48. Republik Indonesia, Departemen Perdagangan, *Ikhtisar Perkembangan Harga-harga dan Data Statistik Perdagangan.*

49. Calculated from data in Biro Pusat Statistik, *Statistik Bongkar Muat Barang di Pelabuhan Indonesia 1982,* Table 1.

50. Biro Pusat Statistik, *Statistik Indonesia 1982,* Table VIII.4.6.

Chapter 5

1. Friedmann, "A General Theory of Polarized Development."

2. Karl J. Pelzer, "The Agricultural Foundation," p. 152.

3. Douglas S. Paauw, "From Colonial to Guided Economy," p. 163.

4. J. A. C. Mackie, "The Indonesian Economy, 1950–1963," p. 19.

5. Gunnar Myrdal, *Asian Drama: An Inquiry into the Poverty of Nations,* vol. 3, p. 1847.

6. Hendra Esmara, "Regional Income Disparities," p. 52.

7. Clifford Geertz, *Agricultural Involution.*

8. R. M. Sundrum, "Manufacturing Employment 1961–71," p. 58.

9. Java's population increased from nine to sixty-three million in the 100 years before 1961.

10. Bruce Glassburner, "The Economy and Economic Policy: General and Historical," pp. 3–4.

11. Achmad T. Birowo and Gary E. Hansen, "Agricultural and Rural Development: An Overview," p. 2.

12. Between 1967 and 1981 the Japanese invested $3.3 billion in 198 projects in Indonesia, and the Americans $570 million in seventy-seven projects. Jean A. Briggs, "A Pint of Blood? Or $20?," p. 96.

13. In addition to the World Bank, the Asian Development Bank and various United Nations programs contribute to Indonesia's development.

14. Contributing countries (in order of descending magnitude for the 1984–1985 fiscal year) are Japan, the United States, the Netherlands, Australia, West Germany, France, Canada, Italy, Belgium, the United Kingdom, Switzerland, and New Zealand. See *Indonesia Development News* 7 (June 1984), p. 2.

15. Republic of Indonesia, Department of Information, *The First Five-Year Development Plan, 1969/70–1973/74.*

16. Esmara, "Regional Income Disparities," p. 41. See also Douglas S. Paauw, "The Indonesian Economy in the 1980s."

17. Republik Indonesia, Departemen Penerangan, *Rencana Pembangunan Lima Tahun Kedua, 1974/75–1978/79.*

18. *Indonesia Development News* 6 (March 1983), pp. 6–7.

19. Ibid. For a fuller discussion of the Third Five-Year Development Plan, see Republic of Indonesia, Department of Information, *Repelita III. The Third Five-Year Development Plan, 1979–84 (Summary).*

20. Republic of Indonesia, *Bappenas* (National Development Planning Agency), *Repelita IV, The Fourth Five-Year Development Plan of Indonesia, 1984/85–1988/89: A Summary,* pp. 6–7. For the complete plan, see Republik Indonesia, Departemen Penerangan, *Rencana Pembangunan Lima Tahun Keempat 1984/85–1988/89.*

21. H. W. Arndt, "Regional Income Estimates"; Esmara, "Regional Income Disparities." They also warn of the weaknesses in and problems of estimating the RGDP, including lack of basic statistical data, and conceptual problems such as how to allocate certain components and how to ascertain the value added in each region.

22. In 1980 the rate of exchange was Rp 615 per U.S. $1. The contrast in RGDP per capita thus ranged from approximately U.S. $1,377 in East Kalimantan to U.S. $170 in East Nusatenggara.

23. Biro Pusat Statistik, *Pendapatan Regional Propinsi-propinsi di Indonesia 1976–80,* Table IIB.9.

24. *Indonesia Development News* 7 (May 1984), p. 2.

25. *Indonesia Development News* 7 (August 1984), p. 6.

26. *Indonesia Development News* 3 (April 1980), pp. 4–6.

27. H. W. Arndt and R. M. Sundrum, "Regional Price Disparities."

28. World Bank, *Indonesia: Selected Aspects of Spatial Development,* p. 84, quoted with permission. However, these figures do not seem to include subsistence agriculture and appear somewhat questionable.

29. Ibid., p. 89.

30. East Nusatenggara suffers from a very dry climate with the lowest and the most variable rainfall in Indonesia. It is unclear to what extent the droughts of the late 1970s are responsible for its shockingly high deprivation figure. East Nusatenggara depends to a greater extent than any other province on agriculture (including livestock raising) for its RGDP; it is the main supplier of livestock for the nation. It has almost no minerals and is one of the least developed provinces.

31. Birowo and Hansen, "Agricultural and Rural Development," p. 7.

32. Biro Pusat Statistik, *Sensus Penduduk 1980,* Series S, no. 2, Table 66.3. However, serious doubts emerge over the reliability of the sample from which these results are extrapolated.

33. Biro Pusat Statistik, *Statistik Keuangan Pemerintah Daerah, Daerah Tingkat I (Propinsi) 1975/76–1980/81,* Table 1.

34. See Colin Rosser, "Training in Regional Development in Indonesia: A Report Prepared for the Regional Development Division of *Bappenas.*" See also Robert van Leeuwan, "Central Government Subsidies for Regional Development: Notes."

35. Esmara, "Regional Income Disparities," p. 56.

36. Friedmann, "A General Theory of Polarized Development."

37. Geoffrey B. Hainsworth, "Dilemmas of Development in Indonesia," p. 190.

38. Gupta, for example, stated in 1975 that Indonesia "is heading towards a more uneven income distribution, unless government intervention occurs." S. Gupta, "Income Distribution, Employment, and Growth: A Case Study of Indonesia," p. 71.

39. Translated into U.S. dollar amounts, the gap in 1972 was over twelvefold, from $45.80 in the poorest province to $562.34 in the richest (using the weighted exchange rate of Rp 393 per U.S. $1); in 1980, it was eightfold, from $169.59 to $1,376.59 (using the exchange rate of Rp 615 per U.S. $1). Data for 1972 from Esmara, "Regional Income Disparities," p. 48. Data for 1980 from Biro Pusat Statistik, *Statistik Indonesia 1983, Buku Saku,* Table X.9.

40. The negative growth rate in North Sulawesi between 1968 and 1972 has been attributed at least in part to the uncertain external market for copra, North Sulawesi's prime export. World Bank, *Indonesia: Selected Aspects,* p. 15, quoted with permission. East Kalimantan's RGDP grew because of the extraction of its timber, oil, and natural gas resources. East Kalimantan also has rich coal and recently discovered tin deposits.

41. Esmara, "Regional Income Disparities," p. 54.

42. Aceh's spectacular growth rate between 1976 and 1980 relates to the

development of its extensive natural gas reserves. Natural gas boosted Aceh's RGDP from $353.2 million in 1977 to $1.03 billion in 1980. Aceh has been the recipient of large amounts of foreign investment, not only for the exploitation of its huge natural gas field at Arun, but also for the development of the Lhokseumawe coastal area, 20 miles north of Arun, into a twenty-square-kilometer port and industrial zone. This reputedly is the single largest concentration of investment in Indonesia; by 1981 $4.1 billion had been invested there. *Indonesia Development News* 5 (August 1982), p. 4.

43. Investment proposals relate to the development of livestock and rain-fed agriculture, onshore marine fisheries, expansion of commercial tree crops, watershed rehabilitation, irrigation development, improvements to infrastructure, and the promotion of industry.

44. Ross Garnaut, "General Repercussions of the Resources Boom in the Segmented Indonesian Economy," p. 415.

45. Ibid., pp. 419–420.

46. Peter McCawley and Chris Manning, "Survey of Recent Developments," p. 36.

47. Ibid., p. 35.

48. Biro Pusat Statistik, *Indikator Ekonomi 1982,* Tables IV.16b and IV.16d.

49. Ibid., Table 16d.

50. Ibid., Table 16b.

51. Torben M. Roepstorff, "Industrial Development in Indonesia: Performance and Prospects," pp. 32–44.

52. Anwar Nasution, "Survey of Recent Developments," p. 2.

53. *Indonesia Development News* 8 (October 1984), p. 5.

54. Peter McCawley, *Industrialization in Indonesia: Development and Prospects,* p. 14.

55. Roepstorff, "Industrial Development in Indonesia," p. 43.

56. Juergen B. Donges, Bernd Stecher, and Frank Wolter, *Industrial Development Policies for Indonesia,* p. 23.

57. Peter McCawley, "The Growth of the Industrial Sector," p. 77.

58. R. B. Suhartono, "Industrial Development in Indonesia," p. 4.

59. H. W. Arndt, "Development and Equality: An Overview," p. 48.

60. Steven J. Keuning, "Farm Size, Land Use, and Profitability of Food Crops in Indonesia," p. 80.

61. Birowo and Hansen, "Agricultural and Rural Development," p. 5.

62. Irma Adelman and Cynthia Taft Morris, *Economic Growth and Social Equity in Developing Countries.*

63. Percentages calculated from Biro Pusat Statistik, *Sensus Penduduk 1980,* Series S, no. 2, Table 44.9.

64. Republic of Indonesia, *Bappenas* (National Development Planning Agency), *Repelita IV, The Fourth Five-Year Development Plan of Indonesia, 1984/85–1988/89: A Summary,* p. 13.

65. The employment data upon which the conclusions in this section are based must be handled with caution because of their questionable accuracy. For example, although the official unemployment figures were as low as 2.2 percent in 1971 (representing a reduction from 5.4 percent in 1961), these do not reflect

the actual situation, partly because of the number of nonregistered unemployed and the high degree of underemployment. The Federation of Indonesian Labor Unions *(Sudono)* estimated that only twelve million (or 30 percent) of the total of forty-four million officially counted as Indonesia's labor force in 1971 were actually fully employed; thirty-two million, or around 70 percent, were either unemployed or underemployed, caught up in the process of agricultural or urban involution. This included about four million out of work, eleven million working half-time, and seventeen million working less than thirty-two hours a week *(Asia Research Bulletin* [December 1974], p. 36). Any attempt to define unemployment is an exercise in ambiguity, partly because approximately 24 percent of the labor force consists of unpaid family workers. In addition, employment figures depend on the month and season in which they are collected, because there is considerable movement between agricultural employment and service industries, especially at off-peak agricultural times.

66. Birowo and Hansen, "Agricultural and Rural Development," pp. 24–25.

67. Hal Hill, "Survey of Recent Developments," pp. 7–8.

68. *Asian Business* (February 1984), p. 59.

69. H. W. Arndt, "Employment, Unemployment, and Underemployment," p. 106.

70. Bela Balassa, "Types of Economic Integration," p. 11.

Chapter 6

1. See Rudolph J. Rummel, *Applied Factor Analysis,* p. 15.

2. Because factor analysis is based on the correlation matrix, which assumes a linear relationship between each pair of variables. See J. Goddard and A. Kirby, *An Introduction to Factor Analysis, Concepts and Techniques in Modern Geography,* no. 7, p. 17.

3. For statistically valid results in an R-type factor analysis it is necessary to have at least twice as many cases (or provinces) as variables. The alternative Q-mode analysis would have grouped cases (provinces) and not variables, and thus not shown the important relationships among the variables.

4. "Correlates significantly" means at least at the 0.01 level of significance.

5. Measuring educational achievement by those over ten years of age who have completed primary school omits the ten to thirteen year olds still in primary school, while those who have completed high school is an index more of the elite (on average 3.1 percent of the population) than of broad-based educational attainment.

6. See Christine Drake, *The Geography of National Integration: A Case Study of Indonesia,* p. 570.

7. East Kalimantan is the most urbanized province after Jakarta and also by far the wealthiest on a per-capita basis. It is therefore not surprising that it ranks first on this factor, which incorporates television and radio ownership, and access to movie theatres and hospital facilities.

8. If the signs on the scores of the fourth factor are reversed to indicate the

real meaning of this factor, that membership in a cooperative is integrative while the presence of non-Indonesian-citizen Asians is a negative or disintegrative force.

9. Ownership of a sideboard probably indicates a higher income level. However, because of cultural differences among the different ethnic groups in the country, it should be viewed as only one representative measure of economic development.

10. See Drake, *The Geography of National Integration,* p. 622.

11. As discussed in chapter 5, East Kalimantan is an extremely resource-rich province, with large reserves of petroleum, natural gas, timber, and coal. Not only are these products exported in their raw state, but the refining and manufacturing of petroleum products (including fertilizers and chemicals), together with the production of liquified natural gas at the Bontang LNG plant, increase East Kalimantan's wealth. In addition, East Kalimantan has the largest plywood manufacturing capacity of any province in Indonesia. See *Indonesia Development News* 6 (December 1982), p. 3.

12. Of –0.20 or more.

13. See note 9 in chapter 1.

14. In 1955–1956, for example, only 12 percent of Indonesia's total foreign exchange earnings came from Java, whereas over 80 percent of these earnings were spent on consumer and capital goods for Java's rapidly expanding population. Fisher, *South-East Asia,* p. 377.

15. Lance Castles, "The Ethnic Profile of Djakarta," p. 153.

16. Gavin Jones, "The Problem of Urbanization in Indonesia," p. 3.

17. Jacqueline Lineton, "Pasompe 'Ugi': Bugis Migrants and Wanderers."

18. Harvey, *Permesta: Half a Rebellion,* p. 21.

19. Barbara S. Harvey, "Tradition, Islam and Rebellion: South Sulawesi: 1950–65," p. 50.

20. Ujung Pandang's population in 1980 was only 709,038, less than 12 percent of the province's population.

21. Drake, *The Geography of National Integration,* pp. 645–646.

22. *Indonesia Development News* 3 (August 1980), pp. 6–7.

Chapter 7

1. Dahm, *History of Indonesia,* p. 145. See also Feith, "Indonesia's Political Symbols."

2. Berry, Conkling, and Ray, *The Geography of Economic Systems,* p. 418.

3. Slamet Sutrisno, *Sedikit Tentang Strategi Kebudayaan Nasional Indonesia,* p. 68.

4. This emphasis on one nationwide, national language began before the Suharto era, in the early 1950s; it has been continued and extended since then.

5. R. Murray Thomas, "Indonesian Education: Communist Strategies (1950–65) and Government Counter Strategies (1966–80)," p. 389.

6. Republik Indonesia, *Rencana Pembangunan Lima Tahun Keempat 1984/85–1988/89,* vol. 2, p. 518.

7. An article in the Indonesian newspaper, *Merdeka* (July 20, 1984), claimed

that almost half of the school-age children were still unable to attend school because of lack of finances or absence of opportunities.

8. The government claims that the percentage of thirteen to fifteen year olds in school has risen from 28.4 percent in 1978–1979 to 44.0 percent in 1983–1984 and the percentage of sixteen to eighteen year olds has increased from 14.7 percent in 1978–1979 to 25.3 percent in 1983–1984. Republik Indonesia, *Rencana Pembangunan Lima Tahun Keempat 1984/85–1988/89*, vol. 2, p. 520. However, these percentages again seem suspiciously high.

9. William K. Cummings, "Notes on Higher Education and Indonesian Society," p. 29.

10. Republik Indonesia, *Rencana Pembangunan Lima Tahun Keempat 1984/85–1988/89*, vol. 2, p. 520.

11. "New University Aiding Indonesian Students," p. 8A.

12. *Indonesia Development News* 8 (December 1984), p. 7.

13. David Jenkins, "What Makes Daud Jusuf Run?," p. 36.

14. Susumu Awanohara, "The New Call to Prayer," p. 26.

15. Peter Rodgers, "Indonesia's Faithful Flex Their Political Muscle," p. 38.

16. Leo Suryadinata, "Indonesia in 1980: Continuity Rather than Change," p. 134.

17. The government claims to have supported equally the other official religions in the country in their building programs. See Republik Indonesia, *Rencana Pembangunan Lima Tahun Keempat 1984/85–1988/89*, vol. 2, p. 476.

18. Guy Sacerdoti, "The Wheel of Fortune Stops."

19. Susumu Awanohara, "On the Defensive in the Pancasila State."

20. Donald E. Weatherbee, "Indonesia in 1984: Pancasila, Politics, and Power," p. 189.

21. Susumu Awanohara, "A Matter of Principles," p. 16.

22. Susumu Awanohara, "A First Warning Shot," p. 15.

23. Awanohara, "The New Call to Prayer," p. 28.

24. Ibid.

25. Thomas, "Indonesian Education," p. 391.

26. Michael Morfit, "Panca Sila: The Indonesian State Ideology According to the New Order Government," pp. 842–843.

27. Ibid., p. 839.

28. As stated by the Minister of Trade and Cooperatives, according to *Kompas*, January 3, 1979, quoted in Leo Suryadinata, "Indonesia in 1979: Controlled Dissent," p. 134.

29. Lincoln Kaye, "Fighting-trim Reforms," p. 24.

30. Ibid.

31. Peter McCawley, "The Devaluation and Structural Change in Indonesia," p. 156.

32. *Kompas* (June 16, 1979).

33. H. W. Arndt, "Growth and Equity Objectives in Economic Thought about Indonesia," p. 432.

34. Indonesian Ministry of Education and Culture, 1977.

35. McCawley, "Survey of Recent Developments" (1985), p. 30.

36. H. W. Dick, "Survey of Recent Developments," p. 35.

37. Ibid.

38. *Indonesia Development News* 8 (September 1984), pp. 4-5.

39. H. W. Dick, "Interisland Shipping: Progress, Problems and Prospects," p. 111.

40. McCawley, "Survey of Recent Developments" (1985), p. 30.

41. Lincoln Kaye, "Anchored in Realism," p. 59; and *Indonesia Development News* 8 (April 1985), pp. 1-2.

42. Nasution, "Survey of Recent Developments," p. 13.

43. Dick, "Interisland Shipping," p. 95.

44. Ibid., p. 96.

45. Ibid., p. 113.

46. *Indonesia Development News* 8 (September 1984), p. 5.

47. Ibid., p. 8.

48. Guy Sacerdoti, "Garuda's Hidden Assets," p. 38.

49. McCawley, "Survey of Recent Developments" (1985), p. 30.

50. Ibid.

51. *Indonesia Development News* 7 (April 1984), p. 6.

52. Republik Indonesia, Departemen Penerangan, *Pidato Kenegaraan Presiden Republik Indonesia Soeharto di depan Sidang Dewan Perwakilan Rakyat 16 Augustus 1984 (pidato dan lampiran)*, p. 1203.

53. Ibid.

54. Paul Handley, "Hamming up the Airways," p. 50.

55. Susumu Awanohara, "More of the Same," p. 15.

56. Susumu Awanohara, "Islam on the Hustings," p. 24.

57. Indonesia's five-year development plans have all been designed by predominantly United States (Berkeley)-trained economists. In addition, international economic advisers from such organizations as the World Bank and the Inter-Governmental Group on Indonesia have helped to shape the direction of Indonesian development.

58. Esmara, "Regional Income Disparities," p. 41.

59. Hidayat, "Peranan Sektor Informal dalam Perekonomian Indonesia."

60. Republik Indonesia, Departemen Penerangan, *Rencana Pembangunan Lima Tahun Kedua, 1974/75-1978/79.*

61. Suharto, *Report to the Nation: Address before the House of the People's Representatives on the 1975/76 State Budget.*

62. It thus reflects the "basic needs" approach of international development agencies of the early 1970s.

63. Republic of Indonesia, Directorate of City and Regional Planning, "A Short Note on Area/Regional Development Studies in Indonesia."

64. Soegijoko Sugijanto and Budhy T. Sugijanto, "Rural-Urban Migration in Indonesia," p. 53.

65. Republic of Indonesia, Department of Information, *Repelita III. The Third Five-Year Development Plan, 1979-84 (Summary)*, p. 4.

66. Ibid., pp. 4-5.

67. Suharto, *Address of State by His Excellency the President of the Republic of Indonesia, Soeharto, before the House of the People's Representatives on the Occasion of the 36th Independence Day, August 17th, 1981*, p. 30.

68. Republic of Indonesia, *Bappenas* (National Development Planning Agency), *Repelita IV, The Fourth Five-Year Development Plan of Indonesia, 1984/85–1988/89: A Summary,* pp. 6–7.

69. Soejatmoko, "Some Thoughts on Higher Education."

70. Nasution, "Survey of Recent Developments," p. 9.

71. *Indonesia Development News* 5 (July 1982), p. 4.

72. "Foreign Economic Trends and their Implications for the U.S.," p. 2. But Ruth Daroesman, in "Survey of Recent Developments," p. 1, recognizes only a 7.1 percent growth in manufacturing production during the years 1975–1980.

73. Production rose from 15.2 million metric tons in 1975 to 25.8 million in 1984. Indeed, rice production has more than doubled since 1969, when production was 12.2 million metric tons. *Indonesia Development News* 9 (November/December 1985), p. 2.

74. McCawley, "Survey of Recent Developments" (1985), p. 29.

75. Ibid., p. 30. During the first three five-year plans electricity was extended to 747,000 new consumers. *Repelita IV* calls for the extension of the electricity network to a further 1.6 million consumers in 7,000 additional villages. Yet only 16.7 percent of the population has access to electricity. *Indonesia Development News* 9 (November/December 1985), p. 4.

76. McCawley, "Survey of Recent Developments" (1985), p. 27. Nasution, "Survey of Recent Developments," p. 1, states that the rate of growth of GDP at constant 1973 prices was 5 percent in 1984, compared with 4.3 percent and 2.2 percent in the two previous years.

77. McCawley, "Survey of Recent Developments" (1985), p. 10.

78. Roepstorff, "Industrial Development in Indonesia," p. 34.

79. *Asian Business* (February 1984), p. 59; and Bruce Glassburner and Mark Poffenberger, "Survey of Recent Developments," pp. 5–6.

80. *Indonesia Development News* 7 (April 1984), p. 1.

81. Suhartono, "Industrial Development in Indonesia," p. 19.

82. Roepstorff, "Industrial Development in Indonesia," p. 55.

83. McCawley, "Survey of Recent Developments" (1985), p. 10.

84. Ibid., pp. 29–31.

85. *Indonesia Development News* 4 (October 1980), p. 5. Indeed, coffee output has changed from 90 percent production on large estates before the Second World War to about 92 percent production by the nation's 1.5 million small holders. *Indonesia Development News* 9 (March/April 1986), p. 6.

86. Daroesman, "Survey of Recent Developments," p. 27.

87. Ibid., p. 12.

88. *Indonesia Development News* 7 (July 1984), p. 6.

89. Republic of Indonesia, Department of Information, *Repelita III.* It is estimated that 70 percent of Indonesian households currently live in low-quality housing.

90. Daroesman, "Survey of Recent Developments," p. 11.

91. Ibid., p. 12.

92. The major criticism of this program has been that little allowance has been made for initiative either in the balance among projects or for innovative responses to local needs.

93. Daroesman, "Survey of Recent Developments," p. 16.

94. Ibid.

95. Susumu Awanohara, Manggi Habir, and Paul Handley, "Focus Indonesia '85," p. 45.

96. Daroesman, "Survey of Recent Developments," p. 17.

97. "Widjojo Nitisastro: Clearing the Jungle," p. 8.

98. Awanohara, Habir, and Handley, "Focus Indonesia '85," p. 50.

99. See chapter 4.

100. "Widjojo Nitisastro," p. 7.

101. Ann Stoler, "Class Structure and Female Autonomy in Rural Java," pp. 87–88.

102. Gary E. Hansen, "Introduction," pp. 177–178.

103. Results reported by Guy J. Pauker, "Indonesia in 1980: Regime Fatigue?," p. 237.

104. *Indonesia Development News* 8 (August 1985), p. 7.

105. Paauw, "The Indonesian Economy in the 1980s," p. 41.

106. John A. MacDougall, "Indonesia 1980: Economic Modernization and Political Discontent," p. 339.

107. Benjamin White, "Political Aspects of Poverty, Income Distribution, and their Measurement: Some Examples from Rural Java."

108. G. A. Hughes and I. Islam, "Inequality in Indonesia: A Decomposition Analysis," p. 60.

109. Ibid. See also R. M. Sundrum, "Income Distribution, 1970–76." Unbalanced growth, the rapid growth of the labor force, displacement of some agricultural labor brought on by changes in cultivation practices associated with the Green Revolution, and erosion of traditional means of income sharing have all contributed to a rising inequality of income distribution in rural areas. See Gustav F. Papanek, ed., *The Indonesian Economy,* Part 1.

110. Guy Sacerdoti, "Running to Stand Still," p. 79.

111. Quoted in Pauker, "Indonesia in 1980," p. 234.

112. Daroesman, "Survey of Recent Developments," p. 1.

113. In addition, the drop in the price of oil (and, to a much lesser extent, of other export commodities) has led to severe cuts in the development budget; for example, by 22 percent in 1986.

114. Guy Sacerdoti, "Taking the Pulse," p. 35.

115. World Bank, *Indonesia: Selected Aspects,* p. 7, quoted with permission.

116. Leo Suryadinata and Sharon Siddique, eds., *Trends in Indonesia II,* p. 4.

117. Njoman Suwidjana, "Indonesia's Rice Policy: Development Patterns, Accomplishments, and Problems," p. 157.

118. Derek Healey, "Survey of Recent Developments," pp. 9–10.

119. Daroesman, "Survey of Recent Developments," p. 29.

120. Phyllis Rosendale, "Survey of Recent Developments," (1984), p. 13.

121. Sid Astbury, "Positive Measures Are Needed to Stimulate a Sagging Economy," p. 56.

122. Mohamed Sobary, "Participation in Practice."

123. Ibnoe Sujono, "Kebijaksanaan Koperasi: Beberapa Masalah dan Prospeknya."

124. Susumu Awanohara, "Jakarta at a Jog," p. 98.

125. "September 1985 Log," p. 18.

126. Max Lane, "Who's Paying for the Recession?," p. 12.

127. Hla Myint, "Inward and Outward Looking Countries Revisited: The Case of Indonesia," p. 40.

128. Garnaut, "General Repercussions," pp. 419–420.

129. Anne Booth and Peter McCawley, "Conclusion: Looking to the Future," p. 321.

130. Nasution, "Survey of Recent Developments," p. 13.

131. Lukas Hendrata, "Bureaucracy, Participation and Distribution in Indonesian Development," p. 25.

132. *Asia Research Bulletin* 14 (October 1984), p. 1216.

133. Awanohara, Habir, and Handley, "Focus Indonesia '85," p. 44.

134. H. W. Arndt, "Prospects for the 1980s," p. 51.

135. Biro Pusat Statistik, *Statistik Indonesia 1983, Buku Saku,* pp. 32–35.

136. Morfit, "Panca Sila," p. 846.

137. Leo Suryadinata, "Indonesia in 1979: Controlled Dissent," p. 125. See also Justus M. van der Kroef, " 'Petrus': Patterns of Prophylactic Murder in Indonesia."

138. Imam Walujo, "Renewing National Consensus." See also Peter Mc-Cawley, "Rural Dualism in Indonesia and China: New Technologies, Institutions, and Welfare," p. 379.

139. Glen Williams, "Community Participation and the Role of Voluntary Agencies in Indonesia," p. 23.

140. Awanohara, Habir, and Handley, "Focus Indonesia '85," p. 44.

141. Ulf Sundhaussen, "Regime Crisis in Indonesia: Facts, Fiction, Predictions," p. 833.

142. Pauker, "Indonesia in 1980," p. 236.

143. Ibid.

144. Steven Jones and Raphael Pura, "Suharto-Linked Monopolies Hobble Economy," p. 8.

145. Guy Sacerdoti, "Overdraft of Inefficiency," p. 44.

146. Even though the World Bank claims that more foreign investment would create jobs and help *pribumi* entrepreneurship, which are two major social aims of *Repelita III.* Guy Sacerdoti, "The Technocrats' Success Story," p. 49.

147. Ibid.

148. Awanohara, Habir, and Handley, "Focus Indonesia '85," p. 43.

149. *Indonesia Development News* 8 (August 1985), p. 6.

Chapter 8

1. Such a study would probably identify greater similarities among coastal areas throughout the archipelago and greater contrasts with the more rugged inland areas of each island. In addition, people in coastal areas could be expected to show far greater integration (through coastal traffic and a common way of life) than inhabitants of more inaccessible, remote, and mountainous interiors ever could.

2. Of the 246 *kabupaten* in the country in the early 1980s, only eighty-two (or 33 percent) were in Java, a marked contrast with the proportion of the population living in Java (62 percent).

3. Sutan Takdir Alisjahbana, "Jakarta, A Fat Leech Sucking on the Head of a Fish," quoted in Feith and Smith, "Indonesia," p. 194.

4. In this chapter the term Javanese refers to all three major ethnic groups living in Java (the Sundanese in West Java, the Javanese in Central and East Java, and the Madurese in East Java), but particularly to the ethnic Javanese and Sundanese.

5. Between 1968 and 1982 Jakarta received 21 percent of all domestic capital investment and West Java a further 22 percent (and 19 and 20 percent, respectively, of the value of all approved foreign investment projects). Percentages calculated from Tables IV.16b and IV.16d in Biro Pusat Statistik, *Indikator Ekonomi 1982*.

6. Even though there is evidence to suggest that the growth rate was higher during the first part of the decade than in the latter half, demographers and planners were taken by surprise at the extra millions.

7. Biro Pusat Statistik, *Statistik Indonesia 1983, Buku Saku,* Table II.1.1.

8. Between 1905 and 1977, 991,100 people had been moved under the official government transmigration program; but during this period the population of Java increased by thirty-five million. During *Repelita II,* 1974–1979, approximately 75,380 people per year were resettled; during *Repelita III,* 1979–1984, the numbers more than tripled to 292,000 per year. Yet Java's population continued to grow at a rate of almost two million a year. Costs have escalated: in 1977 the cost of moving a fully subsidized family of five, including transport, land, housing, materials, tools, seed, and initial food supplies, was $1,200; by 1983–1984, the comparable expense was estimated at $11,663. See Colin MacAndrews, "Transmigration in Indonesia: Prospects and Problems," p. 465; and Arndt, "Transmigration: Achievements, Problems, Prospects," pp. 51, 66.

9. Biro Pusat Statistik, *Penduduk Indonesia 1980 Menurut Propinsi dan Kabupaten/Kotamadya,* Series L, pp. 1–22.

10. Sid Astbury, "Agonizing over Mechanization Down on the Indonesian Farm," p. 85.

11. Beth Rose, *An Overview of the Indonesian Rice Economy,* p. 5.

12. "June 1985 Log," p. 6.

13. In 1961 the population of Jakarta was 2.97 million, in 1971 4.58 million, in 1980 6.50 million, and in 1986 an estimated 8.16 million. Biro Pusat Statistik, *Statistik Indonesia 1983, Buku Saku,* Table II.1.2 and Table II.1.1.

14. Barbara Crossette, "Street Vendors of Jakarta Are Sold on Self-Help."

15. "A Political Undertone to the Anti-Chinese Riots in Java," p. 780.

16. As the example of Sri Lanka illustrates. Alan M. Strout, "Pertumbuhan Pertanian, Tenaga Kerja dan Pembagian Pendapatan: Dilema bagi Repelita III."

17. This widening gap, as well as that between rich and poor, illustrates the contention at the beginning of the book that factors of national integration operate at different levels.

18. Population Reference Bureau, *1985 World Population Data Sheet.*

19. Ross Muir, "Survey of Recent Developments," p. 12.

20. Sacerdoti, "The Wheel of Fortune Stops."

21. See, for example, Mohammed Thaib Hasan's letter, "The Plight of Aceh."

22. Michael Richardson, "Jakarta's Can of Worms."

23. Dunn, *Timor: A People Betrayed,* pp. 336–337.

24. Tengku di Tiro, "Indonesia or Java?," p. 4.

25. Benedict R. Anderson and Audrey Kahin, "Current Data on the Indonesian Military Elite," *Indonesia* 29, p. 157.

26. Undoubtedly, a main motivation for his strong political control is to ensure his own retention of power. In October 1986 Suharto announced his readiness to serve a fifth consecutive five-year term.

27. Harold Crouch, "Patrimonialism and Military Rule in Indonesia," p. 586.

28. Guy Sacerdoti, "Consensus Conundrums," p. 34.

29. Some evidence of this can be seen in the appointment of Benny Murdani, considered to be the most hawkish of the regime's military in the suppression of opposition, dissent, and restlessness, to head the armed forces. The political administration has thus been handed over to the Indonesian security and intelligence establishment *(Kopkamtib),* whereas previously *Kopkamtib* was under the control of career defense-force officers rather than career security and intelligence officers. See Max Lane, "Climate of Fear: The Rise of General Benny Murdani," p. 3.

30. Susumu Awanohara, "Suharto's Kingdom," p. 32.

31. "Indonesia—A Sense of General Disillusionment," p. 647.

32. For example, by October 1986, about sixty of the 800 prospective candidates from *Golkar,* 250 of 800 from the *PPP,* and 259 of 629 from the *PDI* had been judged unfit to run in the April 1987 parliamentary elections. Shim Jae Hoon, "Minority Political Parties Face Struggle for Votes," p. 48.

33. Although the official reason given was to reduce the complexity of the electoral system.

34. This weakness is deliberately encouraged by the government as it thereby keeps the parties more amenable.

35. R. William Liddle, "Indonesia 1977: The New Order's Second Parliamentary Election," p. 178.

36. Lucian W. Pye, *Southeast Asia's Political Systems,* p. 61.

37. Guy Sacerdoti, "A One-Man Consensus?," p. 30.

38. For example, even though only ten of the twenty-four inner cabinet are military personnel, the military is in all the key watchdog positions in the administration; in fact, one-third of the Indonesian army is in urban and administrative duties. Over half of the provincial governors likewise are military men. Ho Kwon Ping, "The Men on White Horses Now Ride a Tiger," p. 42.

39. John A. MacDougall, "Patterns of Military Control in the Indonesian Higher Central Bureaucracy," p. 89.

40. Hong Lee Oey, *Indonesia Facing the 1980's: A Political Analysis,* p. 369.

41. Ibid., p. 370.

42. Ibid., p. 371.

43. See Lane, "Climate of Fear," p. 3; Kieran Cooke, "Suharto Tightens his Political Hold"; and Max Lane, "Suharto Intensifies Clamp-down on Dissent," p. 3. A recent article in the *Far Eastern Economic Review* reported on a deep malaise that has apparently set in, spurred on by the economic downturns, but resulting more profoundly from a combination of events including the continuous crackdowns on Muslim opponents; the closing down of the *Sinar Harapan* newspaper; the failure to bring to justice the murderer of Dice Budimuljono, the mistress of a prominent person connected to the presidential palace; and the increased awareness of the great wealth and corruption of members of the presidential family, government leaders, and their associates. See Shim Jae Hoon, "Breaking Old Ground," pp. 46–47.

44. Indeed, a *Tempo* poll in July 1981 found that over 50 percent of those questioned considered "social disturbances between rich and poor" to be the greatest danger to national unity. Sacerdoti, "Taking the Pulse." See also various issues of *Indonesia Reports* and *Inside Indonesia.*

45. See, for example, Guy J. Pauker, "Indonesia 1979: The Record of Three Decades," pp. 124–127.

46. Although, according to one critic, the amount Sukarno spent is miniscule compared with the misappropriations of funds in recent years.

47. According to World Bank statistics, life expectancy rose from 43 to 52 years for men and from 45 to 55 years for women between 1965 and 1983; infant mortality rates dropped from 138 to 101 per thousand live births, while child death rates (ages one to four years) declined from twenty to thirteen per thousand children over the same period. World Bank, *World Development Report 1985,* Table 23. Per-capita consumption of rice has also increased impressively, from 88 kilograms in 1954 to 107 kilograms in 1970 to 146 kilograms in 1983. Leon A. Mears, "Rice and Food Self-Sufficiency in Indonesia," p. 126. The recent downturn in the economy because of the drop in oil prices will almost inevitably be reflected in lower standards of living in the immediate future.

48. Yuli Ismartino reports slow but steady development over the past eight years in East Nusatenggara. He claims that the economy has registered growth rates above the national average, thanks to increases in coffee and sandalwood oil production and the intensive greening campaign begun in 1979 (in which sturdy, fast-growing lamtaro trees were planted throughout the province, which provide fodder for more than 500,000 head of cattle). See Yuli Ismartono, "Letter from Kupang."

49. In a world that has seen the increasing growth of regionalisms and local ethnic nationalisms in both developing and developed countries (such as the Sikhs, the Eritreans, the Kurds, the Basques, and the Quebecois), such integration is all the more remarkable.

50. Aceh also has experienced some unrest and rebellion in its consistent attempts to throw off all outside control, whether Dutch or Indonesian. However, the costs have been far higher in East Timor and Irian Jaya. An estimated 100,000 people (15 percent of the population) died in East Timor between 1974 and 1980 as a result of war, being forced into villages, disease, and famine. In

Irian Jaya, thousands have been killed and thousands more have fled across the
border to Papua New Guinea, according to local reports. See "West Papua:
Asia or Melanesia? An Interview with Rex Rumakiek"; and Robin Osborne,
"The Flag that Won't Go Away."

51. It is interesting to see that, partly as a result of the policies of the New
Order government of Suharto, which have sought to balance development in
the sociocultural, interaction, and economic dimensions in its attempts to build
a "just and prosperous society," several provinces have changed their relative
status in the country and become more integrated, from a per-capita perspective. In the interaction dimension particularly, Aceh has been drawn more
closely into the nation-state over the past decade. Despite its low integration in
the economic dimension, it stands out for its highest rate of recent economic
growth and foreign investment. West Kalimantan also has experienced closer
integrative ties, particularly in the sociocultural and interaction dimensions.
These two changes are important partly because of the peripheral locations of
these two provinces and their proximity to Malaysia. Southeast Sulawesi has
also become somewhat more integrated, as evidenced in its improved ranking
on one of each of the interaction and economic factor scores. (See Christine
Drake, "The Spatial Pattern of National Integration in Indonesia," p. 485.) By
contrast, between 1971 and 1980 at least, West and especially East Nusatenggara have slipped even further in their status as least integrated and developed
of all the provinces in the country, while the gap between them and the most
highly developed and integrated provinces on many indices has widened.
Bengkulu also declined in its relative level of integration. The provinces of
Java, meanwhile, which stood out as a much more uniform bloc with common
characteristics in the early 1970s, have become less distinctively different on a
per-capita basis.

Glossary

abangan	a Javanese of a heterodox religious orientation; normally a Muslim who is greatly influenced by pre-Islamic Hindu, Buddhist, and indigenous animistic beliefs.
ABRI	*Angkatan Bersenjata Republik Indonesia:* Armed Forces of the Republic of Indonesia.
adat	localized traditional law and custom; one of the major strands of contemporary Indonesian law.
agama	religion.
Akabri	*Akademi ABRI:* Indonesian Armed Forces Academy in Magelang (Central Java).
ani-ani	single-bladed knife traditionally used for cutting rice stalks.
armada	fleet; *armada khusus:* special fleet; *armada lokal:* local fleet; *armada Nusantara:* archipelago fleet; *armada perintis:* pioneer fleet; *armada rakyat:* people's fleet, made up traditionally of wooden sailing vessels, some of which are now equipped with outboard motors.
asimilasi	assimilation.
Badan Pembina Kesatuan Bangsa	Institute for the Advancement of National Unity.
bahan pokok	basic commodity.
bahasa	language; *bahasa Indonesia:* the Indonesian national language, derived from Malay; *bahasa Melayu pasar:* market Malay.
bangsa	nation, a people.
banteng	wild buffalo.
Bappeda	*Badan Perencanaan Pembangunan Daerah:* Regional Development Planning Board. Operates at the provincial level.

311

Bappenas   *Badan Perencanaan Pembangunan Nasional:* the National
                    Development Planning Agency, established in 1965,
                    which has overall responsibility for economic develop-
                    ment plans.

Bhinneka Tunggal Ika   Unity in Diversity. The motto of the Republic of
                    Indonesia (Sanskrit).

Biro Pusat Statistik   Central Bureau of Statistics.

BKK   *Badan Kredit Kecamatan:* subdistrict credit board.

BPKI   *Badan Penyelidikan Kemerdekaan Indonesia:* the Committee
                    for the Investigation of Independence for Indonesia,
                    formed in May 1945, where Sukarno proposed the *Panca
                    Sila.*

Budi Utomo   Glorious Endeavor Society. An early nationalist organiza-
                    tion, founded in 1908.

bupati   district head. Chief officer of a *kabupaten.*

cukong   Chinese businessman. A term used to refer particularly to
                    those Chinese businessmen in collaboration with leading
                    figures in the state bureaucracy or military.

Cultuurstelsel   Cultivation System, instituted by the Dutch, lasting from
                    1830 to 1860, in which the natives were compelled to use
                    part of their land to grow crops in demand on the Euro-
                    pean market.

daerah   territory, region, environs, vicinity, area.

daerah-daerah lemah   economically weak or isolated areas.

dakwah   Muslim missionary activity.

Demokrasi terpimpin   Guided Democracy. The type of government exer-
                    cised under Sukarno from 1957 to 1965.

desa   village.

Dewan Pertimbangan Agung   Advisory Council of State.

DPR   *Dewan Perwakilan Rakyat:* House of People's Representa-
                    tives. One of the two representative bodies provided for in
                    the Constitution of 1945. Cf. *MPR.*

dukun   shaman, traditional healer, magician, fortune-teller, or
                    sorcerer.

Ekonomi terpimpin   Guided Economy.

Fretilin   *Frente Revolucionaria do Timor-Leste Independente:* Revolu-
                    tionary Front for an Independent East Timor. A guerrilla
                    movement seeking the independence of East Timor.

Garis-garis Besar Haluan Negara   Broad Outlines of State Policy.

garuda   eagle, mystical bird, carrier of the god Vishnu; incorpo-
                    rated into the official seal of the Republic of Indonesia.

Gapi   *Gabungan Politik Indonesia:* the Union of Indonesian Politi-
                    cal Associations.

Gestapu   *Gerakan September Tigapuluh:* September 30 Movement.
                 Refers to the abortive pro-Communist coup of 1965 and,
                 by inference, to the bloodshed that followed.

Golkar   *Golongan Karya:* Union of Functional Groups. Groupings
                 within society, such as peasants, workers, and women,
                 that are represented by delegates to the various delibera-
                 tive bodies. *Golkar* functions as an army-instituted and
                 government-supported political party, winning over 60
                 percent of the vote in each of the elections held during the
                 Suharto era.

gotong royong   mutual cooperation, mutual aid; the customary practices
                 of labor and produce exchange as they exist particularly in
                 the Javanese peasant village (based on the hard-headed
                 calculation of expected reciprocity).

Guided Democracy   political system of the period 1957–1965 in which the
                 focal point of political power shifted to the president and
                 the *DPR* was transformed into a nominated body of repre-
                 sentatives of "functional" groups.

Guided Economy   economic policy in the period 1959–1965 that empha-
                 sized state direction of the economy, state ownership of
                 capital, and economic self-sufficiency.

haji   one who has made the pilgrimage to Mecca; a title prefix-
                 ing the name of the *haji,* commanding great respect
                 among *santri.*

hajj   the Muslim pilgrimage to Mecca, expected of every
                 devout Muslim having the means to do so as one of the
                 Five Pillars of Islam.

hukum nasional   national law.

hutan   forest, woods, jungle.

IGGI   Inter-Governmental Group on Indonesia. An informal
                 association of Western and Japanese governmental lend-
                 ing agencies together with international development
                 agencies such as the World Bank, the International Mon-
                 etary Fund, and the United Nations Development Pro-
                 gram, established in 1967 to aid Indonesia's recovery and
                 development. The IGGI included, in order of their total
                 outstanding loan commitments at the end of 1980: Japan,
                 the United States, the World Bank, West Germany, the
                 Netherlands, France, the Asian Development Bank, Can-
                 ada, Belgium, the United Kingdom, Switzerland, Italy,
                 Denmark, Australia, New Zealand, and Austria. For
                 contributing countries for fiscal year 1984–1985 see note
                 14 in chapter 5.

Indess   Indonesian Distance Education Satellite System.

Indische Vereeniging the Indies Association, formed by Indonesian students in the Netherlands, originally promoting the common interests of Indonesian students in the mother country, but later becoming involved in Indonesian politics and nationalism.

indoktrinasi   indoctrination.

Indonesische Vereeniging the Indonesian Association, founded in 1922, which pioneered the Indonesian independence movement in Europe. In 1925 it adopted the Indonesian form of its title, *Perhimpunan Indonesia.*

Inpres   *Instruksi Presiden:* presidential instruction. Program financed through special presidential instructions or authorization for infrastructural works at the local level.

kabupaten   regency in the colonial administration, district since independence; the administrative division below the *propinsi* (province), corresponding approximately to a county in the United States.

Kalimat Syahadat the credo of Islam, consisting of the statement, "I testify that there is no God but Allah, and Muhammed is his prophet." The only ineluctable requirement of Islam.

kampung   village or part of a village; the administrative ward of a city; a neighborhood in a city, often inhabited by migrant villagers, especially one inhabited by the lower classes.

kapal putih   literally "white ships"; ships used by the Dutch colonial government for administrative purposes on noneconomic routes.

kebatinan   mysticism.

kecamatan   subdistrict; the administrative division below the *kabupaten* (regency or district).

kepercayaan   belief; *kepercayaan terhadap Tuhan yang Maha Esa:* belief in the One Supreme Being, the first principle of the *Panca Sila.*

Keppres   *Keputusan Presiden:* presidential decree.

kepribadian   individuality, personality, identity. *Kepribadian Indonesia:* Indonesian identity.

kerudung   veil.

kerukunan   social harmony.

kharisma   term used to refer to the Muslim Sunday lectures.

komunisme   communism.

Konfrontasi   Indonesian hostile confrontation against the formation of Malaysia, involving military action mostly along the eastern Malaysian borders from 1963 through 1965.

Kopkamtib   *Komando Operasi Pemulihan Keamanan dan Ketertiban:* Operational Command for the Restoration of Security and Order; the very powerful military agency for domestic security and intelligence created as a national security organization in the wake of the abortive communist coup of 1965.

kota   city.

kotamadya   municipality or city district; on the same administrative level as the *kabupaten.*

Kowilhan   *Komando Wilayah Pertahanan:* Regional Defense Command.

K.P.M.   *Koninklijke Paketvaart Maatschappij* (the Royal Package Transport Company); the Dutch interisland shipping company, formed in 1891, withdrawn from Indonesia in 1957.

kraton   palace, court (of a Javanese ruler).

KUD   *Koperasi Unit Desa:* village cooperative.

ladang   unirrigated field. Generally associated with swidden cultivation in Indonesia and to be found almost entirely in the Outer Islands. See swidden, *sawah.*

LSD   *Lembaga Sosial Desa:* village social association(s).

Majapahit   the empire founded in 1293 on the eastern part of Java's north coast, expanded under Gajah Mada to include much of present-day Indonesia, dissolved in the early sixteenth century when the courtiers fled to the interior of Java and to Bali.

Manipol USDEK   *Manifesto Politik;* the Political Manifesto of the Republic, as propounded by Sukarno on Independence Day, 1959. It consisted of five ideas: *Undang-undang dasar 1945,* the 1945 Constitution; *Sosialisme Indonesia,* socialism à la Indonesia; *Demokrasi terpimpin,* Guided Democracy; *Ekonomi terpimpin,* Guided Economy; *Kepribadian Indonesia,* Indonesian identity.

merantau   the circular migration pattern of the Minangkabau men (possibly to gain freedom from a matriarchal society), often to Jakarta but always implying a return to their homeland.

merdeka   free, independent; *kemerdekaan:* freedom, independence.

MPR   *Majelis Permusyawaratan Rakyat:* People's Consultative Assembly. One of the two representative bodies provided for in the Constitution of 1945. Cf. *DPR.*

mufakat   consensus; an agreement achieved by the process of *musyawarah.*

musyawarah   discussion; search for a consensus through compromise and synthesis and the reconciling of opposing views.

Nasakom   the national front formed in 1961, based on *nasionalisme, agama,* and *komunisme:* nationalism, religion, and communism.

negara   state.

OPEC   Organization of Petroleum Exporting Countries, the thirteen-member oil cartel, the majority of which are Muslim countries. The great rise in petroleum prices after 1973 focused enormous wealth in the OPEC Muslim world. Indonesia, as a member of the cartel, has benefited from the increased economic and political power also experienced in the other Muslim countries of OPEC.

orang Indonesia asli   native Indonesian(s).

Orde Baru   New Order; term used by the Suharto regime for post-Sukarno policies based on realistic thinking and opposed to the personality cult and alleged lack of constitutionality of the Sukarno regime.

Orde Lama   Old Order; term used by the Suharto regime to refer to the policies of the Sukarno era.

Palapa   Indonesia's domestic satellite communications system, first launched in July 1976. *Palapa* also has symbolic meaning, because Gajah Mada, Prime Minister of the famous Majapahit kingdom, swore not to eat *palapa* (a cake made of coconut and palm sugar) until Indonesia was united.

pamong praja   civil service; regional administrators appointed by the central government.

Panca Sila   the five principles of the Indonesian State; the basic official ideology enunciated by Sukarno and incorporated in the preamble to the 1945 Constitution. The five principles are belief in One Supreme Being, just and civilized humanity, nationalism, democracy, and social justice.

PDI   *Partai Demokrasi Indonesia:* Indonesian Democratic Party.

peci   the small black velvet cap, originally a sign of Islam, but now worn as the national headdress by most Indonesian men.

Pedoman Penghayatan dan Pengamalan Panca Sila   guide to the comprehension and practice of *Panca Sila.*

Pelnas   *Persatuan Pengusaha Pelayaran Niaga Swasta:* Union of owners of private trading vessels.

Pelni   *Pelayaran Nasional Indonesia:* National Shipping Company.

pembangunan   development, construction.

pemerataan   equality.

pemerintah   government.

pengadilan negeri   court of the first instance (secular).

pengadilan tinggi   court of the second instance (appeals).

Pepelra   *Persatuan Pengusaha Pelayaran Rakyat:* Union of People's Shipping Employers. An organization founded in 1971 to serve as a unifying force and communication channel for *perahu* shipping owners (with the government).

perahu   sailing vessel, important especially in eastern Indonesia.

peranakan   Indonesia-born Chinese, often of mixed ancestry, who speak a non-Chinese language by preference, and who have adopted some Indonesian customs and attitudes. The term derived from *Peranakan Tionghoa* (Chinese children of the Indies). See *totok.*

Perhimpunan Indonesia   Indonesian Association, a nationalist youth organization of Indonesian students in the Netherlands that promoted independence for the archipelago and advised Indonesian nationalists in Indonesia on tactics.

Permesta   *Perjuangan Semesta Alam:* Total Struggle (of the Republic of Indonesia's Revolutionary Government); the most serious regional rebellion against the Sukarno administration, by people in West Sumatra and North Sulawesi, 1958–1961.

Perserikatan Komunis Indonesia   the Indonesian Communist Union.

Pertamina   *Perusahaan Negara Pertambangan Minyak dan Gas Bumi Nasional:* the National Petroleum and Natural Gas Company (state-owned).

Perumtel   the state-owned telephone utility.

Peta   *Sukarela Pembela Tanah Air:* Voluntary Defenders of the Homeland. A volunteer army established by the Japanese in 1943.

PKI   *Partai Komunis Indonesia:* the Indonesian Communist Party.

PNI   *Partai Nasional Indonesia:* the Indonesian Nationalist Party.

PPP   *Partai Persatuan Pembangunan:* Development Unity Party.

pribumi   indigenous Indonesian.

priyayi   the entire complex of strongly Hinduized aesthetic canons and theology forms; the *priyayi* variant of the Javanese religion. The term *priyayi* originally referred to the gentry way of life (i.e., the courtiers and officials of the king), but now it implies the whole set of attitudes and moral commitments adhered to by nearly every white-collar Javanese, whatever his social origin.

propinsi   province(s). There are twenty-four true provinces *(propinsi)*, two special autonomous regions *(Daerah Istimewa)* of Aceh and Yogyakarta, and the special capital district of Jakarta *(Daerah Khusus Istimewa)*. In this book the term province is used for all three types.

PRRI   *Pemerintah Revolusioner Republik Indonesia:* Revolutionary Government of the Republic of Indonesia, proclaimed in 1958.

Radio Republik Indonesia   the national radio of the Republic of Indonesia.

rakyat   ordinary people.

Repelita   *Rencana Pembangunan Lima Tahun:* Five-Year Development Plan. *Repelita I:* the first Five-Year Development Plan, 1969–1974; *Repelita II:* the second, 1974–1979; *Repelita III:* the third, 1979–1984; *Repelita IV:* the fourth, 1984–1989.

RGDP   regional gross domestic product.

rukun tetangga   neighborhood association, the smallest administrative unit in the Indonesian system of government.

rupiah (Rp)   basic monetary unit of Indonesia. From 1971 to 1978 Indonesia maintained an exchange rate of Rp 415 to the U.S. dollar. In November 1978 the rupiah was devalued to an exchange rate of Rp 625 to the U.S. dollar. The rate floated slightly to Rp 670 in 1982–1983. It was devalued again in March 1983 to Rp 970 to the U.S. dollar and has floated since. In March 1985 the exchange rate was Rp 1,100 to the U.S. dollar.

santri   a devotee of a strongly Muslim and rather Arab style of life. The *santri* is faithful to the Five Pillars of Islam: repeating the basic creed (the *Kalimat Syahadat*), giving alms, praying five times a day, fasting during the month of Ramadan, and making the pilgrimage to Mecca *(hajj)* if health and finances permit. Used collectively, this term applies also to the group of those having these characteristics.

Sarekat Islam   the Islamic Union, which grew out of the *Sarekat Dagang Islam* (Islamic Trading Union), founded in 1911 to strengthen Indonesian batik manufacturers in Solo (Surakarta) against Chinese competition. The appeal of *Sarekat Islam* to the religious bond between fellow Indonesians was one of the first overt expressions of early nationalist feeling. Its aims were fourfold: promoting a commercial spirit among Muslims, mutual assistance to members,

	encouraging spiritual development and general welfare, and opposition to misunderstanding about Islam.
sawah	irrigated rice field; the method of cultivating rice on irrigated land.
sosialisme	socialism.
statistik	statistics.
Subsidi Daerah Otonomi	autonomous region subsidy.
suku	a tribal, or subtribal or ethnic group.
sukubangsa	ethnic group or tribe.
Susenas	*Survey Sosioekonomi Nasional:* national socioeconomic survey.
swidden	shifting or slash-and-burn cultivation, in which fields are cleared, farmed for one or more years, and then allowed to return to bush for fallowing, usually to be recultivated at a later time.
Syariat	Islamic law based on scholarly interpretation of the Koran and the Hadith (codified Islamic tradition consisting of the sayings and actions of Muhammed as related by those who knew him personally).
tempo	time; also the name of a weekly magazine similar to *Time* magazine in the United States.
toleransi	tolerance.
tonari gumi	neighborhood associations organized by the Japanese during their occupation of Indonesia, 1942–1945.
totok	ethnic Chinese in Indonesia, either China-born or China-oriented, who speak a Chinese language by preference. See *peranakan.*
transmigrasi	transmigration. Government rural resettlement program that seeks to relocate large numbers of Javanese (and some from Bali and Nusatenggara) from overpopulated areas to areas of sparse population in the Outer Islands.
Undang-undang dasar 1945	Constitution of 1945.
Universitas Terbuka	Open University, established in 1984.
Volksraad	People's Council. A body created in 1918, composed of both elected and appointed members to advise the governor-general and apprise him of public opinion. Although it had no real political power, it did serve as a forum for the more moderate of politically active Indonesians in the 1920s and 1930s.
wayang	shadow puppet; Javanese shadow puppet show; any theatrical production based traditionally on the Hindu epics and other traditional literature. *Wayang kulit:* shadow pup-

pet play with leather puppets. *Wayang orang (wong):* Java-nese stage show featuring human dancers; puppets are replaced by live actors whose acting and dancing are for-malized in imitation of the puppets.

zakat　　　religious tax.

Bibliography

Abdullah, Taufik, "The Sociocultural Scene in Indonesia." In *Trends in Indone-sia II,* edited by Leo Suryadinata and Sharon Siddique, pp. 65-76. Athens, Ohio: Ohio University Press, 1981.

Abdullah, Taufik, Shelly Errington, Peggy Lush, James Siegel, Linda Wein-stein, and Elizabeth Witton. "Current Data on the Indonesian Military Elite after the Reorganization of 1969-1970." *Indonesia* 10 (October 1970): 195-208.

Adelman, Irma, and Cynthia Taft Morris. *Economic Growth and Social Equity in Developing Countries.* Stanford: Stanford University Press, 1973.

Agassi, Judith B. "Mass Media in Indonesia." Cambridge: Massachusetts Institute of Technology, 1969. Mimeographed.

Alfian. "Programming for Development in Indonesia." *Journal of Communication* 30 (1980): 50-57.

Alisjahbana, Sutan Takdir. *Indonesia: Social and Cultural Revolution.* 2d ed. Translated by Benedict R. Anderson. Kuala Lumpur: Oxford Univer-sity Press, 1966.

————. "Jakarta, A Fat Leach Sucking on the Head of a Fish." In Herbert Feith and Alan Smith, "Indonesia," pp. 193-196. In *Southeast Asia: Doc-uments of Political Development and Change,* edited by Roger M. Smith, pp. 164-250. Ithaca: Cornell University Press, 1974.

Anderson, Benedict R. "Current Data on the Indonesian Military Elite." *Indo-nesia* 40 (October 1985): 131-162.

————. "Indonesia: Looking Back." *The Wilson Quarterly* 5 (Spring 1981): 113-125.

Anderson, Benedict R., Frederick Bunnell, Lance Castles, Ruth McVey, and James Siegel. "Data on the Current Military Elite." *Indonesia* 3 (April 1967): 205-216.

Anderson, Benedict R., Judith Ecklund, and Audrey Kahin. "Current Data on the Indonesian Military Elite." *Indonesia* 26 (October 1978): 159-177.

Anderson, Benedict R., Elizabeth Graves, Filino Harahap, Mildred Wege-mann, and Elizabeth Witton. "Current Data on the Indonesian Army Elite." *Indonesia* 7 (April 1969): 195-201.

Anderson, Benedict R., and Susan Hatch. "Current Data on the Indonesian Military Elite." *Indonesia* 15 (April 1973): 187–197.

———. "Current Data on the Indonesian Military Elite." *Indonesia* 18 (October 1974): 153–167.

Anderson, Benedict R., and Audrey Kahin. "Current Data on the Indonesian Military Elite." *Indonesia* 29 (April 1980): 155–175.

———. "Current Data on the Indonesian Military Elite." *Indonesia* 33 (April 1982): 129–148.

———. "Current Data on the Indonesian Military Elite." *Indonesia* 36 (October 1983): 99–134.

———. "Current Data on the Indonesian Military Elite." *Indonesia* 37 (April 1984): 145–169.

———. "Indonesia's Territorial Commanders: 1950–March 1983." *Indonesia* 35 (April 1983): 109–124.

Anderson, Michael H. "Transnational Advertising and Politics in Indonesia." *Asian Survey* 20 (December 1980): 1253–1270.

Anwar, Khaidir. *Indonesian: The Development and Use of a National Language.* Yogyakarta: Gadjah Mada University Press, 1980.

Apter, David E. *The Politics of Modernization.* Chicago: University of Chicago Press, 1965.

Arief, Sritna. *Indonesia: Dependency and Underdevelopment.* Kuala Lumpur: Institute for Development Studies, Jakarta, 1981.

Arndt, H. W. "Development and Equality: An Overview." In *The Indonesian Economy: Collected Papers,* edited by H. W. Arndt, pp. 44–60. Singapore: Chopmen Publishers, 1984.

———. "Development and Equality: Themes in Economic Thought about Indonesia." *Journal of Southeast Asian Studies* 12 (1981): 464–475.

———. "Employment, Unemployment, and Underemployment." In *The Indonesian Economy: Collected Papers,* edited by H. W. Arndt, pp. 93–107. Singapore: Chopmen Publishers, 1984.

———. "Growth and Equity Objectives in Economic Thought about Indonesia." In *Indonesia: Australian Perspectives,* edited by James J. Fox, Ross Garnaut, Peter McCawley, and J. A. C. Mackie. Vol. 2, *Indonesia: Dualism, Growth and Poverty,* edited by Ross Garnaut and Peter McCawley, pp. 427–439. Canberra: Australian National University Research School of Pacific Studies, 1980.

———. "The Impact of the International Economic Crisis on the Indonesian Economy." *Economic Bulletin for Asia and the Pacific* 29 (December 1978): 28–36.

———. "Prospects for the 1980s." In *The Indonesian Economy: Collected Papers,* edited by H. W. Arndt, pp. 39–52. Singapore: Chopmen Publishers, 1984.

———. "Regional Income Estimates." *Bulletin of Indonesian Economic Studies* 9 (November 1973): 87–102.

———. "Survey of Recent Developments." *Bulletin of Indonesian Economic Studies* 19 (August 1983): 1–26.

———. "Transmigration: Achievements, Problems, Prospects." *Bulletin of Indonesian Economic Studies* 19 (December 1983): 50–73.

————, ed. *The Indonesian Economy: Collected Papers*. Singapore: Chopmen Publishers, 1984.

Arndt, H. W., and R. M. Sundrum. "Regional Price Disparities." *Bulletin of Indonesian Economic Studies* 11 (July 1975): 30–68.

Asian Business. Various issues.

Asian Research Bulletin. Various issues.

Astbury, Sid. "Agonizing Over Mechanization Down on the Indonesian Farm." *Asian Business* 18 (May 1982): 85–88.

————. "Indonesia: Economic Report." *Asian Business* 19 (May 1983): 67–76.

————. "Indonesia: Economic Report." *Asian Business* 20 (February 1984): 55–71.

————. "Positive Measures Are Needed to Stimulate a Sagging Economy." *Asian Business* 20 (February 1984): 56–59.

Aveling, Harry, ed. *The Development of Indonesian Society*. New York: St. Martin's Press, 1980.

Awanohara, Susumu. "A First Warning Shot." *Far Eastern Economic Review* (September 27, 1984): 14–15.

————. "Islam on the Hustings." *Far Eastern Economic Review* (April 23, 1982): 24–29.

————. "Jakarta at a Jog." *Far Eastern Economic Review* (May 17, 1984): 94, 96–98.

————. "A Matter of Principles." *Far Eastern Economic Review* (October 25, 1984): 16–17.

————. "More of the Same." *Far Eastern Economic Review* (May 14, 1982): 15–16.

————. "The New Call to Prayer." *Far Eastern Economic Review* (January 24, 1985): 26–29.

————. "On the Defensive in the Pancasila State." *Far Eastern Economic Review* (January 24, 1985): 30–31.

————. "Overboard on Ships." *Far Eastern Economic Review* (November 8, 1984): 66–70.

————. "The Perennial Problem." *Far Eastern Economic Review* (September 6, 1984): 26–27.

————. "Points of Contention." *Far Eastern Economic Review* (June 21, 1984): 25–26.

————. "Suharto's Kingdom." *Far Eastern Economic Review* (August 9, 1984): 32–36.

Awanohara, Susumu, Manggi Habir, and Paul Handley. "Focus Indonesia '85." *Far Eastern Economic Review* (February 7, 1985): 43–62.

Bachtiar, Harsja W. *The Indonesian Nation: Some Problems of Integration and Disintegration*. Singapore: Institute of Southeast Asian Studies, 1974.

————. "Masalah Integrasi Nasional di Indonesia." *Prisma* 5 (1976): 3–13.

Balassa, Bela. *The Theory of Economic Integration*. Homewood, Ill.: Richard D. Irwin, 1961.

————. "Types of Economic Integration." World Bank Staff Working Paper, no. 185. Washington, D.C.: World Bank, 1974.

Bank Indonesia. *Report for the Financial Year 1982/83*. Jakarta: Bank Indonesia, 1983.

Baried, S. B. "The World of Islam: Renewal and Reform in Indonesia." *Unesco Courier* 8 (1981): 30–31.

Bee, Ooi Jin. *The Petroleum Resources of Indonesia.* Kuala Lumpur: Oxford University Press, 1982.

Bellwood, Peter. "Plants, Climate and People: The Early Horticultural Prehistory of Austronesia." In *Indonesia: Australian Perspectives,* edited by James J. Fox, Ross Garnaut, Peter McCawley, and J. A. C. Mackie. Vol. 1, *Indonesia: The Making of a Culture,* edited by James J. Fox, pp. 57–74. Canberra: Australian National University Research School of Pacific Studies, 1980.

Berg, C. C. "De sadeng-oorlog en de mythe van Groot-Majapahit." *Indonesie* 5 (1951): 385–422.

———. "The Javanese Picture of the Past." In *An Introduction to Indonesian Historiography,* edited by Soedjatmoko et al., pp. 87–118. Ithaca: Cornell University Press, 1965.

Berry, Brian J. L. "City Size and Economic Development, Conceptual Synthesis and Policy Problems, with Special Reference to South and Southeast Asia." In *Urbanization and National Development,* edited by Leo Jakobson and Ved Prakash, pp. 111–156. Beverly Hills, Calif.: Sage Publications, 1971.

———. "Hierarchical Diffusion: The Basis of Developmental Filtering and Spread in a System of Growth Centers." In *Growth Centers in Regional Economic Development,* edited by Niles M. Hansen, pp. 108–138. New York: The Free Press, 1972.

Berry, Brian J. L., Edgar C. Conkling, and D. Michael Ray. *The Geography of Economic Systems.* Englewood Cliffs, N.J.: Prentice-Hall, 1976.

"Bhinneka Tunggal Ika Terbabar." Jakarta: Badan Penerbitan CV Sabdopalon, n.d.

Bibliografi Surat Kabar dan Majalah di Indonesia. Jakarta: Yayasan Inayu, October 1972.

Biro Pusat Statistik. *Impor Menurut Jenis Barang dan Negeri Asal.* Vol. 2. Jakarta: Biro Pusat Statistik, 1983.

———. *Indikator Ekonomi.* Jakarta: Biro Pusat Statistik, 1976.

———. *Indikator Ekonomi 1982.* Jakarta: Biro Pusat Statistik, 1983.

———. *Indikator Ekonomi 1984.* Jakarta: Biro Pusat Statistik, 1984.

———. *Indikator Sosial 1974.* Jakarta: Biro Pusat Statistik, 1974.

———. *Indikator Sosial 1982.* Jakarta: Biro Pusat Statistik, 1982.

———. *National Income of Indonesia 1975–80.* Jakarta: Biro Pusat Statistik, 1981.

———. *Pendapatan Regional Propinsi-propinsi di Indonesia 1976–80.* Jakarta: Biro Pusat Statistik, 1981.

———. *Penduduk Indonesia 1980 Menurut Propinsi dan Kabupaten/Kotamadya.* Series L. Jakarta: Biro Pusat Statistik, 1981.

———. *Perpindahan Penduduk Antar Propinsi di Indonesia. Hasil Sensus Penduduk 1980.* Jakarta: Biro Pusat Statistik, 1984.

———. *Sensus Industri 1974/75.* Jakarta: Biro Pusat Statistik, 1977.

———. *Sensus Penduduk 1971.* Series D. Jakarta: Biro Pusat Statistik, 1974.

———. *Sensus Penduduk 1971.* Series E. 26 vols. Jakarta: Biro Pusat Statistik, 1974–1975.

————. *Sensus Penduduk 1971*. Series F. 2 vols. Jakarta: Biro Pusat Statistik, 1975.

————. *Sensus Penduduk 1980*. Series L. Jakarta: Biro Pusat Statistik, 1983.

————. *Sensus Penduduk 1980*. Series S. 27 vols. Jakarta: Biro Pusat Statistik, 1981.

————. *Statistik Angkutan Udara 1981*. Jakarta: Biro Pusat Statistik, 1981.

————. *Statistik Bioskop Indonesia 1981 dan 1982*. Jakarta: Biro Pusat Statistik, 1983.

————. *Statistik Bongkar Muat Barang di Pelabuhan Indonesia 1982*. Jakarta: Biro Pusat Statistik, 1983.

————. *Statistik Indonesia: Statistical Pocketbook of Indonesia, 1970 and 1971*. Jakarta: Biro Pusat Statistik, 1972.

————. *Statistik Indonesia 1982*. Jakarta: Biro Pusat Statistik, 1983.

————. *Statistik Indonesia 1983*. Jakarta: Biro Pusat Statistik, 1984.

————. *Statistik Indonesia 1983, Buku Saku*. Jakarta: Biro Pusat Statistik, 1984.

————. *Statistik Industri 1973*. Jakarta: Biro Pusat Statistik, 1975.

————. *Statistik Kendaraan Bermotor dan Panjang Jalan 1974*. Jakarta: Biro Pusat Statistik, 1974.

————. *Statistik Keuangan Pemerintah Daerah 1973/74*. Jakarta: Biro Pusat Statistik, 1975.

————. *Statistik Keuangan Pemerintah Daerah. Daerah Tingkat I (Propinsi) 1975/76–1980/81*. Jakarta: Biro Pusat Statistik, n.d.

————. *Statistik Keuangan 1981/82 dan 1982/83*. Jakarta: Biro Pusat Statistik, 1984.

————. *Statistik Kommunikasi*. Jakarta: Biro Pusat Statistik, 1973 and 1976.

————. *Statistik Kommunikasi 1980*. Jakarta: Biro Pusat Statistik, 1981.

————. *Statistik Pengangkutan Kereta Api 1961–73*. Jakarta: Biro Pusat Statistik, 1975.

Birowo, Achmad T., and Gary E. Hansen. "Agricultural and Rural Development: An Overview." In *Agricultural and Rural Development in Indonesia*, edited by Gary E. Hansen, pp. 1–27. Westview Special Studies in Social, Political, and Economic Development. Boulder, Colo.: Westview Press, 1981.

Blamey, Jeanne. "Ancient Indonesian Empires." Princeton University, 1975. Xeroxed.

Boediono. "Survey of Recent Developments." *Bulletin of Indonesian Economic Studies* 16 (July 1980): 1–30.

Boileau, Julian M. *Golkar: Functional Group Politics in Indonesia*. Jakarta: Yayasan Proklamasi, 1983.

Boothe, Anne. "Survey of Recent Developments." *Bulletin of Indonesian Economic Studies* 20 (December 1984): 1–35.

Booth, Anne, and Peter McCawley. "Conclusion: Looking to the Future." In *The Indonesian Economy During the Soeharto Era*, edited by Anne Booth and Peter McCawley, pp. 315–322. East Asian Social Science Monographs. Kuala Lumpur: Oxford University Press, 1981.

————, eds. *The Indonesian Economy During the Soeharto Era*. East Asian Social Science Monographs. Kuala Lumpur: Oxford University Press, 1981.

Briggs, Jean A. "A Pint of Blood? Or $20?" *Forbes* (October 12, 1981): 91–98.

Bruner, Edward M., and Judith O. Becker, eds. *Art, Ritual and Society in Indonesia.* Athens, Ohio: Ohio University Press, 1979.

Bruyns, A. Morzer. *Glossary of Abbreviations and Acronyms Used in Indonesia.* Jakarta: Penerbit Ichtiar, 1970.

Bunge, Frederica M., ed. *Indonesia: A Country Study.* 4th ed. Area Handbook Series. Washington, D.C.: U.S. Government Printing Office, 1983.

Bunton, John A. W. *Building Indonesia: A Market Survey.* New York: Construction Press, 1983.

Business International Corporation. *Doing Business in the New Indonesia.* New York: Business International Corporation, 1968.

Castles, Lance. "The Ethnic Profile of Djakarta." *Indonesia* 3 (April 1967): 153–204.

Chernichovsky, Dov, and Oey Astra Meesook. *Poverty in Indonesia: A Profile.* World Bank Staff Working Paper, no. 671. Washington, D.C.: World Bank, 1984.

Coleman, James S., ed. *Political Parties and National Integration in Tropical Africa.* Berkeley: University of California Press, 1964.

Constandse, William. *Inside Indonesia: A Practical Guide for Businessmen.* New York: Hippociene Books, 1983.

Conway, G. R., and P. S. McCawley. "Third World Development—Intensifying Tropical Agriculture: The Indonesian Experience." *Nature* 302 (1983): 288–289.

Cooke, Kieran. "Suharto Tightens His Political Hold." *Christian Science Monitor* (February 7, 1986): 9.

Coppel, Charles A. "China and the Ethnic Chinese in Indonesia." In *Indonesia: Australian Perspectives,* edited by James J. Fox, Ross Garnaut, Peter McCawley, and J. A. C. Mackie. Vol. 3, *Indonesia: The Making of a Nation,* edited by J. A. C. Mackie, pp. 729–734. Canberra: Australian National University Research School of Pacific Studies, 1980.

Cribb, Robert. "Elections in Jakarta." *Asian Survey* 24 (February 1984): 655–664.

Crossette, Barbara. "Street Vendors of Jakarta Are Sold on Self-Help." *New York Times* (July 23, 1985): 2.

Crouch, Harold. *The Army and Politics in Indonesia.* Ithaca: Cornell University Press, 1978.

———. "The New Order: the Prospect for Political Stability." In *Indonesia: Australian Perspectives,* edited by James J. Fox, Ross Garnaut, Peter McCawley, and J. A. C. Mackie. Vol. 3, *Indonesia: The Making of a Nation,* edited by J. A. C. Mackie, pp. 657–668. Canberra: Australian National University Research School of Pacific Studies, 1980.

———. "No Enemy in Sight." *Far Eastern Economic Review* (February 14, 1985): 32–34.

———. "Patrimonialism and Military Rule in Indonesia." *World Politics* 31 (July 1979): 571–587.

———. "The People's Army." *Far Eastern Economic Review* (February 14, 1985): 32–33.

Cummings, William K. "Notes on Higher Education and Indonesian Society." *Prisma* 21 (June 1981): 16–39.

Dahm, Bernhard. *History of Indonesia in the Twentieth Century.* Translated by P. S. Falla. New York: Praeger, 1971.

Dapice, David. "Notes. Income Distribution 1970–77: A Comment." *Bulletin of Indonesian Economic Studies* 16 (March 1980): 86–91.

Daroesman, Ruth. "Survey of Recent Developments." *Bulletin of Indonesian Economic Studies* 17 (July 1981): 1–41.

De Blij, Harm. *Systematic Political Geography.* New York: John Wiley & Sons, 1967.

Deutsch, Karl W. *Nationalism and Social Communication.* Cambridge: MIT Press, 1965.

Deutsch, Karl W., Sidney A. Burrell, Robert A. Kann, Maurice Lee, Jr., Martin Lichterman, Raymond E. Lindgren, Francis L. Loewenheim, and Richard W. Van Wagenen. *Political Community and the North Atlantic Area.* Princeton: Princeton University Press, 1957.

Deutsch, Karl W., and William J. Foltz, eds. *Nation-Building.* New York: Atherton Press, 1963.

Deutsch, Karl W., Harold D. Lasswell, Richard L. Merritt, and Bruce M. Russett. "The Yale Political Data Program." In *Comparing Nations: The Use of Quantitative Data in Cross-National Research,* edited by Richard L. Merritt and Stein Rokkan, pp. 81–108. New Haven, Ct.: Yale University Press, 1966.

Deutsch, Karl W., and Richard L. Merritt. *Nationalism and National Development.* Cambridge: MIT Press, 1970.

Dick, H. W. "Interisland Shipping: Progress, Problems and Prospects." *Bulletin of Indonesian Economic Studies* 21 (August 1985): 95–114.

———. "Prahu Shipping in Eastern Indonesia." *Bulletin of Indonesian Economic Studies* 11 (July 1975): 69–107.

———. "Prahu Shipping in Eastern Indonesia." *Bulletin of Indonesian Economic Studies* 11 (November 1975): 81–103.

———. "Survey of Recent Developments." *Bulletin of Indonesian Economic Studies* 18 (March 1982): 1–38.

di Tiro, Tengku. "Indonesia or Java?" *Far Eastern Economic Review* (January 10, 1985): 4–5.

Donges, Juergen B., Bernd Stecher, and Frank Wolter. *Industrial Development Policies for Indonesia.* Tubingen: J. C. B. Mohr, 1974.

Drake, Christine. *The Geography of National Integration: A Case Study of Indonesia.* Ann Arbor, Mich.: University Microfilms, 1977.

———. "National Integration and Public Policies in Indonesia." *Studies in Comparative International Development* 15 (Winter 1980): 59–84.

———. "The Sociocultural Dimension of National Integration in Indonesia." *Tijdschrift voor Economische en Sociale Geografie* 72 (1981): 334–346.

———. "The Spatial Pattern of National Integration in Indonesia." *Transactions, Institute of British Geographers,* n.s. 6 (1981): 471–490.

Dunn, James. *Timor: A People Betrayed.* Milton, Australia: Jacaranda Press, 1983.

Dutt, Ashok K., ed. *Southeast Asia: Realm of Contrasts*. Dubuque, Iowa: Kendall/
    Hunt Publishing Co., 1974.
Economic and Social Commission for Asia and the Pacific. *Migration, Urbaniza-*
    tion and Development in Indonesia, A Comparative Study on Migration, Urbaniza-
    tion and Development in the ESCAP Region. Country Reports III. New York:
    United Nations, 1981.
Ekonomi dan Keuangan Indonesia. Various issues.
Emmerson, Donald K. "Indonesia in 1983: Plus Ca Change. . . ." *Asian Survey*
    24 (1984): 135–148.
———. "Understanding the New Order: Bureaucratic Pluralism in Indone-
    sia." *Asian Survey* 23 (November 1983): 1220–1241.
Esmara, Hendra. "Regional Income Disparities." *Bulletin of Indonesian Economic*
    Studies 11 (March 1975): 41–57.
Etzioni, Amitai. *Political Unification: A Comparative Study of Leaders and Forces*.
    New York: Holt, Rinehart & Winston, 1965.
Evans, Jeremy. "The Growth of Urban Centres in Java Since 1961." *Bulletin of*
    Indonesian Economic Studies 20 (April 1984): 44–58.
Feith, Herbert. "Indonesia." In *Government and Politics of Southeast Asia,* edited
    by George McT. Kahin, pp. 183–278. 2d ed. Ithaca: Cornell University
    Press, 1964.
———. "Indonesia's Political Symbols and Their Wielders." *World Politics* 16
    (October 1963): 79–97.
Feith, Herbert, and Alan Smith. "Indonesia." In *Southeast Asia: Documents of*
    Political Development and Change, edited by Roger M. Smith, pp. 165–250.
    Ithaca: Cornell University Press, 1974.
Fisher, Charles A. "Indonesia—A Giant Astir." *Geographical Journal* 138 (June
    1972): 154–165.
———. *South-East Asia: A Social, Economic and Political Geography*. London:
    Methuen, 1964.
Foley, William A. "History of Migrations in Indonesia as Seen by a Linguist."
    In *Indonesia: Australian Perspectives,* edited by James J. Fox, Ross Gar-
    naut, Peter McCawley, and J. A. C. Mackie. Vol. 1, *Indonesia: The*
    Making of a Culture, edited by James J. Fox, pp. 75–94. Canberra: Aus-
    tralian National University Research School of Pacific Studies, 1980.
Forbes, Dean. "Mobility and Uneven Development in Indonesia: A Critique
    of Explanations of Migration and Circular Migration." In *Population*
    Mobility and Development: Southeast Asia and the Pacific, edited by G. W.
    Jones and H. V. Richter, pp. 51–70. Development Studies Centre
    Monograph no. 27. Canberra: Australian National University, 1981.
"Foreign Economic Trends and Their Implications for the U.S." Jakarta: U.S.
    Embassy, Economic Section/Foreign Commercial Service, December
    1981.
Fox, James J. "The 'Movement of the Spirit' in the Timor Area: Christian
    Traditions and Ethnic Identities." In *Indonesia: Australian Perspectives,*
    edited by James J. Fox, Ross Garnaut, Peter McCawley, and J. A. C.
    Mackie. Vol. 1, *Indonesia: The Making of a Culture,* edited by James J.
    Fox, pp. 235–246. Canberra: Australian National University Research
    School of Pacific Studies, 1980.

————, ed. *Indonesia: The Making of a Culture.* Vol. 1 of *Indonesia: Australian Perspectives,* edited by James J. Fox, Ross Garnaut, Peter McCawley, and J. A. C. Mackie. Canberra: Australian National University Research School of Pacific Studies, 1980.

Fox, James J., Ross Garnaut, Peter McCawley, and J. A. C. Mackie, eds. *Indonesia: Australian Perspectives.* Vol. 1, *Indonesia: The Making of a Culture,* edited by James J. Fox. Vol. 2, *Indonesia: Dualism, Growth and Poverty,* edited by Ross Garnaut and Peter McCawley. Vol. 3, *Indonesia: The Making of a Nation,* edited by J. A. C. Mackie. Canberra: Australian National University Research School of Pacific Studies, 1980.

Friedmann, John. "A General Theory of Polarized Development." In *Growth Centers in Regional Economic Development,* edited by Niles M. Hansen, pp. 82–107. New York: The Free Press, 1972.

Furnivall, J. S. *Netherlands India: A Study of Plural Economy.* Cambridge: Cambridge University Press, 1939.

Garnaut, Ross. "General Repercussions of the Resources Boom in the Segmented Indonesian Economy." In *Indonesia: Australian Perspectives,* edited by James J. Fox, Ross Garnaut, Peter McCawley, and J. A. C. Mackie. Vol. 2, *Indonesia: Dualism, Growth and Poverty,* edited by Ross Garnaut and Peter McCawley, pp. 413–423. Canberra: Australian National University Research School of Pacific Studies, 1980.

————. "Survey of Recent Developments." *Bulletin of Indonesian Economic Studies* 15 (November 1979): 1–42.

Garnaut, Ross, and Peter McCawley, eds. *Indonesia: Dualism, Growth and Poverty.* Vol. 2 of *Indonesia: Australian Perspectives,* edited by James J. Fox, Ross Garnaut, Peter McCawley, and J. A. C. Mackie. Canberra: Australian National University Research School of Pacific Studies, 1980.

"Garuda Takes a Gamble." *Far Eastern Economic Review* (February 6, 1981): 66–67.

Geertz, Clifford. "Afterword: The Politics of Meaning." In *Culture and Politics in Indonesia,* edited by Claire Holt, pp. 319–335. Ithaca: Cornell University Press, 1972.

————. *Agricultural Involution: The Process of Ecological Change in Indonesia.* Berkeley: University of California Press for the Association of Asian Studies, 1963.

————. "The Integrative Revolution: Primordial Sentiments and Civil Politics in the New States." In *Political Modernization: A Reader in Comparative Political Change.* 2d ed., edited by Claude E. Welch, Jr., pp. 197–218. Belmont, Calif.: Wadsworth Publishing Co., 1971.

————. *The Religion of Java.* Glencoe, Ill.: The Free Press, 1960.

Geertz, Hildred. "Indonesian Cultures and Communities." In *Indonesia,* edited by Ruth T. McVey, pp. 24–96. New Haven, Ct.: Human Relations Area Files Press, 1963.

Glassburner, Bruce. "The Economy and Economic Policy: General and Historical." In *The Economy of Indonesia: Selected Readings,* edited by Bruce Glassburner, pp. 1–15. Ithaca: Cornell University Press, 1971.

————, ed. *The Economy of Indonesia: Selected Readings.* Ithaca: Cornell University Press, 1971.

Glassburner, Bruce, and Mark Poffenberger. "The Indonesian Economy: A Review Essay." *Bulletin of Indonesian Economic Studies* 17 (November 1981): 94–107.

———. "Survey of Recent Developments." *Bulletin of Indonesian Economic Studies* 19 (December 1983): 1–27.

Goddard, J., and A. Kirby. *An Introduction to Factor Analysis, Concepts and Techniques in Modern Geography,* no. 7. Norwich: Geo Abstracts Ltd., University of East Anglia, 1976.

Goodland, R. *Indonesia's Environmental Progress in Economic Development.* Bogor, Indonesia: Pusat Studi Pengelolaan Sumberdaya dan Lingkungan, 1981.

Gottmann, Jean. "Geography and International Relations." *World Politics* 3 (January 1951): 153–173.

Grant, Bruce. *Indonesia.* 2d ed. Melbourne: Melbourne University Press, 1966.

Grant, Ronald M. "Indonesia 1978: A Third Term for President Suharto." *Asian Survey* 19 (February 1979): 141–146.

Gray, C. S. "The Jakarta Telephone Connection Charge and Financing Indonesian Telecommunication Development." *Bulletin of Indonesian Economic Studies* 20 (August 1984): 139–150.

Gupta, S. "Income Distribution, Employment, and Growth: A Case Study of Indonesia." World Bank Staff Working Paper, no. 212. Washington, D.C.: World Bank, August 1975.

Haas, Ernst B. "The Uniting of Europe and the Uniting of Latin America." *Journal of Common Market Studies* 5 (June 1967): 315–343.

Habir, Manggi. "Ulamas Change Course." *Far Eastern Economic Review* (January 10, 1985): 37–39.

Hackenberg, Robert A. "New Patterns of Urbanization in South East Asia: An Assessment." *Population and Development Review* 6 (1980): 391–419.

Hainsworth, Geoffrey B. "Dilemmas of Development in Indonesia." *Current History* 79 (December 1980): 189–193, 197–198, 208.

———. "Indonesia: Bonanza Development Amidst Shared Poverty." *Current History* 77 (December 1979): 199–200, 224, 227–230.

———. "The Political Economy of Pancasila in Indonesia." *Current History* 82 (April 1983): 167–171, 178–179.

Handley, Paul. "Hamming up the Airways." *Far Eastern Economic Review* (May 16, 1985): 50–51.

Hansen, Gary E. "Introduction." In *Agricultural and Rural Development in Indonesia,* edited by Gary E. Hansen, pp. 177–179. Westview Special Studies in Social, Political, and Economic Development. Boulder, Colo.: Westview Press, 1981.

———, ed. *Agricultural and Rural Development in Indonesia.* Westview Special Studies in Social, Political, and Economic Development. Boulder, Colo.: Westview Press, 1981.

Hardjono, J. M. "Assisted and Unassisted Transmigration in the Context of Repelita III Targets." *Prisma* 18 (September 1980): 3–16.

———. *Transmigration in Indonesia.* Kuala Lumpur: Oxford University Press, 1977.

Hartshorne, Richard. "The Functional Approach in Political Geography." *Annals of the Association of American Geographers* 40 (June 1950): 95–130.

Harvey, Barbara S. *Permesta: Half a Rebellion.* Monograph Series no. 57. Ithaca: Cornell Modern Indonesia Project, 1977.

―――. "Tradition, Islam, and Rebellion: South Sulawesi: 1950–65." Ph.D. diss., Cornell University, 1974.

Hasan, Mohammed Thaib. "The Plight of Aceh." *Far Eastern Economic Review* (August 21, 1981): 3.

Hastings, Peter. "Timor and West Irian: The Reasons Why." In *Indonesia: Australian Perspectives,* edited by James J. Fox, Ross Garnaut, Peter McCawley, and J. A. C. Mackie. Vol. 3, *Indonesia: The Making of a Nation,* edited by J. A. C. Mackie, pp. 713–719. Canberra: Australian National University Research School of Pacific Studies, 1980.

Hayward, Fred M. "Continuities and Discontinuities Between Studies of National and International Integration: Some Implications for Future Research Efforts." *International Organization* 24 (Autumn 1970): 917–941.

Healey, Derek. "Survey of Recent Developments." *Bulletin of Indonesian Economic Studies* 17 (March 1981): 1–35.

Hein, Gordon R. "Indonesia in 1981: Countdown to the General Elections." *Asian Survey* 22 (February 1982): 200–211.

―――. "Indonesia in 1982: Electoral Victory and Economic Adjustment for the New Order." *Asian Survey* 23 (February 1983): 178–190.

Hendrata, Lukas. "Bureaucracy, Participation and Distribution in Indonesian Development." *Prisma* 28 (June 1983): 21–32.

Hidayat. "Peranan Sektor Informal dalam Perekonomian Indonesia." *Ekonomi dan Keuangan Indonesia* 26 (December 1978).

Hill, Hal. "Survey of Recent Developments." *Bulletin of Indonesian Economic Studies* 20 (August 1984): 1–38.

Hoon, Shim Jae. "Breaking Old Ground." *Far Eastern Economic Review* (November 20, 1986): 45–47.

―――. "Minority Political Parties Face Struggle for Votes." *Far Eastern Economic Review* (November 20, 1986): 48–49.

Hughes, G. A., and I. Islam. "Inequality in Indonesia: A Decomposition Analysis." *Bulletin of Indonesian Economic Studies* 17 (July 1981): 42–71.

Hugo, Graeme J. "Circular Migration in Indonesia." *Population and Development Review* 8 (March 1982): 59–83.

―――. "Levels, Trends, and Patterns of Urbanization." In *Migration, Urbanization and Development in Indonesia, A Comparative Study on Migration, Urbanization and Development in the ESCAP Region.* Country Reports III, pp. 57–80. Economic and Social Commission for Asia and the Pacific. New York: United Nations, 1981.

―――. "Patterns of Interprovincial Migration." In *Migration, Urbanization and Development in Indonesia, A Comparative Study on Migration, Urbanization and Development in the ESCAP Region.* Country Reports III, pp. 81–110. Economic and Social Commission for Asia and the Pacific. New York: United Nations, 1981.

―――. *Population Mobility in West Java.* Yogyakarta: Gadjah Mada University Press, 1978.

―――. "Road Transport, Population Mobility and Development in Indonesia." In *Population Mobility and Development: Southeast Asia and the Pacific,* edited by G. W. Jones and H. V. Richter, pp. 355–386. Development Studies Centre Monograph no. 27. Canberra: Australian National University, 1981.

Hugo, Graeme J., Terence H. Hull, Valerie J. Hull, and Gavin W. Jones. *The Demographic Dimension in Indonesian Development.* Singapore: Oxford University Press, 1987.

Ibrahim, A. Majid, and H. Benjamin Fisher. "Regional Development Studies and Planning in Indonesia." *Bulletin of Indonesian Economic Studies* 15 (July 1979): 113–127.

Ihromi, T. O. "Population and Culture in Indonesia." In *The Cultural Consequences of Population Change: Report on a Seminar Held in Bucharest, Romania, August 14–17, 1974.* Washington, D.C.: Smithsonian Institution Center for the Study of Man, April 1975. Mimeographed.

"Indonesia—A Sense of General Disillusionment." *Asia Research Bulletin* 9 (January 31, 1980): 647–649.

Indonesia Development News. Republic of Indonesia: National Development Information Office. Various issues.

Indonesia Reports. College Park, Md.: Indonesia Publications, 1984–1986. Various issues.

"Indonesia. The Awaking Giant." *Euromoney* 37 (January 1979): 1–37, supplement.

"Indonesia. Trade and Investment Survey." *Journal of Commerce* 357 (August 1983): 1c–6c.

Inside Indonesia. Bulletin of the Indonesia Resources and Information Program (IRIP). Canberra, Australia, 1984–1985. Various issues.

Ismartono, Yuli. "Letter from Kupang." *Far Eastern Economic Review* (November 20, 1986): 110.

Jackson, W. A. Douglas, and Edward J. F. Bergman. "On the Organization of Political Space." *Geographica Polonica* 31 (1975): 149–161.

Jacob, Philip E., and James V. Toscano, eds. *The Integration of Political Communities.* Philadelphia: Lippincott, 1964.

Jenkins, David. "The Aging of the New Order." *Far Eastern Economic Review* (June 27, 1980): 22–24.

———. "Death of a Dream of Freedom: Officials Tackle East Timor's Daunting Economic and Social Problems." *Far Eastern Economic Review* (May 23, 1980): 30–32.

———. "What Makes Daud Jusuf Run?" *Far Eastern Economic Review* (October 10, 1980): 36–39.

Johnstone, John, and Jiyono. "Out of School Factors and Educational Achievement in Indonesia." *Comparative Education Review* 27 (1983): 278–295.

Jones, Gavin W. "Population Growth in Java." In *Indonesia: Australian Perspectives,* edited by James J. Fox, Ross Garnaut, Peter McCawley, and J. A. C. Mackie. Vol. 2, *Indonesia: Dualism, Growth and Poverty,* edited by Ross Garnaut and Peter McCawley, pp. 515–538. Canberra: Australian National University Research School of Pacific Studies, 1980.

———. "The Problem of Urbanization in Indonesia." Jakarta: Lembaga

Demografi, Fakultas Ekonomi, Universitas Indonesia, 1975. Mimeographed.

Jones, Gavin W., and H. V. Richter, eds. *Population Mobility and Development: Southeast Asia and the Pacific.* Development Studies Centre Monograph no. 27. Canberra: Australian National University, 1981.

Jones, Gavin W., and R. Gerard Ward. "Rural Labour Shortages in Southeast Asia and the Pacific: A review of the Evidence." In *Population Mobility and Development: Southeast Asia and the Pacific,* edited by Gavin W. Jones and H. V. Richter, pp. 387–405. Development Studies Centre Monograph no. 27. Canberra: Australian National University, 1981.

Jones, Steven. "Fight for Timor Grows Quiet but Goes On." *Wall Street Journal* (March 20, 1985).

Jones, Steven, and Raphael Pura. "Suharto-Linked Monopolies Hobble Economy." *Asian Wall Street Journal* (November 24, 1986): 1 and 8.

"June 1985 Log." *Indonesia Reports* 9 (July 1985).

Kahin, Audrey, ed. *Regional Dynamics of the Indonesian Revolution: Unity from Diversity.* Honolulu: University of Hawaii Press, 1985.

Kahin, George McT. "Indonesia." In *Major Governments of Asia,* edited by George McT. Kahin, pp. 471–592. Ithaca: Cornell University Press, 1958.

———. *Nationalism and Revolution in Indonesia.* Ithaca: Cornell University Press, 1952.

———, ed. *Governments and Politics of Southeast Asia.* 2d ed. Ithaca: Cornell University Press, 1964.

———. *Major Governments of Asia.* Ithaca: Cornell University Press, 1958.

Kamal, Salih. "Urban Dilemmas in Southeast Asia." *Singapore Journal of Tropical Geography* 3 (1982): 147–161.

Katz, Elihu, and George Wedell. *Broadcasting in the Third World: Promise and Performance.* Cambridge: Harvard University Press, 1977.

Kaye, Lincoln. "Anchored in Realism." *Far Eastern Economic Review* (July 11, 1985): 58–60.

———. "A Change of Customs." *Far Eastern Economic Review* (April 25, 1985): 118–120.

———. "Fighting-trim Reforms." *Far Eastern Economic Review* (October 24, 1985): 23–26.

———. "Happy Father's Day." *Far Eastern Economic Review* (August 29, 1985): 25.

———. "Legislating Harmony." *Far Eastern Economic Review* (June 13, 1985): 14–16.

Kearney, Robert N., ed. *Politics and Modernization in South and Southeast Asia.* New York: John Wiley & Sons, 1975.

Keuning, Steven J. "Farm Size, Land Use, and Profitability of Food Crops in Indonesia." *Bulletin of Indonesian Economic Studies* 20 (April 1984): 58–82.

Kirchbach, Friedrich von. "Transnational Corporations in the Asian Region." *Economic Bulletin for Asia and the Pacific* 33 (June 1982): 16–19.

Kompas. Various issues.

Kronholz, June. "Mass Migration: Indonesia Pushes Plans for Moving Mil-

lions off the Island of Java; Resettling on Other Islands Aims to Ease
Crowding." *Wall Street Journal* 202 (1983): 1 and 56.

Lagerberg, Kees. *West Irian and Jakarta Imperialism.* New York: St. Martin's
Press, 1979.

Lane, Max. "Climate of Fear: The Rise of General Benny Murdani." *Inside
Indonesia* 1 (November 1983): 2-5.

———. "Suharto Intensifies Clamp-down on Dissent." *Inside Indonesia* 2 (May
1984): 3-5.

———. "Who's Paying for the Recession?" *Inside Indonesia* 1 (November
1983): 12-19.

Lee, Khoon Choy. *Indonesia, Between Myth and Reality.* London: Nile & Macken-
zie, 1976.

Legge, John D. *Indonesia.* Englewood Cliffs, N.J.: Prentice-Hall, 1964.

Leinbach, T. R. "Transport Evaluation in Rural Development: An Indonesian Case-Study." *Third World Planning Review* 5 (1983): 23-35.

Leng, Lee Yong. "Southeast Asia: The Political Geography of Economic Imbalance." *Tijdschrift voor Economische en Sociale Geografie* 70 (1979): 339-349.

Lev, Daniel S. "Judicial Institutions and Legal Culture in Indonesia." In *Culture and Politics in Indonesia,* edited by Claire Holt, pp. 246-318. Ithaca:
Cornell University Press, 1972.

Liddle, R. William. *Ethnicity, Party and National Integration: An Indonesian Case
Study.* New Haven, Ct.: Yale University Press, 1970.

———. "Indonesia 1977: The New Order's Second Parliamentary Election."
Asian Survey 18 (1978): 175-185.

———. "The Politics of *Ekonomi Pancasila:* Some Reflections on a Recent
Debate." *Bulletin of Indonesian Economic Studies* 18 (March 1982): 96-101.

Lindberg, Leon N. "Political Integration as a Multidimensional Phenomenon
Requiring Multivariate Measurement." *International Organization* 24 (Autumn 1970): 649-731.

Lineton, Jacqueline. "Pasompe 'Ugi': Bugis Migrants and Wanderers." *Archi-
pel* 10 (1975): 181-201.

Lyon, Peter. *War and Peace in South-East Asia.* London: Oxford University Press,
1969.

MacAndrews, Colin. "Transmigration in Indonesia: Prospects and Problems."
Asian Survey 18 (June 1978): 458-472.

McCawley, Peter. "The Devaluation and Structural Change in Indonesia." In
Southeast Asian Affairs 1980, edited by Leo Suryadinata, pp. 145-157.
Singapore: Institute of Southeast Asian Studies, 1980.

———. "The Economics of *Ekonomi Pancasila.*" *Bulletin of Indonesian Economic
Studies* 18 (March 1982): 102-109.

———. "The Growth of the Industrial Sector." In *The Indonesian Economy During the Soeharto Era,* edited by Anne Booth and Peter McCawley, pp. 62-
101. East Asian Social Science Monographs. Kuala Lumpur: Oxford
University Press, 1981.

———. *Industrialization in Indonesia: Development and Prospects.* Development
Studies Centre, Occasional Paper no. 13. Canberra: Australian National University, 1979.

————. "Rural Dualism in Indonesia and China: New Technologies, Institutions, and Welfare." In *Indonesia: Australian Perspectives,* edited by James J. Fox, Ross Garnaut, Peter McCawley, and J. A. C. Mackie. Vol. 2, *Indonesia: Dualism, Growth and Poverty,* edited by Ross Garnaut and Peter McCawley, pp. 373-397. Canberra: Australian National University Research School of Pacific Studies, 1980.

————. "A Slowdown in Industrial Growth?" *Bulletin of Indonesian Economic Studies* 20 (December 1984): 158-174.

————. "Survey of Recent Developments." *Bulletin of Indonesian Economic Studies* 19 (April 1983): 1-31.

————. "Survey of Recent Developments." *Bulletin of Indonesian Economic Studies* 21 (April 1985): 1-31.

McCawley, Peter, and Chris Manning. "Survey of Recent Developments." *Bulletin of Indonesian Economic Studies* 12 (November 1976): 1-49.

MacDougall, John A. "Indonesia: Economic Growth and Political Order." *Current History* 85 (April 1986): 172-175, 178-179.

————. "Indonesia 1980: Economic Modernization and Political Discontent." *Asian Thought and Society: An International Review* 5 (December 1980): 339-341.

————. "Patterns of Military Control in the Indonesian Higher Central Bureaucracy." *Indonesia* 33 (April 1982): 89-121.

Mackie, J. A. C. "The Indonesian Economy, 1950-1963." In *The Economy of Indonesia: Selected Readings,* edited by Bruce Glassburner, pp. 16-69. Ithaca: Cornell University Press, 1971.

————. "Integrating and Centrifugal Forces in Indonesian Politics Since 1945." In *Indonesia: Australian Perspectives,* edited by James J. Fox, Ross Garnaut, Peter McCawley, and J. A. C. Mackie. Vol. 3, *Indonesia: The Making of a Nation,* edited by J. A. C. Mackie, pp. 669-684. Canberra: Australian National University Research School of Pacific Studies, 1980.

————, ed. *Indonesia: The Making of a Nation.* Vol. 3 of *Indonesia: Australian Perspectives,* edited by James J. Fox, Ross Garnaut, Peter McCawley, and J. A. C. Mackie. Canberra: Australian National University Research School of Pacific Studies, 1980.

McNicoll, G. "Recent Demographic Trends in Indonesia." *Population and Development Review* 8 (1982): 811-819.

McVey, Ruth T. "The Post-Revolutionary Transformation of the Indonesian Army, Part II." *Indonesia* 13 (April 1972): 147-181.

————, ed. *Indonesia.* New Haven, Ct.: Human Relations Area Files Press, 1963.

May, R. J. "Irian Jaya: West Papuan Nationalism in 1979." In *Indonesia: Australian Perspectives,* edited by James J. Fox, Ross Garnaut, Peter McCawley, and J. A. C. Mackie. Vol. 3, *Indonesia: The Making of a Nation,* edited by J. A. C. Mackie, pp. 721-728. Canberra: Australian National University Research School of Pacific Studies, 1980.

Mears, Leon A. "Rice and Food Self-Sufficiency in Indonesia." *Bulletin of Indonesian Economic Studies* 20 (August 1984): 122-138.

Merritt, Richard L., and Stein Rokkan, eds. *Comparing Nations: The Use of Quantitative Data in Cross-National Research.* New Haven, Ct.: Yale University Press, 1966.

Missen, G. J. *Viewpoint on Indonesia: A Geographical Study.* Melbourne: Thomas Nelson, 1972.

Montgomery, Roger D. "Migration, Employment, and Unemployment in Java: Changes from 1961 to 1971 with Particular Reference to the Green Revolution." *Asian Survey* 15 (March 1975): 221–233.

Montgomery, Roger D., and Sugito Toto. "Changes in the Structure of Farms and Farming in Indonesia Between Censuses, 1963–1973: The Issues of Inequality and Near-landlessness." *Journal of Southeast Asian Studies* 11 (September 1980): 348–365.

Morfit, Michael. "Panca Sila: The Indonesian State Ideology According to the New Order Government." *Asian Survey* 21 (August 1981): 838–851.

Moritz, Frederic A. "Indonesia—Will the Volcano Erupt?" *Christian Science Monitor* (May 3, 1979): 1 and 9.

Mubyarto. "Prospek Perekonomian Indonesia dalam Pelita III." *Prisma* (January 1979).

Muir, Ross. "Survey of Recent Developments." *Bulletin of Indonesian Economic Studies* 22 (August 1986): 1–27.

Murai, Y. "The Bima Program and Agricultural Labor in Indonesia." *Developing Economies* 18 (1980): 23–44.

Myint, Hla. "Inward and Outward Looking Countries Revisited: The Case of Indonesia." *Bulletin of Indonesian Economic Studies* 20 (August 1984): 39–52.

Myrdal, Gunnar. *Asian Drama: An Inquiry into the Poverty of Nations.* Vol. 3. New York: Twentieth Century Fund, 1968.

Naim, Mochtar. "Merantau: Causes and Effects of Minangkabau Voluntary Migration." Institute of Southeast Asian Studies Occasional Papers, no. 5. Singapore: Institute of Southeast Asian Studies, 1971.

———. "Voluntary Migration in Indonesia." In *Internal Migration: The New World and the Third World,* edited by A. H. Richmond and D. Kubat, pp. 148–183. London: Sage, 1976.

Nasution, Anwar. "Survey of Recent Developments." *Bulletin of Indonesian Economic Studies* 21 (August 1985): 1–23.

Nawawi, M. A. "The Regions and National Development under the New Order." In *Indonesia: Australian Perspectives,* edited by James J. Fox, Ross Garnaut, Peter McCawley, and J. A. C. Mackie. Vol. 3, *Indonesia: The Making of a Nation,* edited by J. A. C. Mackie, pp. 685–698. Canberra: Australian National University Research School of Pacific Studies, 1980.

Neill, Wilfred T. *Twentieth Century Indonesia.* New York: Columbia University Press, 1973.

"New University Aiding Indonesian Students." *The Evening Post* (Charleston, S.C.) (September 24, 1984): 8A.

Nitisastro, Widjojo. *Population Trends in Indonesia.* Ithaca: Cornell University Press, 1970.

Noer, Deliar. "Islam as a Political Force in Indonesia." In *Indonesia: Australian Perspectives,* edited by James J. Fox, Ross Garnaut, Peter McCawley, and J. A. C. Mackie. Vol. 3, *Indonesia: The Making of a Nation,* edited by J. A. C. Mackie, pp. 633–645. Canberra: Australian National University Research School of Pacific Studies, 1980.

Nye, Joseph S. "Comparative Regional Integration: Concept and Measurement." *International Organization* 22 (Autumn 1968): 856–858.

Oey, Hong Lee. *Indonesia Facing the 1980's: A Political Analysis.* Hull, England: Europress for South-East Asia Research Group, 1979.

O'Malley, William J. "Second Thoughts on Indonesian Nationalism." In *Indonesia: Australian Perspectives,* edited by James J. Fox, Ross Garnaut, Peter McCawley, and J. A. C. Mackie. Vol. 3, *Indonesia: The Making of a Nation,* edited by J. A. C. Mackie, pp. 601–614. Canberra: Australian National University Research School of Pacific Studies, 1980.

Osborne, Robin. "The Flag that Won't Go Away." *Inside Indonesia* 4 (March 1985): 28–31.

Oya, Kenji. "Environmental Dimensions of Rural Regional Development: A Report of a Study in Three Asian Countries (India, Thailand and Indonesia)." *Regional Development Dialogue* 3 (Spring 1982): 72–116.

Paauw, Douglas S. "Economic Growth, Employment, and Productivity: Prospects for Indonesia." *The Singapore Economic Review* 29 (1984): 111–125.

———. "From Colonial to Guided Economy." In *Indonesia,* edited by Ruth T. McVey, pp. 155–247. New Haven, Ct.: Human Relations Area Files Press, 1963.

———. "The Indonesian Economy in the 1980s." *Economic Bulletin for Asia and the Pacific* 31 (December 1980): 31–53.

———. "Recent Economic Trends in Indonesia." *Journal of Southeast Asian Studies* 14 (1983): 248–249.

Panglaykim, J. "Indonesia: Economic Dimensions and Resilience." *Asia Pacific Community* 15 (1982): 76–82.

Papanek, Gustav F., ed. *The Indonesian Economy.* New York: Praeger, 1980.

Pauker, Guy J. "Indonesia 1979: The Record of Three Decades." *Asian Survey* 20 (February 1980): 123–134.

———. "Indonesia in 1980: Regime Fatigue?" *Asian Survey* 21 (February 1981): 232–244.

Peacock, James L. *Indonesia: An Anthropological Perspective.* Pacific Palisades, Calif.: Goodyear Publishing, 1973.

Pelzer, Karl J. "The Agricultural Foundation." In *Indonesia,* edited by Ruth T. McVey, pp. 118–154. New Haven, Ct.: Human Relations Area Files Press, 1963.

Ping, Ho Kwon. "The Men on White Horses Now Ride a Tiger." *Far Eastern Economic Review* (April 11, 1980): 34–48.

"A Political Undertone to the Anti-Chinese Riots in Java." *Asia Research Bulletin* 10 (February 28, 1981): 778–780.

Population Reference Bureau. *1985 World Population Data Sheet.* Washington, D.C.: Population Reference Bureau, Inc., 1985.

Prapanca, Rakawi. *The Nagara-Kertagama,* translated and edited by Theodore

G. Th. Pigeaud. In *Java in the Fourteenth Century: A Study of Cultural History*, pp. 219–250. The Hague: Martinus Nijhoff, 1962.

Premdas, Ralph R. "The Organisasi Papua Merdeka in Irian Jaya." *Asian Survey* 25 (October 1985): 1055–1074.

Pryor, Robin J. "The Migrant to the City in Southeast Asia: Can and Should We Generalize?" *Asian Profile* 5 (1977): 63–89.

———. *Migration and Development in Southeast Asia: A Demographic Perspective.* Kuala Lumpur: Oxford University Press, 1979.

Purcell, Victor. *The Chinese in Southeast Asia.* 2d ed. London: Oxford University Press, 1965.

Pye, Lucian W. *Southeast Asia's Political Systems.* Englewood Cliffs, N.J.: Prentice-Hall, 1974.

Race, Jeffrey. "The Political Economy of New Order Indonesia in a Comparative Regional Perspective." In *Indonesia: Australian Perspectives,* edited by James J. Fox, Ross Garnaut, Peter McCawley, and J. A. C. Mackie. Vol. 3, *Indonesia: The Making of a Nation,* edited by J. A. C. Mackie, pp. 699–709. Canberra: Australian National University Research School of Pacific Studies, 1980.

Reinhardt, Jon M. *Foreign Policy and National Integration: The Case of Indonesia.* Southeast Asia Studies Monograph Series, no. 17. New Haven, Ct.: Yale University Press, 1971.

Reksohadiprodjo, Sukanto. "Oil and Other Energy Resources for Development: The Indonesian Case." *Journal of Energy and Development* 5 (1980): 289–325.

———. "Tata Guna Tanah dan Pengembangan Perkotaan." *Prisma* 16 (1984): 14–18.

Republic of Indonesia, *Bappenas* (National Development Planning Agency). *Repelita IV, The Fourth Five-Year Development Plan of Indonesia 1984/85–1988/89: A Summary. Policies and Prospects for Sustained Development under Challenging Conditions.* Jakarta: National Development Planning Agency, 1984.

Republic of Indonesia, Department of Information. *The First Five-Year Development Plan, 1969/70–1973/74.* Jakarta: Department of Information, 1969.

———. *Indonesia 1979: An Official Handbook.* Jakarta: Department of Information, 1980.

———. *Repelita III. The Third Five-Year Development Plan, 1979–84 (Summary).* Jakarta: Department of Information, n.d.

Republic of Indonesia, Directorate of City and Regional Planning. "A Short Note on Area/Regional Development Studies in Indonesia." Jakarta: Directorate of City and Regional Planning, 1978.

Republik Indonesia, Departemen Penerangan, Proyek Penelitian dan Pengembangan. *Hasil-hasil Polling Pendapat Umum Pelita Tahun Ke-IV.* Jakarta: Departemen Penerangan, 1972.

———. *Pidato Kenegaraan Presiden Republik Indonesia Soeharto di depan Sidang Dewan Perwakilan Rakyat 16 Agustus 1984 (pidato dan lampiran).* Jakarta: Departemen Penerangan, 1984.

————. *Rencana Pembangunan Lima Tahun Kedua, 1974/75-1978/79.* Jakarta: Departemen Penerangan, 1973.

————. *Rencana Pembangunan Lima Tahun Keempat 1984/85-1988/89.* 4 vols. Jakarta: Departemen Penerangan, 1984.

Republik Indonesia, Departemen Perdagangan. *Ikhtisar Perkembangan Harga-harga dan Data Statistik Perdagangan.* Jakarta: Departemen Perdagangan, 1974.

Republik Indonesia, Departemen Perhubungan Laut. Direktorat Perkapalan dan Pelayaran SubDit. Kebandaran dan Awak Kapal, Seksi P.U. *File No. TH 1981/82.* 2 vols. Jakarta: Departemen Perhubungan Laut, 1983.

Republik Indonesia, Direktorat Jenderal Perhubungan Udara. "Airport Traffic Statistics, Domestic and International." Jakarta: Direktorat Jenderal Perhubungan Udara, 1977. Mimeographed.

Republik Indonesia, Perusahaan Negara PELNI. *Facts and Figures of P.N. PELNI.* Jakarta: Perusahaan Negara PELNI, 1971.

Republik Indonesia. *Prospek Perekonomian Indonesia.* Jakarta, 1973.

Resink, Gertrude J. *Indonesia's History Between the Myths.* The Hague: W. van Hoeve, 1968.

Richardson, Michael. "Jakarta's Can of Worms." *Far Eastern Economic Review* (January 1, 1982): 26.

Robison, Richard. *Indonesia: The Rise of Capital.* Asian Studies Association of Australia, Southeast Asia Publications Series no. 13. North Sydney: Allen & Unwin, 1987.

Rodgers, Peter. "Indonesia's Faithful Flex Their Political Muscle." *Far Eastern Economic Review* (November 28, 1980): 37-39.

Roeder, O. G., comp. *Who's Who in Indonesia: Biographies of Prominent Indonesian Personalities in All Fields.* Jakarta: Gunung Agung, 1971.

Roepstorff, Torben M. "Industrial Development in Indonesia: Performance and Prospects." *Bulletin of Indonesian Economic Studies* 21 (April 1985): 32-62.

Rose, Beth. *An Overview of the Indonesian Rice Economy.* Ithaca: Cornell International Agricultural Economics Study, 1982.

Rosendale, Phyllis. "Survey of Recent Developments." *Bulletin of Indonesian Economic Studies* 16 (March 1980): 1-33.

————. "Survey of Recent Developments." *Bulletin of Indonesian Economic Studies* 20 (April 1984): 1-31.

Rosser, Colin. "The Evolving Role of a National Agency for Housing and Urban Development in Indonesia." *Habitat International* 7 (1983): 137-149.

————. "Training in Regional Development in Indonesia: A Report Prepared for the Regional Development Division of *Bappenas.*" Jakarta, 1974. Mimeographed.

Royal Dutch Geographical Society. *Atlas van Tropisch Nederland.* The Hague: Royal Dutch Geographical Society, 1938.

Rummel, Rudolph J. *Applied Factor Analysis.* Evanston: Northwestern University Press, 1970.

————. "The Dimensionality of Nations Project." In *Comparing Nations: The Use of Quantitative Data in Cross-National Research,* edited by Richard L. Merritt and Stein Rokkan, pp. 109–130. New Haven, Ct.: Yale University Press, 1966.

————. *Dimensions of Nations Series.* Vol. 3, *National Attributes and Behavior.* Beverly Hills, Calif.: Sage Publications, 1979.

Sacerdoti, Guy. "Consensus Conundrums." *Far Eastern Economic Review* (August 21, 1981): 34–35.

————. "Garuda's Hidden Assets." *Far Eastern Economic Review* (May 1, 1981): 38–40.

————. "A One-Man Consensus?" *Far Eastern Economic Review* (May 22, 1981): 30–31.

————. "Overdraft of Inefficiency." *Far Eastern Economic Review* (May 29, 1981): 41–47.

————. "Running to Stand Still." *Far Eastern Economic Review* (August 28, 1981): 78–79.

————. "Taking the Pulse." *Far Eastern Economic Review* (August 28, 1981): 34–35.

————. "The Technocrats' Success Story." *Far Eastern Economic Review* (May 29, 1981): 8–49.

————. "The Wheel of Fortune Stops." *Far Eastern Economic Review* (January 16, 1981): 14.

Salim, Emil. "Trends in the Indonesian Economy." In *Trends in Indonesia II,* edited by Leo Suryadinata and Sharon Siddique, pp. 101–116. Athens, Ohio: Ohio University Press, 1981.

Schiller, A. Arthur. *The Formation of Federal Indonesia, 1945–1949.* The Hague: W. van Hoeve, 1955.

Seda, Frans. "The Progress of Economic Integration During Two Decades." *Prisma* 4 (November 1976): 7–26.

"September 1985 Log." *Indonesia Reports* 12 (October 1985).

Sethuraman, S. V. *Jakarta: Urban Development and Employment.* Geneva: International Labor Organization, 1976.

Shakhs, Salah El. "Development, Primacy, and Systems of Cities." *Journal of Developing Areas* 7 (October 1972): 11–36.

Sharif, M. N., and V. Sundararayan. "Assessment of Technological Appropriateness: The Case of Indonesian Rural Development." *Technological Forecasting and Social Change* 25 (1984): 225–237.

Siddique, S., and L. Suryadinata. "Bumiputra and Pribumi: Economic Nationalism (indiginism) in Malaysia and Indonesia." *Pacific Affairs* 54 (1981): 662–687.

Skinner, G. William. "Change and Persistence in Chinese Culture Overseas: A Comparison of Thailand and Java." In *Southeast Asia: The Politics of National Integration,* edited by John T. McAlister, Jr., pp. 339–415. New York: Random House, 1973.

————. "The Chinese Minority." In *Indonesia,* edited by Ruth T. McVey, pp. 97–117. New Haven, Ct.: Human Relations Area Files Press, 1963.

————, ed. *Local, Ethnic, and National Loyalties in Village Indonesia: A Symposium.*

Yale University Cultural Report Series, no. 8. New Haven, Ct.: Yale University Southeast Asia Studies, 1959.

Smith, Roger M., ed. *Southeast Asia: Documents of Political Development and Change.* Ithaca: Cornell University Press, 1974.

Sobary, Mohamed. "Participation in Practice." *Kompas* (February 4, 1981).

Soedjatmoko. "Some Thoughts on Higher Education." *Prisma* 2 (November 1978).

Soedjatmoko, Mohammed Ali, G. J. Resink, and G. McT. Kahin. *An Introduction to Indonesian Historiography.* Ithaca: Cornell University Press, 1965.

Soemarwoto, Otto. "Interrelations among Population, Resources, Environment and Development." *Economic Bulletin for Asia and the Pacific* 32 (June 1981): 1-33.

Speare, Alden J. "Rural and Urban Migration: A National Overview." In *Agricultural and Rural Development in Indonesia,* edited by Gary E. Hansen, pp. 202-235. Westview Special Studies in Social, Political, and Economic Development. Boulder, Colo.: Westview Press, 1981.

Speed, Frank W. *Indonesia Today.* Sydney: Angus & Robertson, 1971.

Stoler, Ann. "Class Structure and Female Autonomy in Rural Java." In *Women and National Development: The Complexities of Change,* edited by the Wellesley Editorial Committee, pp. 74-89. Chicago: University of Chicago Press, 1977.

Strout, Alan M. "Pertumbuhan Pertanian, Tenaga Kerja dan Pembagian Pendapatan: Dilema bagi Repelita III." *Ekonomi dan Keuangan Indonesia* 25 (December 1977).

———. "Some Comments on the 1969 Input-Output Table for Indonesia." *Ekonomi dan Keuangan Indonesia* 21 (1973): 51-61.

Sudarsono, Juwono. "Political Changes and Developments in Indonesia." In *Trends in Indonesia II,* edited by Leo Suryadinata and Sharon Siddique, pp. 55-64. Athens, Ohio: Ohio University Press, 1981.

Sugijanto, Soegijoko, and Budhy T. Sugijanto. *Rural-Urban Migration in Indonesia.* Monograph Series. Jakarta: LEKNAS-LIPI, 1976.

Suharso, Alden Speare, Han R. Redmana, and Imron Husin. *Rural-Urban Migration in Indonesia.* Monograph Series. Jakarta: LEKNAS-LIPI, 1972.

Suharto. *Address of State by His Excellency the President of the Republic of Indonesia, Soeharto, Before the House of the People's Representatives on the Occasion of the 36th Independence Day, August 17th, 1981.* Jakarta: Department of Information, 1981.

———. *Report to the Nation: Address Before the House of the People's Representatives on the 1975/76 State Budget.* Jakarta: Department of Information, 1975.

Suhartono, R. B. "Industrial Development in Indonesia." *The Indonesian Quarterly* 8 (January 1980): 3-20.

Sujono, Ibnoe. "Kebijaksanaan Koperasi: Beberapa Masalah dan Prospeknya." *Prisma* 6 (July 1977): 3-16.

Sumarlin, J. B. *Indonesia: Economic Update 1984.* Jakarta: National Development Economic Office, 1984.

Sundhaussen, Ulf. "Regime Crisis in Indonesia: Facts, Fiction, Predictions." *Asian Survey* 21 (August 1981): 815-837.

Sundrum, R. M. "Income Distribution, 1970–76." *Bulletin of Indonesian Economic Studies* 15 (March 1979): 137–141.

———. "Manufacturing Employment 1961–71." *Bulletin of Indonesian Economic Studies* 11 (March 1975): 58–65.

Suparlan, Parsudi, and Harianto Sigit. *The Case of Indonesia.* Farnborough, U.K.: Gower, 1980.

Suryadinata, Leo. "Indonesia in 1979: Controlled Dissent." In *Southeast Asian Affairs 1980,* edited by Leo Suryadinata, pp. 121–144. Singapore: Institute of Southeast Asian Studies, 1980.

———. "Indonesia in 1980: Continuity Rather than Change." In *Southeast Asian Affairs 1981,* edited by Leo Suryadinata, pp. 129–145. Singapore: Institute of Southeast Asian Studies, 1981.

Suryadinata, Leo, and Sharon Siddique, eds. *Trends in Indonesia II.* Athens, Ohio: Ohio University Press, 1981.

Sutrisno, Slamet. *Sedikit Tentang Strategi Kebudayaan Nasional Indonesia.* Yogyakarta: Liberty, 1983.

Suwidjana, Njoman. "Indonesia's Rice Policy: Development Patterns, Accomplishments, and Problems." In *Southeast Asian Affairs 1981,* edited by Leo Suryadinata, pp. 146–157. Singapore: Institute of Southeast Asian Studies, 1981.

Syamaprased, Gupta. *A Model for Income Distribution, Employment and Growth: A Case Study of Indonesia.* Baltimore: Johns Hopkins University Press, 1977.

Tate, D. J. M. *The Making of Modern South-East Asia.* Vol. 1, *The European Conquest.* Kuala Lumpur: Oxford University Press, 1971.

Taylor, Peter J. *Quantitative Methods in Geography: An Introduction to Spatial Analysis.* Boston: Houghton Mifflin Co., 1977.

Thomas, R. Murray. "Indonesian Education: Communist Strategies (1950–65) and Government Counter Strategies (1966–80)." *Asian Survey* 21 (March 1981): 369–392.

Thorne, A. G. "Indonesia: Cultural Pluralism and Education." *Educational Research Quarterly* 6 (1981): 75–85.

———. "The Longest Link: Human Evolution in Southeast Asia and the Settlement of Australia." In *Indonesia: Australian Perspectives,* edited by James J. Fox, Ross Garnaut, Peter McCawley, and J. A. C. Mackie. Vol. 1, *Indonesia: The Making of a Culture,* edited by James J. Fox, pp. 35–43. Canberra: Australian National University Research School of Pacific Studies, 1980.

Tinker, Irene, and Milledge Walker. "Planning for Regional Development in Indonesia." *Asian Survey* 13 (December 1973): 1102–1120.

U.S. House of Representatives. "Famine Relief for East Timor." Hearings before the Subcommittee on Asian and Pacific Affairs of the Committee on Foreign Affairs, House of Representatives, 96th Congress. December 4, 1979, pp. 12–30. Washington, D.C.: House of Representatives, 1979.

van der Kroef, Justus M. "Indonesia: Centrifugal Economies." In *Foreign Aid Reexamined,* edited by James W. Wiggins and Helmut Schoeck, pp. 197–220. Washington, D.C.: Public Affairs Press, 1958.

————. " 'Petrus': Patterns of Prophylactic Murder in Indonesia." *Asian Survey* 25 (July 1985): 745–759.

Van Leeuwan, Robert. "Central Government Subsidies for Regional Development: Notes." *Bulletin of Indonesian Economic Studies* 11 (March 1975): 66–75.

Vlekke, Bernhard H. M. *Nusantara: A History of Indonesia.* The Hague: W. van Hoeve, 1965.

Vreeland, Nena, Peter Just, Kenneth W. Martindale, Philip W. Moeller, and Rinn-Sup Shinn. *Area Handbook for Indonesia.* 3d ed. Foreign Area Studies Series. Washington, D.C.: U.S. Government Printing Office, 1975.

Waldack, Albert C. "Dwi-Fungsi: The Indonesian Army in Civil Affairs." *Military Review* 61 (Spring 1981): 13–19.

Wallerstein, Immanuel. "Ethnicity and National Integration in West Africa." In *Comparative Politics,* edited by Harry Eckstein and David Apter, pp. 665–670. Glencoe, Ill.: The Free Press, 1963.

Walujo, Imam. "Renewing National Consensus." *Kompas* (March 9, 1981).

Weatherbee, Donald E. "Indonesia in 1984: Pancasila, Politics, and Power." *Asian Survey* 25 (February 1985): 187–197.

Weiner, Myron. "Political Integration and Political Development." In *Political Modernization: A Reader in Comparative Political Change.* 2d ed., edited by Claude E. Welch, Jr., pp. 180–196. Belmont, Calif.: Wadsworth Publishing Co., 1971.

"West Papua: Asia or Melanesia? An Interview with Rex Rumakiek." *Inside Indonesia* 4 (March 1985): 22–26.

Wheatley, Paul. *The Golden Khersonese: Studies in the Historical Geography of the Malay Peninsula Before A.D. 1500.* Kuala Lumpur: University of Malaya Press, 1966.

White, Benjamin. "Agricultural Involution and Its Critics: Twenty Years After." *Bulletin of Concerned Asian Scholars* 15 (1983): 18–31.

————. "Political Aspects of Poverty, Income Distribution, and Their Measurement: Some Examples from Rural Java." *Development and Change* 10 (January 1979): 91–114.

————. "Population, Involution, and Employment in Rural Java." In *Agricultural and Rural Development in Indonesia,* edited by Gary E. Hansen, pp. 130–146. Westview Special Studies in Social, Political, and Economic Development. Boulder, Colo.: Westview Press, 1981.

Wickman, Stephen B. "The Economy." In *Indonesia: A Country Study.* 4th ed., edited by Frederica M. Bunge, pp. 119–174. Area Handbook Series. Washington, D.C.: U.S. Government Printing Office, 1983.

Widjaja, Albert. "Impact of Multinational Corporations on Social and Political Conditions in Indonesia." *Asia Pacific Community* 8 (1980): 44–57.

————. "Worker Participation in Socio-Economic Development." *Prisma* 16 (March 1980): 79–90.

"Widjojo Nitisastro: Clearing the Jungle." *Euromoney* (January 1979): 7–10.

Wijarso. "National Energy Planning in Indonesia." *Energy* 6 (1981): 737–744.

Williams, Glen. "Community Participation and the Role of Voluntary Agencies in Indonesia." *Prisma* 16 (March 1980): 11–31.

Willner, Ann Ruth. "The Neotraditional Accommodation to Political Independence: The Case of Indonesia." In *Southeast Asia: The Politics of National Integration*, edited by John T. McAlister, Jr., pp. 517–541. New York: Random House, 1973.

———. "Repetition in Change: Cyclical Movement and Indonesian Development." *Economic Development and Cultural Change* 29 (1981): 409–417.

Withington, William A. "The Economic Infrastructure." In *Southeast Asia: Realm of Contrasts*, edited by Ashok K. Dutt, pp. 55–70. Dubuque, Iowa: Kendall/Hunt Publishing Co., 1974.

———. "Indonesia: Insular Contrasts of the Java Core with the Outer Islands." In *Southeast Asia: Realm of Contrasts*, edited by Ashok K. Dutt, pp. 97–111. Dubuque, Iowa: Kendall/Hunt Publishing Co., 1974.

World Bank. "Current Economic Position and Prospects of Indonesia." Report no. AS-143a. Washington, D.C.: World Bank, October 1, 1968.

———. *Indonesia: Selected Aspects of Spatial Development*. Washington, D.C.: World Bank, 1984. Restricted circulation.

———. *World Development Report 1985*. New York: Oxford University Press, 1985.

World Bank Country Study. *Indonesia: Employment and Income Distribution in Indonesia*. Washington, D.C.: World Bank, 1978.

Yasunaka, Akio. "Basic Data on Indonesian Political Leaders." *Indonesia* 10 (October 1970): 107–142.

Zainu'ddin, Ailsa G. *A Short History of Indonesia*. Melbourne: Cassell, 1968.

Index

About the Author

Christine Drake was educated at Walthamstow Hall and Oxford University. She received her doctorate from Rutgers University and is currently an associate professor at Old Dominion University, Norfolk, Virginia. Professor Drake has broad and longstanding experience in the Third World: she has taught in Khartoum, Sudan and North Sulawesi, Indonesia; and field research has taken her to Côte d'Ivoire and Tanzania in Africa, to the United Arab Emirates, Oman, and North Yemen in the Middle East, and to Indonesia. Among her publications are articles on Indonesia, Oman, Third World women, educating for responsible global citizenship, and coastal land use.

Production Notes

This book was designed by Roger Eggers.
Composition and paging were done on the
Quadex Composing System and typesetting on
the Compugraphic 8400 by the design and
production staff of University of Hawaii Press.

The text typeface is Baskerville and the display
typeface is Caslon Bold.

Offset presswork and binding were done by
Vail-Ballou Press, Inc. Text paper is Writers
RR Offset, basis 50.